Arc of Empire

Arc of Empire America's Wars in Asia from the Philippines to Vietnam

MICHAEL H. HUNT & STEVEN I. LEVINE

The University of North Carolina Press *Chapel Hill*

3 1336 08972 7458

This book was published with the assistance of the H. Eugene and Lillian Youngs Lehman Fund of the University of North Carolina Press. A complete list of books published in the Lehman Series appears at the end of the book.

© 2012 The University of North Carolina Press

Designed by Richard Hendel
Set in Charter and Aller types
by Tseng Information Systems, Inc.
Manufactured in the United States of America

The paper in this book meets the guidelines for permanence and durability of the Committee on Production Guidelines for Book Longevity of the Council on Library Resources.

The University of North Carolina Press has been a member of the Green Press Initiative since 2003.

Library of Congress Cataloging-in-Publication Data
Hunt, Michael H.
Arc of empire : America's wars in Asia from the Philippines to Vietnam / Michael H. Hunt and Steven I. Levine.
p. cm.
Includes bibliographical references and index.
ISBN 978-0-8078-3528-9 (cloth : alk. paper)
1. Asia—History, Military—20th century. 2. United States—History, Military—20th century. 3. Asia—Strategic aspects—History—20th century. 4. Philippines—History—Philippine American War, 1899–1902. 5. World War, 1939–1945—Japan. 6. Korean War, 1950–1953. 7. Vietnam War, 1961–1975. I. Levine, Steven I. II. Title.
DS35.H96 2012
355.02095'0904—dc23
2011031532

16 15 14 13 12   5 4 3 2 1

To Allen Whiting—

mentor, inspiration, and friend

—SL

To the memory of Sam and Betsy Hunt—

caring, smart, and much missed

—MH

Contents

Illustrations and Maps

Introduction

Between 1899 and 1973 Americans fought four wars in eastern Asia. This prolonged though intermittent military engagement began with a brutal and now barely remembered struggle in the Philippines (1899–1902). As that conflict was winding down, tension began building between the United States and Japan, another rising Asian power. It exploded at Pearl Harbor. Nearly four years of savage fighting followed, culminating in the atomic bombing of Hiroshima and Nagasaki and in the addition of U.S. strong points in eastern Asia, including occupied Japan. Five years after Japan's surrender, Korea became the third link in this chain of conflict. Civil war in a country divided by Cold War rivalry turned in 1950 into an international conflict pitting American troops against Chinese forces backed by the Soviet Union. The Korean War in turn helped push U.S. policymakers, anxious about China's seemingly aggressive communism, toward a major commitment in Indochina. The war there that U.S. troops took over in 1965 proved the most protracted and frustrating of all. It ended in a humiliating defeat that wrote finis to U.S. dreams of dominance in eastern Asia.

These four wars—in the Philippines, against Japan, in Korea, and in Vietnam—were not separate and unconnected, although they are conventionally treated as such. They were phases in a U.S. attempt to establish and maintain a dominant position in eastern Asia sustained over some seven decades against considerable resistance. These wars, along with other conflicts in which Americans had a part, such as the Boxer expedition (1900), the Chinese civil war (1946–49), the Huk insurgency in the Philippines (1947 to mid-1950s), and the Cambodian revolution (1970–79) constitute a single historical drama in four acts. The Philippines set the scene, Japan's defeat brought the American protagonists to the apogee of their dominance, soon challenged in Korea and then broken in Vietnam. These developments carried profound consequences for eastern Asia as well as the United States. Ultimately the political and social changes transforming the region proved beyond the control of Americans despite the military advantage that their vastly superior weaponry and material resources conferred.

This study approaches the U.S. project with a strong international emphasis. It devotes as much attention to the Asian as to the American side of the wars in large measure to highlight the role of ethnocentrism and to suggest a version of the past that transcends it. No analysis that depicts Americans as the only significant actors can do justice to the ramifications of these conflicts. While rising regional resistance ultimately caused the American drive into eastern Asia to falter and collapse, the cost of defying the United States proved exorbitant. The lands where Americans and Asians fought and died in large numbers remain of vital concern to us today. We forget at our peril the wars that the Asians—friends as well as former and current foes—have certainly not forgotten. Bloody, disruptive, and cruel, those conflicts are etched deeply in their sense of their national pasts.

This account uses the term "eastern Asia" to identify a zone of sustained conflict. The term is not standard geographical usage, blurring the lines, as it does, for what is conventionally referred to as East Asia (including Northeast Asia) and Southeast Asia. The eastern Asia here originated in the minds of Americans, a kind of geographical imaginary, as they cultivated expansive ambitions on the other side of the Pacific, and it became clearly demarcated on the ground not only by the arrival of U.S. armed forces and proconsuls but also by their intense interaction with and impact on the lands and peoples over a distinct area. War creates its own geography, especially when it is waged by a rich, technologically potent state with a clear sense of its own mission and when it generates a complex pattern of sympathy and hostility, cooperation and resistance, both within and across borders. The Americans eventually retreated, their imaginary drained of the meaning it once had had for them, but the legacy of their presence would persist in all sorts of ways so that eastern Asia is more than a historical artifact. It retains its pertinence for the present.

This study also provides a comparative perspective on the U.S. drive by treating it in terms of *empire*. Our decision to give prominence to this much controverted term requires an explanation. Imperial references have evoked anxieties for as long as Americans have debated their role in the world. Early generations of American leaders, steeped in classical traditions, regarded empire as a fundamental threat to the survival of republics, which history told them were inherently fragile. The fear of imperial tendencies repeatedly sounded in U.S. political debate through the nineteenth century, and though attenuated today, that fear can still be heard. American leaders, loath to acknowledge the existence of an American empire, have been quick to deny even its possibility. To some considerable extent they are captives of the broader popular view of the United States as an exceptional country immune to imperial temptation and frequently at odds with those who have sought dominion over others. Indeed, in major conflicts from the late nineteenth century onward Washington has sought to rally international support by drawing a clear line between its commitment to national liberation and its foes' record of imperial subjugation. Much of the indictment of Spain in 1898, Germany over the first half of the twentieth century, Japan during the 1930s and early 1940s, and the Soviet Union and China during the Cold War was couched in terms of their imperial ambitions. The avowed U.S. goal was to check empire, not create it.

Only in the last decade or so have the proponents of the uninhibited exercise of U.S. global power sought to sweep aside popular hesitations and doubt. Wearing empire as a badge of honor, they have challenged their fellow citizens to match the standards of service and sophistication set by the British in the nineteenth century. Yet, this argument has had virtually no impact on the outlook of the foreign policy establishment, journalists, policymakers, or the broader public. These latter-day champions of empire have ignored what American leaders have learned the hard way over the last half century. Citizens in a society devoted to the pleasures of personal consumption have proven averse to the personal sacrifices required by distant, dirty wars. The consumer-citizen's lack of enthusiasm for what it takes to impose and sustain dominance can be measured at the ballot box and by attitudes toward the draft. So even as the classical fears of empire have faded in U.S. political culture, powerful social trends have helped to maintain the allergy to the E word.

Regardless of this long-standing tendency to consider *empire* a loaded term, it remains a valuable concept capturing a major phenomenon in human history—the assertion by major powers across the millennia of control over other lands and peoples. An examination of empires as diverse as ancient Rome, Han and Tang dynasty China, Russia and the Soviet Union, and Britain suggests a basic working definition that is neither value-laden nor confusing. Empire is fundamentally a centrally directed political enterprise in which a state employs coercion (violence or at least the threat of violence) to subjugate an alien population within a territorially delimited area governed by another state or organized political force. Once created, empires acquire other structural features. Maintaining control depends on collaboration between metropolitan and colonial elites (with each exercising disproportionate influence within their own societies) supplemented by a variety of other mechanisms. These mechanisms include an army ready to do the dirty work of repressing "restless natives," a network of proximate military bases to facilitate the movement and rapid response of that army to insurgent threats, a system of intelligence and police to serve as the eyes and arms trained on sources of subversion, a class of imperial administrators to oversee elite clients and monitor social developments, and ideological orthodoxies that rationalize dominance both at home and in the field.

This notion of empire helps make sense of the long U.S. transpacific encounter. Americans followed a familiar imperial path marked by four features. One is the strength and persistence of a strong ideological impulse that stirred dreams of dominance and animated U.S. policy. Nationalist visions together with a commitment to sweeping political, social, and cultural transformation in other lands inspired an ambitious regional project similar to those undertaken by other imperial powers. Infusing this project was a sense of superiority that helped reconcile a people dedicated to freedom to taking freedom, however provisionally, from others and to exercising control, sometimes uneasily.

A second feature is the importance of colonialism and third-world nationalism in defining the context for the U.S. project. By the time the United States became seriously involved in eastern Asia at the start of the twentieth century, the heyday of European colonialism had already passed. Declining empires, restive subjects, and late-arriving challengers combined to create a volatile environment for Americans to operate in. The Philippines drama began with a transfer of colonial control from one power (Spain) to another (the United States) even as Filipino nationalists objected vehemently. The struggle against Japan involved two empires on the rise at the very time that the Europeans' grip on their colonies was weakening. Tokyo's imperial aggrandizement helped ignite conflict, which ended with direct U.S. rule over Japan and a concerted effort to tame and redirect Japanese nationalism. From these two strong points—the Philippines and Japan—Washington set about creating client regimes in a region gripped by revolution and with nationalism at flood tide. But by then the embryonic nationalism evident in the Philippines at the turn of the century had developed into a vigorous regionwide force fatal to imperial aspirations.

A third feature is the massive and indiscriminate destruction of modern warfare even as it feeds the illusion of control. American mastery of military technology resulted in the deaths of millions. It also inspired confidence, seemingly confirmed by success in wars against the Philippines and Japan, that superior weaponry guaranteed the subjugation of even the most willful foe. This illusion was painfully punctured in Korea and Vietnam.

The final feature is the emergence of a strong, stable, and prosperous eastern Asia from the cauldron of conflict. The "Asian Miracle" of the last half century developed against the backdrop of the American wars and gave rise to a region whose cultural, political, and even economic preferences diverged markedly from the visions of American reformers. China looms especially large in a revived region that has blazed its own path to modernity. China was at the beginning of our story a passive player with a market to exploit and souls to win. It became a beleaguered client and then to the astonishment of Americans a potent adversary in Korea and in Vietnam.

A couple of commonplace misconceptions about empire, at least when applied to the United States, are worth considering here. By bringing these misconceptions to the surface, we hope to anticipate some likely questions and answer possible objections to our claims.

First, we do not emphasize the motives behind empire. There is a venerable body of writing linking imperialism to the pressures generated by a maturing capitalist economy. A highly influential body of theoretical writing going back to the liberal Hobson and Marxist Lenin may or may not be right that overproduction has prompted a drive to secure colonies for overseas markets in order to avert crisis at home. The definition of *empire* proposed here purposefully avoids ascribing a particular motivation to those who create empire any more than to those who resist it. Motives for creating empire are worth examining but only in the context of a clear, historically informed, easily tested definition that can be flexibly applied in an analytic way to examine and compare a variety of cases. The motivation for the rise of empires is distinctly a second-order matter; our larger task is to define empire in terms that make comparative historical sense.

Put differently, we do not insist that empire builders acknowledge their creation for what it is or even have explicit imperial plans or intentions. Indeed, defining empire as a purposive project pursued consistently and consciously by leaders over time might leave in doubt many historical instances of what historians today would unequivocally consider empire. In other words, the history of empire for the United States as for others has to allow for multiple, even contradictory motives but also for accident, confusion, improvisation, and unintended consequences.

Second, skeptics may want to argue that informal control, so prominent a feature of the U.S. case, does not qualify as empire. This objection does not withstand scrutiny. Rome's eastern frontier, China's subordination of lands beyond the line of direct imperial authority, and Soviet control over eastern European client states leap to mind as imperial cases in which informal control was an integral part of the imperial system. That American empire has been largely informal is easily explained. As a people with a strongly professed commitment to freedom, Americans have tended to balk at the prospect of directly ruling others. Compounding the discomfort has been a frequent resort over the last century to the rallying cry of self-determination. Quite naturally Americans have found indirect control a less blatantly offensive way to have empire. It is cheaper too—an attractive feature in a country with a strong preference for low taxes. Finally, informal control keeps the official bureaucracy to a minimum—another plus for the many American advocates of small government.

Rather than focus on distinctions between formal and informal control, we might more fruitfully think instead about how control is exercised—within the limits imposed by imperial resources, by the technologies of the time, and by the tolerance of subject peoples. Formal no less than informal control has depended on enlisting subordinated groups in the imperial enterprise. Negotiating terms and making concessions are integral to the imperial process, for the simple reason that they make dominance more manageable and cost effective. Under some circumstances formal control is the outcome; under others informal control; and circumstances may change so that one form of dominance gives way to the other. Rather than make the test formal or informal control, we ask who ultimately decides whether local rulers stay or go, who has the final word on alliances and foreign military bases, and from what quarter do indigenous military forces take their cue.

The last recurrent misconception is to view empire as a broad and potentially diffuse form of influence. We think this approach mistaken because it fails to draw distinctions among the diverse kinds of impact any great power can have in international affairs, especially a power with influence as diverse and far-reaching as the United States. Our notion of empire is essentially military and political, in keeping with the coercive nature of the imperial condition, with its state-dominated proceedings, and with the continuing and inevitable challenges of managing a subjugated population and sustaining a collaborative relationship with at least some of that population. Imperial conquest may have behind it economic objectives (e.g., access to a potential market) or cultural calculations (e.g., attitudes of superiority over other peoples). Conquests once effected may create economic stakes, transform cultural attitudes in the colony or the metropole, or set in motion long-lasting social change among the subjects. But the advance of the imperial enterprise is itself ultimately dependent on armed might and comes to an end only when the mailed fist is voluntarily withdrawn or breaks against local resistance.

We insist on a distinction between empire and what might be called hegemony in the interest of a more fine-grained understanding of the U.S. role on the world stage. The wide envy, admiration, resistance, and adaptation prompted by the U.S. consumer society model across the twentieth century are not themselves imperial in any meaningful sense of the term. Rather than involving coercion applied by Washington, the spread of that model has been marked by unstructured diffusion and negotiation among a wide range of nonstate actors, with states playing only a limited role. The same could be said for other forms of U.S. influence abroad, such as tourism, trade, investment, and promotion of democracy and a variety of other international norms through consensus building within international organizations and through formal international conventions. All these activities can be made to fit only by making *empire* a synonym for "great power," thus draining the term of meaning and foreclosing comparative possibilities as well as practical insights.

The notion of empire taken seriously and used in a clear, grounded fashion can help us do some serious analytic work. First, this book seeks to highlight the relation of the past to a set of present problems. The history of one long, bloody, and ultimately failed regional project speaks directly to another regional project now in progress. The U.S. withdrawal from Vietnam in 1973 and acquiescence in the conquest of South Vietnam in 1975 seemed like the end of a pattern. It was not. To a degree that too few American observers recognize, the United States has replicated in the greater Middle East—in the battle against the Taliban in Afghanistan and the bungled occupation in Iraq—the course that it followed earlier in eastern Asia.

This history of American empire building and warfare in one region speaks to the current imbroglio across the Middle East and Central Asia in a striking variety of ways. U.S. policymakers have ignored or have deliberately forgotten the lessons from the conflicts in eastern Asia. They have revived a misplaced faith in the efficacy of military power to shape a regional agenda to American liking. And as a consequence, they have once more demonstrated how ignorance begets ineffectual and counterproductive policies and how beautiful dreams of democracy and development can easily turn into nightmares of death and destruction. As in the Pacific Wars treated here, Americans are rediscovering in another regional context the constraints under which even the most dominant of powers labor. The present does not replicate the past, but historical parallels can provide fresh ways of understanding and dealing with current challenges.

Second, thinking about empire in a clear, grounded way forces our attention beyond the issues of origins and management to the inevitable and practical problem of retreat. Once constructed, empires are challenging to maintain and ultimately hard to let go. "Natives" become restive, the resolve at home may falter, and available resources for management and defense, always limited, may shrink and force hard choices. The prospect of retreat has perennially wrapped empire builders in a blanket of fears. They worry about diminished prestige and about declining national potency and character that other powers are sure to exploit. They blanch at the idea of humiliation at the hands of upstart subjects or unworthy clients. They quail in the face of the likely backlash from a disillusioned public or angry imperial administrators and warriors. They wring their hands over the loss of markets and natural resources and the betrayal of loyal collaborators. Imperial dissolution does indeed carry consequences, though perhaps overall less serious than proponents of empire imagine and some perhaps even beneficial to the power freed of its burdens. While talk of the fall of empire is often clichéd, thinking about that process is essential to understanding how empire works and thus deserves careful consideration. That the U.S. adventure in the Middle East and Central Asia may be approaching an end makes the study of retreat from eastern Asia a matter of some practical urgency.

Readers may want to know a bit about the authors advancing these propositions about war and empire in eastern Asia. We came of age, amid the ferment of the 1960s, deeply concerned with the Vietnam War. Hunt lived in Vietnam early in that decade and began studying and teaching the history of U.S. foreign relations while the war was still in progress. As a graduate student, Levine was an activist in the antiwar and civil rights movements. He too completed his academic training and began teaching under the shadow of Vietnam. As colleagues for nearly thirty years, we have sought to make sense of those times and to use our insights to illuminate the policy choices facing Americans. Our personal stake in this past is considerable but so also is our commitment to follow the evidence and to adjust our views accordingly. This book has its origins in a jointly authored and widely cited article on the U.S. Cold War collision with Asian revolutions and in graduate and undergraduate courses taught together at the University of North Carolina at Chapel Hill. In these and other contexts we have wrestled with the evidence on these four wars with the results to appear in the pages that follow.

Our four core chapters tackle our four wars each in turn. Each chapter begins with the origins of the conflict and includes the conduct of the war, the experience of the war for combatants and civilians, the repercussions in the United States, and, finally, the consequences of the war, including political lessons, social transformations, and postwar memory. This format will facilitate comparisons across the wars and the development of major analytic themes. But alongside analysis and structured comparison we want to bring to life the experience of individuals—the obscure as well as the famous—and evoke the drama inherent in this long, bloody crusade. The stories are too good and too numerous to neglect. A substantial conclusion briefly recapitulates the argument about the rise and fall of a U.S. empire in eastern Asia and examines some of the main features of this imperial project. It then addresses the U.S. relationship to a region that has shed empire and increasingly come into its own as a dynamic center of prosperity and power. Finally, the conclusion tackles the tough issues of what happens when an imperial project collapses and of what insights the U.S. Asian imbroglio offers on the current U.S. involvement in the Middle East and Central Asia. The endnotes and an essay on the historical literature provide opportunities to acknowledge the historical accounts, documents, memoirs, and oral histories essential to telling our story and allow us to express our debt to other scholars whose work we draw on.

1 | **The Philippines,** 1899–1902

THE IMPERIAL IMPULSE UNLEASHED

n the early evening of 4 February 1899, just outside Manila, the war began that fixed formal U.S. control over the Philippines and thereby plunged the United States into a deepening involvement in eastern Asia. According to a generally accepted U.S. version, a foot patrol sent out by Company D of the First Nebraska Regiment encountered Philippine soldiers. When the advancing Filipinos failed to halt as ordered, someone on the American side—very likely Private William Grayson—made a split-second decision to fire. Grayson, a British immigrant who had left a hotel job to join the army, later claimed that he had taken several more shots at other figures and then taken stock of the situation. "Line up, fellows," he said, "the niggers are here all through these yards." Within minutes the trenches around the city had erupted in gun battles that continued into the next day.[1]

What Grayson helped unleash was a distinctly colonial struggle—from conception to execution to consequences—just as the larger U.S. enterprise in the Pacific that it inaugurated was bound up at every turn by issues of colonialism and empire. To be sure, the presiding presence, William McKinley, expressed his heartfelt belief that "no imperial designs lurk in the American mind."[2] And nothing in the biography of this strikingly reserved Ohio lawyer and Civil War veteran hinted at bold imperial impulses. He had served fourteen years in the House of Representatives and four years as governor before making his successful presidential bid under the Republican Party banner. During that time he had not ventured beyond his country's borders or taken any interest in world affairs. Yet he conducted his presidency as though thoroughly versed in the logic of empire so prominent a feature of his age: great powers had a clear claim to colonies; native peoples had no legitimate say in their own future; and superior arms of the one could justifiably put to rest any objections from the other. Almost overnight he would bring his country in line with the prevailing practices of that imperial age. He struck at the last vestiges of Spain's empire in the Pacific as well as in the Caribbean, fully conscious of its vulnerability. He made the case for annexation using nationalist language—invoking a cause sweep-

ing, grand, and noble—commonplace among other eager empire builders of the time. He dispatched across the Pacific an army as practiced in
putting down the "natives" as any the Europeans could field. By embracing
an overtly imperial policy in the Pacific no less than in the Caribbean, he
initiated the rise of the strong executive able to challenge empires as well
as create and manage them.

IMPLICATED IN EMPIRE

It should come as no surprise that empire emerged as a defining feature
of the U.S. push into the Pacific. The United States had emerged from and
been profoundly shaped by its origins as a settler colony with a strong sense
of nationalism and a pronounced feeling of cultural superiority. These were
prerequisites for any imperial calling. Settlers from England had proved unusually adept at asserting control over eastern North America during the
seventeenth and eighteenth centuries. They had squeezed out the Spanish,
French, and Dutch and eliminated or subordinated indigenous peoples. As
the United States expanded westward across the continent, political and
cultural control remained in the hands of the descendants of the English
and in time the Scottish and the Welsh of broadly British background. These
transplants spoke glowingly if imprecisely of their new country as a great
empire in embryo. The subjugation of native peoples and the enslavement
of Africans were indispensable to the making of this settler colony—in the
acquisition of great tracts of land and in the creation from that land of
a wealth-generating plantation economy. Their nationalist self-conception
incorporated a strong sense of racial superiority and entitlement justify-
ing Anglo dominance over other, supposedly lesser peoples. Was not God,
a prominent Protestant evangelist rhetorically asked in 1885, "preparing in
our Anglo-Saxon civilization the die with which to stamp the peoples of the
earth?"[3] By ethnic background and nationalist outlook, McKinley and his
circle were connected to this tradition of settler empire.

Nowhere was the U.S. settler experience more relevant to what was to
come in the Philippines than the process of turning Native Americans into
unwilling subjects. Informing that process at every step of the way was a
sturdy settler assumption of superiority over lesser peoples that justified,
even compelled, securing control of their land and lives in the name of
progress and civilization. Native Americans who refused to acknowledge
these claims and resisted were invariably met with coercion. Countering
irregular warfare required prolonged and brutal fighting that led to dehumanization of the enemy and ample opportunity for atrocities directed

at a population of "savages" in which civilians were indistinguishable from combatants. The struggle usually ended with the army's corralling whole populations in a strategy of removal and concentration that proved effective in disrupting and undermining resistance. Bargains struck with amenable Native American leaders could hasten the end by creating divisions that isolated and demoralized the resistance. Carrying this process of conquest to the Philippines were those most intimately familiar with it: a corps of career officers steeped in small-unit Indian fighting and a strong representation of volunteer units drawn from Western states that had recently witnessed the last phase of frontier warfare. Of the thirty generals who served in the Philippines between 1898 and 1902, twenty-six (including all four commanding officers) were experienced Indian fighters, and the remainder had some other kind of connection to the American West.[4]

By McKinley's day, Americans had already proved proficient at playing the imperial game on a steadily expanding stage. Growing national strength and confidence made it possible for assertive U.S. leaders to gather up great stretches of territory from France, Spain, and Russia as well as from Spain's successor regime in Mexico. Only the imperial prizes of Cuba and Canada escaped the U.S. grasp. What Americans did not seize, they shielded from the clutches of other powers. After much of Spanish Latin America declared independence, President James Monroe proclaimed in 1823 that the European powers were to keep their hands off. By the time of McKinley's presidency Monroe's doctrine had become internationally respected even by Great Britain. Americans who had begun the century hemmed in by other empires had become adept at poaching on them. Guided by their "manifest destiny," they had fastened control over a vast stretch of North America and fenced the hemisphere off from European ambitions.

By the time McKinley took office in 1897, Americans' outlook on imperial expansion in the Pacific was still in flux, though the general tendency was telling. Acquiring Pacific Ocean frontage seemed to set the stage for a new phase in the westward advance of civilization with Americans the prime agents and China the ultimate objective. At the same time, European and Japanese ambitions across the Pacific seemed ever more threatening, not just to American dreams but also to American strategic and trade interests. New naval technology—not least steam-driven armored warships with accurate long-range guns—had made the world seem smaller and more dangerous. Territory once considered remote now mattered. American missionaries and commercial interests active in China and Hawaii were joined by big-navy advocates in promoting the notion of an American Pacific destiny and warning against European schemes that might deny Americans their proper influence in the region. U.S. naval expeditions regularly prowled the western Pacific bolstering national prestige, keeping an eye on the other powers, and beating down doors to foreign trade. The demonstration of force led by Commodore Matthew Perry against Japan in 1853–54 was the best known of these, but other naval officers tried their luck in Chinese and Korean waters with less success than Perry.

Following the Civil War, the breadth and tempo of American involvement in eastern Asia increased. Washington began acquiring maritime outposts (Midway in 1867 and Pearl Harbor in 1887), and in 1885 sharply challenged German claims in Samoa. After a narrowly averted naval clash, Washington and Berlin joined London in putting Samoa under a temporary three-way protectorate. Equally notable was the rising presence of private citizens, some hired to help with Asian modernization initiatives and others bent on saving souls. By 1889 nearly five hundred American missionaries were at work in China alone. During the following decade levels of domestic support for proselytizing reached a crescendo, and so did Chinese harassment and violence directed against an exposed network of mission stations spreading into the interior. The resulting incidents prompted missionary calls for U.S. government protection. Increasingly officials obliged.

Against this backdrop, Hawaii became the scene of the first overtly imperial U.S. exercise in the Pacific. The results were ambiguous. By 1893 American sugar plantation owners and their missionary allies had gained control of the economic and cultural life of the islands. While curbing the Hawaiian monarch, they promoted an ever tighter relationship with the United States. When this settler minority overthrew the monarchy that year and approached Washington on joining the union, the outgoing administration of Benjamin Harrison responded favorably. A takeover would foreclose any British, German, or Japanese claims on the islands. But the newly elected President Grover Cleveland regarded the coup as illegitimate; outspoken West Coast nativists wanted nothing to do with an Asia that sent hordes of cheap Chinese labor their way; and important leaders in Congress shared these reservations and added their concerns about the difficulty of defending distant island possessions. Frustrated, the settlers in Hawaii set up their own republic. They would wait for the political winds on the mainland to shift.

A confrontation with Spain over Cuba kicked up the squall that they were waiting for. It carried U.S. ambitions all the way to the Philippines, an archipelago of some seven thousand tropical islands about seven thousand miles from the U.S. mainland. McKinley took office facing a stale-mated struggle between Cubans demanding independence and a Spanish ruling class clinging to the remains of a once great empire even though the treasury was empty and Spain's armed forces were unable to pacify restive subjects. Demands for independence had flared into armed resis-tance in 1868, subsided following the promise of autonomy in 1878, and then erupted again in the early 1890s. By 1896 Spanish forces faced a small but stubborn guerrilla resistance, which even draconian measures failed to extinguish. While the fighting in Cuba—grinding, destructive, and cruel—failed to restore Spain's upper hand, it did disrupt American business and investments there and generate humanitarian outrage in the United States. McKinley at first sought to resolve the conflict through diplomatic pres-sure. But Madrid's half-hearted offer of autonomy was now unacceptable to Cubans, while significant concessions to Cubans collided with a strong current of opinion in Spain determined to hang on to Cuba even at the risk of war with the United States. By February 1898 McKinley was facing at home a rising chorus of jingoists demanding armed intervention and charg-ing Madrid with not negotiating in good faith. The chorus grew louder after Spanish authorities were implicated (falsely as it turned out) in the sinking of the American battleship *Maine* in Havana harbor on 15 February 1898. In late April 1898, with fellow Republicans pressing for action and Congress in near revolt, McKinley asked for an authorization to go to war. Congress quickly obliged.

To this point McKinley had been conflicted and hesitant over the pros-pects of war with all its terrible and unknown consequences. His combat experience during the Civil War had taught him what happened once the guns began to fire. He was in addition temperamentally cautious as he had demonstrated in a political career spanning three decades. But like other Americans he was susceptible to an expansive nationalism that envisioned a great future for his country on the world stage. He also could appreciate the political advantages that accrued to a war president and the leeway it allowed him to advance the interests of the nation. The president now wheeled into action, carried along by the almost instant successes against Spanish forces and the enthusiasm that news of one victory after another produced at home.

Following the war declaration, an energized president directed U.S. forces to take Cuba and Puerto Rico and to seek out the Spanish fleet de-fending the Philippines. McKinley's actions followed navy contingency plans going back to mid-1896. These plans anticipated that a successful strike at the Philippines would deprive Spain of both a base of operations and a source of revenue. In short order—on 1 May 1898—U.S. warships under the command of Commodore George Dewey scored a fateful victory in Manila Bay. By July the administration had scooped up Puerto Rico without resistance, gotten the campaign in Cuba well under way, and pushed Hawaii's annexation through Congress. War had strengthened the argument for the importance of a Pacific stronghold to protect the West Coast and to serve as a way station for the U.S. advance into the western Pacific. The next month Manila, the last Spanish bastion in the Philippines, fell to U.S. forces, giving them a foothold in a land otherwise under the control of the Filipino forces fighting for independence. The United States was having "a splendid little war," so observed John Hay (the man about to become McKinley's secretary of state).[5] On 12 August Madrid bowed to Washington's cease-fire terms. The president proceeded to gather up the spoils of war. He subjected Cuba to a U.S. military occupation that would end in 1902 with the island formally independent but in fact politically and economically subordinate to the United States. He insisted that the peace treaty concluded with Spain on 10 December hand over the Philippines, Guam, and Puerto Rico. On 6 February 1899, the president won Senate approval of his handiwork.

McKinley's transpacific push continued in 1899 and 1900, driven by rising alarm over the major powers' carving up of China into ever more distinct spheres of influence. Trade groups warned against the prospect of restrictions against U.S. commerce in a China threatened by formal partition. In September 1899 Secretary of State Hay issued a formal warning to the powers against obstructing U.S. commercial access within their spheres of influence. In December McKinley diverted his attention from China long enough to reach an agreement with Germany to partition Samoa but then shifted back the next year as an armed popular movement, what came to be known as the Boxer Rebellion, spread like wildfire across northern China. Washington at first watched incredulous as Boxer bands took hold in the countryside, attacked foreign missionaries and their Chinese converts, and finally won the support of court officials seething over years of foreign intervention. With Boxers and sympathetic imperial forces dominating the capital and laying siege to its diplomatic quarter, McKinley decided to dispatch U.S. troops as a part of an international army assembled to pacify and punish.

McKinley wanted to make clear that the United States was a formidable Pacific power. Some four thousand American troops helped take Beijing, quell the Boxers, and bring the ruling dynasty to account. With China's future still unsettled, Hay issued a second, more broadly drawn open-door note in September. This time he warned the powers against converting their informal spheres into a formal partition. Privately he dismissed as "mere flap-doodle" the notion that the United States was in any position to dictate.[6] But in fact his call to preserve a faltering Chinese empire as a political entity gave voice to an emerging conviction that preserving American influence was essential to China's progress and to the U.S. future as a Pacific power. While China was emerging in the closing decades of the nineteenth century as the part of eastern Asia that Americans most prized, it was also proving a difficult catch. The country was enormous, its elites were highly politicized and averse to foreign control, and other powers with their own agendas were well entrenched. The Philippines was a different story.

Of all these initiatives that began to stake out American claims in the mid- and western Pacific, the taking of the Philippines was the most surprising and unsettling. Here was a land at great remove from the U.S. mainland and with no prospect of cultural or political amalgamation through settlement. A colonial commitment was sure to plunge the administration into serious controversy. Complicating the prospects of annexation, the islands were in the grip of independence fever. The Spanish had answered reform demands with repression, finally precipitating an armed uprising in August 1896. The resistance forces had not fared well in the fighting around Manila and in nearby provinces, so the revolutionary leaders had struck a deal with the colonial authorities. They would go into exile in exchange for cash payments and the promise of reform. This deal marked a pause in the push for independence, not its death knell. Later, with the Spanish preoccupied by U.S. ambitions, armed resistance would resume, this time with greater success.

With good reason, McKinley moved toward his decision incrementally. As commander in chief, he created compelling facts on the ground. His order in April to attack the Spanish fleet defending the Philippines not only yielded a quick naval victory but also paved the way for the president's equally quick decision to dispatch U.S. forces to secure a U.S. foothold there. At minimum he could use the islands as a pawn in any peace settlement. On 4 May he ordered the first contingent of U.S. troops to deploy, and he added more in the course of the month. By 3 June, McKinley was eyeing Manila as a commercial entrepôt and naval base along with the main island of Luzon, on which that colonial capital was located. Just as Madrid sued for peace in early August, U.S. forces secured the surrender of Manila, and McKinley insisted that the cease-fire agreement leave the future of the Philippines a matter for resolution in the final peace talks. On 16 September he told his negotiating team in Paris that he wanted all of Luzon. On 28 October he went a step further, instructing them to claim the entire Philippines.[7] To soften this blow to Spain, McKinley authorized the payment of $20 million (included as a provision in the final treaty). Converted to its present-day value, his outlay came to about half a billion dollars.

McKinley supplied posterity a rough sense of the logic that guided those decisions. Taking only Manila or Luzon was impractical. Those who knew the islands had convinced him that both places were integrally tied to the rest of the archipelago. He could not return the islands to the brutal and benighted Spaniards. Independence would not work. The childlike nature of the Filipinos, according to the president's recital, would lead them into "anarchy and misrule." Walking away and letting the now vulnerable islands go to some other power struck McKinley as "bad business and discreditable." The British, the leading imperial power of the day, were already dominant in the Philippine banking and export sector and conveniently ensconced in nearby Hong Kong. They could take quick, decisive action. The Japanese with their nascent empire, including Taiwan just to the north, would be closely eyeing the Philippines. German ambitions were also a cause for worry, as the naval face-off over Samoa had dramatically made clear. Finally, McKinley knew that hanging onto the Philippines would appeal to naval strategists looking for bases to secure the Pacific and to the business community interested in the China market.[8]

McKinley made his intentions public in the same incremental fashion that he had set his goals. He assumed at first a posture of indecision and only gradually revealed his hand while carefully gauging popular attitudes. In this process he made the most of the new technologies of the time: the mass press and the telegraph to reach a national audience; and the railroad network to help him canvas a wide sweep of the country quickly and conveniently. All the while his staff fed him informal surveys of press and letters from the public, which served as a substitute for opinion polling. Encouraged by what he saw, he began gingerly to appeal in public in the same terms that he also used in private. His message repeated in ever more emphatic terms was that his policy toward the Philippines followed the dictates of "destiny" and "duty." What he meant was that the course of the war had created for Americans obligations which they as an honorable people could not evade.

McKinley discovered that the public needed little prodding. His repeated references to colonial duties undertaken with national pride elicited consistently enthusiastic public responses. During a tour of the Midwest in October, he avoided explicit references to the Philippines, thus depriving critics, already then mobilizing, a good target. But he said enough to thrill the large crowds he attracted and to buoy Republican chances in the November congressional elections. For example, in Iowa on 13 October he observed obliquely, "Territory sometimes comes to us when we go to war in a holy cause, and whenever it does the banner of liberty will float over it and bring, I trust, the blessings and benefits to all people." Following the conclusion of his peace treaty with Spain in December, McKinley again went before the public, now to explain why he had included transfer of the Philippines. Touring the South, he sounded even more emphatically than earlier the themes of destiny and duty. On 15 December in Atlanta he talked of planting the American flag "in two hemispheres" in the name "of liberty and law, of peace and progress." Now defiant, he asked, "Who will haul it down?" The audience responded (according to the contemporary record) with "tremendous applause."[9]

From what we know of late-nineteenth-century public opinion, McKinley depended heavily on community, business, and professional leaders around the country to get a favorable response to his rhetorical question. These influential people were preponderantly Protestant and Anglo and generally urban and well educated, with higher incomes and high-status jobs as lawyers, clergy, and professors. Those who had served in Washington or spent time abroad commanded special deference in discussions of the annexation issue. Before radio and television gave a president's voice national and instantaneous reach, this attentive, knowledgeable public could shape opinion within their communities and circles of contacts. They could sway the broader electorate—some 12 million adult white males (perhaps 20 percent of the total population), including some three-quarters of the voters (heavily rural and working class) who were uninformed or barely informed and harder for national leaders to reach.[10]

The influential minority of the voting public and probably the mass base were predisposed to the kind of nationalist arguments McKinley made. The narrative of a once small, weak country whose territorial, political, and economic success had made it the wonder of the world was by the end of the nineteenth century widely disseminated and accepted in U.S. political culture. Sympathy for the Cuban independence struggle had set the fire under the nationalist kettle and gotten it simmering. War with Spain, ending in a quick, glorious victory, brought it to full boil. By the time the president began to sort out his Philippine options, the passions driving American politics made his nationalist appeal a winning strategy. Republicans hoping to win elections in a country closely divided along partisan lines needed an argument that would evoke broad popular support. McKinley's theme of duty and destiny, with its overtones of piety and racial superiority, nicely fit the ticket. Taking in hand backward but redeemable "Orientals" and demonstrating the fitness of Americans as a leading people of the world had an appeal that transcended turn-of-the-century regional, party, religious, and ethnic divides. War had done more than teach Americans geography (to paraphrase McKinley's contemporary, the satirist Ambrose Bierce); it had also directed them down a new path of self-righteousness.

Having made his case for securing an American colony on the far shore of the Pacific, McKinley still had to overcome strong opposition in the Senate inspired by a powerful undercurrent of public doubt about the president's plans. Here he caught a couple of lucky breaks. William Jennings Bryan, the leader of the Democratic Party, decided against a showdown on the issue despite personal and party opposition to taking the Philippines. Looking to the 1900 election (his second face-off against McKinley), Bryan calculated that his chances would be better if he kept the focus on domestic economic issues. Even with Bryan's decision to stand aside on the treaty, a worried McKinley had to engage in some vigorous backstage deal-making to win over enough wavering senators to secure ratification.

Just as the Senate was about to vote after a month of debate, McKinley got his second break—news of the outbreak of fighting in Manila between American troops and the forces of the Philippine independence movement. Private Grayson's shot echoed through the capital. Opponents of annexation had to ask if they were prepared to turn their back on American forces now engaged in battle. On 6 February McKinley's treaty scraped by 57 to 27, one vote over the two-thirds constitutionally required for ratification. The president celebrated his victory ten days later in Boston before an assemblage of almost six thousand. He once more sounded the themes of duty and destiny. Denying any imperial ambitions of the sort his critics accused him of, he posed as a liberator. Filipinos "shall for ages hence bless the American republic because it emancipated and redeemed their fatherland, and set them in the pathway of the world's best civilization."[11]

As he moved from one critical decision to another, McKinley had the support of a small team. By comparison with the gargantuan White House staff of recent times, his was minuscule. He relied heavily on his chief of staff and press secretary, George B. Cortelyou. Under the press of business (including the telegraphic and telephone traffic that allowed the president to follow and shape events), the clerks under Cortelyou would expand from a handful to a total of thirty by early 1901.[12] McKinley also turned for help to his cabinet secretaries. His long-time associate, William R. Day, served him first as secretary of state during the war with Spain and then as head of the commission to negotiate the peace in Paris. Later in managing the Philippines conflict, McKinley depended on Secretary of War Elihu Root and on a couple of small, presidentially appointed ad hoc commissions to assess the situation on the islands and make recommendations. William Howard Taft at the head of the second commission would round out the group of influential figures. The president was ringmaster in a very small circus.

ROOTS OF RESISTANCE

Wanting a colony was one thing, securing it another. By February 1899 McKinley had already learned this home truth known to empire builders from time immemorial. No matter how high-sounding the professed motives of the conqueror, peoples under the sword may not willingly submit. The problem, as the humorist Peter Finley Dunne phrased it, was that McKinley might want to give his new charges a measure of freedom, but he first had to get them to stand still long enough to be measured. Most fidgety of all was a burgeoning Philippine independence movement. It had taken up arms in 1896 in response to Spanish repression. When the Americans burst on the scene in 1898, leaders of the independence cause sought to head off a U.S. takeover that promised to perpetuate their country's subjugation.

The land that the American president had claimed had undergone a dramatic transformation in the course of the nineteenth century. Expanding global demand for hemp (used for rope), coconuts, sugar, and tobacco had brought an economic revolution to the islands in the form of plantation agriculture. A new class of Filipinos emerged in Manila, the rapidly growing center of economic and political activity, and in other commercial nodes across the islands raising, selling, and transporting cash crops. These Filipinos grew wealthy, began to participate in local governance, and sought education for their sons in local secondary schools. A few attended Spanish schools in Manila and even Madrid.

This new class added one more layer to an already socially segmented society of nearly 7 million people. The Spanish-born had long claimed pride of place, followed by Spaniards born and raised in the Philippines. Chinese hailing from southern Fujian province had established themselves alongside the Spanish from the outset of the colonial era and emerged as eco-nomic middlemen between the rising port of Manila and the native (*indio*) population practicing subsistence agriculture in the hinterlands. The all-male Chinese population came under Spanish pressure to assimilate. Those who refused to convert to Catholicism and otherwise clung to their cultural practices became the target of prejudice and occasional physical assault. Colonial authorities finally imposed a ban on immigration that lasted into the middle of the nineteenth century. By then expanding trade had resulted in a reopening of migration from China while also attracting a community of foreign businessmen and investors (with the British especially promi-nent). The Filipinos claiming a prominent place in this social mosaic were all Hispanicized and many were mestizo—primarily the offspring of *indio*-Chinese unions.

Filipinos on the rise within the colonial system had by the late 1880s and early 1890s become restive under Spanish rule. Commerce and education had broadened their personal vistas. Their taste for greater influence set them at odds with aristocratic Spanish overlords claiming privileged status and with Catholic religious orders deeply entrenched in local society and in control of large landholdings. Nationalist notions acquired in Manila and Madrid gave language and legitimacy to their discontents. The signs of the European political influence on Philippine nationalists were pervasive—in their marked obsession with constitutions as the key to a well-ordered polity; in their florid, romantic language about national identity rooted in the native land and in a mythic past; in their melodramatically professed readiness to make the ultimate sacrifice on behalf of the people; and in their paradoxical mix of sharply anticlerical sentiments with frequent invo-cations of divine favor. Nationalist ideas became a critical part of the elite's vision for the future, and by degrees these ideas permeated the islands' lit-erature, press, and schools.

José Rizal was the leading voice of educated Filipinos demanding re-forms—greater freedom at home, an end to abusive and discriminatory colonial practices, and representation in the Spanish legislature. Born in 1861 into a mestizo family of middling means, he had studied in his birth-place just south of Manila (in Laguna province) and then with the Jesuits in Manila. In 1882 Rizal left for Europe, where he studied in Madrid as well as Paris and Heidelberg and won a reputation as a Renaissance man as much at home in the arts and literature as in science. A prolific writer who expressed himself in Spanish rather than his native Tagalog, Rizal spoke for an elite that was learning to transcend its regional differences and that would (he hoped) function collectively as "the brain of the country."[13] He warned that Spain would either have to grant the reforms this elite was demanding or face a revolt that a decrepit empire was bound to lose. On his return to the Philippines in 1892, Rizal was arrested for sedition, condemned to internal exile, and then executed in 1896. The foremost voice of the nationalist cause became at once its greatest martyr.

Rizal's death coincided with the shift in anticolonial sentiment from reform to insurrection under the auspices of the Katipunan. This secret revolutionary brotherhood, founded in 1892, emphasized social solidarity and social equality. By August 1896, when the fighting with Spanish forces began, the Katipunan membership probably totaled in the thousands, concentrated in Manila and areas just to the south. Its leader was Andrés Bonifacio, a clerk of fairly humble origins with little formal education. Drawing on a tradition of folk religion, he fashioned a nationalist appeal attractive to the "ignorant and poor" in central and southern Luzon. He denounced the treacherous Spanish for "contaminating us with their lowly behavior, forcibly destroying the good customs of the land." According to the statement of the society's principles, the task of redeeming the Mother Country from three centuries of political abuse and cultural corruption fell to the kind of man who treats others with "dignity and honor, does not oppress nor allows himself to be oppressed, . . . and loves his native land." In this formulation the well-born and powerful—those with "a high aquiline nose and a white skin" or who occupied "an exalted and privileged position on earth"—were suspect.[14]

The local elites who rallied to the Katipunan were to emerge as some of the most prominent nationalist leaders. They would capture the Katipunan and use its language even as they pushed aside its founding figures and ignored its commitment to social justice. None was more prominent than Emilio Aguinaldo. Born in 1869 into a mestizo family with substantial resources, Aguinaldo received some secondary education and then in his late teens entered local politics and interisland trade. He joined the Katipunan in 1895, and in 1896 he emerged as a relatively effective resistance commander thanks to his previous experience leading police operations against bandits. The times called, he argued, for a "centralized military committee" headed by a president to direct the fighting, a distinct break from Bonifacio's decentralized, consultative approach.[15] In March 1897, with Spanish forces rapidly regaining control in Cavite (just to the south of Manila), the leaders of the resistance in the area came together to accept Aguinaldo's plan for a top-down command organization. They elected him head of the revolutionary movement. Bonifacio was already in eclipse as a result of the defeats forces under his command had suffered. When he resisted Aguinaldo's authority and his efforts to assemble the state machinery critical to defeating the Spanish and securing independence, Aguinaldo ordered Bonifacio's arrest and after some indecision his execution in May. These events ended the Katipunan's leading organizational role. Aguinaldo and other regional leaders would henceforth dominate the nationalist cause.

No sooner had Aguinaldo secured his commanding position than he suffered defeat in May 1897 in his home province of Cavite. With his conventional military campaign in trouble, he belatedly shifted in September to guerrilla warfare of the sort that he knew the Cubans were waging to wear down the Spanish. Finally, in December he accepted a face-saving deal with Spanish authorities. He agreed to go into exile in exchange for cash payments into the revolutionary coffers. Aguinaldo and his close associates moved to the British colony of Hong Kong. Their revolutionary committee in exile continued to plot while guerrilla operations against the Spanish spread with increasing effect.

News of the outbreak of the Spanish-American War must have struck the exiles like a bolt of lightning quickly followed by the thunderous report of the Americans' smashing of the Spanish fleet. This news prompted the revolutionary committee on 4 May 1898 to agree that Aguinaldo should return home to renew the struggle. But on whose side? Spanish images of Americans as ruthless and racist circulated among influential, well-to-do Filipinos and made them wary of U.S. intentions. Stories of the extermination of Native Americans in particular gave rise to doubts about the Americans that would increasingly figure in revolutionary commentary.[16]

Apolinario Mabini, one of the most determined and acute proponents of independence, argued for caution. Born in 1864 in the southern Luzon province of Laguna, he had risen to prominence despite his family's poverty. He had managed to get his schooling in Manila, where he earned a law degree. In 1896 Mabini embraced the nationalist cause, and his political brilliance quickly made him Aguinaldo's chief adviser and ghostwriter. (He came to be known affectionately as the "sublime paralytic" because illness contracted in 1896 left his lower limbs paralyzed but his mind as sharp as ever.) Writing in April 1898, he asked his colleagues to imagine Spain's winning the test with the United States and in the process so exhausting itself that Philippine independence would follow with relative ease. Alternatively, he reasoned, if Philippine forces helped defeat the Spanish, this would create an opening for the Americans, who were as prone to seizin

Imperial Ambitions and National Ferment

"COLOSSUS OF THE PACIFIC," *Chicago Tribune*, 24 August 1898. This expression of Pacific dreams that became reality in the wake of the war with Spain was modeled on a famous British cartoon of the time in which empire builder Cecil Rhodes is depicted standing athwart all of Africa.

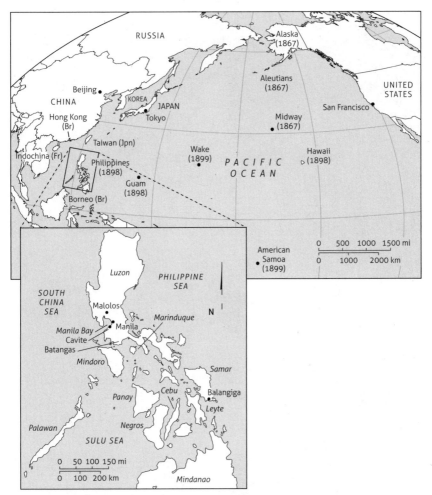

The Philippines in a vast new field for imperial ambitions. While Americans were taking the first bold steps in the making of an overseas empire, nationalist sentiment was on the upswing in the Philippines. Nationalism and by extension resistance to the U.S. takeover was strongest among elites on the island of Luzon, especially in Manila and adjoining areas, including notably the provinces of Cavite and Batangas.

Emilio Aguinaldo, probably 1898 or early 1899. This resistance leader and head of state hailed from Cavite. McKinley's secretary of war, Elihu Root, dismissed him as "a Chinese half-breed" at the head of the Tagalog "tribe." (*From* Rockett, *Our Boys in the Philippines* [1899])

Miguel Malvar, circa 1902. This skillful resistance leader hailed from Batangas. He led the opposition there until finally in 1902 succumbing to U.S. pacification pressures. (Photograph courtesy of Glenn May)

vulnerable territory as were Spain and the other European powers. The best strategy was to preempt U.S. ambitions by convincing the Americans they faced "a strong and organized people who know how to defend the laws of justice and their honor."[17]

Pedro Paterno, a nationalist leader noted for his caution, was equally skeptical of U.S. intentions. But he drew different conclusions. Born into a wealthy Chinese-mestizo merchant family, the young Paterno moved as a youth to Spain. There he lived for nearly a quarter century, becoming culturally assimilated and politically well connected. He came to regard Spanish and Filipinos as peoples of "one blood," with the colonized capable of rising to the level of the civilized and cultivated colonizers. He returned home to Manila in 1893 and following the outbreak of the revolution made himself useful to the colonial government by helping broker the 1897 agreement by which Spain purchased Aguinaldo's exile. In a revealing moment while talking to the revolutionaries, Paterno reportedly suggested that rebellion would bring "certain ruin." Aguinaldo is supposed to have flared: "You who, with your superior education, should be guides to us blind ones who gladly struggle to reconquer the liberty of the land, are the ones who put most obstacles in the way and are the worst enemies of the insurrection."[18]

Writing in mid-1898 following the U.S. declaration of war, Paterno still wanted to stick to the safer course, and that meant siding with the Spanish. They were a known quantity, culturally familiar from nearly four centuries of colonial contact, while their declining power left them vulnerable to nationalist demands. The Americans were by contrast strangers who could pose considerable peril to the Philippines. "We neither know that nation nor its language. The Americans will endeavour by all imaginable means to induce us to help them against Spain. And then, alas! they, the all powerful, will absorb us and reward our treachery to Spain by betraying us, making us slaves and imposing upon us all the evils of a new colonization."[19]

Aguinaldo decided to seize the moment—to finish off the Spanish—but also to keep a wary eye on the Americans. He would renew the military campaign against a colonial force now distracted by the Americans. Victories on the ground would in turn, he hoped, bolster the authority and legitimacy of the independence cause and enable him to forestall any U.S. takeover of the islands. Through the remaining months of Spain's war with the United States (May to August) and in the six months following, Aguinaldo directed at Americans—from local commanders to McKinley himself— a campaign of flattery, professions of goodwill and gratitude, and veiled threats of armed resistance. He wanted their acceptance of Philippine independence. If necessary, he confessed to his representative in Washington, he was ready at least to consider some form of negotiated "protection or annexation."[20]

The caution that marked this emergent Philippine nationalism—from the 1897 truce with Spain to Mabini's and Paterno's analysis in mid-1898 to Aguinaldo's strategy in the later half of 1898—reflected its leaders' sense of vulnerability. Internationally they were isolated, with no real patrons and with the great powers circling like buzzards ready to feast on the expiring Spanish empire. Domestically they were beset by deep divisions. One critical and enduring fault line was religious, pitting a Catholic majority against a Muslim minority in the south (Mindanao and the string of islands to its southwest). Muslims had stoutly resisted the imposition of direct Spanish control and would continue to jealously defend their autonomy against outsiders, whether Americans or Filipinos. A second fault line was cultural. A population scattered across an array of islands was divided into eleven major language groups and poorly integrated by transport and communications. Even the predominantly Muslim area split along tribal and clan loyalties. From the outset of the nationalist movement Tagalog speakers dominated the nationalist political and military leadership, with Tagalog areas (notably central and southern Luzon but also Mindoro, Marinduque, and part of Palawan) most active in the resistance. Filipinos outside these core areas felt less of a stake in the nationalist cause. Finally, the Philippines was socially fractured. The privileged new class—with its wealth from commerce and land, its rising ambitions, and its initiation into the Spanish world of learning and politics—had grown apart from an uneducated and poor peasant majority. While the elites claimed to speak for the people, their visions derived from their own distinct experiences and interests.

Of these divisions, the one along class lines would most debilitate the nationalist cause. The elites envisioned a political revolution whose goals reflected European influences and whose outcome would consolidate the position of prominent Philippine families as the new masters of the nation. The privileged men who led the revolution were accustomed to a sharply limited suffrage that had allowed them to dominate local government under the Spanish. They had no interest in changing the electoral system to allow broader participation in voting, not to mention officeholding. They would now control the national as well as the local administration. Most ordinary Filipinos were, in contrast, intensely preoccupied with securing a livelihood from the land. The landless and tenant farmers wanted above all to improve their lives. Their notion of a better future thus involved access to land, tax relief, and an end to coerced labor. They also wanted local communities to be protected from the exactions of corrupt officials and the abuses of powerful, land-hungry local notables. The political goals to which elites aspired meant little to the masses, while popular dreams of security, equality, and justice seemed to elites a harbinger of social disorder. When war with the United States came, some ordinary Filipinos may have fought because they disliked the invaders or wanted adventure. But most of them probably followed the directions of local patrons. Pressed on this point, a man preoccupied with taking care of his land explained, "We were fighting because our officers told us to fight. We obeyed our officers."[21] He and other ordinary Filipinos had scant personal investment in a cause that depended on prolonged popular sacrifice to wear down the Americans.

Aguinaldo's strategy of cultivating, accommodating, and neutralizing the Americans began promisingly. The outbreak of war had found Aguinaldo in Singapore, where he secured meetings with the American consul general, E. Spencer Pratt, on 24 and 25 April. Pratt reported to Washington his favorable impression of the Philippine leader ("a man of intelligence, ability, and courage") and noted that his troops might prove helpful in the looming Spanish-American battle for the Philippines. Aguinaldo encouraged Pratt with expressions of interest in American "protection" as well as "advice and assistance" as the Filipinos set up their own government. Influenced by Pratt, Commodore Dewey arranged Aguinaldo's return home on 19 May and quickly established what he described as "cordial" relations. In late June he reported to Washington his favorable impressions: "These people are far superior in their intelligence and more capable of self-government than the natives of Cuba."[22]

Hardly a month after he returned home, Aguinaldo had raised an army and launched military operations. He declared national independence on 12 June as one more in the string of steps intended to convince Americans that independence was a foregone conclusion. He tried to drive that point home in a letter to McKinley (probably drafted by Mabini). Aguinaldo expressed his thanks for help in throwing off the Spanish yoke and praised the United States for serving Filipinos as "the harbinger of their liberty." But he also declared that his country "should not be sold as if it were a lamb to be sacrificed and exploited for the greed of another nation." U.S. traditions, principles, and constitution ruled out such a course, the Philippine leader hopefully suggested. Also standing in the way, he warned, was the will of a people both "warlike" and "thoroughly civilized."[23]

Revolutionary forces soon had the Spanish on the run and their Manila stronghold besieged. In September Aguinaldo summoned an assembly in Malolos (some twenty miles north of Manila) to form a Philippine revolutionary government. With the last vestiges of Spanish authority gone, Paterno the respectable moderate showed up to embrace the revolutionary cause. He was elected president of the assembly and at once threw his literary skills and considerable wealth behind popularizing the nationalist cause. Now invested by the assembly with a claim to national legitimacy, Aguinaldo and his associates set about substantiating that claim by building up government administrative and military functions through the second half of 1898 and early 1899.

Nationalist achievements and suasion counted for less and less as American troops massed in ever greater numbers on the islands between late June and early August. It became increasingly clear that McKinley was in the Philippines, as in Cuba, determined to rule unencumbered by native claims. During late May and early June, the president cautioned Dewey and Pratt against making any commitments to Aguinaldo that would compromise U.S. freedom of action, and he himself parried Philippine claims to independence. Confirmation that the president would insist on a free hand came on 13 August when U.S. forces took Manila without involving Aguinaldo's troops, even though the latter's siege of the city predated the American arrival. After the Spanish garrison had surrendered following a pro forma defense, the president informed his commanders that there would be no joint occupation. Americans troops thus deployed around the city to keep Philippine units out while U.S. commanders pressed Aguinaldo during the fall to pull his troops back a safe distance from U.S. lines. While Philippine soldiers gave vent to anti-American sentiments, Aguinaldo and his lieutenants swallowed their anger and gave the Americans the space they demanded. But McKinley continued to move forward. By October, with annexation settled, he was categorically rejecting the legitimacy of the Philippine government and having nothing to do with the Philippine representative in Washington, Felipe Agoncillo. The peace treaty concluded with Spain in early December incorporated a transfer provision ignoring the preferences of Filipinos and the existence of a functioning Philippine government. On 21 December McKinley issued orders to extend military government over the entire territory.

With an American takeover looming, the Filipino campaign to avert an armed conflict entered its last desperate phase. In December and January Agoncillo in Washington made the case for his country's independence as a foregone conclusion and for annexation as inconsistent with U.S. principles. The briefs prepared by this lawyer from Batangas sought to sway not the McKinley administration, which ignored him, but its critics, above all senators who were looking for information that might help defeat the treaty effecting annexation. At home Aguinaldo actively prepared for a possible clash of arms. Early in January he sought to solidify popular support by proclaiming the end of the forced labor regime carried over from the Spanish era. (At no point was Aguinaldo prepared to address the other pressing social issues of taxation, corruption, or redistribution of land taken from the Spanish friars.) Later that month in Malolos, Aguinaldo oversaw the inauguration of the Republic of the Philippines.

Even as he sought to consolidate his domestic base, Aguinaldo sent emissaries to the U.S. command of General Elwell Otis in a desperate attempt to avert conflict. They dangled the prospect of a U.S. protectorate limited to foreign affairs and defense. Americans could not, they warned, impose control over Filipinos "in the same manner as over savages." Otis's agents insisted on full U.S. sovereignty over the islands. The Filipinos would have to accept that they were as much subjects now as under Spanish rule but also take heart in the knowledge that their new masters would proceed "in substantial harmony" with the interests of their subjects.[24]

A TEST OF ARMS

Aguinaldo did not want the collision between U.S. and Philippine forces that came on 4 February. Nor was he prepared for battle that day with his commanders away from the lines around Manila. By contrast, General Otis was keen to resolve the anomalous military situation on the islands, in which two armies glared across the lines at each other. His forces had grown edgy as the tension entered its sixth month. The first exchange of gunfire broke that tension and gave Otis an opportunity to establish his preeminent authority. He told Aguinaldo that the only way to avert further fighting was to disband Philippine forces. The next day Aguinaldo assumed a publicly defiant tone. Enough of "the constant outrages and taunts, which have caused the misery of the people of Manila, and . . . the useless conferences and the contempt shown the Philippine government."[25] The only way to turn back the invaders was through bloodshed and sacrifice. Word that the U.S. Senate had approved annexation on 6 February confirmed for Aguinaldo and his colleagues the stark choice they faced between capitulation and resistance. They would resist.

The U.S. conquest was already under way. The Americans had begun by capturing Manila, excluding Philippine forces from the operation, and gradually pushing their lines away from the city. Consolidating control of Luzon was on the agenda for 1899, and the pacification of the entire archipelago was to follow. At each stage U.S. forces enjoyed an edge of the sort common to other Western armies asserting colonial claims. In gross terms U.S. resources far exceeded anything Philippine nationalists could tap. By the turn of the century the United States was the world's leading economic power with a total output about sixty times that of the Philippines and a population about ten times greater.[26] Without these resources, not to mention a strong state to direct them, McKinley and his administration could not have raised and maintained a substantial force operating at a great distance from the continental United States, not only in the Philippines but also in Cuba and north China. In the conflict in the Philippines alone, the War Department sustained a force at peak numbering some 70,000 but usually closer to 40,000. By contrast, Philippine nationalists were scrambling to patch together an administrative system that could field and sustain a modern army. An estimate of the total Philippine forces during the war ranges from about 80,000 to 100,000 poorly trained, ill-equipped, ill-supplied regulars backed by a substantial but even less well-prepared local militia.

The Americans had an additional edge in the rich and varied professional experience of its officer corps. The most senior had learned the art of war in that most rigorous of courses, the Civil War, while virtually all career officers had additional training in the frontier wars waged against Native Americans into the early 1890s. Some officers arrived in the Philippines with the additional benefit of having participated in the invasion and occupation of Cuba. Preparing men for combat, keeping them supplied, directing small as well as large unit operations, and seeing to the pacification of subject peoples were all in their bag of tricks. The men who led McKinley's army were also eager for action. For decades a sharply downsized force had offered limited opportunities for advancement and distinction. Philippine military leaders from Aguinaldo down were by comparison amateurs on the battlefield and in the operations of a centralized command and keenly aware of the odds against them.

The U.S. advantages first came into play during the spring and summer of 1898 as the army mobilized for war with Spain and then hurriedly diverted troops to the Philippines. McKinley called on 23 April for 125,000 volunteers and then on 25 May for an additional 75,000. The regular army was small, capped by Congress at 28,000 in the post–Civil War decades.

It now expanded by assimilating into federal service units of the National Guard (generally considered unfit to operate on its own) and by adding raw recruits. Career soldiers then turned the mix into an effective, quickly deployed fighting force despite limited stockpiles of uniforms and equipment and an improvised system of supply and transport across the Pacific. With regular army units assigned to operations in Cuba, roughly half the initial forces reaching the Philippines in the course of the summer were volunteer units organized along regimental lines. Some carried the names of the states in which they had been raised (mainly in the western part of the country). Others were federally controlled and commanded.

Minnesota's Thirteenth Volunteer Regiment provides insight into this popular army. In response to McKinley's call at the start of the war with Spain, enough Minnesotans had flocked to arms to form four regiments. Some were moved to volunteer by veterans' tales of the Civil War as a grand adventure, a chance to win personal glory and community esteem. Others wanted to see more of the world, to escape a deadening job, or to strike a blow against an oppressive colonial power. Assigned to service in the Philippines rather than Cuba, the Minnesota Thirteenth set off from St. Paul amid public hoopla. Once in San Francisco the regiment began training and outfitting in earnest. In late June nearly fourteen hundred men began the long transpacific journey. During the thirty-five days at sea they endured cramped quarters, poor provisioning, and seasickness. In early August they finally disembarked south of Manila—and at once they tasted what was ahead: rain and heat that made their camp a dank, muddy agony infested with ants and mosquitoes and plagued by dysentery, malaria, cholera, and dengue fever. Despite these difficulties, the Minnesota Thirteenth maintained its morale and demonstrated its mettle. It helped make quick work of the Spanish garrison on 13 August and then stayed in Manila to keep order and fix up the city. This meant disposing of the refuse accumulated during the siege, rebuilding roads, repairing streetlights and the water system, attending to public health, reopening schools, repressing gambling, and regulating prostitution. Members of the regiment also kept an eye on nearby Philippine forces—an annoyance at best and a future enemy at worst.[27]

In February 1899, following Private Grayson's fateful shot, the Thirteenth and other U.S. units in the Manila area shifted from occupation duties to combat. The first round of fighting, which encompassed much of the year, entailed large units clashing in set piece battles for control of Luzon north of Manila. The results were predictably one-sided. These encounters followed a fairly consistent pattern. Philippine troops would assume defensive positions either in trenches or along natural obstacles such as rivers. The U.S. attack would begin with an artillery barrage—sometimes from guns on ships just offshore, sometimes from guns manned by two special batteries, and sometimes from guns integral to the attacking infantry unit. Their shells would pound the Philippine lines with percussion and shrapnel and quickly silence any counter fire from the few artillery pieces on the other side. The effects were devastating. Those in the trenches who were not killed were soon in retreat with U.S. soldiers in close pursuit. Both sides would then regroup and prepare for the next encounter, though with the Philippine side diminished at each step in numbers and morale. By contrast, U.S. soldiers suffered few casualties, and the wounded had a good chance of survival. Only 6.3 per thousand died during the Spanish-American War, close to the 4.5 figure for World War II and a big improvement over the Civil War rate of 13.3.[28]

The first months of campaigning between February and March resulted in the capture of Malolos, the capital of the Philippine Republic. U.S. forces took a break for the rainy season, then resumed the northward offensive in October and November. By then Aguinaldo's republic had lost any semblance of central organization and much of its army. The president himself was on the run, seeking safety in remote Luzon locations barely one step ahead of the pursuing Americans.

To achieve these victories the U.S. Army had to overcome several handicaps. One was the distinctly outmoded Springfield rifle that ordinary infantrymen carried. Dating back to 1873, the Springfield was single shot and used black powder that betrayed the shooter's position. Only gradually were these weapons replaced by the Krag-Jorgensen rifles, which were higher powered, repeat firing, and smokeless. The rifles in the hands of the Filipinos were at the outset at least as good—a mix of Remingtons (similar to the American Springfields) and the even better Mausers (repeat firing with smokeless powder). Fortunately for U.S. soldiers, Philippine infantrymen were notoriously poor shots. In any case, the limited number of rifles meant that some substantial part of any unit was composed of "bolomen" who wielded nothing more than large knives normally used in harvesting.

The other U.S. handicap was persistent supply difficulties and constant illness that hobbled forces fighting in the field. While units located on the coast or along rivers were easily reached by ships or rafts, getting food, ammunition, and mail to units operating inland required trains of ox carts or pack animals traversing rugged trails often turned by rain into quagmires and constantly subject to ambush. Microbes were an even greater threat than enemy bullets. They had begun their attack in the training camps stateside and intensified the assault once troops reached the Philippines and moved into rural areas. Medical staff could do little except provide rest and for the worst cases a ticket home. The damage was impressive. Half of a unit's roster could be ill at any one point and cumulatively disease accounted for more casualties than the enemy. For example, with some 1,400 men the Thirteenth Minnesota suffered a total of forty-four deaths, only eight from combat. Most of the rest were from disease.

The Minnesotans' experience in the spring campaigning demonstrates how the U.S. Army fought effectively despite these handicaps. In their first clash with the enemy in late February, they inflicted heavy losses while suffering light casualties (all wounded). A month later, still in high spirits, the regiment joined the northward advance. The familiar heat and disease now mixed with hard marches, unpredictable food supplies, and anxiety over the sharp but short encounters with the enemy. By the time campaigning ended on 18 May with the line of advance some fifty miles north of Manila, the romantic gloss once eager volunteers had put on war had lost its sheen. Private George W. Kurtz wrote, "We got what we have been praying for a long time and we found that it was not as much fun as we expected." Another trooper, John Bowe, recorded in his diary what war now meant to him: "double-timing across country under tropical skies, going hungry several days at a stretch, lying in trenches soaked to the skin, and pushing buffalo carts across country."[29]

These impressions echo in the accounts left by men from other units who participated in the first months of the Philippine-American War. Capt. Jacob Kreps, a regular army officer, watched his company of men with sympathy as they endured the trial that weather and terrain imposed. During the day he observed troopers "standing on one foot, then the other, attempting to keep dry, while at the same time trying to keep a fire going and fry bacon." During the night typhoon rains left all "drenched to the skin, trying vainly to rest comfortably on the rough, muddy ground." The next morning they "rose from their muddy beds and sat around campfires until the hot sun finally appeared and dried the clothes on their backs." Private Walter R. Combs, a voice from the ranks, recorded the toll campaigning took on his volunteer unit. "Most of the boys are suffering from diarrhea or other diseases. Clothing is rotting on our backs, and some men are without shoes. Those of us who have been in battle can say with certainty [sic] that 'war is hell.' It's no fun to wade through rivers and swamps with bullets playing music over your head—and then rest in the sun just long enough for the mud to dry on your body before orders come through to resume the attack." What soldiers had to look forward to was mainly mail call and payday, which set off a spasm of gambling, drinking, and brawling. Sex was also on their minds as the influx of "cosmopolitan harlotry" (as one observer put it) and the army's quick resort to a medical inspection regime both indicate.[30]

By the summer of 1899 the war for the Minnesotans and others in state regiments was over. They had signed up to fight Spain, not to engage in an open-ended war of conquest. They were ready to leave. This refrain in their letters home was soon taken up by state political leaders and even senior officers. After a bit more than a year in Luzon, the Thirteenth joined other state volunteers in saying farewell to the Philippines. Once back in the States, they were feted at stops along the way home, climaxing in a grand parade in Minneapolis. There the state's Democratic governor, John Lind, dueled with visiting President McKinley over whether the Philippines was a war of "conquest and subjugation" or an advantageous war fought "without changing our republican character."[31] The celebrations and the rhetorical fireworks done, the citizen-soldiers resumed civilian life, most in their old jobs.

The quick and clear American victories in the course of 1899 had achieved much—but not an end to the war. With his writ sharply circumscribed and his available resources virtually exhausted, Aguinaldo came to the belated and seemingly reluctant decision to wage a guerrilla-style war. This shift to irregular warfare, accepted by some commanders at once and others later, gave the balance of the conflict in the Philippines a crazy-quilt quality. The degree and kind of resistance varied from region to region, in turn evoking differing responses from the U.S. military.

Where guerrillas were strong, U.S. forces lost some of their advantages evident during the first phase of the fighting. Resorting to a strategy suited to the weak, the remaining Philippine regular units and the local irregulars began avoiding head-on confrontations. They instead played a waiting game, launching only occasional surprise attacks and putting the resistance on a more sustainable basis. Guerrillas operated on terrain that they knew and where sympathetic locals would supply manpower, food, and intelligence. Above all, this new strategy inspired hope, critical to maintaining resistance morale. Simply keeping forces active in the field might ultimately embolden domestic critics of McKinley's colonial adventure and induce the U.S. electorate to put an anti-imperialist Democrat in the White House. One soldier fighting with a small band in Batangas recalled years later his leader's encouraging words: "If we held out long enough, the Americans would get tired and go home."[32]

The first year of the guerrilla phase—1900—proved a time of transition for U.S. forces. Their makeup was changing. The departure in mid-1899 of the state volunteer regiments left a mix of federal volunteer and regular army regiments to extinguish the resistance. When the federal volunteers deactivated in the latter part of 1901, the regular army stayed behind to wage the last stage of the war with the assistance of the growing ranks of Philippine Scouts. In this realignment, African American soldiers assumed a prominent role. They made up six regiments (four regular and two volunteer) that had a substantial hand in the fighting. By December 1900 they totaled 6,000 men, or nearly a tenth of the overall U.S. force.[33] These units, like the rest of the U.S. Army, endured the hardships of the guerrilla phase of the fighting with its exhausting small unit patrolling, debilitating disease, sapping heat, and erratic supply. African American soldiers remained until early 1902, when colonial administrators intent on laying down a clear color line in the Philippines sent them home to face another color line marked by intensifying segregation and disenfranchisement.

The attitude of African American soldiers was filled with ironies that distinguished them from their white counterparts while also embodying prevalent American attitudes about uplift and mission. Blacks were, to begin with, eager to prove themselves as worthy citizens whose manliness, martial skill, patriotism, and good discipline were beyond question and who thus deserved respect and full equality at home. "We moisten the soil with our precious blood, stain the colors with our oozing brains," one noted in what was a steady and revealing stream of letters to hometown black newspapers. Even so, they understood that their demonstration of personal sacrifice came at the expense of another people's claim to citizenship. Indeed, they noted and resented the physical and verbal abuse whites directed against Filipinos. No matter that Filipinos seemed clean, industrious, and thrifty, whites hurled at them "the same vile epithet they hurl at us." "The first thing in the morning is 'Nigger' and the last thing at night is 'Nigger.'" Yet despite this sympathy for Filipinos as "men of our own hue and color," black troopers embraced the imperial presumption that these people were but half civilized and required tutelage in order to expunge the Spanish influence and promote Americanization. Finally, while they sympathized with the cause of Philippine independence, they also imagined the islands—a rich and beautiful land—as a kind of new frontier of commerce and missionary work open to them.[34]

In this second phase of the war U.S. commanders experimented with a variety of strategies, looking for the most effective way to pacify their regions. Civic action that focused on the judicial and legal system, sanitation, schools, and local government offered one way to win popular gratitude and draw elites to the U.S. side. Guerrilla forces left isolated would be easier to find and subdue. Commanders could also take advantage of the U.S. Navy's command of the sea-lanes to blockade food and arms from areas with well-entrenched guerrillas. Finally, U.S. troops took up the tedious task of chasing guerrillas in a grueling round of patrolling— plodding through rain, across rice fields, and into forbidding mountainous terrain. Ambush was a constant risk, and telegraph and supply lines were subject to regular disruption. Even camps were vulnerable to enemy raids and rioting prisoners. In most places the combination of civic action, control of commerce, and patrolling began to produce the desired result— acquiescence to U.S. rule. But in a few areas an especially well-organized and well-led resistance gave every evidence that it would hang on for the long term.

For example, in Batangas in central Luzon, General Miguel Malvar had created an unusually successful resistance base. Born in 1865, Malvar was not among the best educated of the nationalist leaders. Like Aguinaldo, he had not gotten beyond high school. But he had considerable business acumen and political popularity, which put him at the forefront of the revolution in his home region. At first tied to the Katipunan, he threw his backing to Aguinaldo, followed him into exile in Hong Kong, returned to the Philippines with him in 1898, and took charge of revolutionary forces in Batangas as well as two adjoining provinces to the east. Following the appearance of U.S. military units in early 1900, Malvar's men fought well with strong local support. By the end of the year the Americans had managed to occupy but not pacify the area.

As the nature of the war changed, so too did the U.S. soldiers' views of the Filipinos and their culture. The first arrivals expected the people to be like African Americans or Native Americans. They thus expected to find an inferior people who were "black," "primitive," and "savage." Simple preconceptions quickly dissolved on direct contact. Newcomers discovered ethnic diversity—a Spanish and Chinese presence alongside the "natives" (Filipinos). The women could be surprisingly attractive, and the men were "quick of thought and action—not dull and stupid as expected in such climes." Some observers settled on a comparison of Filipinos with Japanese or "dwarfed Indians," while others more repulsed described the natives as "a dirty and filthy lot," "the ugliest people you can imagine," and "a lazy, shiftless set who would rather steal than work." Some found their churches grand edifices; others saw nothing but symbols of "religious souls manacled to the Church of Rome."[35]

The standoff between U.S. and Philippine forces from late 1898 followed by fighting in 1899 produced a shift back to simpler, essentially racist views. Angry, frustrated soldiers increasingly described the enemy as "niggers" while occasionally expressing sympathy for a foe who seemed to want no more than self-government and who was sometimes capable of "great bravery." Dehumanization became more pronounced as the war entered its difficult guerrilla phase in 1900. The wear and tear of patrolling for an elusive but deadly enemy and of dealing with a civilian population whose loyalties were suspect further hardened soldiers' attitudes. The enemy became "Mr. Nig" and "coons," while armed forays into the countryside were commonly called "nigger hunts."[36]

At the same time, a new term—"Gugu"—crept into soldier usage. Its origins are not entirely clear. It may have at first applied to "tarts" and camp-following prostitutes and thus meant someone trampy or low. Alternatively, "gugu" may have originated in soldiers' mocking imitation of Filipino speech. "Gugu," along with its variant "gook," would travel with soldiers all around the world. As a reference to nonwhite people, the term was part of the vocabulary of Marines doing occupation duty in the Caribbean and Central America in the 1910s and 1920s and among servicemen during World War II in North Africa as well as the Pacific. The wars in Korea and Vietnam seem to have finally narrowed the meaning of "gook" to Asians specifically.[37]

Mistreatment of civilians and captured soldiers had been a feature of the war from its first weeks. Volunteer units in particular had a reputation for firing wildly at civilians and impressing them into work gangs without pay, burning houses and forcing villagers to relocate to eliminate concealment for ambushes, and shooting prisoners. Livestock—mainly chickens, turkeys, and pigs—often ended up in soldiers' cooking pots. Horses and carriages were taken for army use. Men poked around in smoldering huts looking for trophies. Officers did not formally sanction this misbehavior, and some such as Kreps lamented the "looting and plundering" as a "lasting disgrace to our uniform."[38]

The trying guerrilla phase of the fighting intensified the pattern of mistreatment—and more often U.S. commanders on the scene condoned if not encouraged it. Filipinos, including prominent local citizens, suspected

U.S. Soldiers and the White Man's Burden

A burial detail, mid-March 1899. While U.S. political leaders spoke grandly of civilizational uplift, U.S. soldiers more likely saw the war through the prism of hunting and the long, cruel Indian wars familiar to the many from the western part of the United States. This posed photo, taken after fighting around the Pasig River south of Manila, puts in the center foreground their trophies, four dead Filipino soldiers, neatly laid out for the camera and ready for the graves that their countrymen were preparing. (*From* Neely, *Fighting in the Philippines* [1899])

African American troopers, circa 1898. These veterans of the Indian wars, pictured while stationed on Long Island, went to the Philippines to carry "the white man's burden." There they found themselves caught (as one put it in September 1899) between "the Devil and the Deep Blue"—determined to prove their own mettle yet sympathetic to "our colored brothers" fighting for independence. (Courtesy of U.S. National Archives)

of colluding with the enemy were detained. Villages suspected of providing money, recruits, or information were torched and the inhabitants deprived of food, subject to collective punishment, and on occasion forced to relocate to where the military could keep a better eye on them. Prisoners reluctant to talk were subjected to the "water cure," what is now known as waterboarding. One trooper who both witnessed and performed it gave this description: "The victim is laid flat on his back and held down by his tormentors. Then a bamboo tube is thrust into his mouth and some dirty water, the filthier the better, is poured down his unwilling throat." The lyrics from a soldier's notebook suggest the war was turning ugly: "Get the good old syringe boys and fill it to the brim. / We've caught another nigger and we'll operate on him. / Let someone take the handle who can work it with a vim / Shouting the battle cry of freedom."[39] While atrocities during the period of irregular warfare were commonplace, it is impossible to calculate their incidence. Officers were not likely to report the excesses committed by their angry and racist troops, nor were troops likely to mention transgressions in letters home. What is clear is that individual atrocities pale in comparison with the effects of the officially sanctioned policies in the provinces where the Americans encountered the most intense resistance. Cutting off food supplies and relocating entire populations spawned economic and social disruption, disease, and starvation. The loss of life was devastating—to be measured in the hundreds of thousands.

TOWARD ACCOMMODATION AND PACIFICATION

Completing the subjugation of the entire Philippines required more than military muscle applied against the more recalcitrant regions. It took exploiting fissures among Filipinos. McKinley and his agents pursued a divide-and-conquer approach familiar to all empire builders. Sowing disaffection within the ranks of the local leadership and drawing defectors to the American cause made pacification possible by means other than brute force. It also reduced the cost and vexation of empire. The conquered could participate in their own subordination by bearing much of the burden of administration and policing. Turning potential or actual foes into collaborators required working out mutually acceptable terms. Between 1899 and 1901, the McKinley administration and prominent Filipinos concluded their tacit bargain. It put an end to talk of immediate independence and in exchange promised local elites at once substantial and increasing scope in running their country and in time full independence. This deal had by 1901 substantially undercut the resistance, leaving the U.S. military to apply brutal and ultimately irresistible force on hard-core pockets of guerrilla activity. By 1902 the flame of the Philippine national revolution was flickering out.

McKinley laid the basis for collaboration in 1898—even as he made his decision on annexation. He repeatedly signaled his commitment to enlightened rule. His first instructions to his military commander in the Philippines in May stressed that the Americans came to the islands guided by a "beneficent purpose" and determined to respect existing laws, rights, and administration. McKinley stuck to this theme in the more elaborate set of instructions he sent in December. He now spoke of pursuing a policy of "benevolent assimilation" and sought to get Filipinos to weigh the potential benefits of U.S. control against the possible costs of resistance. "We come, not as invaders or conquerors, but as friends, to protect the natives in their homes, in their employments, and in their personal and religious rights." He promised "support and protection" to all Filipinos who fell in line.[40]

McKinley and his agents on the islands hewed to this policy of benevolence in 1899 and 1900. Even before the Senate had agreed to annexation, McKinley had assembled a commission headed by Cornell University's president, Jacob Gould Schurman, to tackle the task of putting a colonial regime together. On 4 April 1899 that commission issued a proclamation demanding acceptance of American supremacy while pledging numerous benefits. Notable among the incentives to collaborate were the promise of substantial and expanding self-government, protection of civil rights (including religious tolerance and legal equality), promotion of the material welfare of the islands, a civil service with slots reserved for Filipinos, limited taxes honestly administered, public works to improve communications and transport, the promotion of foreign trade, and the support of education at all levels. The proclamation emphasized what had become a now familiar refrain: American rule was guided by a commitment to "the well-being, the prosperity, and the happiness of the Philippine people and their elevation and advancement to a position among the most civilized peoples of the world." In their private communications with the president, the commissioners referred to the Philippines not as a nation but as "only a collection of different peoples." Those most likely to accommodate to U.S. dominance were, they concluded, "the men of property and education, who alone interest themselves in public affairs."[41]

McKinley created a second commission in January 1900 to turn the notion of collaboration based on enlightened administration, economic development, and increasing political participation into a workable plan. Two eminent Republicans helped him put the plan into practice. Secretary of

War Elihu Root drafted for the president's approval the second commission's instructions: to advance the policy of attraction. This meant transferring authority from military to civilian hands and building from the bottom up an administrative mechanism with increasing room for Philippine participation and with sensitivity to "their customs, their habits, and even [t]heir prejudices." McKinley then pressed William Howard Taft into heading that commission, which included four other members with political, legal, and academic backgrounds. Taft was more interested in the U.S. judiciary than in colonial governance and in any case had harbored some initial doubts about annexing the Philippines. But after some arm twisting he agreed to tackle the tough job of making good on the quid pro quo now on offer to the elite. Once a deal on self-government was struck, the U.S. task was just begun. In the empire of liberty that Taft imagined, the Philippines with its childlike masses and glib leaders was capable of taking only baby steps toward self-rule. He foresaw "the training of fifty or a hundred years before they shall ever realize what Anglo Saxon liberty is." And even then they would surely not want to separate entirely from so enlightened a patron.[42]

Taft's more immediate problem following his arrival in the Philippines in June 1900 was getting the military to cooperate in a pacification strategy that relied heavily on political suasion. Otis's successor as commander of U.S. forces in the Philippines, General Arthur MacArthur, was impatient with civilian interference. He made clear from the arrival of the Taft commission that he resented what he regarded as a challenge to his authority. He disagreed with Taft's view that most of the islanders would respond to positive incentives. Only relentless force would bring to heel a population united in its hostility to the American presence. MacArthur's pompous and egotistical personality made a troubled relationship even worse. Determined to secure and maintain civilian control, Taft put his skills as a bureaucratic infighter to work. He won the support of Secretary of War Root and McKinley. In July 1901, when power passed formally to civilian hands, MacArthur was unceremoniously replaced with a more amenable Adna Chaffee.

If the continued fighting in the Philippines had not given the McKinley administration adequate reason to adopt a mollifying course, a stubborn antiwar movement in the United States certainly did. Suspicions that the president would opt for annexation had spurred the creation of the Anti-Imperialist League. It emerged in Boston in November 1898 as the umbrella organization for a wide range of groups with diverse objections. In the lead were dissident Republicans convinced that foreign adventures would result in dangerous abuses of executive power. In October 1899, with McKinley's conquest of the Philippines well under way, league members gathered in Chicago to advance what was by then a widely shared proposition among opponents: "the policy known as imperialism is hostile to liberty and tends toward militarism, an evil from which it has been our glory to be free."[43]

This grand anti-imperialist coalition emphasized the theme of liberty imperiled and militarism on the march—but with distinct differences from one member to another. Democrats, especially those from the South, recoiled before initiatives that strengthened the federal government relative to the states, and that might bring more people of color into the union. They had supplied the largest bloc of "no" votes when the Senate considered annexation, and these defenders of liberty and white supremacy remained staunch opponents of McKinley's policy. One of their number, Senator Benjamin R. ("Pitchfork Ben") Tillman, spoke as a South Carolina Democrat and also as a vice president of the Anti-Imperialist League when he asked in October 1900, "Confronted, as we are, within our own borders with this perplexing problem [of race], why do we seek to incorporate nine millions more of brown men under the flag?" Other prominent Americans representing varied causes and social groups—women's social reform and peace organizations, fiscal conservatives fearful of ballooning government spending, academics, industrialists, and popular writers—added to the chorus objecting to acquiring an empire in the Pacific. The industrialist Andrew Carnegie warned that taking the Philippines not only meant assuming the cost of ruling peoples "bitterly hostile to one another, alien races, ignorant of our language and institutions." It also meant betraying U.S. values and plunging into dangerous great power rivalries in Asia. Mark Twain, writing in a sardonic mood, warned that McKinley's betrayal of American principles in favor of the colonial game was so obvious that even "the People who Sit in Darkness" would notice and conclude, "There must be two Americas: one that sets the captive free, and one that takes a once-captive's new freedom away from him, and picks a quarrel with him with nothing to found it on; then kills him to get his land."[44]

The anti-imperialists made life difficult for McKinley. Their initial objections to his policy reached a crescendo in February 1899 with the approach of the Senate vote on the peace treaty, including the hated annexation provision. McKinley's narrow victory had been a blow, but the reported excesses associated with military pacification kept anti-imperialist sentiment alive. The opposition vowed to make the presidential election in 1900 a referendum on imperialism. But the Democratic Party, the most eligible instrument for undoing McKinley's conquest, proved a disappointment. Its election platform put stability in the Philippines ahead of independence and ruled out U.S. citizenship for a people inimical to American civilization. The party's candidate, William Jennings Bryan, decided to downplay his anti-imperialist principles and focus instead on domestic issues unpopular with many anti-imperialists. McKinley won reelection handily. Despite this second defeat, antiwar leaders vowed to continue their fight.

McKinley was keen to quiet the clamor and neutralize the charges of brutality and exploitation lodged against his policy. This domestic political strategy made it all the more important not only to profess benevolence but also to translate good intentions into convincing action in the Philippines and thereby to hasten the end of a military campaign that so agitated the critics. Essential to that end was pushing ahead with the divide-and-conquer strategy and putting a stop to armed resistance. Pacified Filipinos would help pacify McKinley's antiwar opponents.

Already in 1899 Aguinaldo's associates began to disagree on how to react to U.S. blandishments. Mabini as prime minister and foreign secretary in the revolutionary government between January and May 1899 was fiercely committed to independence. He appealed to Filipinos to "fight until the last breath." Otherwise, they faced domination by "a nation whose manners and customs are distinct from ours, which hates mortally the colored race." He rejected the inducements the first U.S. commission held out to secure unconditional surrender. How "eccentric" was the American view that "even though we may be their slaves, we shall not in fact be slaves, for we shall be under the rule of a free people." The Americans "promise us the most ample autonomy and the greatest political liberties, that they might afterwards oppress us at their whim," but their offers "signify nothing in practice."[45]

By May 1899, with Aguinaldo's troops having taken a beating, calls for resistance had become more muted. In a telling move, Aguinaldo had transferred Mabini's official duties to a pair of colleagues—men of property and education. Pedro Paterno, a latecomer to the revolution who had been reluctant to break violently with Spain and had arranged the 1897 truce, became prime minister. The new foreign minister was Felipe Buencamino, a leading figure in the revolutionary leadership. They were precisely the sort the Americans had pinned their hopes on and to whom the first commission's appeal had been directed. Mabini had good reason to fear that they would weaken the revolutionary cause. He dismissed them as "pliant, easily

Making the Case against Empire

"THE WHITE (?) MAN'S BURDEN," *Life*, 16 March 1899. Early opposition
to the Philippines project emphasized annexation's betrayal of claims of
humanitarianism and U.S. leaders' cynical disavowal of imperial ambitions. The
cartoonist, William H. Walker, supplied a title that appealed to the periodical's
antiwar readers. It mocked the poem by Rudyard Kipling, published in February
1899, that called Americans to their imperial destiny. Joining the march of empire
made them as bad as the self-satisfied British and Germans.

frightened." Even so, Aguinaldo had given them the task (as he delicately put it) "to seek a remedy for the evils which afflict our unfortunate country." Accordingly, Buencamino presented the U.S. Congress a memorial in August that made the case for independence in a mild, almost pleading tone. Paterno for his part made overtures to the recently arrived U.S. commissioners suggesting home rule as a basis for ending the conflict. By early October government emissaries were engaging in talks with Otis to find a way out of the fighting short of unconditional surrender.[46]

The dual American strategy—military repression and political suasion— was by late 1899 beginning to cripple the nationalist cause. Elites in some regions had from the outset of the conflict decided to opt out of what was clearly going to be a one-sided contest. For example, already by May 1899 leaders on the island of Negros saw their interests better served by accommodating a country that "is the incarnation of work and material progress, and is the generator of moral progress also."[47] McKinley's reelection victory in November 1900 added to the pressure on wavering nationalists to accept the bargain offered by determined American empire builders. Reaching the end of their resources, some resistance leaders fell into the hands of the Americans; others, recognizing the mounting costs and doubtful long-term viability of their cause, decided to defect. Mabini was captured in December 1899. (Exiled to Guam in 1901, he took an oath of allegiance to the United States in 1903 in order to regain his freedom, but cholera took his life shortly thereafter.) Paterno fell into U.S. hands in April 1900 and promptly went to work drumming up support for U.S. rule, preferably with ample Philippine autonomy.

The formation of the Federal Party in December 1900 reflected the rising impulse to embrace the islands' new foreign masters. Paterno, Buencamino, and others of their persuasion met in Manila in the aftermath of McKinley's electoral victory to form the party and thus bring the first batch of influential leaders to the American side and formally into the political process. They expressed to their new overlord dedication to "Americanizing ourselves," by which they meant adopting from the United States "its principles, its political customs and its peculiar civilization that our redemption may be complete and radical." The party's professed aim was to become a state in the American union. From the resistance side came denunciations of these "sycophants and cowards" who had been as quick to embrace the revolution when it was on the upswing as they were now ready to abandon it in favor of the ascendant Americans. These "skillful traitors" were to be found "groveling at the feet of whomsoever happens to be their master."[48]

But revolutionary leaders continued to fall by the wayside. Aguinaldo's life on the run ended in March 1901 after a small U.S. force tracked him down in his hiding place. His capture was a serious symbolic loss, and it was soon followed by his decision to reconcile himself to the new American order. He took a loyalty oath and appealed publicly for an end to the conflict. "Enough of blood; enough of tears and desolation." He in effect conceded that the collaborationists had it right. Filipinos faced "an irresistible force—a force which, while it restrains them, yet enlightens the mind and opens another course by presenting to them the cause of peace." Reflecting the widespread pressure the resistance was under, the commander in Cavite, Mariano Trías, announced his surrender. He was determined to spare his people "misery, tears and wails, and ruin in general." Guerrillas on Cebu had lost the backing of the island's upper classes and suffered from relentless and socially destructive U.S. operations. By October 1901 the resistance leader Arcadio Maxilom and his chief lieutenants had surrendered. He later came to the fatalistic conclusion that this outcome reflected "the wishes of heaven."[49]

On 4 July 1901 the strategy of accommodation reached a turning point with the transfer of primary control of the Philippines from the U.S. military to a civilian administration headed by Taft. As governor, he would embark on a program whose key elements McKinley and the two commissions had already elaborated. In assuming his role, Taft paid tribute to "the sympathetic and patriotic patience of those educated Philippine people who have already rendered us such tremendous aid."[50] He made clear those same people would play an important role in the next phase of the islands' development. He promised them a stake at the municipal level at once and in time a role in provincial and national governance. Indeed, those associated with the pro-Taft Federal Party at once assumed a prominent administrative place at his side. A man who had undertaken to rule the Philippines despite doubts about empire was proving deft at convincing wealthy and educated Filipinos that they should work with a U.S. administration itself dominated by the wealthy and educated. He built a sturdy alliance based on the two groups' commonalities—their aversion to revolutionary change, their belief in a restricted electorate, and their devotion to large-scale enterprise. Over the following decade, first as governor of the Philippines, then as Theodore Roosevelt's secretary of war with a portfolio that included the colonies (1904–8), and finally as president (1909–13), Taft would keep a close eye on his old bailiwick—and keep the collaborative arrangement in good working order.

lated in 1863 as guidance for Civil War operations and later established as fundamental to U.S. military law and the international laws of war. Intent on drawing a distinction between modern, civilized warfare and barbarous conduct, General Order 100 stipulated that "the unarmed citizen is to be spared in person, property, and honor as much as the exigencies of law will admit." That last phrase provided a barn door big enough to get most any harsh measure through. The Marinduque strategy, sanctioned by MacArthur and proven in the field, would be embraced by his successor, Adna Chaffee. The accumulated experience of campaigning in the Philippines as well as China, where he had commanded U.S. troops, was bringing into focus some hard but simple truths. Chaffee distilled these for the benefit of Secretary of War Root: "the Asiatic . . . respects only power." He added for good measure, "Human life all over the East is cheap. One life more or less does not matter." Soon Samar and Batangas would feel the effects of this widely shared bit of imperial folk wisdom. During late 1901 and early 1902 they would be the scenes of the dirtiest part of the entire conquest of the Philippines.[52]

Resistance in Samar under the command of General Vicente Lukban had proved frustratingly stubborn. The massacre of Americans garrisoning the village of Balangiga on Samar's southern coast in September 1901 finally galvanized the U.S. Army into taking strong measures. After the garrison commander had imposed forced labor on the village, angry locals joined guerrillas in a surprise attack on the Americans. Surprised as they ate breakfast, some of the Americans died on the spot, others later from wounds. The loss of over half the garrison (forty-eight men) caused outrage up and down the chain of command. Chaffee concluded that he faced "a treacherous, lying, half-civilized community" and that its "natural instinct is hatred of the white race." He ordered Brigadier General Jacob H. Smith, a man not known for a cool, humane temperament, to get Samar under control. Smith in turn told his subordinates to turn the interior where the guerrillas operated into a "howling wilderness." His "kill and burn" approach meant in practice targeting food supplies, animals, and homes, while also cracking down with courts martial on wanton violence against civilians. In February 1902 Lukban fell into U.S. hands. He was malnourished, his family was suffering, his forces were decimated, and his civilian supporters were demoralized. The costs of resistance had risen so high that Samar fell quiet.[53]

Batangas was the other province needing attention. Under the leadership of Miguel Malvar, it had become the site of the most sustained and best-organized opposition to U.S. control. Malvar himself assumed greater visibility in 1901, when, following Aguinaldo's capture, he became the nominal leader of the Philippine army and government. He recognized and spoke openly of the "deception and treason together with the hazards of warfare" that were threatening to overwhelm the national resistance. Local men of property and education were moving to the side of the invaders out of fear of popular anarchy, social disorder, and personal loss. Malvar's response was to appeal to the still potent populist spirit of the Katipunan while also warning against American sweet talk: "independence cannot be expected of one who begins by suppressing us, by killing the defenders of the country and razing to the ground the towns which support them."[54]

In January 1902 General J. Franklin Bell imposed a reconcentration policy that would shake the determination of Malvar and his followers. Following the Marinduque model, Bell had his troops round up populations in suspect areas and resettle them where the Americans could keep an eye on them. As a result, the guerrillas were increasingly cut off from sources of support. At the same time, prominent Filipinos sympathetic to the nationalist cause faced detention and torture, while civilians under confinement increasingly felt the effects of malnutrition and disease. The brutal and broad pressure Bell applied accentuated in Batangas the kinds of divisions that had bedeviled the Philippine independence movement from the outset — above all the gap between the local elites, whom limited suffrage gave a stranglehold on political power, and the conscript rank and file, who were mainly young, poor peasants. With his forces and the local population exhausted, Malvar surrendered to Bell in April 1902. Though treated well after his surrender, Malvar refused to hold office under the Americans. He died in 1911, aged forty-six and widely honored in his region.

McKinley had left a deep stamp on the Philippine project. He had not just created the preconditions for taking the Philippines by going to war with Spain and then quickly positioning U.S. forces to take advantage of the opportunity that the war had created. He had also maneuvered himself and his country after the war into a decision to annex and then found a way to pacify the islanders and circumvent his domestic critics. Taft's inauguration as civil governor and the capitulations in Batangas and Samar marked the consummation of his project. McKinley's success demonstrated that empire and democracy were hardly antithetical. To the contrary, the president's well-honed political skills — his sensitivity to the public mood, his grasp of the language of U.S. nationalism, his appeal to respectable and influential segments of the electorate, his command of party loyalists, and his consummate sense of caution and timing—all combined to make him a potent advocate for the cause of empire in the democratic mode.

McKinley was felled by an assassin's bullet in September 1901, leaving in the hands of his successor the further development of the colonial project. Theodore Roosevelt, a former New York governor and influential maverick in the Republican Party, stayed on course. He had been a staunch defender of the colonial enterprise from the outset. Speaking in Chicago on 10 April 1899, Roosevelt, then assistant secretary of the navy, had justified the new American possession as a valuable strategic strong point, as an inspiring commitment to "the cause of civilization," and as a contribution to "the great work of uplifting mankind" pioneered by British empire builders. Like other proponents of the Philippine project, he saw it as an extension of U.S. westward expansion, thus making Filipinos inferiors and wards to be treated just as Native Americans had been. To critics who called for Philippine independence, Roosevelt responded in 1900 as McKinley's running mate by drawing on an analogy he prized. Conceding self-government under Aguinaldo "would be like granting self-government to an Apache reservation under some chief." He turned on the critics, charging them with giving aid and comfort "to a syndicate of corrupt Chinese half-breeds and ferocious Tagal bandits."[55]

As president, Roosevelt followed the course McKinley had charted. In the Philippines he accepted the wisdom of incorporating the Philippine elite into American rule. At home he had to face the critics of the war, who reacted to news of Samar and above all General Smith's inflammatory language with a third and final round of activism. They pressed the Senate into hearings on the conduct of the war, held between January and June 1902 just as the fighting wound down. Senators listened to sometimes shocking eyewitness accounts of brutality, and some lamented the heavy loss of civilian life. But the president's allies managed to limit the damage by hearing testimony behind closed doors. Finally in July, with harsh pacification well advanced, Roosevelt could plausibly proclaim the formal end of the "insurrection" and not incidentally the irrelevance of any lingering anti-imperialist complaints. Now Americans had, in the president's view, to turn to "the task of working for the actual betterment, moral, industrial, social, and political, of the Filipinos." Only with instruction could these dependent peoples escape the tendency to swing between "despotism and anarchy" and become ready for independence at some distant date.[56]

The calm that at last began settling over the islands proved uneasy. Discontent with the social order, opposition to U.S. rule, charismatic figures appealing to folk religion, and bandit groups helped keep the countryside in ferment. These sources of disorder, notably in Luzon in 1905 and on Samar and Leyte between 1905 and 1907, met a firm and effective response from the U.S. military assisted by colonial police and paramilitary organizations. U.S. military governors were at the same time bringing the "Moros" to heel by ordering an end to slavery, imposing a legal code in line with "civilized standards," and raising taxes (in effect overturning the permissive Bates agreement). The result was nearly a decade of sporadic resistance met by a mix of armed repression and political conciliation. Not until 1913 was the Muslim region calm enough that a civilian administration backed by Philippine forces could take over from the U.S. military.

Meanwhile the collaborative bargain held, with its promise of a gradually increasing role for the elites in the affairs of the island. For some Filipinos, participation in administration and legislation following the first election in 1907 was not enough. They wanted an explicit promise of ultimate independence. This demand set off repeated rounds of public if empty anti-American posturing by rival Philippine politicians, while in the United States it became entangled in partisan wrangling. Democrats continued battering away at a Republican colonial creation. On the other side, some Republicans wanted to retain control of the Philippines and to withhold any formal commitment to ultimate independence. Any hope that a rush of U.S. settlers would stem independence talk was soon dashed. The 1903 census found some 8,000 U.S.-born residents, overwhelmingly male and probably most ex-soldiers or colonial officials. By the time of the 1918 census the total had dwindled to 5,700 (still heavily male).[57] Democrats dealt an additional blow in 1916 by passing the Jones Act, an explicit congressional promise of independence. President Woodrow Wilson's appointee to run the islands, Francis B. Harrison, moved aggressively to increase Philippine control over the government and the economy. During the 1920s Republicans, once again in control of the White House, sought to reverse this process only to get thrown on the defensive by agitated Philippine nationalists. In 1934 Democrats, returned to power, reaffirmed the commitment to ultimate independence that remained at the heart of the U.S.-Philippine bargain and set 1946 as the date for the end of U.S. rule.

PARTIALLY FORGOTTEN BUT HARDLY GONE

The war fought in the Philippines between 1899 and 1902 would have weighty consequences. Securing the Philippines created a significant U.S. stake in eastern Asia, inspired expansive visions of influence in the region, and thus set the stage for a string of conflicts that Americans in 1899 could not have anticipated in their wildest imaginings.

Paradoxically, Americans have turned their back on the war despite its significance. It disappeared almost at once. Part of the reason can be found in the long shadow cast by the Civil War. Strongly imprinted and increasingly romanticized in living memory, that grand contest had great captains commanding massive forces (around 3 million men) and inflicting unprecedented losses (half a million dead) for momentous principles. The Philippines was by comparison distinctly small potatoes. Only 126,500 soldiers served on the islands between February 1899 and July 1902 with only 4,165 losing their lives (and only a quarter of those deaths occurred in combat). Even the near contemporaneous and tellingly labeled "splendid little war" with Spain has attracted more public attention, despite the fact that the fighting in the Philippines lasted longer and resulted in more U.S. deaths.[58]

More important in erasing the memory of the war in the Philippines was the taint that attached to it. Blatantly imperial in its objectives, McKinley's project set off intense, stubborn, broad-based opposition at home. Even the champions of duty and destiny suffered early buyer's remorse. A dirty colonial war had a higher price than they expected. They were surprised to find the Philippines a strategic liability. Its precise future remained a bone of contention well into the 1930s. The controversial war and its messy aftermath fit poorly in a national pageant which could accommodate conquest of an "empty" continent but not a distant land filled with surly natives who could be quelled only by armed force and the promise of ultimate independence.

There was thus not much reason to remember, and celebration was out of the question. In textbooks and popular treatments the conquest became something of an embarrassment, to be minimized as an "insurrection" rather than a full-fledged war or an aberration to be redeemed by the generous decision to set Filipinos toward full freedom. U.S. veterans of this war were not honored with public monuments or celebrations, and oral histories did not record their achievements. Despite its relevance as an exercise in conquest, occupation, and armed pacification, no army manual encapsulated the lessons learned in the Philippines, and by the time of war in Vietnam, the Philippines had disappeared from active official memory. A prominent military historian described the denial baldly: "The army made almost no effort to incorporate the lessons of the Philippine experience into its professional education system."[59] Even today the authoritative compilation of U.S. data prepared by the Bureau of the Census assimilates this war as well as the Boxer expedition into the war with Spain. The U.S. Army Center of Military History does not even acknowledge the fighting in the Philippines as an official campaign. Nor does the U.S. Military Academy include it in its fine online collection of maps covering major American wars.

What Americans managed to forget Filipinos have had no trouble remembering. They paid a heavy price for their resistance—some 20,000 combatants dead and the broader population suffering a far heavier toll, as it invariably does in a guerrilla war. The total of those lost directly as a result of the fighting or indirectly as a consequence of conditions created or exacerbated by the conflict is hard to calculate. The estimates fall somewhere between 200,000 and 1 million out of a population of 7 to 8 million. The best guess is that between 1899 and 1903 the death rate exceeded normal mortality by 775,000. This figure reflects war-related hardships such as severe food shortages and outbreaks of diseases such as malaria, dysentery, typhoid, smallpox, and cholera that shortened the lives of adults, raised infant mortality, disrupted pregnancies, and reduced fertility. These effects persisted well into peacetime.[60]

Those who have done the most to keep alive bitter memories of the American conquest have been nationalists seeking a fundamental transformation of their country. Since the late 1950s they have developed a version of the conquest that highlights mass struggle and elite collaboration. Rejecting the collaborators' view of U.S. tutelage as progressive and resistance as foredoomed, they have charged that the resistance failed not just because the U.S. forces were strong and brutal but also because prominent countrymen betrayed a patriotic people by striking a deal with the invaders. This self-interested class (so the critique has gone) continued to protect its position by manipulating nationalist sentiment in order to blunt demands for greater popular political control and social welfare. During World War II those who had collaborated with the Americans proved just as amenable to working with Japanese conquerors. Even after formal independence in 1946, so the nationalists argue, members of this self-serving elite maintained a neocolonial relationship with Washington while vying with each other for control of the state and the means of enrichment it has offered. The result was a weak government and a poorly integrated nation.

This critical nationalist perspective contains an important insight. The colonial bargain that elites struck with Taft set the Philippines on a development path that did more in the long run to advance the interests of the well-to-do than to realize the soaring promises of U.S. annexationists. The consequences can be seen in the economic and political dominance of regionally based family dynasties. At the same time, the American colonizers, who discovered that uplift was tedious, costly, and slow, faltered in their commitments. The U.S. Congress had better things to do than worry about the welfare of a distant colony. Basic education remained underfunded and in any case poorly served popular needs. Little capital investment arrived for industry and infrastructure. Per capita income remained stagnant, and social inequalities, whether measured in wealth or power, persisted as a glaring feature of everyday life. Taft and others committed to "uplift" could see early on that the dream of broad participation in a democratic system was running up against elite-dominated politics. One percent of the population consisting of the very upper classes dominant in the late Spanish period elected the first national assembly in 1907.[61] Though the electorate expanded thereafter, the political system retained its early features, including notably corruption, sharp rivalries for personal advantage, and flagrant manipulation. American reformers had no remedy for this deeply flawed, persistent class-based system.

However hard to impose and however controversial at home, the imperial position Americans had created in the Philippines carried powerful consequences that would contribute importantly to later wars in the Pacific. Taking the Philippines along with Hawaii and Guam had substantiated U.S. claims as a Pacific power and fed an appetite for the further development of the U.S. position in the region. China figured prominently. Vocal groups—business, missionary, and nationalist diplomats—joined in advocating a greater U.S. voice in the future of a country that anchored the far reaches of the Pacific frontier and whose ancient civilization seemed ready for the animating touch of a progressive force. During the Boxer crisis in China in 1900, the presence of U.S. troops in the Philippines demonstrated the value of that advanced outpost. They made it possible for the McKinley administration to claim a significant role not only in the Allied Expedition to restore calm and punish wrongdoers but also in the diplomatic councils formulating conditions to impose on the chastened dynasty. In the process John Hay underlined the seriousness of the U.S. commitment in China by advancing a new and far more ambitious version of the open-door doctrine first formulated the year before.

Rising American ambitions and presence in eastern Asia set off powerful and unanticipated reverberations in the region, nowhere more than in Japan and China. Observers and political leaders in these two countries had to contend with the entry into the imperial fray of a previously marginal but now powerful player behaving with the cruelty and arrogance associated with other intruders from outside the region. The American drive at its very inception dramatically altered their estimate of the United States, with long-term consequences we will trace in the chapters to follow.

For Japanese observers the conquest of the Philippines helped undercut positive views of the United States. Before 1898 Americans not only seemed free of the taint of empire that attached to the European powers. They also offered an example of a well-ordered polity respectful of the people's rights and of rapid economic development attractive to the more liberal-minded of the Japanese elites who began in the 1860s to transform Japan's institutions. One of the most influential minds of what is known as the Meiji restoration, Fukuzawa Yukichi, expressed amazement in 1884: "America's richness is one of the wonders of the world. . . . As the population grew, wealth increased. As wealth increased, the population swelled. The pace of progress quickened. It continued, day and night, swiftly and without letup, until eventually, all Europe, hitherto the center of civilization, stood astounded. This can only be termed an unprecedented phenomenon."[62] Japanese touring the United States during the late nineteenth century qualified this praise as they discovered a society shockingly at odds with core Japanese values. They noted the chaos of democracy, unrestrained individualism, an indifference to social ritual, and women's far too public presence.

The American initiatives of 1898 added significantly to these negative features. They revealed that the Americans had as much taste for empire as anyone. "To use force to suppress another people's desires and plunder their territory and wealth—does such a thing not bring shame to America's glorious history of civilization and liberty?" This was the question Kotoku Shusui posed in a popular 1901 treatment of the "monster" of imperialism. The acquisition of Hawaii, with its substantial Japanese immigrant presence, and then the Philippines was more than a betrayal of U.S. values; these territorial additions were also a direct challenge to Japan's future as a first-class regional power with interests in expanding its commerce and foreign settlements. Over the previous decade Japanese officials and observers had begun to think of the Pacific as an emerging "great theater of world politics and trade" (in the words of Inagaki Manjiro, a foreign affairs expert writing in 1890). Japan was to play a major role on that stage, a conviction strengthened by its easy victory over China in 1894–95. The resulting acquisition of Taiwan directed attention to the "South Seas" (including the nearby Philippines), where the prospects for expanding national influence seemed bright. Fears of being muscled aside so close to home deepened as Americans enthusiastically proclaimed their Pacific destiny, took Hawaii and closed it to further Japanese immigration, and preempted the development of a Japanese presence in the Philippines. The points of friction that would help carry the two countries to Pearl Harbor were beginning to take shape.[63]

The U.S. takeover of the Philippines also registered powerfully among a class of politically engaged Chinese intellectuals. Their once positive picture turned quickly and distinctly negative. The United States had been the "beautiful country" (*Meiguo*) thanks to the widely circulated views of a pair of scholar-officials, Wei Yuan and Xu Jiyu. Their writings, published in the 1840s and influenced by information supplied by U.S. missionaries, depicted the United States as a developmental model and as a rising Pacific power at odds with Britain and other powers encroaching on China. In the oft-repeated Wei-Xu rendition, George Washington figured as a virtual "sage-ruler" who was admirably attuned to the popular will ("no different than the rule of the worthy emperors"). This educated, technologically adept country had rapidly developed its North American holdings, gained "wealth and power," and become one of the "powerful countries of the West," a rival to Britain. In its dealings with China it had proved accommodating, and its citizens had shown themselves, in the formula of the day, "most amicable and obedient."[64]

The war of conquest in the Philippines helped discredit this admiring view and gave rise to a picture of American imperialism (*Meidi*) that would in time gain wide currency. An anonymous essayist in 1901 saw the United States undergoing a fundamental transformation. "From the founding of the country, America has preserved republicanism and non-aggressionism [as its two basic principles]. . . . And yet, in these past several years, it has emerged to swallow Cuba, annex Hawaii, defeat Spain, and take over Luzon. It also recently participated in the allied troop assault on our country [against the Boxers]. In one blow, they have abandoned the memory of their esteemed founder, Washington, and the principles inherited from him in order to compete on the world stage with the other powers."[65] The Philippines thus appeared as one piece of evidence that Chinese collected during the last years of the Qing dynasty (1901–12) to support a notably negative view of the United States. Events touching closer to home, including defense of treaty rights and the continuing abuse of Chinese immigrants helped make this imperialist label stick.

In formulating and promoting a menacing picture of the United States, the late Qing intellectual, Liang Qichao, was pivotal. His visits to Hawaii and the U.S. mainland at the turn of the century dispelled residual views of an attractive U.S. developmental model. American politics, he discovered, were dominated by mediocre leaders, a corrupt patronage system, and a variety of electoral excesses, including campaign violence. American society was no less troubling. Glaring inequalities of wealth disturbed him. So too did the new economic servitude that blacks were falling under and the constant threat of lynch mobs that they faced. At the same time, Liang discovered that the driving force behind McKinley's expansionist foreign policy was the rise of the industrial trust, that "great spirit of the twentieth century." Under its sway "the Americans' desire for expanding external markets is as urgent as that of the people suffering the drought for the rains. . . . As a result, the imperialist ideology has captured the imagination of America." Liang was especially interested in the Philippines for its longtime ties to China and even more for its inspiring example of resistance to Western domination. By snuffing out this liberation movement, the Americans had revealed their contempt for democracy and national independence for Asians. Liang warned that "the expansionist policies of the United States will go far beyond the confines of the rather insignificant regions like Cuba, Hawaii, and the Philippines." He saw China as the ultimate target of this westward U.S. drive and cautioned against looking for sympathy or support from Washington.[66]

While the Philippines undercut the standing of the United States as a model and a potential strategic partner, the struggle there also encouraged the view that China was part of a community of weak and oppressed people who might combine to resist foreign conquest. The Chinese conception of their place in this community began to take shape in the latter part of the nineteenth century out of sympathy for Chinese immigrants subjected to abuse in Southeast Asia and the Americas. It was a short step to incorporate into this solidarity such oppressed weak countries as Hawaii and the Philippines that had been gobbled up by the United States at the turn of the century. In this incipient dream of third-world solidarity, Chinese commentators would in the years ahead identify a long string of other countries "conquered, ruled, and enslaved by powerful nations": Poland, Egypt, Turkey, South Africa, India, Burma, and Vietnam.[67]

By the 1920s observers of world affairs in China, whether on the right or the left, saw the United States through the prism of empire. The vogue of Marxism in the wake of the Russian revolution added to the appeal of an already well-established understanding of the international system while lending that understanding a supposedly scientific authority and conceptual consistency. From its establishment in 1921, China's Communist Party became the keeper of this refined version of imperialism, and it propagated its basic tenets as a matter of faith among the party rank and file. The United States, like all the major powers (with the notable exception of the Soviet Union), was driven to aggression by relentless internal economic pressures generated by a dynamic capitalism. But the United States as a potent latecomer to the imperial game was on the wrong side of history. The capitalist system as a whole was moving toward crisis and collapse brought on by overproduction and war while (as an early party primer explained) "the proletariat and poor peasantry of all countries" were lining up against "the bourgeoisie of all capitalist countries and their imperialist governments."[68] These notions of implacable but vulnerable imperialism and the certain faith that the weak and oppressed could achieve liberation carried critical implications that would not begin to become apparent until the 1940s—long after the end of the war in the Philippines. But they would profoundly alter the course of U.S. empire.

As Japanese and Chinese observers clearly saw, the United States had become an imperial presence in eastern Asia. The debut came at a pivotal moment. Nationalist currents were in motion all across the region, and nowhere did they manifest themselves so early, so directly, or so violently as in the Philippines. Americans professed themselves champions of liberty but also demanded a larger part on the world stage and so collided with Asia's first national liberation movement. That the Americans imagined their brand of colonialism different—benevolent, self-limiting, and self-liquidating was of little importance. The very fact of conquest dramatically signaled the emergence of a powerful and confident country on the shores of the western Pacific. The consequences would shake the region, with effects that Americans would increasingly feel.

2 | **Japan,** 1941–1945

SECURING DOMINANCE

The seventh of December 1941. Dawn. The central Pacific. Altitude 9,800 feet. In the cockpit of his east-bound bomber Commander Fuchida Mitsuo hailed the sun rising in a clear sky. It seemed a divine omen. It was still early when Fuchida, now bearing south over the island of Oahu, a green emerald ringed by a sapphire sea, sighted Pearl Harbor through his field glasses. Shortly before 8:00 A.M. he telegraphed a code phrase indicating that the attackers had reached their target and achieved surprise. The first wave of Japan's aerial armada, consisting of fighters, high altitude bombers, dive bombers, and torpedo bombers—183 aircraft in all—unleashed a devastating assault on the American warships riding at anchor off Ford Island, on the neatly parked rows of planes at Hickam and Wheeler Fields, and on the Schofield Barracks where many American servicemen were still sleeping that Sunday morning.[1]

The Americans on the ground were stunned. Nicholas Gaynos, a young U.S. Army radio operator stationed at Hickam Field, was awakened by a terrific blast and concussion. In a letter hastily scribbled to his parents two days later, he mentioned seeing "flames about five hundred feet high and huge clouds of smoke coming from Pearl Harbor" and Japanese planes sweeping by "only from fifty to one hundred feet off the ground." Marine corporal James Jenkins later recalled that "the planes came in so low you could see the goggles on the pilots' heads." By the time the last wave of Japanese attackers departed Pearl Harbor at 9:45 A.M., eighteen American warships had been sunk or badly damaged and 188 American planes destroyed. In the blasted ships and wrecked barracks, 2,251 American sailors, marines, soldiers, and airmen lay dead or dying.[2]

The next day a no less stunned nation listened to the radio broadcast of President Franklin Delano Roosevelt speaking to a joint session of Congress. He condemned this "unprovoked and dastardly attack" and pronounced it "a date which will live in infamy."[3] He asked for a declaration of war; Congress quickly complied. Two days later, Japan's European allies,

Germany and Italy, declared war against the United States. The circle of global conflict was complete. The war in Asia that Japan had begun against China in September 1931 was now joined with the war in Europe that Germany had ignited with its invasion of Poland in September 1939. All the major powers, including the United States, were now embroiled in the vast conflict. By the time World War II ended in August 1945, some 60 million persons had died and great tracts of Europe, North Africa, Asia, and the Pacific islands had been laid waste. A vast sweep of littoral Asia was now under U.S. sway, marking the high-water point for the U.S. drive toward regional dominance. The conflict Commander Fuchida helped set in motion had consequences far from those he expected.

THE ROOTS OF REGIONAL RIVALRY

The Pacific component of World War II had its roots in the long smoldering question of which of two rising powers—Japan or the United States— would secure the paramount position in eastern Asia. Though fought as part of a worldwide conflict between opposing coalitions in multiple theaters of battle, the Pacific War was in essence a war between empires with mutually exclusive regional ambitions. Both were ultimately inspired and sustained by a vision of national destiny that had gripped the imagination of political elites for decades.

Japan's imperial program took shape in the late nineteenth century, driven by a sense of foreign peril and encirclement. In 1868, provincial leaders from an influential warrior class (samurai) launched the Meiji restoration, so named because it concentrated political power in a government operating under the nominal control of the Meiji emperor. The reformers created a centralized bureaucratic state deriving its legitimacy from the imperial institution. They pursued the task of "enriching the country and strengthening the army" (as the famous slogan of the times had it) by stimulating popular nationalism, training a professional armed force, promoting economic development and mass education, adopting modern technology, and rolling back treaties sanctioning foreign interference in Japanese domestic affairs. The ultimate goal was to make Japan the equal of the other world powers.

With that aspiration went a determination to dominate the neighborhood as a matter of necessity and right. The weakness and incapacity of China and Korea left the region vulnerable to penetration by outside powers. The latter's machinations not only closed off opportunities in Japan's backyard but also created potential security threats to the home islands. The solution was to assert Japanese interests and to assume the task of guiding and protecting an imperiled Asia. Japan shared with its neighbors a cultural outlook and a nonwhite identity, and it had demonstrated its fitness to lead by forging ahead in its development as a modern state. Acting on these concerns, imperial leaders set about creating an empire in parallel with their pursuit of domestic reform. This empire arose largely at China's expense. Tokyo established a foothold in one Chinese protectorate, Korea, by imposing a treaty on the moribund monarchy in 1876. It seized another protectorate, the Ryukyu (Liuchiu) Islands including Okinawa, in 1879. And finally, after a decisive victory in the Sino-Japanese war of 1894–95, it eliminated Chinese influence at the Korean court and annexed the Chinese province of Taiwan.

Tokyo's empire building continued unabated after the turn of the century. The U.S. annexation of the Philippines merely confirmed the need for an assertive policy. In 1902 Japan secured an alliance with Britain—a recognition of Japan's emergence as a leading regional power and the only Asian member of the great power club. War with Russia in 1904–5 ended in victory, proving that Asians could humble Westerners with their grating pretensions to superiority. These achievements in turn helped Tokyo take further advantage of China's weakness. Japan staked out a sphere of influence in China's northeast provinces known collectively as Manchuria and in the coastal province of Fujian across from Taiwan. In 1910 it formally annexed Korea. The collapse of the Qing dynasty in 1912 and the disorder and weakness that characterized the succeeding republican era opened up fresh opportunities to strengthen Japan's strategic and economic positions, especially in Manchuria and North China.

Americans, meanwhile, were building on what they had achieved during the McKinley years. They were determined to maintain access to a reputedly boundless China market and to preserve China's territorial and administrative integrity. They were also now convinced, thanks in part to the advocacy of missionaries, that China's ultimate salvation—material no less than spiritual—depended on benevolent U.S. involvement. This strong focus on China's future alerted American political and opinion leaders to Japan's ambitions. The sweeping reforms launched in 1868 initially seemed to bring Western-style development. But Japan's increasingly assertive role in the region—its decisive victory over Russia, its takeover of Korea, and its tightening grip on China's northeast provinces—fed American anxiety. Some alarmists charged that Westernization was making Japan stronger yet not transforming its feudal, militaristic outlook. Even as Japan's over-seas ambitions challenged U.S. China policy, a controversy over Japanese immigration to the U.S. West Coast further inflamed relations. In a reprise of the earlier anti-Chinese agitation, West Coast nativists sought to repel the "invasion" of another allegedly inferior and unassimilable group of Asians.

In this increasingly tense relationship, the Philippines played a critical role by trapping Washington and Tokyo in a strategic quandary. Any U.S. fleet strong enough to defend the Philippines was also strong enough to threaten Japan. And any Japanese fleet strong enough to counter the U.S. threat could also command the entire Pacific. Naval planners on both sides began thinking of the other as the principal Pacific danger, inspiring calls for more ships even at the risk of igniting an arms race. Japanese planners decided that the Philippine archipelago could be a U.S. strong point and a supply base for operations against Japan, and that it had to be an early tar-get in case of war. U.S. naval strategists, for their part, recognized the stra-tegic vulnerability of the distant colony as early as 1907 when they drew up the first contingency plans for the conduct of a war with Japan. Regularly updated until the very eve of Pearl Harbor, Plan ORANGE highlighted the problem of rapidly deploying sufficient battle-ready units of the U.S. Navy across the Pacific to the Philippines in time to inflict a decisive defeat on the Japanese fleet. Compounding the sense of the Philippines' vulnerability, U.S. authorities there worried that the outbreak of war would activate seri-ous internal threats: "a system of Japanese espionage that is minute and exhaustive, coupled with political agitation having for its apparent object the destruction of American sovereignty in these islands."[4] Abandoning the Philippines and pulling back to a mid-Pacific defensive line anchored by Hawaii might make strategic sense, but such a retreat from dreams of Pacific destiny was politically unpalatable.

Once in the White House, that arch-imperialist, Theodore Roosevelt, had to face this strategic challenge. He chose to conciliate rather than confront Japan and to avoid a dangerous and costly naval race. His appraisal of the Japanese achievements and prospects had done much to dim his ardor for Pacific empire. As a people, they had the virtues of manliness and vigor that commanded his respect. In private he foresaw that "Japan will develop herself, and seek to develop China, along paths which will make the first and possibly the second great civilized powers; but the civilization must of course be of a different type from our civilizations." The clear implication of these insights was that Japan was entitled to "paramount interest in what surrounds the Yellow Sea, just as the United States has a paramount interest in what surrounds the Caribbean."[5]

Roosevelt's policy initiatives reflected these views. He volunteered as a mediator to end the Russo-Japanese War, wishing to create a restraining balance between the two regional powers. In July 1905 he sent William Howard Taft to Tokyo. Taft persuaded Foreign Minister Katsura Taro to recognize the U.S. position in the Philippines in exchange for Taft's recognition of Japan's special claims in Manchuria and Korea. Tensions over the control Japan exercised over the southern part of Manchuria and U.S. discriminatory treatment of Japanese immigrants threatened to sour relations and inspired hotheads on both sides to talk of war. Roosevelt sought to calm matters by having Secretary of State Root strike an informal "gentleman's agreement" with Tokyo in 1907–8 that provided for a sharp reduction in Japanese immigration, affirmed the earlier Philippines-Manchuria deal, and endorsed the principle of China's territorial integrity. This renewed bargain reflected the president's firm conviction that Japan was a civilized power deserving of a dominant regional role. The Philippines, once a gratifying symbol of national fitness, had become a source of strategic anxiety— "our heel of Achilles" and easy pickings in case of war with Japan.[6]

Once in the White House, Taft rejected his predecessor's modest version of America's Pacific destiny and set in motion an oscillation in U.S. policy that would persist through the 1920s. Taft and his secretary of state, Philander C. Knox, were determined to contest Japanese pretensions to regional hegemony, promote American economic and cultural influence in China, and vindicate the "traditional" open-door policy with its commitment to defend China's political and territorial integrity. To advance these goals they promoted what they called dollar diplomacy, in which U.S. bankers and hard-line diplomats pressed U.S. interests and challenged Japanese claims to a sphere of influence. Taft and Knox saw no reason to treat Japanese immigration as anything but a purely domestic matter. Reinforcing the Taft administration's tough stance was the continuing domestic clamor against what a California legislator described in 1909 as "Japs, with their base minds, their lascivious thoughts" threatening "the pure maids of California."[7]

Predictably, the Japanese public and officials seethed over U.S. insults, and Tokyo countered by joining its Russian rival in a united front against the Chinese and the Americans. Roosevelt warned Taft against his fixation with China, a country that was in his view a mess, not a market. If Taft really wanted to challenge Japan in Manchuria, then he would have to be "prepared to go to war," and then he would need "a fleet as good as that of England, plus an army as good as that of Germany."[8] The Taft-Knox policy collapsed in a shambles.

Woodrow Wilson initially revived the confrontational approach but, increasingly distracted by war in Europe, toned down his open-door rhetoric and conceded Japan's "special position" in China, particularly in Manchuria and Fujian. This more conciliatory approach remained in place once Republicans regained the White House in 1921. The Harding administration struck a new bargain at an international conference in Washington in 1921–22 that affirmed the status quo in the Pacific and committed Tokyo and Washington to consult each other in case of crisis. It added a naval agreement as part of a broader effort (including Britain, France, and Italy) to avert an expensive arms race and the U.S.-sponsored open door as an internationally recognized principle. Japanese leaders agreed to return to China the German concessions in Shandong seized during the war, while keeping German islands in the South Pacific. To relieve American anxiety, Tokyo and London terminated their alliance.

But familiar irritants persisted. U.S. tariff increases in 1922 and 1930 harmed Japanese exports, and immigration restrictions formally imposed by Congress in 1924 sowed resentment in Japan. China remained a sharp bone of contention, especially as a newly assertive Chinese nationalism targeted foreign influence and the treaties earlier imposed on China guaranteeing foreigners special privileges. Japan, with the biggest investments and the largest number of expatriates living in China, was the most unwilling to accommodate China's new nationalism and, therefore, became its chief target. Americans generally favored the Chinese and embraced General Chiang Kai-shek, leader of the Nationalist Party, who after more than a decade of internal conflict had managed by 1927 to nominally reunify the country.

Japan's foreign policy tilted toward confrontation in the 1930s. Chinese nationalism threatened to terminate Japan's privileged economic position in China and discredit its political collaborators. Tokyo had to repel these attacks if it were to preserve its claims to regional dominance (what Japanese liked to call an Asian Monroe doctrine). The world economic depression, which devastated Japan's export markets, deepened rural hardship, and sowed popular unrest, was no less important in reorienting Japanese foreign as well as domestic policy. Already on the defensive internationally and worried about communists exploiting social instability, Japanese

leaders lurched toward a nativist right-wing authoritarianism that preserved only the semblance of parliamentary government and that gave
senior army and navy leaders an increasingly important role. The Meiji
Constitution of 1889 had stipulated that the army and navy ministers had
to be serving military officers and that they should enjoy direct access to the
emperor. Leaders of the armed forces now used their privileged position to
push their security concerns, make growing claims on the budget, margin
alize cautious civilians, and exercise a veto to immobilize and topple governments. Junior officers aided by ultranationalist groups conducted what
amounted to a coup by assassination, threatening politicians and intellectuals perceived as too liberal and cosmopolitan. This purging of the elite
was part of a broader drive to cleanse society of its supposed corruption and
restore the simple virtues of an idealized Japanese past.

The foreign policy promoted by the military rejected cooperation with
the Western democracies in favor of unilateral military expansion to
secure Japan's position in Asia. The duplicitous Americans, in the view of
expansionists, claimed dominance within their hemisphere while rejecting Japan's claim to preeminence in its neighborhood and a preponder-
ant position in China. Despite their lofty rhetoric, the Anglo-Americans
clung to their Asian colonies, pursued their economic self-interest, and despised Asians. Taking advantage of nationalist unrest in China to undercut
Japan's position, the Anglo-American "white imperialists" pursued policies
of diplomatic, strategic, and territorial encirclement to deny Japan the regional influence it had earned.

Military leaders, however, disagreed on strategy. The army eyed China,
initially just Manchuria and Mongolia, as a natural site for Japanese enterprise and colonization. The proximity of the Soviet Union to China and
communist inroads there intensified the army's determination to eliminate
resistance to Japanese policy. The navy, by contrast, looked increasingly to
Southeast Asia for the resources critical to the prosperity of a resource-poor
nation. The prospect of liberating Asians from white colonial control added
to the appeal of a southern advance. These divergent priorities together
with intense factionalism within both armed services made policy consensus difficult even as the military tightened its grip on decision making.

Under the new authoritarian, military-dominated dispensation, policy
turned distinctively more assertive. The negotiation of a new naval agreement in 1930, essential to preserving good relations with the British and
the Americans, angered the navy and riled patriots. The prime minister,
accused of betraying his country's security, was the target of an assassina-

tion attempt. In September 1931, quasi-autonomous Japanese forces based in Manchuria attacked and quickly occupied the entire region. The government in Tokyo reluctantly bowed to this fait accompli despite justifiable fear of an eruption of international criticism. Ignoring its pledge to respect China's territorial integrity, Japan proceeded to establish in Manchuria the ostensibly independent state of Manchukuo. In this de facto colony, Chinese puppets did the bidding of the Japanese military.

The Hoover administration was conflicted over how vigorously to resist this aggression. U.S. secretary of state Henry L. Stimson, who boasted an understanding of the "Oriental" mind, believed that U.S. pressure could moderate Japanese behavior. The key was to encourage pro-Western, modern Japanese liberals to resist the reactionary, antiforeign, feudal-minded types who favored militaristic and expansionist policies. When quiet, gentle prodding failed to push Tokyo toward a more enlightened, cooperative stance, Stimson tried formally invoking the Hay open-door principles, openly condemning Japanese actions, and vowing that the United States would not recognize territorial changes wrought by force. This Stimson doctrine, announced in January 1932, had no effect. Indeed, the next month Japanese forces invaded Shanghai to crush Chinese resistance. Stimson now moved from moral disapprobation to a veiled threat of a U.S. naval buildup. This was as far as his boss, President Herbert Hoover, preoccupied with an economic crisis at home, would go.

The outbreak of full-scale war in China intensified the ill will accumulating between Japan and the United States. Following the loss of Manchuria in 1931–32, Chiang Kai-shek had focused on battling his domestic opponents, including the Communists, while repeatedly yielding to Japanese pressure. This choice emboldened his critics. A patriotic student movement demanded resistance. The Chinese leader finally obliged even though his army, which he had begun to modernize with help from abroad, was still a work in progress. A minor clash between Japanese and Chinese troops just west of Beijing on 7 July 1937 provided the spark for war. Chinese soldiers fought valiantly, but they could not prevent the better-trained and better-equipped Japanese expeditionary forces from occupying major coastal cities. The invaders commonly committed atrocities whether they faced resistance or not. The most notorious and largest-scale atrocity occurred in the capital city of Nanjing in December 1937. There Japanese troops indiscriminately slaughtered many scores of thousands of surrendered Chinese soldiers and civilians and raped and in many cases mutilated thousands of girls and women. Instead of surrendering following the fall of Nanjing,

Chiang moved his government up the Yangtze River to Wuhan, and when that city fell in October 1938, further upriver to Chongqing, fifteen hundred miles inland from the coast. From there he fought on, pursuing a strategy of protracted war designed to wear down and outlast his more powerful enemy. To sustain that strategy, the Nationalists had entered into uneasy alliance with the Chinese Communists, their historic enemies.

By the late 1930s U.S. officials and the foreign policy public had turned decisively against Japan. On coming into office in 1933, Franklin Roosevelt had adopted the Hoover-Stimson position of condemning but taking no forceful action against the steady Japanese inroads in China. Finally, in October 1937, the president made his first major public statement, describing Japanese actions in China as part of a "reign of terror and international lawlessness" that he saw threatening "the very foundations of civilization."[9] Yet he issued no more than a vague call for the world to quarantine aggression, and he did little to assist China during the first few years of its struggle against Japan. Like Hoover, he was focused on ameliorating the domestic ravages of the Great Depression, and he was cognizant of America's military unpreparedness.

The public was less restrained in expressing its sympathy for China. Older negative stereotypes associated with anti-Chinese agitation and disdain for a country that had fallen behind the march of civilization had given way to a distinctly more attractive image. This shift is evident in the popularity of two fictional creations—the Honolulu detective Charlie Chan and the peasants of *The Good Earth*. The sleuth with his stilted diction, ancient wisdom, and sharp insight debuted in mainstream media in 1926 and went on to inhabit books, movies, radio, and television. Perhaps even more important was Pearl Buck's 1931 novel, which would help her win a Nobel Prize and establish this daughter of a China missionary as a favorite author. Asked in October 1936 what was "the most interesting book [they had] ever read," Americans put in sixth place her heart-warming story of simple, long-suffering peasants struggling for survival in an exotic and timeless rural world. Her story proved no less popular as a 1937 movie. Public opinion polls captured the policy implications of this popular engagement with China. Asked in October 1937, just after the outbreak of fighting, about their sympathies, 59 percent of Americans sided with China (with a mere 1 percent leaning toward Japan). By May 1939 those professing pro-Chinese feelings had risen to 74 percent.[10]

Missionary influence figured prominently in shaping the views of the mass public and in legitimizing Washington's policy of verbal resistance. At the peak of their activity in the mid-1920s, some five thousand U.S. missionaries worked in Chinese higher education, medical training, and social reform. Their numbers were subsequently reduced, but those that remained supported China, viewed as an American ward, and embraced Chiang Kai-shek, a Christian convert, as the savior of China. Prominent public figures with missionary ties, such as Buck and Henry Luce, the publisher of *Time* and *Life*, favored a special U.S. commitment to China's security and welfare. American missionaries as well as journalists who witnessed Japanese atrocities reported them in the American press, evoking widespread shock and revulsion. Missionary boards and periodicals joined domestic pressure groups in campaigning for tough U.S. countermeasures.

By the late 1930s Japan was caught in a bind, its army bogged down in China, pursuing an impossible campaign of pacification. The Soviet Union made the task more difficult by providing Chiang Kai-shek's government substantial financial support, military advisers, aircraft, pilots, weapons, and ammunition. The magnitude of the Soviet threat became fully apparent in 1938 and 1939, when the Red Army soundly defeated Japanese units in two large-scale battles along the Mongolian and Soviet-Manchurian borders. These setbacks dampened the enthusiasm of the Japanese army for the strategy of striking north. But there were glimmers of hope. The Western democracies had sunk into immobilizing economic and political crises, while the concurrent upsurge of fascism in Europe was pushing international politics in a direction favorable to Japan.

Gradually Tokyo moved toward an alliance with Berlin and Rome. In 1936 Japan joined Germany in the Anti-Comintern Pact, an ideological precursor of the Axis alliance four years later. Japanese leaders in effect gambled that Adolf Hitler would become the master of Europe and thus put Japan in a favorable position to dominate Asia. The gamble seemed to pay off. The success of German arms between September 1939 and June 1940—the conquest of Poland, the Low Countries, Denmark, Norway, and France—did indeed open opportunities in French Indochina and the Dutch East Indies. Britain's inability to defend Malaya, Singapore, or Hong Kong presented a powerful temptation to Tokyo. Seizing an exposed Southeast Asia with its petroleum, rubber, tin, rice, and other necessities of war would assure access to vital resources while also putting Japanese forces in a position to choke off supplies reaching the Chinese resistance through Burma and Indochina.

On 27 September 1940, Japan formally cast its lot with Germany as well as its junior partner Italy. Their Tripartite Pact pledged the parties to come to the assistance of any of the others that was attacked. Matsuoka Yosuke, foreign minister in the cabinet of Prime Minister Konoe Fumimaro, saw this crowning diplomatic achievement as a message to the United States of Japanese resolve. "Only a firm stand on our part will prevent war."[11] As the pact's main sponsor, Matsuoka had convinced his colleagues to make a reckless wager that would doom the Japanese empire. By casting its lot with the European fascist powers, Tokyo had fatally entangled itself in the net of global war and sealed the enmity of the United States, the only significant obstacle to the realization of Japan's imperial objectives.

The question now hanging over U.S.-Japan relations was whether some kind of last-minute diplomatic modus vivendi could avert war. The Roosevelt administration rejected the idea of any settlement inimical to U.S. values and commitments, but it also wanted to avoid a Pacific war the better to concentrate on the Atlantic. Down to the very eve of Pearl Harbor, the president gave priority to combating Germany and preventing Britain's collapse even as he kept the pressure on Japan, hoping to curb its expansion without sparking armed conflict. In July 1938, the Roosevelt administration called for an embargo on the shipment of aircraft and spare parts to Japan; two months later it prohibited the sale of scrap iron. In July 1939 it terminated the U.S. commercial treaty with Japan, paving the way for additional retaliatory measures. In August and September 1940, following the Japanese occupation of air and naval bases in French Indochina, Washington banned the sale of high-octane aviation fuel and lubricants. In April 1941 it authorized army and navy personnel to transfer to the American Volunteer Group, the "Flying Tigers," to assist in the defense of China.

Tokyo responded to U.S. pressure in mid-April 1941 by sending a special envoy to Washington, Nomura Kichisaburo, to explore a compromise settlement that would preserve most of Japan's gains. At the same time Tokyo was taking out insurance against failure by concluding a nonaggression pact with Moscow. This deal, cut with the concurrence of Berlin, freed the army not only to concentrate on the pacification of China but also to prepare for a possible drive into Southeast Asia.

Germany's surprise attack on the Soviet Union on 22 June 1941 helped resolve the mounting tension between war and peace. It buoyed Tokyo's confidence in its German ally while sharpening Washington's fears that the Axis Powers might soon control all of continental Europe. Such an outcome would further jeopardize England and ultimately imperil America's own security. On 25 July 1941, the Roosevelt administration retaliated by bringing its campaign of economic pressure to a climax. It froze all Japanese assets in the United States, in effect halting trade and cutting off the largest single source of Japan's oil. Mounting U.S. pressure now pushed Japanese leaders toward war. The loss of U.S. oil exports was an especially critical blow that would in time cripple the Japanese navy and air force. The ring of war was now closing fast.

These developments hardened the views of the two leading U.S. policy-makers. Secretary of State Cordell Hull was horrified by Japan's barbaric behavior and felt the United States was obligated to act in the name of civilization and the open door. He tongue-lashed the emissaries Tokyo had sent to avert war, bluntly charging their country with following a "policy of force and conquest." Compromise was impossible unless Tokyo abandoned its immoral policy and withdrew from China. Roosevelt echoed this indictment, characterizing the Japanese as "the Prussians of the East, and just as drunk with their dream of dominion." Tokyo's decision to join the Axis particularly stuck in the president's throat. By this action Japan had become more than a peril to U.S. regional interests; it was now an integral part of a global threat to peace, the principles of democratic governance, and the European and global balance of power on which America's own security ultimately rested. Writing privately to his ambassador in Tokyo, he stressed that "the problems which we face are so vast and so interrelated that any attempt even to state them compels one to think in terms of five continents and seven seas."[12]

Elite and mass opinion were behind the administration. Luce had captured the increasingly militant national mood in early 1941 in his celebrated essay "The American Century." This China-born missionary's son summoned Americans to assume their duty as "the powerhouse of the ideals of Freedom and Justice" throughout the world. By the fall the public felt intense antagonism toward Japan. Roughly two-thirds to three-quarters of those surveyed on the eve of Pearl Harbor supported standing up to Japan even at the risk of war, and nearly half believed that if war came it would be fairly easy to wage. Contemporary attitudes toward Germany offer a striking contrast. Nearly two-thirds shied away from the notion of a declaration of war against that country.[13]

The unyielding U.S. position intensified pressure in Tokyo for bold action. Navy leaders, the chief proponents of the push south, were goaded to action by the need for oil. They viewed the European colonies in Southeast Asia as a rich, irresistible prize that could be easily taken thanks to German victories. In July, the Japanese Imperial Conference, Tokyo's key decision-making body, inched toward war with the United States, starting with the decision to occupy French Indochina. By September the die for war was cast. Preparations for an attack on Pearl Harbor and targets throughout Southeast Asia now accelerated.

Japanese leaders were plagued by doubts about the looming conflict with the Americans. A skeptical emperor kept asking through the late summer and fall why diplomacy could not resolve the crisis with the United States and whether a war would in fact go well. Doubting military assurances, he had objected in July, "But our national strength, especially material strength, is not sufficient. Can we achieve our objectives through use of force in such a condition?" In early September navy chief of staff Admiral Nagano Osami warned his colleagues that once attacked "America will attempt to prolong the war, utilizing her impregnable position, her superior industrial power, and her abundant resources." Driving his pessimistic view home, he added: "Our Empire does not have the means to take the offensive, overcome the enemy, and make them give up their will to fight. Moreover, we are short of resources at home." General Tojo Hideki, the army minister who took over as prime minister from Konoe in October, told an imperial conference early the next month that war was the only alternative to accepting Japan's decline to the status of "a third-class nation." But at the same time he confessed, "I see no end to difficulties. We can talk about austerity and suffering, but can our people endure such a life for a long time?" Early the next month he closed the imperial conference that gave the green light for the Pearl Harbor attack with the grim observation: "At the moment our Empire stands at the threshold of glory or oblivion." On 7 December 1941, Japanese leaders crossed the threshold and onto a path that would end in terrible destruction.[14]

AN UNEQUAL TEST OF STRENGTH

In one fundamental sense the U.S. war with Japan was a replay, to be sure on a much grander scale, of the war with the Philippines. As earlier, the United States could bring to bear overwhelming military and material superiority. Unlike Aguinaldo, Japanese prime minister Tojo had at his disposal a strong, well-established state, a mobilized population, and a seemingly successful regional project. But Roosevelt's America was also far stronger than McKinley's and far more able to translate that strength into military force. Tojo was tackling the leading global economy and a people with a keen sense of their might and virtue. Little wonder given U.S. material advantages and clarity of purpose that the United States prevailed.

Just as in McKinley's war, Roosevelt managed to beat the foe into complete submission within less than four years. Step by relentless step, a powerful and aroused country first stopped and then overwhelmed its foe. But victory did not come easily. The Japanese resisted fiercely at every one of those steps, exacting a high price in American lives and treasure as they fought desperately to hold on to the empire they had only recently acquired.

In the end, of course, no amount of the "Yamato spirit" that Japanese leaders celebrated as their distinctive virtue could offset the American advantage in manpower and matériel once Washington determined to force an unconditional surrender upon Japan whatever the cost. Compared to U.S. industrial capacity, Japan's was minuscule, about one-sixth that of the United States. What was at best a second-rate industrial power faced a giant whose production of such key commodities as motor vehicles, steel, aluminum, and oil exceeded the combined total of all the other industrialized nations. The population that could be mobilized to maintain production while filling the ranks of the military was also skewed in favor of the United States: 134 million Americans in 1941 versus 74 million Japanese.[15]

These comparisons are complicated by the fact that the two countries were not fighting only each other. U.S. forces were engaged on two fronts. Even before Pearl Harbor, the U.S. Navy was covertly defending British shipping in the Atlantic, but there was no U.S. ground campaign on the European front until the invasion of North Africa in November 1942. Japanese forces were tied down on three fronts: China, in which a third of the army had been embattled since 1937; Southeast Asia, which the military occupied after easily sweeping aside British and Dutch forces; and in the Pacific, where the Japanese faced the Americans. While the United States worked intimately with the British and sustained Chinese and Soviet resistance, the Japanese got no significant outside help. The Axis alliance proved useless with respect to strategic planning, military coordination, the sharing of military intelligence, and the provision of supplies.

U.S. military leaders had prepared well during the interwar years to make the most of their technological advantages and mobilization capabilities. They had combed through the World War I experience for lessons applicable to the next mobilization. At the same time they pressed ahead on the latest in the technology of warfare. Pinched interwar budgets did not impede work on an impressive range of innovations — from aircraft carriers and long-range bombers to advanced submarines and landing craft for newly devised amphibious operations to sonar and radar. In addition, they developed an unrivaled capacity to decode encrypted Japanese radio traffic that enabled them to read the strategic plans of Japanese commanders and the movement of Japanese naval vessels, troopships, and supply convoys.

Even before the Pearl Harbor attack, the Roosevelt administration had begun to unleash U.S. productive power and enlisted the captains of industry such as Henry Ford and Henry J. Kaiser in the task of creating a large and technologically advanced military force. The conversion from civilian to military production occurred rapidly and efficiently. Modern equipment and innovative assembly-line techniques made American workers several times more productive than their Japanese counterparts. Even before the intensive U.S. bombing took its toll, Japanese output fell well short in every significant kind of military hardware. In 1941, for example, U.S. factories manufactured 26,277 military aircraft; Japan built only 5,088. Three years later U.S. aircraft plants turned out 96,318 aircraft, Japan only 28,180. An even greater disparity existed with respect to naval vessels and tanks. In 1941 U.S. shipyards launched 544 major naval vessels to Japan's 49; in 1944 the ratio was 2,654 to 248. That year the United States manufactured 17,565 tanks, Japan a mere 401.[16] In the final analysis, Japan fell well short of the United States in every significant indicator of military output.

This disparity meant that on this occasion, as in other American wars in eastern Asia, U.S. forces were much better supplied than their opponents with all the necessities of war and even some of the luxuries. While U.S. combat troops in the field subsisted on cold C-rations consisting of canned beans and franks and the like, rear-echelon troops and troops resting on rotation could usually count on nourishing hot meals including steak, eggs, fresh-baked bread, fruit, desserts, and ample supplies of coffee and cigarettes. Later in the war there was even a special navy ship in the Pacific supplying ice cream. American soldiers, sailors, airmen, and marines received mail from home regularly. Also sustaining morale were visits to the front lines by troupes of Hollywood personalities, most famously Bob Hope, and special wartime editions of comic books and popular magazines. American medical services were greatly improved over those in World War I, not to mention the Philippines War. Well-trained army, navy, and marine medical corpsmen administered battlefield first aid, including sulfa drugs and morphine. The sick and wounded were quickly conveyed by stretcher or motorized transport to the beaches and then ferried to offshore hospital ships providing first-rate medical treatment.

Japanese troops by contrast fought a war of scarcity and hardship. They subsisted in the field on short rations of inferior-grade rice, dried fish, and pickled vegetables. As the war dragged on and supply lines from mainland Japan frayed and snapped, many Japanese forces, especially those isolated on islands in the Pacific, were reduced to near starvation and ate whatever they could lay their hands on. Cases of cannibalism were reported in the waning months of the war. Servicemen heard from their loved ones rarely, if ever. Enlisted men in the field endured on top of all this a harsh military discipline, including routine corporal punishment, that mirrored the brutal regimen of boot camps. Japanese wounded, lacking an advanced medical infrastructure, were much more likely than their foe to die from their wounds as well as from numerous tropical diseases.

Given the massive, advanced U.S. war machine, it made little difference that the quality of some Japanese weapons substantially exceeded their generally poor reputation in the West. The Japanese navy's main fighter, the Mitsubishi A6M2, known as the Zero, outperformed American aircraft in speed and maneuverability. The Japanese navy's cruisers and destroyers were excellent and its torpedoes superior to those of the U.S. Navy, with a range nearly five times that of the standard American issue. Japanese medium and heavy bombers, however, were limited by short ranges and small bomb loads, and Japan never developed long-range strategic bombers equivalent to the Americans' B-24 or B-29 (the latter with a range in excess of four thousand miles). Japanese tanks, artillery, rifles, and machine guns were vastly inferior to those in the American arsenal. To compound the problem, shortage of matériel and damage to factories meant in the latter stages of the war that weapons, however good, were produced in small numbers, often in makeshift fashion. The resort to attacks by *kamikaze* ("divine wind") pilots reflected the dire straits of the armed forces by the last year of the war. With its corps of elite pilots long since decimated, aviation fuel running out, the navy at the bottom of the sea, and only jerry-built aircraft left, the only remaining serious counter to American warships were young, poorly trained pilots ready to embark on suicide missions.

These basic disparities meant that Japanese and American strategies in the Pacific War would be fundamentally different. A protracted conflict would inevitably place a heavy burden on the Japanese economy and give an advantage to the much larger and wealthier American economy. This is precisely why Japanese leaders hoped to fight a short war and secure a quick peace. By contrast, the U.S. goal was to secure victory in a grinding war in which U.S. abundance would in time totally overwhelm the enemy. The national sports of Japan and the United States—sumo wrestling and football—encapsulate the difference between their approaches. Victory in sumo, a contest between two contestants in a small ring, depends much more on tactical surprise than on the strength of the jumbo-sized gladiators. Bouts last from as little as a few seconds to at most a few minutes. The winner seizes an opportunity to throw his opponent off balance and out of the ring. By contrast, American football is a test of endurance, a lengthy campaign involving scores of players and plays. The winning team grinds out victory by making incremental territorial gains through a series of engagements in the air and on the ground.

When Japan's military and political leaders made the decision for war, they gambled that a blitzkrieg would bring a quick victory. They calculated that a combination of strategic surprise, their own superior determination, and their enemy's preoccupation with the war in Europe would result in the rapid conquest of Southeast Asia and the enemy's island territories in the western and central Pacific. Possession of the former would enable Japan to exploit their natural resources and mobilize additional labor power; control of the latter would provide an outer defensive perimeter for Japan's expanding empire. After suffering heavy losses of men, ships, planes, and equipment, a dispirited enemy would be ready to negotiate a quick end to the war. The Americans would then acknowledge Japan's regional dominance, accept all or most of its territorial gains, and concede Japanese forces a free hand to conclude the China war without outside interference.

Tokyo's plan to defend its newly established Asian perimeter depended heavily on the cooperation of Asian nationalists. Japanese imperialists had long arrogated for themselves a special liberating role in Asia. They wanted an end to colonial control and the emancipation of the peoples of the region from their white overlords. Nationalists at the head of increasingly potent anticolonial movements seemed Japan's natural allies. Many of them viewed the Japanese conquest of colonial Southeast Asia in the six months after Pearl Harbor as the harbinger of their own independence. Japanese victories shattered the myth of Western invincibility and Japanese forces deliberately humiliated the Americans, British, Dutch, and French in the bargain. In the occupations that followed, Japan sought to win over Asian nationalists by promising various forms of subordinate independence within the Japanese imperium. The same strategy of cooptation was supposed to work in China. Tokyo hoped that a China cut off from foreign sources of financial and military support would fall under the control of pro-Japanese nationalists, who in turn would bring the stubborn resistance to an end.

The U.S. "football" strategy was to move patiently, using vastly superior might to wear down a smaller opponent. But U.S. strategists fell into some disarray over which front in the war should take priority. Roosevelt and his military advisers had initially placed war against Germany first. But Pearl Harbor and the Japanese thrust toward Australia and New Zealand inspired second thoughts. The head of the navy, Admiral Ernest J. King, bristled at the prospect of these two "white man's countries" falling to the Japanese and worried about the resulting "repercussions among the non-white races of the world" (as he put it to the president).[17] When the British put the brakes on an early cross-channel attack strongly favored by Washington, King and Admiral William D. Leahy, the president's personal military adviser, pressed for accelerating action on the Pacific front. Focusing there was popular with the navy. It also offered an outlet for those wanting revenge for Pearl Harbor. And it promised to reestablish control in a region considered more of an American preserve than Europe. Army chief of staff George C. Marshall and Roosevelt acquiesced in a recalibration of strategy that would in effect create a rough equality between the Pacific and Europe. They, too, were dismayed by British foot dragging, and they worried about the Chinese dropping out of the war unless the United States actively engaged in the anti-Japanese struggle. Overextended Japanese lines, rapid ramping up of U.S. production, early U.S. successes against the Japanese navy, and declining fears about a separate Soviet peace with Germany facilitated this shift.

Ultimately the war in Europe did indeed account for the bulk of the American war effort. But in the short term, while preparations for the main thrust against Germany continued, most U.S. fighting men and military resources went to the Pacific. Troops in the Pacific equaled those in Europe by late 1942 (350,000 each) and surpassed them the next year, while the bulk of the navy's valuable carrier task forces was taking the fight to Japan. And as American factories rapidly increased production, more and more resources were available to direct westward, overcoming initial shortages and permitting offensive operations far sooner than initially thought possible.

Although the Japanese and the Germans were different foes, U.S. strategists viewed them as kernels in the same hard-shelled nut. They methodically went about cracking the tough outer shell before reaching inside. This nutcracker strategy played out on the two fronts in roughly parallel fashion. While the United States and its British and Soviet allies began penetrating the German Reich's outer perimeter, eager U.S. commanders in the Pacific were able to launch seaborne operations against Japanese-held territory in the central and southwestern Pacific. By the end of 1943, they were on the offensive. By the beginning of 1945, while Allied forces were bearing down on the German homeland, U.S. air power and the American naval blockade had enveloped Japan and made invasion and defeat only a matter of time.

The first phase of the war, from December 1941 to June 1942, followed the optimistic Japanese plan. It was marked by a string of victories on land and sea. The army and navy in a series of rapid thrusts overran mainland and insular Southeast Asia, devastated Pearl Harbor, and occupied Burma, Malaya, Singapore, the Philippines, and the Dutch East Indies. The conquest of New Guinea, New Britain, and the northern Solomon Islands jeopardized the security and maritime lifeline of nearby Australia and New Zealand, while the seizure of America's Pacific Ocean territories, Wake Island in the central Pacific and Guam in the Marianas Islands, some thirteen hundred nautical miles to the southwest, threatened to make the Pacific a Japanese lake. These skillfully executed attacks threw the United States and its Pacific partners—Australia, Britain, China, the Netherlands, and New Zealand—off balance and cast a pall of gloom over the Allies. Japanese garrisons transformed the Pacific islands, as planned, into a multilayered defensive perimeter shielding the Japanese homeland from seaborne and airborne attacks.

The war presented U.S. forces with what seemed from the outset a tall order. Thrown back to Hawaii, they faced the daunting task of mounting an offensive across a vast ocean. They had to take entrenched Japanese positions in the Solomon, Gilbert, Marianas, and Caroline Island chains that guarded the approaches to the Japanese heartland, and they had to sink the Japanese navy and merchant marine that held the empire together. Not until this was done would American strategic bombers be able to come within range of Japan's home islands. Yet by July 1942 U.S. forces were able to blunt the Japanese thrust and launch their own counterthrust, putting Japan almost continuously on the defensive. In a series of naval, air, and land battles across the Pacific, American and allied forces tightened the circle around the Japanese homeland. In these savage battles Japanese forces suffered losses that could not be long sustained even as they exacted a heavy price in American and allied lives. Yamamoto Isoroku, architect of the Pearl Harbor attack, watched his navy suffer steady attrition after its initial dramatic successes. By early 1945 the disastrous end was coming into sight. But by then Yamamoto was dead, killed in April 1943 when a U.S. fighter, alerted by code breakers, shot him from the air.

American naval victories in mid-1942 were the first sign of the fundamental disparity between the industrial and military power of the United

States and that of Japan. The battles of the Coral Sea (May), northeast of Australia, and Midway (June) in the central Pacific began to degrade Japan's carrier fleet. In these and subsequent naval engagements in the southwestern and central Pacific, carrier-based U.S. fighter pilots proved decisive in putting Japanese naval and merchant ships out of action. These fliers got better training as the war proceeded, had more experience, and had improved aircraft. These advantages contrasted with the disappearing pool of well-trained veteran Japanese fliers and the diminishing stock of replacement aircraft.

In exploiting their advantage, U.S. commanders followed two invasion routes to Japan. This development reflected not just the preferences of the two commanders themselves but also of the armed services they represented. Admiral Chester W. Nimitz operated from Hawaii. He would move westward across the central Pacific to Wake Island, the Marshalls (Kwajalein), the Marianas (Saipan), and the Bonin Islands (Iwo Jima). He enjoyed the backing of Admiral King, and the rest of the navy brass. General Douglas MacArthur was in charge of the southwestern Pacific. A bold and headstrong strategist but also a prima donna, he had famously said, "I shall return," when ordered to evacuate the Philippines' fortress island of Corregidor in March 1942, and he was determined to redeem that promise. MacArthur would advance from Australia via New Guinea to the Philippines. The two drives converged at Okinawa, with Kyushu, the southernmost of Japan's main islands, the penultimate objective prior to an anticipated invasion of Honshu, the island where Tokyo was situated.

The battle that marked the turning point took place on Guadalcanal, a steaming tropical island in the Solomons. Japanese forces began in July 1942 to fortify the island as part of their effort to cut American supply lines to Australia and New Zealand. An American landing the next month spearheaded by elements of the First and Fifth Marine Divisions set off the longest encounter of the Pacific War. While air and naval battles raged, U.S. soldiers and marines engaged Japanese troops in close combat, enduring stifling heat and humidity while tracking through almost impenetrable jungle terrain teeming with crocodiles, scorpions, lizards, wasps, spiders, and mosquitoes. Tropical diseases, above all malaria, depleted the ranks on both sides. The Japanese suffered in addition from starvation as their supply lines gradually broke down under U.S. attack. Officers lamented that their men were sinking to the "very bottom of the human condition" and denounced the situation the high command had put them in as "beyond outrageous." A second lieutenant created a grim formula for predicting im-

The Struggle for the Western Pacific

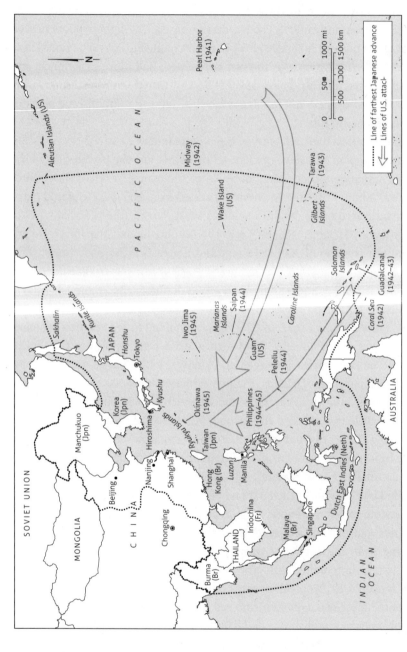

The changing lines of control in the Pacific, 1942–1945. Japan's surprise offensive extended the outer lines of empire deep into the Pacific and Southeast Asia. The U.S. counteroffensive following two lines of advance quickly reversed those gains, putting the home islands themselves in danger.

minent death based on watching the suffering all around him: "Those who can stand—30 days / Those who can sit—3 weeks / Those who cannot sit up—1 week / Those who urinate lying down—3 days / Those who have stopped speaking—2 days / Those who have stopped blinking—tomorrow." When the fighting concluded in February 1943, over 30,000 Japanese servicemen—army, navy, and air force—had been killed in combat. U.S. and Allied dead numbered 7,100, of which over 4,900 were seamen. This widely disproportionate ratio of Japanese to American battle casualties held throughout the war, reflecting differences in levels of technology, tactics, medical care, and codes of military conduct.[18]

Terrible as it was, Guadalcanal was only a foretaste of even worse to come, as the Americans launched a series of powerful counterthrusts. MacArthur's forces operating in the southwestern Pacific reconquered New Guinea in the first half of 1944 and attacked the southern Philippines in the fall. It was not until early March 1945, however, that the main island of Luzon and the city of Manila were liberated. Before they surrendered, Japanese troops committed countless atrocities against the civilian population, some 100,000 of whom were killed. The city itself was left in ruins. Meanwhile, Nimitz's command took aim at the Pacific islands that Japan had conquered early in the war. Once under attack, the garrisons on these widely dispersed islands were ordered to fight to the death, with no prospect of relief or reinforcement from a fatally weakened Japanese navy and with no air support. The ferocious fighting at points such as Tarawa, Saipan, Peleliu, Iwo Jima, and Okinawa ended in American victories and brought the war ever closer to Japan's doorstep.

Typically, massive naval gunfire and relentless air strikes on Japanese positions preceded the amphibious landings by U.S. marines and soldiers, but they caused relatively little damage to the dug-in defenders. In the earlier of these battles, the Japanese tried to stop the invading forces on the beaches as the Americans scrambled out of their landing craft into the shallow waters of the landing zones. "The world was a nightmare of flashes, violent explosions, and snapping bullets," wrote Eugene Sledge, a twenty-one-year-old marine who landed on Peleliu in the Palau Islands of the southwestern Pacific.[19] Those who made it onto the beaches fought their way forward, crawling, crouching, and running past the mangled bodies of their dead and dying comrades.

In later battles Japanese commanders changed tactics. They conceded the beaches to the invaders and entrenched their forces in caves, well-camouflaged and reinforced concrete blockhouses, pillboxes, bunkers, and tunnels. From these places of concealment, Japanese defenders directed withering and accurate gunfire against the advancing Americans even after heavy bombardment from air and sea and intensive artillery and mortar barrages. By night, Japanese warriors, shod in rubber-soled canvas shoes, silently infiltrated American lines to pick off troops one by one. By day they faced attacking U.S. infantry armed with flamethrowers shooting long tongues of fire at a range of fifteen yards that literally incinerated or asphyxiated defenders trapped in their bunkers and other defensive positions. Even when their hopes of victory had vanished, most Japanese soldiers fought to the death or committed suicide. On islands with substantial civilian populations such as Saipan, Japanese officers often coerced noncombatants, including women, children, and the elderly, to commit suicide rather than submit to the Americans, whom Japanese propaganda had depicted as rapists and murderers.

The defining spirit of ground combat in the Pacific War was what one combatant described as "a brutish, primitive hatred." This perceptive U.S. marine who got more than his fill of the front line spoke for warriors on both sides when he recalled, "The war was a nether world of horror from which escape seemed less and less likely. . . . The fierce struggle for survival . . . eroded the veneer of civilization and made savages of us all."[20] The battlefields were stench-laden abattoirs of rotting corpses on which maggots and clouds of bloated flies feasted, littered with rotted rations and human feces that could not be buried in the coral or volcanic island soils. Each island taken cost U.S. forces thousands of lives. Japanese losses were always many times higher.

In this world of brutal combat, U.S. soldiers saw the enemy as lesser beings whose eradication was of little moral moment. Fighting in Europe, Americans were engaged in mobile warfare, often exchanging fire at a distance and with ample opportunity for rest and resupply and with prisoners respected on both sides. In the Pacific, by contrast, combat was at close quarters, progress often slow, hardship intense and prolonged, and the enemy unforgiving and unforgiven. The hatred this kind of combat generated was amplified by preexisting views of Japanese as inferiors who, unlike the culturally close Germans, could easily seem less than human. "I wish we were fighting against Germans," observed a marine on Guadalcanal. "They are human beings, like us. . . . But the Japanese are like animals." A partial list of the names by which GIs referred to the Japanese revealed the animosity and contempt that had taken hold early in the war: "*fucking Japs, Nips, yellow-bellied bastards, rattlesnakes, vipers, vermin, human cock-*

roaches, mad dogs, crazed gorillas, jaundiced baboons, and monkey men." As in the Philippines at the turn of the century, racist assumptions carried to the battlefield quickly came to the surface in combat. American troops routinely stripped enemy corpses of valuables like gold teeth and swords; macabre souvenirs like severed ears, hands, and even skulls likewise found their way back to the States. The ability of Japanese fighters to persevere in the face of incredible hardships won the respect of only some Americans and even then only grudgingly.[21]

In this grim struggle, Japanese troops routinely engaged in their own horrific practices. On the Bataan Death March, following the surrender of American and Filipino forces in April 1942, tens of thousands of exhausted, emaciated, and disease-ridden prisoners were force-marched one hundred miles to prison camps in searing tropical heat with almost no food or water. Thousands died en route. Guards used dying men for bayonet practice, strung them up from trees, and shot those who stumbled and fell. As fighting spread across the Pacific, Japanese troops took no prisoners and mutilated American dead by stuffing the penises of corpses into their own mouths.[22]

Japanese soldiers were brutalized by the Pacific War even as they dealt brutally with the enemy. The recollections of one defender on Saipan, Yamauchi Takeo, provide a glimpse into their special hell. He recalled the invading U.S. armada in June 1944 seemed to leave "the sea completely black[,] . . . like a large city had suddenly appeared offshore." The first of many salvos from sea and air left his unit cowering and shaken. "We just clung to the earth in our shallow trenches. We were half buried. Soil filled my mouth many times. Blinded me. The fumes and flying dirt almost choked you. The next moment I might get it!" The defenders were hungry, thirsty, and short on ammunition. His officers insisted their men fight to the death rather than suffer the ignominy of surrender. Most of the emperor's soldiers accepted the notion, ingrained through official propaganda and reinforced during basic training, that because Japan's was a pure cause against a brutal, immoral enemy, they were duty bound to make the ultimate sacrifice. Those like Yamauchi who contemplated surrender still thought of the shame to their family, felt the gibes of their comrades, and knew they risked a bullet in the back from their superiors.[23]

Few soldiers on Saipan and other island redoubts cheated death amid the rain of shells and close-quarter infantry assaults. By the end, Yamauchi's company of 250 men was destroyed except for him and two others. This ratio of dead to living was a microcosm of the island's defense as a whole.

Out of a force of nearly 44,000, the dead exceeded 41,000. Some 12,000–14,000 civilians, out of a population of 20,000, also died. Yamauchi was a rare survivor because he had the good luck to fall into the hands of a U.S. unit that safeguarded its prisoners. Overwhelmed by his experience, this college-educated soldier finally managed to ask his captor in English, "Will peace come soon?" In a glimmer of the humanity that occasionally broke through the pervasive brutality, the American soldier responded, "I hope so."[24]

Japanese forces fought with grim if hopeless determination to the very last minute of the war. Some refused to surrender even after the formal capitulation in August 1945. The army mounted a desperate defense on one island position after another until totally overwhelmed. (Forces that had resisted to the death were poetically known as "shattered jewels" [gyokusai].) On Iwo Jima in February and March 1945, with the war turning decisively against Japan, its army did not falter. Almost 20,000 Japanese were killed defending that four and a half-mile by two and a half-mile volcanic rock, taking with them the lives of 6,821 marines in the costliest battle in the history of the Corps. The following month the even greater battle of Okinawa began, and again the Japanese units did not flinch in the face of certain annihilation. Similarly, the Japanese navy, though reduced to a shell of its former self, continued to steam into battle motivated by a hopeless sense of fealty to emperor and homeland. Pilots were no less intensely committed. A veteran, Itabashi Yasuo, recognized in early 1945 the arrival of grim times—"the autumn of emergencies when the Yamato race, one million strong, will choose death and make a last stand."[25] Clinging to the faith that Japan could still win if its people only willed it, he and others performed the ultimate act of defiance. Just five days before the end of the war, he set off to "body crash" into a U.S. ship.

A TALE OF TWO HOME FRONTS

Japanese subjects and American citizens alike rallied round their flags and their political and military leaders. In Japan pride in the empire and devotion to the emperor gave rise to a national unity that held remarkably firm until nearly the end despite signs the war was not going well. In the United States, Pearl Harbor triggered a spirit of bipartisan patriotism that only increased with news of the victories marking the U.S. advance toward the Japanese home islands. But the similarities end there. As the war unfolded, life for the civilian population increasingly reflected the disparity in the fundamental strength and resources of the two sides. For one, war meant ever heavier sacrifice and suffering; for the other, sacrifice was limited and the benefits notable.

By 1941 Japan was already approaching total mobilization. Heavy industry was churning out warplanes, ships, tanks, artillery, and other weapons needed at a time when American industry was still focused on manufacturing automobiles, tractors, and other civilian goods. The imperial government demanded sacrifice from everyone and brooked no dissent. It dissolved labor unions, consolidated businesses, imposed production priorities, rationed food, censored the media, and spun a web of state-dominated organizations covering the workplace, urban neighborhoods, rural villages, and schools. These initiatives made the war more and more the focal point of almost everyone's life.

Mobilization on this scale involved a trade-off. A people driven hard to sustain the war effort were a resource deserving of the state's solicitude. Already at the start of the China war, a sophisticated military-dominated bureaucracy began putting in place the rudiments of a state welfare system intended to fill the ranks of the military with able-bodied recruits and to ensure the labor force essential to feeding, clothing, and arming a nation at war. Military needs provided the impetus to implement measures earlier favored by progressives but opposed by the business community. A health plan begun in 1938 was by 1944 covering two-thirds of the population (with soldiers attended to separately). A pension insurance plan became compulsory for part of the workforce. Public assistance for soldiers' families evolved into a public-private relief program for the poor. Public housing for workers and for those rendered homeless by the bombing became a priority. What began in wartime would continue to develop without a break in peacetime, creating the foundation for Japan's postwar system of state-directed welfare capitalism.

Even so, the demands of war gradually eroded living standards as ever larger supplies of fuel, foodstuffs, and other resources went to the battlefront. A war undertaken in part to secure natural resources ended up exacerbating Japan's resource problems. At the very time that the demands of the military rose, attacks on Japan's merchant marine reduced it from 5 million tons in 1942 to just 670,000 tons in 1945, choking off supplies of oil, food, and raw materials from Southeast Asia and other overseas sources.[26] Living conditions further deteriorated. Despite rationing, food shortages had become acute by 1943, and malnutrition and attendant illness were soon commonplace. Japanese scrabbled to collect all kinds of edible plants and creatures to supplement their increasingly meager diets.

For some food became an obsession. For all but the privileged few, life in the cities became a constant struggle for food, clothing, shelter, and basic amenities. Only the countryside, safe from bombing and with food more readily available, was spared the heavy privations of the time.

The war also decimated the domestic labor force as conscripts departed for battlefronts along an arc stretching from Burma eastward to the central Pacific and from the Aleutians southward to the Solomon Islands. Ever larger numbers of civilians became involved in the war effort irrespective of age, gender, or ethnicity. By the summer of 1945, men as old as sixty and boys as young as twelve were serving in the home guard, a reserve force that the army bitter-enders intended to deploy in a last-ditch effort to defend the home islands from the expected American invasion. Women, children, and the elderly filled the ranks of farm and factory workers in a country stripped of able-bodied adult men.

The systematic destruction of Japanese cities by U.S. strategic bombers from late 1944 on marked a new, more desperate stage. As those attacks escalated in February 1945, the distinction between the home front and the battle lines, between combatants and civilians disappeared. They caused massive loss of life and property and left survivors in a state of permanent anxiety. Life for city dwellers turned into a struggle for survival, and the countryside became a refuge for large numbers of children and other urban evacuees. Nearly half a million children had by March 1945 evacuated to the countryside. Many of their schools were turned into factories for war production, and children over age ten were put to work on farms or in factories. Neighborhood associations were organized in cities to enforce sumptuary laws and blackout regulations. Local wardens supervised civil defense shelters and formed neighborhood fire brigades to cope with incendiary bombing. Bucket brigades, however, were no match for the firestorms that saturation area bombing ignited among the flimsy wood and paper dwellings of urban Japan.

The home front displayed the same resolve as the battlefield. Patriotism, social conformity, and the constant barrage of state propaganda combined to maintain a high degree of social order despite the extraordinary tumult and suffering that most Japanese experienced in their daily lives. The euphoria that attended the early victories in the Pacific in late 1941 and 1942 permeated the community rituals of sending recruits off to war or receiving their remains, facilitated accommodation to the net of officially sponsored organizations laid atop society, and promoted acceptance at face value of news from the censored media. Even as the end neared, some remained strikingly defiant. Children organized into resistance groups were ready to face the invaders with bamboo spears and (as one dutifully recorded in her diary) to follow the official injunction that "we are to kill at least one person before we die." Araki Shigeko, married hurriedly in April 1945 to a close friend on the eve of his suicide mission in defense of Okinawa, recalled with pride a half century later the spirit of the war years. At her plant producing rice cakes for the navy, "we'd put on our headband with the rising sun emblazoned on it. Then we'd bow deeply in the direction of the Imperial Palace. Next, we drilled with our bamboo spears. Finally, we'd start our work. But I enjoyed it. It was for Japan, it was to preserve and protect the country. We were sending our loved ones off to die to protect the country. . . . At the time we had an unbounded faith in Japan. We felt the Yamato race was unequaled."[27]

But as the imperial crusade flared out, disillusion set in. Some began to cultivate quiet doubts about the imperial cause and the sacrifices it now required. By mid-1944, Tamura Tsunejiro, an elderly operator of a billiard parlor in Kyoto, was seething with resentment toward the wealthy and price-gouging merchants whose behavior undermined national solidarity. He reacted testily to news of the resignation of Tojo, the prime minister who had abandoned the country he had taken to war: "What a spineless general!" Takahashi Aiko, a woman in her late forties married to a doctor and living in Tokyo, began turning against the war earlier. Already by June 1942 she was worrying that Japan had overreached. "What in the world are we doing extending the battle zones to such distant places?" A year later, watching fresh recruits marching down the street, she confided to her diary, "I have the wrenching thought that today once again, a funeral of living people is passing." By July 1944, with the tide running strongly against Japan, she wrote, "We should have the courage, come hell or high water, to give up the fight."[28]

By the spring of 1945, as the struggle for Okinawa got under way and massive B-29 raids intensified, official propaganda could no longer conceal the tangible evidence of defeat in the mantle of spurious victories, as it had done when the war was being fought at long range. The theme song of a 1944 propaganda film *Wipe Out Americans and Britons!* could melodramatically describe the war in terms of a terrible tumult—"waves roar," "winds howl," and "fields burn"—that would surely overwhelm the vicious, degraded enemy and bring victory in "the sacred war to revive Asia." But claims of ultimate victory seemed hollow to a population contemplating an American invasion and facing deepening hunger, cities burning under a rain of bombs, and roads and rail clogged with refugees seeking food and safety. Tamura described city life under bombing as "a living hell," and Takahashi lashed out at her country's "feudalistic thinking" and her people's sheep-like mentality.[29]

A country pushed to the breaking point found it easy to push subjugated peoples even harder. The new masters of Asia—the Yamato race—situated themselves at the top of a racial hierarchy that rationalized treating those below them as expendable, according to the needs of the time. The resulting suffering of Japan's colonial and conquered subjects far exceeded that of the Japanese people, even if one takes into account the atomic bombing of Hiroshima and Nagasaki. Privation, brutalization, and starvation befell tens of millions in Korea, Taiwan, and Manchuria as well as in Occupied China, Indochina, Burma, the Dutch East Indies, and the islands of the central and South Pacific. Hundreds of thousands of Koreans and Taiwanese were forcibly recruited as virtual slave laborers in Japanese fields, mines, and factories. In Manchuria and North China, Chinese laborers were likewise pressed into working for Japanese-controlled enterprises on starvation rations in conditions that approximated slavery. Mortality rates soared. Japanese officials and their collaborators in mainland Asia levied extortionate taxes and resorted to coercive confiscation in order to funnel large quantities of rice, oil, and other foodstuffs to the armed forces. Local populations were left without sufficient means to survive. In China and in Indochina in 1944 and 1945 several million died as a result.

Women in areas of conquest were especially vulnerable. The Japanese army and independent contractors lured, tricked, kidnapped, and coerced some 200,000 girls and women, mostly Korean and Chinese but also Taiwanese, Burmese, Filipina, and Dutch to work as so-called comfort women in brothels run by or catering to the army. Conditions varied widely in these establishments as did the behavior of the soldier clients. In the worst cases, each comfort woman was raped by as many as forty to fifty men per day. Maria Rosa Henson, a young Filipina, recalled her first day as a sexual slave. "Twelve soldiers raped me in quick succession, after which I was given half an hour to rest. Then twelve more soldiers followed. . . . I bled so much and was in such pain, I could not even stand up."[30]

While the Japanese people paid dearly in material terms for their leaders' audacious bid for empire, Americans on the home front managed to support their forces advancing across the Pacific as well as Europe at considerably less cost. Even at the war's peak, when the U.S. economy was producing for a large coalition fighting on multiple fronts, sacrifices were minimal

All is well on the home front, January 1941. On New Year's a mother and happy son attend to the duties of flag-raising normally handled by the husband, who is presumably doing his duty at the front. The caption on the cover of *Asahigraph*, a long-lived and popular Tokyo-based periodical, reads: "The Rising Sun Flag Dyes the Hearts of One Hundred Million." (*From* David C. Earhart, *Certain Victory*)

Fantasies of revenge, September 1943. The book cover for Noyori Shuichi, *Air Raids on the Continental United States* (1944) overlaid on a photograph of the U.S. capital a drawing of Japanese bombers in action. (*From* David C. Earhart, *Certain Victory*) compared to what the Japanese endured. Sacrifice for many Americans was limited to substituting margarine for butter and drinking chicory "coffee." Rather than facing saturation bombing or anticipating an invasion, they prospered during wartime. Rapid expansion of defense industries provided full employment at good wages after the bleak years of the Great Depression. While the Office of Price Administration enforced the rationing of scarce goods such as gasoline, soap, meat, butter, and sugar, Americans could still do their shopping on the black market or sock away their earnings in expectation of a postwar consumption binge.

The outrage occasioned by Pearl Harbor brought Americans together in a spirit of collective purpose and national unity. Film and print media alike, subjected to censorship by the Office of War Information, helped sustain that spirit. Reports airbrushed out most of the grim and gory reality of combat. Instead, the media celebrated heroism and promoted a positive view of the Allied cause. Conversely, it made light of the enemy. *Bugs Bunny Nips the Nip* showed the buck-toothed lagomorph blowing up Japanese soldiers on a Pacific island. Tin Pan Alley took a similarly light-hearted tone, declaring, "You're a sap, Mr. Jap, you don't know Uncle Sammy, / When he fights for his rights, you will take it on the lammy."[31] No one mined this dismissive stereotype more assiduously than Theodore Seuss Geisel. Working under the pen name Dr. Seuss, this author and graphic artist best known for his children's books produced over four hundred cartoons supporting the war effort between 1941 and 1943.

Other media productions taught hatred of the enemy, depicting the Japanese as a fanatical race of subhumans akin to apes or cockroaches. The message was that extermination was the only way to deal with such loathsome creatures. Brutal Japanese treatment of conquered peoples and POWs and Japanese troops who often committed suicide rather than surrender helped perpetuate such stereotypes. Children were caught up in wartime fervor, imbibing adult racism from their parents, including stereotypes of the Japanese as sneaky and cruel.

Wartime propaganda put a premium on drawing a distinction between bad Asians (the Japanese) and good ones (the Chinese). This sorting of Asians into good and bad built on a century of paternalistic fantasies of tutelage, on the one side, and "Yellow Peril" imagery, on the other. Increasingly lionized even before Pearl Harbor, the Chinese as wartime allies loomed large as convenient foils for the cruel Japanese enemy. *The Battle of China*, a government-sponsored documentary directed by Frank Capra and released in 1944, distilled the attractive stereotypes bestowed at least for the moment on the Chinese. A large and peaceful people, they had a long history of learning and invention. They were now engaged in coming to terms with "Western civilization." Unlike the Japanese, who had responded to the outside challenge in a troubled, militaristic fashion, the Chinese were proving promising students, even as they sacrificed on the first line of defense in Asia against aggression. For citizens worried about distinguishing good Asians from bad, *Time* magazine offered pointers just weeks after Pearl Harbor: "The Chinese expression is likely to be more placid, kindly, open; the Japanese more positive, dogmatic, arrogant. Japanese are hesitant, nervous in conversation, laugh loudly at the wrong time. Japanese walk stiffly erect, hard heeled. Chinese, more relaxed, have an easy gait, sometimes shuffle." Taking no chances, Chinese storekeepers displayed signs reading, "This is a Chinese shop," and many Chinese wore buttons saying, "I am Chinese."[32]

The broader war effort of which the Pacific was only a part set off far-reaching social change that touched categories of Americans in quite distinct ways. Young men felt the effects at once. An upwelling of patriotism led some to recruiting stations, hoping to enlist in the service of their choice before they were drafted, while others wondered how long before the Selective Service system, set up by Congress in September 1940, called them to arms. Eventually, 18 percent of American families would have one or more members among the 16 million who saw service during World War II.[33]

The war opened new opportunities for women. For the first time in U.S. history substantial numbers went into uniform. Over 150,000 women served as mechanics, drivers, radio operators, weather forecasters, and cryptographers as well as in more traditional female occupations such as clerks, typists, and stenographers. But only 5,500 of the total served in the Pacific theater, most in administrative and office positions; to protect them from predatory American males, the army confined them outside of work hours to barbed-wire compounds and denied them leaves or passes, restrictions women naturally resented.[34] At the same time labor shortages drew women into jobs in such traditionally male sectors as manufacturing and mining. The experience of millions of women was symbolized by the iconic Rosie the Riveter, modeled on Rose Will Monroe, a real-life riveter at the Willow Run Aircraft Factory in Ypsilanti, Michigan. This advance into the workforce had its limits. Women were paid only two-thirds of what men earned, and after the war women had to make way for returning servicemen. But the experience of wartime economic empowerment fractured the myth of female incapacity. While women venturing out of the domestic sphere raised social anxieties, the presence of women in the workforce continued to rise in the immediate postwar years (even if in less desirable jobs), setting the stage for the feminist revolution of the 1960s.

For African Americans as well, the war set in motion social changes with long-term consequences. The war accelerated the Great Migration from the rural South to the urban industrial North and West that had begun early in the twentieth century. Black workers took jobs in war industries and moved into previously white neighborhoods. The parents often encountered appalling race hatred at work while their children suffered prejudice in their new schools. In June 1943 race tensions exploded into riots in Detroit (anti-black) and Los Angeles (anti-Hispanic). The U.S. armed forces remained segregated throughout the war. African American men who went into the military and got assigned to the Pacific found themselves restricted to service roles including construction, stevedoring, and food preparation. Yet U.S. wartime propaganda condemning the racist ideology of fascism sharpened these soldiers' sense of the need to redress the economic and social injustices of segregation at home. The pride and sense of entitlement to full rights as citizens gained through military service would find expression in the postwar civil rights and black liberation movements.

The black migration was part of an even larger wartime migration of some 30 million Americans. They moved from rural to urban areas and from the South to the West and the North. The West Coast as well as the Intermountain West entered a new stage of development. Cities from Los Angeles and Long Beach to Portland and Seattle boomed as sites for new factories, military training camps, transportation hubs, and places of embarkation for troops bound for the Pacific. The center of gravity of American politics, industry, religion, and culture shifted westward and regional integration increased.

Social scientists and linguists were among those mobilized for the war effort in what amounted to a coming-of-age of American social science, with a strong but controversial bond with the U.S. government. Academics organized intensive Japanese-language courses at colleges and universities across the country. The Office of War Information employed substantial numbers of anthropologists, economists, ethnographers, historians, political scientists, and sociologists to lecture at military training camps, engage in policy-oriented studies of Japanese society and psychology, assess Japanese morale, and produce propaganda for broadcast to Japanese troops in the field and the Japanese home islands. Not surprisingly, specialists in agreement with the fundamentals of policy tended to be heard at the highest levels. Some dressed up in respectable clothes the "racial stereotypes of maniacal Japanese soldiers and civilians fighting to the death" that (according to one study) dominated officialdom. Others, such as Edwin O. Reischauer, who served in army intelligence, articulated the influential position that Japan was the embodiment of "an ideology which is threatening to drive the ideas of democracy, equality, and individual freedom from the Far East." He, like the outlook he expressed, would help shape the postwar field of Japanese studies and policy toward Japan.[35]

Of all the groups, Japanese Americans—citizens and resident aliens—were the most deeply touched by the war in what proved one of the most shameful episodes in American history. Japanese Americans already were associated in the popular imagination with cheap labor and aggression against China; Pearl Harbor tarred them with the brush of treachery. As a result of this cumulative set of negative views, a fetid geyser of racism, prejudice, and paranoia erupted on the West Coast, the traditional stronghold of anti-Japanese feeling. Hysterical rumors about an imminent Japanese invasion fed the calumny that all Japanese were potential spies and saboteurs. An avatar of racism, Lieutenant General John L. DeWitt, head of the Western Defense Command, labeled Japanese "an enemy race" and sought authority to exclude all Japanese from the coastal sections of California, Oregon, and Washington state. Patriotic organizations like the American Legion, the jingoist press, local and state politicians, and white farmers eager to take over their Japanese neighbors' holdings mounted a virulent anti-Japanese crusade. President Roosevelt, who himself viewed the Japanese as untrustworthy and semicivilized, had long contemplated interning Japanese Americans in concentration camps in the event of war. On 19 February 1942, he issued Executive Order 9066, granting the army the open-ended authority to sweep the West Coast that DeWitt had sought. Despite the lack of evidence that Japanese Americans posed a security threat, prejudice carried the day on the U.S. mainland. By contrast, an even larger population of Japanese and Japanese Americans in Hawaii was largely left alone.

On the U.S. mainland, some 110,000 native-born U.S. citizens as well as resident aliens—from babes-in-arms to the elderly and infirm—were directed to report on short notice to designated assembly points with only hand luggage. These domestic scapegoats of the Pacific War constituted the entire Japanese American population of California, Oregon, and Washington and almost all in the other parts of the United States. Not knowing when or even if they would return to their homes, farms, and shops, they hastily disposed of their possessions at fire-sale prices. The evacuees, as they were euphemistically referred to, were temporarily bedded down in horse stables, fairgrounds, and stockyards. Then they were moved under armed guard into a system of internment camps, most situated in remote inland Western locations operated by the War Relocation Authority, a civilian agency established in March 1942. There they were crowded together in jerry-built wood and tar-paper barracks housing four to six families, each of which was allotted one drafty room. Upon the insistence of local officials in nearby towns, the camps were enclosed in barbed wire, patrolled by armed sentries, and illuminated at night with searchlights like a prison yard. Once the camps were smoothly running, the camp administrators sought to make life bearable, and some among them who were familiar with Japanese culture even opposed internment. For example, anthropologist Morris Opler characterized it as "Nazi-type nonsense and hysteria."[36] As policy softened in 1943, some four thousand young people were allowed to leave for college, others did temporary farm labor, and some even returned to civilian life (only to encounter prejudice again).

The social upheaval, public humiliation, and daily hardship produced by internment created strains within families and open conflict within the camps. One line of division pitted those born and educated in the United States (*nisei*) against the older immigrant generation (*issei*), with strong cultural ties to Japan, and also against the American born who had gone to school in Japan (*kibei*) and thus were less assimilated and more sympathetic to the Japanese cause. The other major split developed among the nisei, who made up two-thirds of those interned. Feeling American, they were in various degrees puzzled, angry, and disillusioned by imputations of disloyalty. Some with citizenship were determined to prove their loyalty. Others were so offended by what they perceived as the implication of "once a Jap, always a Jap" that they resisted the camp administrators and even bitterly renounced their citizenship. Joseph Yoshisuke Kurihara, a Hawaiian-born nisei from southern California, found himself detained even though he was a World War I veteran, a successful businessman, and a devout Catholic with no links to Japan. Disgusted, he "swore to become a Jap 100 percent, and never to do another day's work to help this country fight this war." He did just that, participating in camp protests and resettling in Japan in 1946. Washington's decision in 1943 to draft internees intensified tensions among nisei, with some reacting as Kurihara did. They asked why citizens betrayed should feel any obligation to serve. Others volunteered for military duty. In all thirty-three thousand entered the U.S. armed forces.

Dr. Seuss Puts Away Childish Things

"Beware of the Ferocious Nipponese Tiger," 22 August 1941. This cartoon by Theodore Seuss Geisel suggests how the light side of stereotyping could carry serious consequences, in this case underestimating the Japanese by making them into a laughable paper tiger several months before the Pearl Harbor attack. (Courtesy of Mandeville Special Collections Library, University of California at San Diego)

"Waiting for the Signal from Home . . . ," 13 February 1942. This cartoon by Geisel, published just days before the federally authorized roundup of dangerous "aliens" on the West Coast, depicted all Japanese as stamped from the same mold with no distinction between citizens and resident aliens. All were disloyal. (Courtesy of Mandeville Special Collections Library, University of California at San Diego)

Most served in Europe, in the highly decorated all-nisei 442nd Regiment, with great distinction. But 6,000 were assigned to Asia and the Pacific as Japanese-language interpreters, translators, interrogators, and scouts.[37]

Paradoxically the war that led to the abuse of one Asian American community opened up opportunities for others. Chinese especially benefited. They broke through employment barriers that had largely confined them to menial, low-wage ethnic labor markets. Restaurant workers and laundrymen found better paying jobs in defense industries. Chinese contributions to the war effort, including exemplary service in the armed forces, helped to soften the prejudice of white Americans against the Chinese in their midst. In 1943, to counter Japanese propaganda that the Pacific War was a conflict between the so-called white and yellow races, Congress repealed the Chinese Exclusion Act, first passed in 1882, and granted China a tiny but symbolically significant immigration quota. Chinese immigrants were also now able to become naturalized citizens. This was a small step toward equality in a society still acutely conscious of skin color as a marker of status. Other minorities, including Filipinos and Asian Indians, made similar gains in occupation and status because they too were convenient foils—good Asians whose newfound virtues highlighted the depth of Japanese depravity. Koreans occupied an ambiguous position. Though officially classified after Pearl Harbor as enemy aliens simply because their homeland was a Japanese colony, their knowledge of the Japanese language proved valuable to a U.S. government in need of teachers, translators, broadcasters, and military interrogators.

ENDGAME

The uneven contest between rival Pacific powers moved toward its inevitable conclusion between April and August 1945. A holocaust from the sky set the stage for the endgame. Already by the autumn of 1944, B-29s based on Saipan had begun intensive high-altitude bombing of Japan's urban industrial infrastructure, much of it small-scale and usually interspersed among residential areas. In February 1945, General Curtis LeMay directed the planes under his command to switch to low-altitude saturation area bombing. On the night of 9–10 March 1945, 334 B-29s attacked Tokyo with incendiary bombs, igniting a firestorm that killed upward of 100,000 persons, destroyed almost 300,000 homes, and obliterated nearly 16 square miles of the city. According to the most recent treatment of this new approach to destruction, crews flying over the city could smell charred flesh, and those approaching "at the end of the two-hundred-mile-long bomber stream beheld an awesome sight—from more than one hundred miles away, the horizon glowed a bright yellow." And this was only one of the nine raids U.S. air fleets would carry out against the Japanese capital. Almost every other significant population center, including Nagoya, Osaka, and Kobe, would be subjected to comparable devastation.[38]

To men like LeMay, the time-honored distinction between military and civilian targets was meaningless in a war whose outcome ultimately depended as much on the efforts of civilians working in arms factories as it did on those wielding weapons. But he was hardly alone in these views. In August 1937, Japanese aircraft had strafed and bombed civilian targets in Shanghai and later throughout China, meeting widespread international condemnation. During the war in Europe, British and then American bombers had pounded German cities in an equally indiscriminate fashion. By 1945 so degraded were the moral sensibilities on all sides that the obliteration of cities and the incineration of their civilian populations were considered unexceptional. Devotion to the broad application of U.S. air power had become a defining feature of U.S. military strategy.

The fall in late June of Okinawa, the last bastion before mainland Japan, signaled that the end was near. This battle looms in significance alongside Pearl Harbor, Midway, and Guadalcanal. Okinawa, some sixty miles long and from two to eighteen miles wide, offered Americans a sense of what the invasion of the Japanese home islands some 350 miles to the north would be like. Japanese commanders had no hope of defeating the vast U.S. naval armada—over 1,200 ships, including 40 aircraft carriers of varying sizes and 18 battleships—bearing nearly 200,000 men into battle against a defending force roughly a third that size. The Japanese strategy was to delay the enemy and win time for defensive preparations in Japan itself. To that end, the Americans were allowed to land virtually unopposed while the defenders waited in deep bunkers ready to resist to the death. The American advance, begun in early April, did not end in victory until mid-June, and along the way cost 12,000 U.S. dead (including almost 5,000 sailors lost to repeated and punishing waves of kamikaze attacks). Those losses paled in comparison with Japanese military losses of 70,000 (all but 7,000 of the force on the island) and the still longer list of civilian dead (some 80,000).[39]

As the systematic aerial annihilation proceeded and an American invasion of the home islands drew closer, leaders in Tokyo were deadlocked over what to do. Prime Minister Suzuki Kantaro, an elderly admiral who took office in early April, presided over the official stalemate, which grew more desperate with news in mid-June of the loss of Okinawa. Those who sought to prolong the war and those who wished to end it were evenly split within the Supreme War Council, the six-member inner cabinet that was the highest policy-making organ of government. Whether pro-war or pro-peace, those on the council were performers in a drama staged for an audience of one man, namely, Emperor Hirohito. He possessed, but almost never used, the ultimate decision-making authority in his realm. In a political system where circumlocution was often the preferred means of expression, the meaning of the unfolding drama had to be intuited from words not spoken as much as from those that were.

The army high command rejected surrender as dishonorable. Army Minister Anami Korechika, Chief of Staff Umezu Yoshijiro, and other advocates of continued resistance knew that unconditional surrender would doom the Imperial Armed Forces and subject its surviving leaders to humiliation, imprisonment, or a dishonorable death at the hands of the enemy. Calculation as well as the instinct for self-preservation informed the views of these bitter-enders. They pointed to the immense casualties that Japanese defenders had inflicted on victorious American forces on Iwo Jima and Okinawa. Now that Japan had its back to the wall, they counted on a final epic battle to defeat the anticipated American landing on the southernmost island of Kyushu, where a U.S. invasion force ultimately set at three-quarters of a million men would face nearly as many regular Japanese troops backed by civilian auxiliaries. Resistance would begin on the beaches and then continue from prepared defensive positions in the interior.[40] By inflicting enormous losses, they believed they could persuade Washington to modify its demand for unconditional surrender and agree to negotiate a peace that would preserve the nation, its imperial institution, and its armed forces. Hirohito, too, his own mind divided, clung to this illusory hope.

On the other side, those eager to find a diplomatic way out of the deepening disaster, led by Foreign Minister Togo Shigenori, Navy Minister Yonai Mitsumasa, and Lord Keeper of the Privy Seal Kido Koichi, moved cautiously. Keenly aware of the political power of the army, Togo and his allies realized that, if sufficiently provoked, Anami might resign and bring down the cabinet, precipitating a political crisis. An even more dire possibility was that the army might seize power and, whatever the cost in civilian lives, fight to the death in the name of the emperor and the nation. Conscious that exposing their hand prematurely might increase this danger, the peace seekers temporized and maneuvered behind the scenes. They desperately sought some broadly acceptable plan that would save their country from the tightening U.S. vise.

Admitting defeat was inherently difficult, and the U.S. insistence on unconditional surrender made it harder. At the Casablanca Conference in January 1943, Roosevelt had proclaimed that there would be no negotiated surrender of the Axis Powers. He sought to avoid a repeat of World War I, from which a defeated Germany had escaped unreformed, resentful, and susceptible to the appeal of Nazism. This time the victors would destroy the taproot of militarism and to that end had to exercise unfettered power over the cultural, social, and political life of the Axis countries. The Allied aims posed a threat to Japan's very survival as a nation and to its defining core, Japan's imperial institution embodied in the person of the emperor himself.

Foreign Minister Togo at first looked toward Moscow to broker a negotiated end to the war that would preserve the nation and the emperor. With the Soviet-Japanese Neutrality Treaty good for another year and with rumored strains between the USSR and its allies, it seemed safe to assume that Moscow might respond favorably, especially if offered territorial and economic concessions in eastern Asia. Togo's ambassador in Moscow, Sato Naotake, was unconvinced. In blunt, undiplomatic language, he repeatedly warned his boss that the hope for help from Moscow was a pipe dream. But Togo was undeterred even after learning that Moscow did not intend to renew the Neutrality Treaty. Finally, on 22 June an increasingly desperate Hirohito approved this effort to engage the Soviet Union. Stalin had absolutely no intention of acting as a mediator. As recently as February at the Yalta Conference, he had renewed his pledge to Roosevelt to enter the war against Japan three months after Germany's surrender. In exchange he secured the return of the southern half of Sakhalin and of the railroad and port concessions in southern Manchuria (both taken by Japan in 1905) and in addition the transfer of the Kuriles. The Soviet leader skillfully strung the Japanese along while he prepared for war against them.

Meanwhile, American military and political leaders were reviewing detailed plans for the invasion of the home islands. On 18 June, President Harry Truman gave his approval to Operation Olympic, the invasion of Kyushu scheduled to commence in early November. Operation Coronet, the invasion of the Tokyo plain (Honshu), would begin the following March if Japan had not surrendered by then. An authoritative briefing paper submitted to the Joint Chiefs of Staff estimated 25,000–46,000 American combat deaths in the two operations. An estimate Marshall gave Truman at this time suggested the Kyushu operation would cost 16,000–19,000 American lives.[41]

While considering these plans, U.S. policymakers contemplated modification of their demand for unconditional surrender as a way to avoid a bloody invasion. The most prominent advocates of softer terms were Stimson, who had entered Roosevelt's cabinet as secretary of war, and Undersecretary of State Joseph Grew, who had been ambassador to Japan from 1931 to 1941. They argued that Japanese leaders would be more likely to surrender if they received advance assurance on the preservation of the emperor-based political system. The opposition to this suggestion was led by the newly appointed secretary of state, James F. Byrnes, the former South Carolina senator whom Roosevelt had passed over in favor of Truman as his vice-presidential running mate in 1944. Byrnes, a confidant whom Truman added to his cabinet in early July 1945, cited the likely domestic uproar that sparing the emperor would create. The American public regarded Hirohito and former prime minister Tojo as personifications of Japanese militarism, so both had to go. Truman remained noncommittal as the issue was discussed in Washington prior to the Big Three summit scheduled for mid-July in Potsdam, amid the ruins of Hitler's capital.

The atomic bomb now took center stage. It epitomized the U.S. material advantage that had characterized the entire war. The epochal theoretical advances in nuclear physics by a brilliant constellation of European and American scientists were internationally understood, and so too was the corollary that weapons of unprecedented destructive power were within the grasp of any industrialized country with the theoretical knowledge, engineering know-how, and financial resources. Japan's small-scale effort to develop nuclear weapons had gone nowhere, while President Roosevelt had authorized a secret crash program, lavishing on it the requisite money and skilled manpower. Only a handful of top officials in the American and British governments was apprised of the program. Most of those involved in developing the plans for the invasion of Japan and in the discussion of surrender terms were not privy to this tightly held secret.

Roosevelt's vice president and successor, Harry S. Truman, would reap the practical benefits of this program. Born in 1884, he had grown up on a Missouri farm and saw service as a field artillery captain in France during World War I. He entered politics and with support from the Democratic machine in Kansas City was elected first to a judgeship and in 1934 to the U.S. Senate. A moderate New Dealer with few political enemies, Truman was drafted by Franklin Delano Roosevelt as his running mate in 1944. With FDR's death on 12 April 1945, this American everyman, plain-spoken, pugnacious, and feisty, found himself in the White House. He knew nothing about the weapon being rushed to completion at Los Alamos in the high desert of New Mexico. Indeed, the new president knew little about foreign affairs and war strategy, and so at first depended on Roosevelt's key advisors to show him the way.

By the time Truman was briefed on the atomic secret, work on two types of weapons, a uranium bomb and a plutonium bomb, was nearing completion. On 1 June, the high-level Interim Committee that Truman had appointed to advise him on all aspects of the bomb adopted a decision to employ atomic bombs against Japan as soon as they were ready. This decision set in motion a series of events that led inexorably to the atomic bombing of Hiroshima and Nagasaki. There is no record that President Truman himself, contrary to his subsequent assertions, ever made a decision regarding whether and where the bombs would be dropped. That they would be used as soon as they were ready was a foregone conclusion based on military considerations. Truman's retrospective claim seems right: "I regarded the bomb as a military weapon and never had any doubt that it should be used." The closest student of Truman's controversial decision agrees: "American lives were the pre-eminent concern, the atomic bomb was deemed a legitimate weapon, especially to be used on a hated enemy, and Japanese lives were deemed unimportant."[42]

The Big Three summit in Potsdam set the stage for the atomic bombing. Truman received news on 17 July of the first successful atomic weapons test in Alamogordo, New Mexico, and was informed that two operational weapons would be available for use in early August. Awestruck, he wrote in his diary, "We have discovered the most terrible bomb in the history of the world. It may be the fire of destruction prophesied in the Euphrates Valley Era, after Noah and his fabulous Ark." With invasion plans moving forward and the atomic bomb in hand, Truman gave the enemy a last chance to surrender. The president now joined Byrnes in rejecting Stimson's renewed attempt to modify unconditional surrender and permit the Japanese to retain the emperor system. The Potsdam Proclamation, broadcast to Japan on 26 July, repeated the demand for unconditional surrender and in a nod to the terrible new weapon now available warned that otherwise Japan faced "prompt and utter destruction." The Japanese government temporized. It was still not prepared to accept unconditional surrender, but neither did it reject the Potsdam Proclamation. Truman, eager to end the war, interpreted

Tokyo's non-response as a rejection, and so preparations moved ahead to use the bomb on a target selected by a special committee from one of a handful of urban centers not yet destroyed by conventional bombing.[43]

Such high-level politics were far from the concerns of the residents of Hiroshima on the morning of 6 August. They were in the midst of their morning routines when they saw a single American bomber—the *Enola Gay*—overhead and then the flash of light. The city shook, its center evaporated, and fires ignited that would rage over a wide area. Stunned and wounded survivors wandered among the ruins, seeking relief from their terrible burns, and searching for traces of loved ones. Ryoso Fujie, a peasant woman venturing into the city in search of her husband the next day, found charred bodies everywhere she looked—scene after scene that "was like something out of hell." The living were "groaning and asking for water. . . . In their agony, you could hear them calling out over and over again: 'Mum! . . . Mum!'"[44]

The atomic devastation visited on Hiroshima followed by the atomic attack on Nagasaki on 9 August hardened the determination of the Japanese peace party. On 10 August Emperor Hirohito proposed an immediate end to the war on the sole condition that the imperial prerogative be preserved. The U.S. reply offered no definite assurances on that point, and so the split within the leadership persisted. It finally took the shock of Soviet entry into the war followed by the devastation of Nagasaki to precipitate the last moves in this painfully slow, tortured end game. Stalin had decided to advance the date of Soviet entry into the war so he could claim his territorial prizes and other concessions before Japan surrendered. Just after midnight on 9 August, Soviet mechanized armies crossed into China and Korea and rapidly advanced against depleted Japanese forces. With this action, a violation of the Soviet-Japanese Neutrality Treaty, the chimera of Soviet mediation that Hirohito and Togo had clung to finally vanished. Later that same day Nagasaki was destroyed by a second atomic bomb. By then Truman's realization that he was vaporizing entire cities, not just military targets, roused his conscience. He told his cabinet that "he had given orders to stop atomic bombing. He said the thought of wiping out another 100,000 people was too horrible. He didn't like the idea of killing, as he said, 'all those kids.'"[45]

Now only Army Minister Anami still opposed surrender, yet he could still stymie a decision. Over the next several days Kido, Suzuki, and Togo succeeded in persuading the emperor to end the impasse. The thin reed of hope to which Hirohito had clung that Stalin would mediate a negotiated end to the war had been snapped by the Soviet entry. The emperor finally resolved to exercise his imperial will. On the morning of 14 August, an imperial conference was convened in the basement shelter of the palace. Hirohito, dressed in his marshal's uniform and white gloves, informed the assembled political and military leaders of his decision to accept the terms of the Potsdam Proclamation on the tacit understanding that the imperial institution would be preserved. This intervention by Emperor Hirohito brought to an end this distinctly Japanese tragedy. Army Minister Anami and the military high command bowed to the emperor's will. On 15 August the emperor went on the air to concede (in a striking understatement) that the war "did not turn in Japan's favor" and to ask his people to "endure the unendurable and bear the unbearable" in what was to come. Hearing his voice for the first time, Japanese all over the country fell silent, rose to their feet, uncovered and bowed their heads, and listened respectfully. Even the disillusioned were gripped by deep emotion. "As each word and phrase was etched on my heart, my eyes got quite warm and tears welled up," so Takahashi, a decided critic of the war, recorded in her diary that day. At the same time surrender had brought the exhilarating realization of "the lives we had regained."[46]

But the game was not quite over. A group of die-hards—mid-ranking and junior officers in the Imperial Guard—attempted a coup. They seized the palace grounds and searched unsuccessfully for the recording of the emperor's surrender address before it could be broadcast to the nation. But ranking army officers, including General Anami, refused their support. On the early morning of 15 August, just hours before the emperor's noon broadcast, Anami committed *seppuku*, the ritual suicide via disembowelment of a samurai warrior. Japanese commanders all across Asia reluctantly laid down their arms in obedience to the emperor's command. On 2 September 1945, on the quarterdeck of the battleship USS *Missouri* riding at anchor in Tokyo Bay, General MacArthur presided over the formal ceremony of surrender. Now the war was truly over. Paul Fussell, who famously quipped, "Thank God for the atomic bomb," recalls how U.S. troops reacted to the electrifying realization that the war was at an end: "We cried with relief and joy. We were going to live. We were going to grow up to adulthood after all." This was something beyond the hope of 93,000 American combatants and 1,589,000 Japanese lost in battle, not to mention the 659,000 Japanese noncombatant dead.[47]

THE RISING TIDE OF EMPIRE

By launching a war that would prove their undoing, Japan's leaders had created an opening that their American rival would exploit to the hilt. Victory had made the United States preeminent in eastern Asia. The thoroughness of Japan's defeat, following soon after the destruction of Hitler's Third Reich, seemed to offer assurances for a future defined by the power of American arms and the rectitude of American ideals. More broadly, victory represented a triumph for those with a strong sense of a U.S. Pacific destiny going back to McKinley and Taft and continuing with Stimson, Douglas MacArthur, and Henry Luce. The time, it seemed, had come to fulfill Luce's summons to America to become the "Good Samaritan of the entire world" dedicated to "lifting the life of mankind from the level of beasts." His was a vision now widely shared of a peaceful world remade along the lines of such American ideals as freedom, equality of opportunity, self-reliance and independence, and cooperation.[48] What was true in broad global terms was especially true in eastern Asia.

Japan, rendered docile and subordinate by defeat, was the obvious place to start the building of a greater eastern Asia liberal prosperity sphere. This entailed nothing less than the dissolution of the Japanese empire, the reduction of Japan to its four main islands, the abolition of the Japanese form of government prescribed in the Meiji Constitution of 1889, and its replacement by a modified form of American-style democracy. These far-reaching objectives emerged from discussions during the war as U.S. policymakers and their advisors contemplated how to eliminate the roots of Japanese militarism. They assumed that the Japanese were ready to turn over a new leaf. And to a considerable degree they were right. The experience of war had created a wide range of deep discontents—from the oppressive political and cultural atmosphere to arrogant, venal, and incompetent officials to war's cruel waste and inhumanity to flaws in the Japanese character. Here was fertile ground for the reforms the American occupiers would promote.

The occupation of Japan, lasting from September 1945 to April 1952, was essentially an American enterprise in which the wartime allies played a nominal role. Presiding over this enterprise from atop the Dai-ichi Building in downtown Tokyo was an American proconsul. Acting in the best imperial tradition, General MacArthur served as Supreme Commander of Allied Powers. The sixty-five-year-old general was just the man for turning devilish delinquents into good pupils of the American way. The son of General Arthur MacArthur, military governor of the Philippines in 1900–1901, he had graduated at the top of his West Point class. After serving in France during World War I and as army chief of staff from 1930 to 1935, he returned to the Philippines as head of its army. Steeped in the mores of the colonial Philippines, he even more than Stimson had a deep emotional investment in the U.S. project in eastern Asia and a conviction that he understood the "Orient." An aloof self-promoter with a Messiah complex and a flair for the theatrical, he used his position as supreme commander in the southwestern Pacific and his political influence to ensure that he would preside over the remaking of Japan.

The Japanese people treated their new overlord as one part substitute emperor, one part Santa Claus, and one part Dear Abby. While showing him the deference appropriate to a high official, they also saw him as the patron of economic recovery and democratization; they solicited his advice on all manner of purely personal matters, invited him to weddings, and showered him with gifts of harvest fruit and local handicrafts. Letters to MacArthur covered an amazing variety of issues reflecting the range and depth of the occupation's grip as well as the awe in which MacArthur was held. Some wished MacArthur good health and praised him for his service to Japan or announced that U.S. cultural and political influence had helped to alter their political views. Some complained about peeping toms among U.S. troops and about abuses of the ordinary people by Japanese officials. "What bothers me is that those in high positions use their power and money to have mistresses and buy expensive things on the black market and lead extravagant lives." Writing in a similar vein, another instructed MacArthur in the sins of "those former military leaders who forced us into war and still make us suffer." Some wanted help in getting work or getting children to the United States. Some prayed for help with relatives who had served overseas. One fearing the loss of a son in Burma confessed that "I am worried because he was taught by the Japanese state to fight to the death." Another with a husband scheduled for execution in the Philippines for war crimes asked for help in letting him know that she had borne him a son and heir.[49]

The New Dealers from Washington who staffed the occupation set to work on a broad front guided by a directive approved by Truman in early September 1945. They began with the dismantling of the Japanese war machine and the partial purge of Japanese political elites and bureaucrats. In place of this old discredited Japan, they envisioned a more democratic and egalitarian society based on small farmers, small merchants, shopkeepers, and handicraft workers. They acted on a faith that popular government—encouraged and shaped by Americans—would engender an immunity to the disease of militarism and imperialism. The franchise was extended to women. Left-wing parties, including the Communist Party, were legalized for the first time. A new constitution, written by the Americans and based on the principles of popular sovereignty and democratic governance, was adopted by the Japanese Diet (parliament). Article IX, a decided novelty, renounced war as an instrument of national policy and stated that Japan would not maintain armed forces. The emperor was reduced from a virtual god-king to a living symbol of the nation. The power of the industrial barons and rural landlords was diluted by the legalization of trade unions and the implementation of land reform. A program of American-style trust-busting began to dissolve the *zaibatsu*, the industrial conglomerates that had earlier enjoyed an economic oligopoly and worked hand in glove with the military.

In a program aimed at purging all traces of militarism, the leaders who had fomented that militarism became prime targets. They were hauled before war crimes courts modeled on the International Military Tribunal at Nuremberg set up to judge Nazi leaders. These trials sidestepped the tangled issue of broad national responsibility. Like other peoples beguiled or dragged into war, Americans not excepted, the Japanese were both victims of the ambitions and delusions of their leaders as well as complicit in their crimes. It was far easier politically and legally to assign blame to a relatively small segment of the Japanese elite. Altogether more than 2,200 trials of 5,600 accused war criminals were held in fifty-one locations throughout former Japanese-occupied territories as well as in Tokyo. The vast majority of these trials charged military officers with a long list of conventional war crimes including torture, abuse of POWs, atrocities committed against civilians, and use of slave labor.

The centerpiece was the International Military Tribunal for the Far East. The U.S. government both organized the tribunal and set the terms for its conduct. In proceedings that commenced in May 1946 and finally adjourned in November 1948, a panel of eleven justices from each of the Allied countries sat in judgment over twenty-eight high-ranking defendants accused of planning and executing a war of aggression, crimes against humanity, and war crimes. The defendants included former prime minister Tojo, Lord Keeper of the Privy Seal Kido, and former foreign minister Togo. They were represented by Allied as well as Japanese counsels who conducted a vigorous if ultimately unsuccessful defense. All the indicted were found guilty and seven were sentenced to be hanged. Although evidence was gathered against Emperor Hirohito, Washington ultimately instructed U.S. chief prosecutor Joseph Keenan not to bring charges against him in the interest of maintaining political stability. General MacArthur, commonly though incorrectly deemed personally responsible for the decision to shield Hirohito, did agree with Washington on this matter.

The Tokyo tribunal was not without serious flaws. Its conspiracy narrative regarding the origins of the Pacific War is historically dubious. Moreover, since the winners sat in judgment over the vanquished, some scholars have condemned the proceedings as an example of victors' justice—a thinly disguised exercise in exacting revenge. Nevertheless, the tribunal did expose and render necessary judgment on a multitude of extremely serious war crimes. The trials also served to remove prominent members of the wartime elite from public life and offer vital civics lessons about accountability and responsibility. More broadly, along with the Nuremberg tribunal, the Japanese trials helped to establish as part of the postwar system of international justice the personal responsibility of state leaders for their official actions.

With an official verdict on the war enunciated by the Tokyo tribunal, MacArthur's regime was content to put aside the brutality of Japan's imperial project. Why disrupt the cooperative spirit on which the occupation practically depended by constantly raising wartime transgressions? Only after the occupation did Japanese begin to wrestle with the basic moral questions raised by the war. They have continued the contest over memory right down to the present with perspectives divided along political lines. In the country's public life, the history of the war has kept washing up like trash dumped in coastal waters that every tide redeposits on the shore.

The most contentious point has been war guilt. The postwar peace movement, active from the 1950s onward, blamed the authoritarian, militarist elites who destroyed democracy, deceived their own people, subjected them to prolonged privation, and trampled conquered nations. Advocates of this critical perspective drew attention to what others wanted to omit or deny—the Nanjing massacre, the abuse of enemy soldiers, and the biological experiments conducted in China as part of a systematic pattern of official brutality. At the same time, the peace movement invoked Hiroshima and Nagasaki and more broadly the bombing of cities as irrefutable evidence for the proposition that the Japanese people were innocent victims whose suffering was a stark warning to a world imperiled by nuclear war. Memories of the dead and the testimony of survivors became the instruments for waging campaigns against nuclear weapons, nuclear proliferation, and the acquisition of nuclear weapons by Japan itself.

Right-wing patriots countered by rejecting the verdicts of the Tokyo trials and instead echoing the wartime claims of Japan's imperial government. They depicted Pearl Harbor as the response of a country put on the defensive and threatened by powerful outsiders. Rejecting charges of militarism run rampant, these neonationalists preferred to emphasize Japan's supposedly high-minded effort to liberate Asia from Western colonial domination and exploitation and celebrated the glorious record of military successes and valor. The symbolic focal point for neonationalists was the Yasukuni shrine in Tokyo, where the souls of some 2.5 million war dead are supposed to reside. There officials, including half of the postwar prime ministers, have honored the sacrifice of soldiers defending the nation and serving the emperor. Similarly, educational bureaucrats gave their approval to textbooks written to replace what neonationalists have decried as "too gloomy" or "excessively critical of Japan's position and actions in World War II."[50] School materials needed instead to instill national confidence and pride. Mainstream and leftist historians protested the texts' denial of such events as the Nanjing massacre and their general justification of Japan's prewar policy, and very few schools actually chose to use these neonationalist textbooks from among the wide array of textbooks on the approved list. The pattern of officialdom in denial was also evident on the issue of "comfort women," those forced into the sexual service of Japanese troops. For several decades the Japanese government covered up these war crimes, which the women themselves were too ashamed to raise publicly. When in their old age some of them stepped forward, Japanese courts rejected their suits for official apology and compensation on the grounds that the matter had long since been closed.

Repeated attempts by high government officials to wrap an ugly past in brocaded cloth have infuriated neighbors who had been on the receiving end of Japanese aggression. For example, in 1994 the minister of justice dismissed the women complaining of wartime abuse as "public prostitutes" and for good measure added that the Nanjing massacre was a "fabrication."[51] Remarks of this sort have helped members of the wartime generations in China, Korea, and the Philippines to keep alive their animosity and transmit their anti-Japanese sentiments to their children and grandchildren. These sentiments, stoked by nationalist politicians, have entered into the national identities of Japan's former victims.

The Japanese public has developed its own version of its controversial past. It has sidestepped the debate over war guilt by cultivating a collective national amnesia regarding the fifty years of Japanese colonization and aggression. Its only concession on this point, according to an opinion poll conducted in 1991, was the agreement by roughly half of the respondents that Americans were due an official apology for the Pearl Harbor attack. What really dominated the public imagination was the suffering of ordinary Japanese in the atomic bombings and more broadly in the incendiary attack on cities in the last year of the war. Reflecting this intense engagement, nearly two-thirds of the respondents in the 1991 poll endorsed the idea of an official U.S. apology for the atomic bombing. Implicitly, that transgression balanced the fault for Pearl Harbor. More evidence for the appeal of this victim mentality can be found in the novels, reminiscences, poems, museum exhibits, paintings, and movies that have elaborated in great and vivid detail since the 1950s the ways in which ordinary Japanese suffered during the war. As recently as 1997, an autobiographical novel focusing on the plight of the city dwellers helpless before the rain of death from the air proved a best seller. It tellingly if incidentally blames officialdom for misleading the public with "a pack of lies."[52]

American memory has proven just as selective as Japan's—and strikingly antithetical on fundamentals. The lines of difference, drawn during the occupation, were still holding firm a half century later. One point of divergence was over the suggestion that the Japanese were victims of war. The American occupation would have none of it, banning all discussion and images of the atomic aftermath. Later attempts to get Americans to focus on the topic in ways that suggested Japanese victimization have set off controversy, most strikingly on the fiftieth anniversary of Pearl Harbor. To mark the occasion the Smithsonian National Air and Space Museum in Washington planned an exhibit around the *Enola Gay* meant to explore a range of difficult questions surrounding the atomic bombing. The critical reaction was intense. The man who had piloted the *Enola Gay* pronounced the exhibit "a package of insults." The American Legion agreed. The hostility soon blazed out of control, fanned by a media that sympathized with aggrieved veterans. The *Wall Street Journal* announced that the Smithsonian had fallen "in[to] the hands of academics unable to view American history as anything other than a woeful catalog of crimes and aggressions against the helpless peoples of the earth." Republican conservatives eagerly took up the charge, with presidential candidate Pat Buchanan claiming to see in the exhibit evidence of a "sleepless campaign to inculcate in American youth a revulsion toward America's past." Senator Wendell Ford (R-Ky.) worried about what happens to America's view of its history "when you start mixing in other countries' perspectives." Threatened with prolonged congressional hearings by an outraged Congress and a cut in funding, a shaken museum head resigned, and the exhibit was sanitized to avoid uncomfortable questions about what the "good war" did to enemy civilians.[53]

A second point of divergence over memory relates to war guilt. Americans have clung to the notion of the war as a morality tale. The Tokyo trials established the basic version of Japanese aggression against an innocent America and uniquely brutal wartime conduct. Hollywood films have proven a powerful vehicle for perpetuating the war-guilt verdict, with Pearl Harbor the favorite exhibit. As late as 2001, the movie *Pearl Harbor* offered a comforting and familiar picture of Japanese militarism and American victimization with strong public appeal. Conversely, *Tora! Tora! Tora!*, a 1970 attempt to provide a perspective on the attack as both sides saw it, proved a commercial flop.[54] In American memory, the bookend to Pearl Harbor has been the postwar occupation (not Hiroshima and Nagasaki) — an object lesson in how to redeem an autocratic nation run amok. As in the textbook version of America's colonial stewardship of the Philippines, so too in Japan Americans imagined themselves selflessly bestowing the blessings of liberty, democracy, and prosperity upon a wayward but ultimately grateful Asian nation.

Coming to terms with Japanese internment, an event closer to home that had called into question the U.S. system of civil rights, proved easier to confront than shared responsibility for war or the moral implications of the atomic bombing. Repairing the injustice of the internment began immediately after the war with token compensation of approximately $38 million for actual property losses in the range of $400 million. The wartime breach of civil liberties got more serious attention only after young Japanese Americans made it their cause in the context of the 1960s florescence of ethnic identity movements. Responding to mounting pressure in 1976, President Gerald Ford publicly described the detention as a grave mistake. This judgment was confirmed by a presidential commission in 1981, which pronounced internment "not justified by military necessity" but rather prompted by "race prejudice, war hysteria, and a failure of political leadership."[55] Finally, in 1988 Congress tendered an official apology and offered additional compensation to the surviving victims ($20,000 per person for an ultimate total of $1.6 billion).

Toward the end of World War II, Woody Guthrie, the left-leaning American folk bard best known for "This Land Is Your Land," captured the spirit of the times when he sang, "Well, there's a better world that's a-coming."

One War, Two Meanings

Marine Corps War Memorial, Arlington, Virginia. This tribute to the troops who wrested control of Iwo Jima was based on the iconic photo by combat photographer Joe Rosenthal taken in the midst of the brutal battle for the island. The monument, designed by Felix de Weldon and dedicated in 1954, evokes the warrior ethic that Americans have come to associate with the "good war." (Courtesy of Prints and Photographs Division, Library of Congress)

Hiroshima Peace Memorial. What is commonly known as the A-Bomb Dome is the last remnant of the destruction from a nuclear weapon that detonated on 6 August 1945 almost directly overhead. After extended uncertainty, the city council decided in 1966 to preserve the building, which had had its beginnings as a commercial exhibition hall. In 1996 it was declared a UNESCO World Heritage site over U.S. objections. The memorial serves at once as a universal warning of the nuclear peril looming over all people and as a particular reminder of the aerial devastation visited on virtually every Japanese city. (*From* WikiCommons)

As Guthrie's "Better World" promised, the United States and its allies did indeed "beat 'em on the land in the sea and in the sky." Forty-five months of bitter fighting across a vast amphitheater of war had determined who was the overlord of the western Pacific. The entire ocean had become an American lake—or in the words of a popular song, "To be specific, it's our Pacific." With both opportunity and motive to exploit this opportunity, U.S. leaders executed what was in effect an imperial substitution program extending well beyond Japan.[56]

The arc of American power in eastern Asia had reached its apogee. McKinley had launched Americans on an imperial enterprise marked by concerns with duty and destiny. He had fastened a firm grip on the Philippine outpost as well as Hawaii and helped lay down a claim to a stake in China's future. Confronted by a strong Japanese state with its own imperial vision for the future of eastern Asia, his successors had first vacillated and then gone to war. Having stymied Japan's ambitions, U.S. policymakers asserted their own claim to regional dominance. The Japanese empire was no more, the remnants of European empires struggled to survive, China was still weak and divided. In the countries all along the Pacific's western shore, securely ensconced U.S. agents now had an open field. Guided by the old dream of destiny and duty, they could now turn to the tasks of exercising the requisite control and advancing the liberal values that McKinley had first articulated and Franklin Roosevelt had affirmed. They would provide instruction in democracy, help build states, encourage a market economy tied to the United States, and above all demand respect and compliance. Directing and uplifting Asians in all these ways was a practical expression of a paternalism evident in the U.S. advance across the Pacific from the outset.

The greatest bloodletting in world history, however, was followed not by peace and the Asian embrace of this liberal vision but by conflict. Two fundamental challenges to the newly won U.S. position would emerge. The lesser one came from the Soviet Union. Joseph Stalin entered the Pacific War at the eleventh hour, occupying strategic territories on the Soviet Union's far eastern periphery. This signaled his and his successors' interest in having a voice in the future of Northeast Asia. More important, as prescient observers understood at the time, was the challenge issuing from within eastern Asia itself. The forces of revolution, decolonization, and anti-imperialism were in full play by the war's end. "There is no peace in Asia," Harold R. Isaacs wrote in 1947. "As long as the social, political, and economic problems of Asia remain unsolved, Asia will remain the scene of conflict, and while there is no peace in Asia there can be no peace for

America or for the world."[57] Between 1945 and 1975, the swells of popular nationalism and communism washed over the new U.S. imperium and dashed hopes for a docile U.S.-dominated region. Yet, America's belief in its Pacific destiny was deeply rooted. It took two more wars over the next quarter century, the first in Korea, the second in Vietnam, before U.S. policymakers reluctantly came to terms with the unwelcome reality that their power, like that of the empires that had preceded them, was limited.

3 | **Korea,** 1950–1953
DOMINANCE CHALLENGED

A t precisely 10:00 A.M. on 27 July 1953, U.S. Army general William K. Harrison Jr. and Korean People's Army general Nam Il entered from opposite sides of a specially constructed building in the border village of Panmunjom, the site of long-running truce talks aimed at ending the Korean War. They represented, respectively, the U.S.-led sixteen-nation U.N. coalition and North Korean and Chinese forces backed by the Soviet Union. Without uttering a word to each other, the two men affixed their signatures to nine blue-covered and nine maroon-covered copies of an armistice agreement. Twelve hours later, when the cease-fire took effect, Sergeant William D. Dannenmaier, a radio scout with the U.S. Army's Fifteenth Infantry Regiment, was disconcerted: "The silence was startling. So was the darkness, no longer broken by the lights of exploding shells. Then, slowly, lights began appearing, a cigarette here, a flashlight there. . . . I never felt more desolate or empty in my life. . . . There were no cheers[,] no laughter." Although both sides claimed a kind of victory, Dannenmaier's reaction was closer to the truth.[1]

Several years of intense civil conflict on the Korean peninsula preceded the North Korean invasion of South Korea on 25 June 1950. The ensuing war raged up and down the peninsula for more than three years, quickly drawing in the United States and its allies on the side of South Korea and China on the side of North Korea. Grinding land warfare, savage atrocities committed by both sides, and indiscriminate bombing by the U.S. Air Force inflicted massive death on civilians as well as combatants. Korea's cities and industries were destroyed and the land itself horribly scarred. Finally, the combatants, unable to enforce their will without risking a wider war, settled for a cease-fire line that ran like a jagged scar across the midsection of the Korean peninsula, not far from the line that had separated rival regimes before the invasion. An inconclusive war doomed the divided country to a future of continued antagonism and tension.

In broader terms, the Korean War marked a distinct downward turn in the arc of America's protracted engagement in eastern Asia. Only a few years earlier that arc had reached its apogee. With Japan subordinated and European empires in postwar retreat, no other power in eastern Asia seemed capable of challenging America's dominance. But in fact the war in Korea would demonstrate the limits of U.S. power in a region undergoing profound changes. By 1950 nationalist movements in South Asia, Indonesia, the Philippines, Malaya, and Indochina had already gained or were rapidly advancing toward independence. A renascent China, driven by a species of the revolutionary impulse increasingly ascendant in the region, was beginning to reassert its historic interest in its border areas. America's major Cold War adversary, the Soviet Union, aligned with China in supporting the cause of liberation. Amid these adverse currents, U.S. policymakers would find themselves first drawn onto the Korean battlefield, then constrained there, and finally compelled to accept a frustrating settlement.

A REGION IN FERMENT

From the high optimism of the fall of 1945, American leaders had descended rapidly into fear and pessimism. Relations with the World War II Soviet ally soured in late 1945 and early 1946 as the Kremlin fastened its grip on Eastern Europe and probed for advantage in Iran and northeast China. Gradually, President Harry S. Truman resolved to take a stand. His growing hostility toward Moscow was first evident in personal outbursts and comments to close advisers. Then in March 1947 he went public. In a landmark speech to Congress, he asserted the world was deeply divided ideologically and proclaimed a sweeping commitment to support free peoples everywhere threatened by communism. His dramatic affirmation quickly translated into the Marshall Plan to ensure the economic recovery of Western Europe. By 1949, his administration had lined up governments there behind an anti-Soviet position and stitched together the North Atlantic Treaty Organization as a basis for military coordination.

While the Truman administration gave priority to the defense of Western Europe and relegated eastern Asia to a distinctly secondary position, its fundamental views were so sweeping that the distinction between one region and the other proved hard to maintain. U.S. leaders subscribed to a potent set of axioms that trumped neat distinctions between primary and secondary areas. They had internalized the dangers of appeasement from the Munich agreement concluded by Britain's Neville Chamberlain with Adolf Hitler on the eve of World War II in Europe. They were quick to see in Stalin and other communist leaders the same impulse to aggression earlier demonstrated by Hitler. Weakness or hesitation, they believed, would only encourage the boundless territorial ambitions of totalitarians: confronting them was the surest way to security and peace. Washington reinforced this first axiom with a second built on the hard logic of geopolitics already prominent in Franklin Roosevelt's thinking in the late 1930s: security was indivisible. A defeat at one point was certain to spread around the world, toppling countries like dominoes. Since any struggle was now inherently global, the defense of Asian lands might prove as consequential as those of Europe. Finally, and perhaps most important of all, Truman and his advisers believed they were engaged in an ideological contest with monumental stakes. The president's March 1947 assertion of a fundamental contradiction between the world of slavery (the Soviet Union and its satellites) and the world of freedom (the United States, its allies, and its protectorates) swept aside geographical limits. With the fate of humanity seemingly hanging in the balance, the Truman administration viewed the prospect of communist victories anywhere as potentially catastrophic.

These axiomatic views inspired the U.S. Cold War strategy known as containment. It dictated resolute resistance at virtually any point at which communists might threaten. Quickly, a score of imperiled points contended for the attention and resources of U.S. policymakers, and those in eastern Asia steadily moved toward the top of Washington's list. Step by step, the Truman administration tightened its grip on the region to ward off possible disasters.

The rising level of tension registered earliest and most decisively in Japan, where U.S. occupation policy underwent a sharp reversal in 1947–48. Reform of yesterday's enemy gave way to creating tomorrow's Cold War ally. What the American proconsul, Douglas MacArthur, had imagined as the "Switzerland of Asia" was to become an anticommunist bastion. To secure the bastion, the occupation began to crack down on labor unions and the Left, halted the dissolution of the economic conglomerates known as *zaibatsu*, stopped reparations promised to victims of Japanese aggression to speed Japan's recovery, and encouraged the recentralization of authority in Tokyo in the hands of the conservative Yoshida Shigeru, who before the war had served as a senior official in the imperial foreign ministry. Yoshida was in tune with the anticommunist impulse behind the U.S. reverse course even if he differed at times with the Americans on details.

Looking beyond Japan, American observers saw young nations in Asia needing the guidance of a more mature, benevolent power, especially in an unstable environment rife with revolutionary possibilities. Even as the war was coming to a close, U.S. policymakers began to worry about how communists and radical nationalists might exploit this time of transition. They thus set to work weaving a regionwide web consisting of military occupations, military bases, trade agreements, and alliances. Once limited to a strategically vulnerable Philippines, the new sphere extended across some 3,000 miles along the western Pacific.

If Japan with its deferential political elite, its reviving economy, and its valuable naval, air, and ground bases was the northern anchor, the Philippines was the southern strong point. There Washington was determined to deliver on its prior commitment to formal independence. Ending colonial control made good economic sense, and granting independence would also demonstrate to hopeful Asians and doubtful Europeans how enlightened colonialism was supposed to work. But a strong residue of the colonial relationship remained. The new Philippine state was dominated by the old collection of powerful families who saw U.S. aid and military assistance as essential underpinnings of the status quo. The U.S. military, in a shift of thinking, likewise thought close ties essential. The Philippines seemed no longer a vulnerability but an asset in the postwar defense system. The bestowal of independence was thus conditioned on the granting of a ninety-nine-year lease on twenty-three U.S. bases including the air force's Clark Field and the navy's Subic Bay.

Elsewhere in Asia, Washington was keenly concerned that the clash between weakened colonial regimes and impatient nationalists carried the risk of regionwide instability. In British lands, from which rapidly emerged Pakistan, Burma, and Ceylon as well as India, the colonials promptly packed up. But in Southeast Asia European dominion died hard—and put Washington in a quandary. Its wartime endorsement of self-determination clashed with the assumption that a lengthy period of tutelage was required before subject peoples could be granted independence. The specter of communist revolution steadily pushed the Truman administration toward an indulgent view of the remnant European claims.

The Dutch East Indies confronted Washington with what was to become a familiar choice: back the colonial stake of European allies or make good on the rhetoric of self-determination. In this case, constructing a stable, U.S.-aligned Europe initially was given priority as the Truman administration lent quiet support to the Dutch attempt at reconquest. But the Japanese occupation had created an opening for a two-decades-old independence movement, which quickly took advantage of Japan's surrender in August 1945 to establish the Indonesian Republic. Washington's subsequent call for a benign colonial restoration was as out of date as Dutch dreams of bringing back the old order. In 1948 Secretary of State George C. Marshall switched gears, fearing that Stalin might seek to exploit anticolonial sentiment in Southeast Asia. The moderate nationalist Indonesian government led by Sukarno and Mohammad Hatta gave every promise of keeping homegrown communists in check, the Soviet Union at arm's length, the islands' strategic position safe, and their rich supply of oil, rubber, and tin accessible. Under U.S. pressure the Dutch, dependent on U.S. aid for postwar recovery, grudgingly agreed in 1949 to pack up and go home.

In British-ruled Malaya, an insurgency gathered steam in the late 1940s and exacerbated anxieties about a communist breakthrough. In 1952 the British adopted a multifaceted counterinsurgency strategy that by the end of the decade had defused the danger. They were helped considerably by the narrowness of the insurgent appeal, confined to a rural ethnic Chinese minority. Malaya moved smoothly toward independence and a place within the British Commonwealth.

By contrast, the situation in Indochina, also beset by a Communist insurgency, looked bleak. The French refused to abandon their colony, and France's importance to European defense precluded Washington from exerting the degree of pressure it had on the Netherlands. In any case, Washington increasingly worried that a French departure would simply clear the way for a takeover by the Communist movement led by Ho Chi Minh. While continuing to talk of ultimate self-determination, the Truman administration shifted steadily toward supporting France's effort to retain its colony. In early 1950 Indochina won a formal place within the containment line, signaling its emergence as a new U.S. salient in the region.

Further darkening Washington's mood was the dramatic Communist victory in China in 1949. That victory capped a half century of tortuous inquiry, debate, and organizing by public intellectuals committed to the regeneration of their country. They had watched the great powers (including the United States) colonize some of their neighbors, stake out informal spheres of influence in others, and (most serious of all) steadily extend their control in China itself. The prerequisite for overcoming this crisis, Chinese intellectuals and political leaders alike concluded, was the creation of a strong government determined to repossess Taiwan, Manchuria, Mongolia, Xinjiang, and Tibet, cut foreigners down to size, restore Chinese pride, and regain China's status as a respected world power. This program of national revitalization gained momentum in the last decade (1901–11) of the Qing dynasty. The political disarray following the fall of the dynasty in 1912 and its replacement by a weak republican government led many nationalists to turn to various schools of Western thought, including revolutionary Marxism, to understand their country's domestic and international woes. It also led them to adopt the incandescent language of anti-imperialism.

The 1940s witnessed a sea change in the politics of Chinese nationalism, with grim consequences for the United States. Chiang Kai-shek had embodied nationalism during the late 1920s and the 1930s. But the Sino-Japanese War (1937–45) fatally weakened his government while his Communist foes, led by Mao Zedong, matured into a powerful military and political force. In June 1946, civil war erupted from which three years later the Communists emerged victorious. Their new regime quickly radicalized the old nationalist program and identified the United States as its major international foe. At home it sought to eliminate U.S. influence that had accumulated since the days of the Open Door notes. Abroad, the new government backed Ho Chi Minh in Vietnam, denounced U.S. occupation policy in Japan, and supported the North Korean Communist regime led by Kim Il Sung. As devoted Marxist-Leninists, Mao Zedong and his comrades looked to the Soviet Union for support in building and securing a new China. Just two months after inaugurating the People's Republic of China on 1 October 1949, Mao journeyed to Moscow. There in February 1950 he and Stalin concluded a formal alliance that included a mutual security commitment and provided for a $300 million low-interest Soviet loan to jump-start China's recovery from the ravages of war.

The man who presided over this sudden shift in China's fortunes was born in 1893 to a moderately wealthy peasant family in the inland province of Hunan. Mao had dallied with Western liberalism and anarchism before settling on Marxism-Leninism. A founding member of the Chinese Communist Party in 1921, he was quick to recognize the revolutionary potential of China's rootless and landless rural masses, the wretched of the earth. Over the next dozen years Mao survived political attacks by rival Moscow-trained leaders who viewed him as an undereducated country bumpkin with a primitive understanding of party doctrine and a penchant for warfare over politics. They underestimated his talents as a shrewd political infighter, his skill as a guerrilla warrior, and his charisma as a leader. By 1935 he had outmaneuvered his enemies and assumed the leadership of his party.

Stalin took note and recognized Mao as the head of the Chinese party. Mao in turn made clear his acceptance of the Kremlin boss as leader of the worldwide communist movement and his devotion to the revolutionary cause. This acknowledgment of Soviet leadership did not mean complete obedience to Soviet directives. Already during the last phase of the Chinese civil war, Mao and Stalin had diverged on strategy, with Mao sometimes going his own way.[2] Like all alliances, this one subordinated but did not eliminate differing priorities, interests, and even world views.

By the late 1940s, Mao's success had come to represent a serious danger to the American imperium. A weak and poor China with its large population and land mass occupied a central place in the dream of an American era in the Pacific. Communist dominance had been the nightmare preying on the minds of U.S. officials ever since the Bolshevist contagion had "infected" China in the early 1920s. They had then interpreted anti-imperialist attacks on the onerous, much resented unequal treaties as an expression of rising Soviet influence threatening to American missionary, business, and diplomatic interests. Ultimately, the U.S. goal had to be (as one diplomat put it in 1926) "saving the Chinese from their own folly."[3]

Chiang Kai-shek, with his sterling credentials as an anticommunist and Christian, emerged as the best U.S. hope. After taking power in 1927, Chiang set about exterminating his Communist rivals and cultivating American missionaries, educators, and diplomats. President Franklin Roosevelt had cast Chiang in the role of a postwar ally who should be built up and who could help stabilize Asia. FDR had observed in 1943 that "China was at least a potential world Power and anarchy in China would be so grave a misfortune that Chiang Kai-shek must be given the fullest support."[4] Through the fall of 1945 Truman administration officials sought ways to shore up their client weakened by its eight-year war against Japan. Washington posted U.S. marines to North China, supplied humanitarian and reconstruction aid, and transported Nationalist units into position to accept the surrender of Japanese forces all across China and thus box out the rival Communists.

As the Chinese Communists clawed their way to power in the late 1940s, U.S. leaders engaged in a spasmodic, painful, and ultimately unsuccessful attempt to save Chiang and (Truman added in a nod to McKinley and Hay) to "carry out the policy of 1898." The president first sent General George C. Marshall to China in December 1945 to mediate a peaceful resolution of the looming civil conflict. It was mission impossible. By mid-1946 civil war engulfed China. Marshall abandoned his efforts in January 1947, blaming both sides for their obduracy. Thereafter, Washington, disenchanted with Chiang but implacably hostile toward Mao, provided a modicum of financial and military support to the Nationalists while trying to nudge the generalissimo in the direction of reform thought essential to saving a corrupt, unpopular, ill-led regime. By 1949 some $3 billion in U.S. aid had failed to revive Chiang's fortunes. The Truman administration, lacking sufficient forces even to defend Europe, refused to send American troops to China in a last-ditch rescue effort.[5]

The retreat of Chiang's defeated armies to Taiwan changed U.S. calculations. China's island province was squarely in the sights of Mao's People's Liberation Army, which was planning an invasion to bring it inside the new China. Because of its location athwart the sea-lanes of communication in the western Pacific, U.S. officials viewed Taiwan as an important strategic asset, but with U.S. power spread thin worldwide, Truman still hesitated to make a strong commitment to a regime with such a poor track record. Washington, however, maintained diplomatic ties to Chiang's "Republic of China" and recognized its claim to be the rightful government of all of China. Meanwhile, powerful Republicans in Congress, backed by Henry Luce's media empire, charged the Democratic administration with the "loss of China" and demanded forceful action to save a long-time ally.

No ambiguity crept into Truman policy toward the mainland. Chiang Kai-shek's defeat had not just cost Washington a proxy in its worldwide battle against communism; it had also opened a massive breach in the containment line. U.S. cold warriors feared a Communist China tied tightly to the Soviet Union posed a strategic threat not seen since the rise of the Axis powers in 1940. Reinforcing these strategic anxieties were attitudes of condescension and contempt for the new regime. Truman lamented that the pro-American Chinese "liberals" had lost out, leaving China saddled with a "totalitarian state." Its new leaders were (according to a 1949 assessment by the State Department's policy guru, George Kennan) a bunch of "grievously misguided and confused people," who bore an "attitude of arrogancy, contempt for the West." Dean Acheson, who succeeded Marshall as head of the State Department, regarded the Chinese revolution as a Russian takeover. He charged, "The Communist leaders have forsworn their Chinese heritage." Still nursing the forlorn hope of bringing China back into the U.S. fold, he predicted, "Ultimately the profound civilization and the democratic individualism of China will reassert themselves and she will throw off the foreign yoke."[6]

With Truman's backing, Acheson shaped a hard-line policy of diplomatic and economic isolation, punctuated by public scoldings of the new Chinese leadership, meant to undermine support by the Chinese people, induce the true nationalists within the party leadership to break with Moscow, and ultimately drive the Communists from power. By 1949 the predominant view of the U.S. public professing some knowledge of the China problem was in line with the administration. It was skeptical of providing aid to the Nationalists and opposed recognizing the Communists.[7]

Compared to the upheaval in China, Korea seemed a sideshow of limited consequence to the broader U.S. position. Yet, in the context of Cold War rivalry and Sino-American tensions the fierce struggle among Koreans over the future of their country would create the conditions for the third American war in Asia. This harsh, mountainous, relatively resource-poor land had a reputation as a focal point of regional conflict, and its position made it an invasion route between Northeast Asia and Japan. In the late nineteenth century, Korea lived up to that reputation as an expansionist Russia pressed from the north, a modernizing Japan bent on empire from the east, and an enfeebled China, trying to play protector, from the west. The Yi dynasty, a 500-year-old Confucian monarchy challenged internally by reformers and wracked by warring court factions, was gradually overwhelmed. In 1905 Japan gained undisputed mastery on the peninsula following victory over Russia, and in 1910 Japan formally incorporated Korea into its empire.

Four decades of Japanese colonialism left a deep mark. It stymied the emergence of an indigenous Korean leadership class as well as autonomous political organizations. Colonial administrators implemented policies of cultural genocide, suppressing Korean language and culture and forcing assimilation and servitude on a recalcitrant people. Tokyo bound Korea's economy to the Japanese empire and impressed millions of Koreans into compulsory labor service tantamount to slavery. While Japan brought a modicum of industrialization to the north, the colony remained predominantly agricultural, with low levels of education and technology and a population living close to the margin of survival.

U.S. policymakers, who had merely looked on as Japan took control in 1910, were initially sympathetic toward Japan's "civilizing mission." But World War II left them resolved on the destruction of the Japanese empire, and this forced them to consider the postwar future of Korea. Franklin Roosevelt envisioned independence, but only after several decades of "democratic tutelage" under a great power trusteeship. His attitude followed the Philippine model, which assumed that Asians were politically immature and required a long season of benevolent guardianship before they could govern themselves. This assumption, rooted in elite as well as popular American thinking, deeply offended educated and patriotic Koreans.

In any case, Roosevelt's plan was stillborn. As the Pacific War drew rapidly to a close, the new Truman administration had to improvise a policy. Anticipating the imminent surrender of Japanese forces in Korea, two U.S. military officers—one of whom was future secretary of state Dean Rusk—were tasked on 10 August with choosing a line to divide the American and Soviet zones of military occupation. Their choice of the thirty-eighth parallel, a line with no prior significance in Korean history, placed the capital city of Seoul in the American zone. In early August, the Soviet army routed Japanese forces and quickly occupied Korea down to the thirty-eighth parallel. A month later U.S. forces commanded by General John R. Hodge arrived from Okinawa to manage the U.S. zone.

Without experts to offer advice, American military and civilian officials scrambled to devise a policy for a land in social and political ferment. The economy was in shambles. The countryside, marked by high tenancy rates, was a battleground between the landless and landlords. The politically active elite was split between those who had collaborated with Japan and those on the left who had played a leading role in the resistance. Political loyalties on both sides were fragmented. Fearful of political turbulence, Hodge at once pushed aside radical Korean nationalists, including a bewildering assortment of leftists and communists, almost all of whom wanted immediate independence. For help in imposing order, he turned to the defeated but intact Japanese forces, their despised Korean collaborators, and English-speaking Koreans keen to trade on their American connections.

The politician who emerged as Washington's default choice to head an interim southern government was Syngman Rhee. Born in 1875 into an aristocratic family from northern Korea, Rhee received a classical Confucian education before entering a Methodist missionary school, where he became a devout Christian and acquired fluency in English. As a young man he spent seven years in prison because of his nationalist politics. Released in 1904, he traveled to the United States to pursue his studies. In 1910, the year Japan annexed his homeland, Rhee earned a PhD in political science at Princeton, where he was befriended by university president Woodrow Wilson. During his long years in exile in the United States, he lobbied tirelessly but in vain to win American support for Korean independence.

The upheaval at the end of the Pacific War finally provided Rhee an opening. Though a prickly conservative not easily controlled, he had strong U.S. credentials, a useful command of English, and a strong Protestant faith that commended him to Hodge and the U.S. military government. Rhee and a shifting coalition of conservative nationalists would work with the Americans to build an anticommunist bastion south of the thirty-eighth parallel. Aligned with landlords and local notables, many of them former collaborators with the Japanese, Rhee's government focused on eliminating the mainly leftist opposition. The army, the police, and progovernment vigilante groups brutally suppressed armed leftists, labor unions, and farmers' associations at a cost of roughly 100,000 lives *prior* to the outbreak of war in June 1950.[8]

As the southern government struggled to establish its authority in the South, Soviet-backed Communists took control north of the thirty-eighth parallel. Although nominally consisting of a three-party coalition including the Korean Democratic Party and the Young Friends Party, the northern government was actually controlled by the North Korean Workers Party, a communist party first cousin to those in the process of seizing power in the Soviet-occupied nations of Eastern Europe.

At the head of the party stood the youthful Kim Il Sung. He was born in northern Korea in 1912 as Kim Song Ju into a Christian family of modest means. When he was eight, his family moved across the border into Manchuria, where he learned Chinese and became interested in communism in middle school, his highest level of formal education. As a teenager in the late 1920s, Kim took part in underground anti-Japanese activities and became a political commissar and then military officer in a Chinese Communist–led guerrilla army, where he eventually commanded some 300 troops. Taking the nom de guerre Kim Il Sung in 1935, he scored some dramatic if small-scale successes as a guerrilla leader before being driven into eastern Siberia by Japanese counterinsurgency forces in 1940. In the Soviet Union Kim received military training and a major's commission in the Red Army's Far East Command. Unlike Syngman Rhee, two generations his senior, Kim was little known outside his immediate circle of followers. After returning by ship from Siberia, Kim made his first public appearance at a Soviet-sponsored rally in Pyongyang in October 1945.

Thereafter, Kim ascended like a rocket, guided by General Terentii F. Shtykov, the Soviet emissary who became the first ambassador to North Korea. Within two months Kim had become the de facto head of the North Korean Communist Party, and in February 1946 he was chosen as chairman of the North Korean Provisional People's Committee, the nucleus of the future North Korean state. Kim's regime, like Rhee's, could not have survived without outside political, economic, and military support and technical assistance. In other words, at this early stage of its development, the dependent regime in the north was being integrated into Stalin's Eurasian empire. Like other Soviet clients, the rulers of North Korea proceeded forcibly to implement a socialist revolution, to suppress opposition ruthlessly, and to introduce a thorough and generally popular land reform that, in Charles Armstrong's words, "took place with very little violence." This was likely because during the revolutionary upheaval in the North as many as 800,000 persons, presumably most opposed to the Kim regime, managed to flee to the South.[9]

As the two competing regimes consolidated their power, what were initially merely zones of military occupation hardened into separate states. By 1947 Soviet-American talks to bring about a unified Korea had stalled. The impasse had less to do with satisfying clients than with retaining potentially strategic zones of control and avoiding any concessions that might signal weakness. Accordingly, despite their view that Korea was not worth becoming "a *casus belli* for the U.S.," and that its people were handicapped by "political immaturity," U.S. policymakers set about building up the Rhee regime.[10] They first sponsored a U.N. Temporary Commission on Korea and then bullied it into validating what was in essence a rigged election in the South in May 1948 that confirmed Syngman Rhee in power. The Soviet-backed North refused to take part in this election or to recognize the outcome. Rhee was installed as the first president of the Republic of Korea, officially established on 15 August 1948 with its capital in Seoul. Despite the veneer of democratic legitimacy, Rhee's was a police state, a good example of the many right-wing dictatorships that Washington supported during as well as before the Cold War. The final step in Korea's formal division followed with the proclamation on 9 September of the Democratic People's Republic of Korea led by Kim Il Sung with its capital in Pyongyang. With their client regimes seemingly firmly in place, Washington and Moscow were disposed to focus on more strategically important areas.

The tacit accommodation that Moscow and Washington had reached failed to account for the fierce nationalism of their respective clients. The two separate Korean states were like Siamese twins joined, rather than separated, by the thirty-eighth parallel, each convinced its own long-term survival necessitated the elimination of the other and committed to restoring the historical unity of the Korean nation. Although men from very different backgrounds and generations, both Rhee and Kim had come of age in the difficult, tenacious struggle against Japanese control. Like other patriots, they took profound pride in a rich, distinctive, ethnically homogeneous culture and in their country's long history of independence (much longer in fact than that of either the United States or Russia). They harbored a deep-seated mistrust of outsiders with their deplorable record of demeaning Korean culture and disrupting Korean unity. Rhee and Kim alike had embraced the World War II promise of a new era for their country and wanted to make the most of the postwar chance for independence. They regarded the division of their country as an aberration, a historical anomaly that no Korean patriot could accept. To emerge from Japanese domination only to suffer division as a result of great-power diktat grated on the sensibilities of patriots north and south. Reunification, therefore, became the paramount goal of leaders in both Pyongyang and Seoul.

Between 1946 and 1950, each regime maneuvered to advance its own version of unification. Both were prepared to use force. Political instability in the South presented attractive opportunities for Pyongyang to extend its control by supporting popular insurrections, waging guerrilla warfare, and conducting cross-border raids. Yet, by the spring of 1950, despite his growing unpopularity, Rhee had largely succeeded in crushing his opponents. He matched North Korean provocations by launching his own cross-border operations. Rhee in addition had a distinct resource advantage—a population of 21 million (twice that of the North). The South's economic output was also twice as large.[11]

In this deadly dance, both rival regimes sought and received aid from their patrons even as foreign forces began their withdrawal (completed by the Soviets in late 1948 and by the Americans by June 1949). Both powers sought to bolster their clients by transferring arms and embarking on military training programs. A 500-man U.S. Army Korean Military Advisory Group went to work in August 1948 to create a southern army on the American model. Downplaying the likelihood of a full-scale North Korean invasion, the U.S. military supplied the 100,000-strong South Korean force mainly with light arms. U.S. leaders decided to withhold tanks, armor, and heavy artillery because these items seemed unnecessary, were too expensive, and might tempt Rhee into mounting a full-scale attack against North Korea. Even so, by 1950 U.S. aid to South Korea totaled $100 million. The Soviet effort had begun even earlier, in 1946, when Soviet advisers midwived the birth of the North Korean army and oversaw the delivery of some equipment. In September 1947, a school was opened in Pyongyang to train guerrilla leaders for operations in the South. Moscow considerably raised its level of support in the several months prior to June 1950, making significant deliveries of artillery, armor, and aircraft. Contributions from both sides in the Cold War were raising the chances for a conflagration.

ILLUSIONS OF VICTORY

A country divided by Cold War rivalry and irreconcilable nationalist dreams plunged into war in June 1950. During the year that followed, the illusion of victory repeatedly tempted commanders on both sides. North Korean leaders were the first to grasp for a total victory, seeking to bring to a close the struggle for unification. The second to try were the Americans hoping to unify the country on Rhee's terms and to roll back communism. This overt internationalization of the war prompted the third attempt, this time by China's leader, to score a decisive victory. The result was yet a third failure and at last a willingness on the part of the exhausted belligerents to seriously contemplate peace.

Revolutionaries, like skilled gamblers, try to gauge when the odds are shifting in their favor. Kim Il Sung performed just such a calculation in 1949 and early 1950. He took the measure of Rhee's unpopularity, his army's shortcomings, and political turmoil in South Korea, and concluded that the North Korean army could conquer the South in a matter of weeks. The risk of American intervention seemed slight. The Truman administration had acquiesced in the Chinese Communists' victory. If China weighed so little in America's strategic balance, Korea surely counted for less. The National Security Council confirmed this view in March 1949 when it decided that the withdrawal of American troops should be completed by June so they could be redeployed to points more strategically important in case of war with the Soviet Union. Far East commander General Douglas MacArthur and Secretary of State Dean Acheson publicly spelled out the implications of this strategic approach in speeches in December 1949 and January 1950. Acheson famously omitted Korea from his detailed survey of America's Pacific defense perimeter. Pyongyang as well as Moscow took note.

Before Kim could take the offensive, he needed Stalin's approval and assurances of Soviet material support. Badgered by his cocky and importunate Korean client, the Kremlin boss responded cautiously. Stalin's vast Soviet empire was still recovering from the ravages of the German invasion. The United States and its allies were much more powerful than the rickety socialist camp. There was no reason for rushing to confrontation. Indeed, Stalin's communist faith taught him that time was on the Soviet side. The contradictions afflicting a mature capitalist system were bound to intensify, ultimately trigger that system's global collapse, and deliver victory to socialism. But Stalin at seventy was still a Leninist revolutionary at heart, one who did not wait on history but wanted to make it happen. He was ready to make history on the Korean peninsula—but only if the Soviet risk was minimal.

Calculation of the risk began to turn in an adventurist direction during 1949. In the spring Moscow promised a major arms package and endorsed Pyongyang's request for the transfer home of Korean troops fighting on the Communist side in the Chinese civil war. Accordingly, Mao repatriated some 75,000 battle-hardened Korean veterans along with their units' equipment, with the first group arriving in July and August 1949 and the second in the spring of 1950. These men comprised more than half of Kim's soldiers.

Thus, substantially bolstered, Kim began pressing for action; Stalin enjoined him to be patient. For example, in September 1949 the Soviet Politburo told Kim that a military attack on the South was not only "ill-timed" but also "impermissible." It would fail while also giving the Americans an excuse for interfering. Yet Kim kept pressing, promising that the combination of his regular army and his partisans in the South would win a quick victory—well before the Americans could intervene. By January 1950, the prospect of U.S. resistance seemed remote, especially after Acheson's speech excluding Korea from the U.S. defense perimeter. Stalin, his anxiety alleviated, now agreed to an attack. He merely stipulated in an April meeting with Kim in Moscow that his Korean protégé first secure the approval of Mao Zedong. "If you should get kicked in the teeth, I shall not lift a finger. You have to ask Mao for all the help." At the same time, Moscow sped up deliveries of heavy military equipment including T-34 battle tanks and long-range artillery that would give the North a military capacity the South lacked.[12]

To clear the last hurdle standing in the way of his invasion, Kim dutifully journeyed to Beijing in mid-May to secure the endorsement of fellow Communists with whom he had a correct but distant relationship. Mao, only now made formally aware of the advanced state of Soviet-Korean planning for the invasion, was not enthusiastic. He understood even then that if the invasion miscarried he could find a major conflict on his doorstep, possibly involving U.S. forces. Moreover, a Korean crisis could disrupt preparations to invade Taiwan, the last province remaining in Nationalist hands. Even more than the Korean attack, that operation would require Soviet air and naval support. At the same time his forces were preoccupied with regaining control of China's inner Asian frontier, notably Tibet and Xinjiang. Nevertheless, Mao told Kim, "If the Americans take part in military action, then China will provide troops to North Korea."[13]

At 4:00 A.M. on a rainy Sunday, 25 June 1950, ten divisions of the North

Korean army, some 90,000 troops spearheaded by tanks and mobile artillery, launched a multipronged offensive. Advancing across the thirty-eighth parallel, they caught officers of the Republic of Korea Army off guard after a Saturday night on the town. As it quickly became clear that this was not another limited probe but a full-scale invasion, Rhee called for U.S. assistance. Three days into the attack, with his defenses crumbling and North Korean troops on the outskirts of Seoul, his government fled southward followed by more than a quarter of the city's population, the vast majority of which was composed of refugees from North Korea. Early on the morning of 28 June, South Korean sappers in their haste to evacuate Seoul blew up the city's main bridge. They had given no warning, killing hundreds of civilians trapped on the structure and cutting off many of their own troops.

As they retreated, South Korean police and army units emptied the prisons of some 30,000 political prisoners whom they summarily executed, including as many as 7,000 in the city of Taejon, where the victims' bodies were dumped in mass graves. Over the next several months, Rhee's men rounded up and massacred in cold blood many tens of thousands of suspected leftists and presumptive communist collaborators, including 3,500 near Kyongsan City whose corpses were sealed in a cobalt mine. U.S. military personnel who witnessed and reported these atrocities up the chain of command did nothing to stop them. Nor did their superiors. Instead, the killings, excused as a military necessity, were conveniently blamed on the North Koreans and covered up for decades.[14]

With Kim Il Sung's gamble on the verge of succeeding, the fate of South Korea rested in the hands of Harry Truman. In deciding whether to authorize quick and effective military assistance, he was guided above all by Dean Acheson, that elegantly mustachioed Anglophile whom Republicans loathed. Consistent with core Cold War convictions, both the president and his secretary of state viewed North Korea's invasion not as the escalation of a civil war but as a blatant act of aggression across an international boundary. A failure to respond forcefully, they reasoned, would not only constitute appeasement but invite aggression at other points and weaken the U.S. position worldwide.

Impressed with the urgency of the situation, Truman hesitated just long enough to ascertain that North Korea's attack was not the opening move in a wider Soviet challenge. On 27 June, with no sign of a global war in the offing, he authorized MacArthur to deploy Japan-based U.S. air and naval units in the defense of South Korea. On 30 June, with the North Koreans still advancing, the president authorized throwing U.S. ground forces stationed in Japan into battle. Not wishing to inflame U.S. public opinion, stir up a Republican hornets' nest, or provoke Moscow, Truman declined to ask Congress for a declaration of war. He consulted just a handful of legislative leaders before committing U.S. troops. Refusing to call the Korean conflict a war, he concurred with a reporter's proposed definition of it as a "U.N. police action," a term that later grated on the sensibilities of the troops. Truman acted solely under his authority as commander in chief. At this point he and his advisers, notably Acheson, thought that U.S. troops could quickly stop the invasion force. They had underestimated its strength and momentum. At the same time, Truman, on Acheson's suggestion, authorized deployment of the U.S. Seventh Fleet in the Taiwan Strait to prevent the Chinese Communists from taking Taiwan and stepped up assistance to the French fighting Communist forces in Vietnam.

The Truman administration quickly turned to the task of securing international legitimacy at the United Nations. Founded in 1945 as a key element of Franklin Roosevelt's plan for postwar peace and security, it was under effective U.S. control at this time except for the Security Council, where the Soviet Union could exercise a veto. Fortunately for Truman, the Soviet delegation had been boycotting meetings since January 1950 over the failure to seat a delegation from Communist China and thus could not veto U.S. calls for U.N. action in Korea. The Kremlin boss justified this continuing absence from the Security Council as an important signal of Soviet solidarity with its Chinese ally while also undermining the legitimacy of any U.N. action. Let the Americans plunge ahead, draining their resources, damaging their reputation, diverting their attention from the main European theater, and (in the bargain) enhancing the prospects for revolution in Asia. The result, Stalin boasted, would be to "give us an advantage in the global balance of power."[15]

On 27 June, with Soviet chief U.N. delegate Jacob Malik still absent, the Security Council by a vote of 9 to 0, with Yugoslavia abstaining, gave Truman the resolution he wanted. It condemned North Korea, demanded that Pyongyang withdraw its army from the south and restore the status quo ante, and called on U.N. member states to render South Korea necessary assistance. Acting on this resolution, Truman appointed MacArthur as commander of U.N. forces. Eventually sixteen nations contributed combat forces to his command, and an additional five provided medical personnel. The United States supplied by far the largest number of U.N. troops. Roughly 1.6 million American soldiers, sailors, airmen, and marines served in Korea during the war, peaking at 440,000 at the time of the armistice in

July 1953. Other major contributors included the United Kingdom, Canada, Turkey, Australia, and Thailand.[16]

Now it was MacArthur's show. A temperamental and aloof septuagenarian, the general cloistered himself in the Dai-ichi Building in downtown Tokyo and ran the Korean War by remote control. He rarely made the short flight to Korea and never stayed there overnight. He was to prove a headstrong commander ill-suited to waging a war on which Washington set limits. World War II had taught him nothing about managing the often trying complexities of coalition warfare, especially when harnessed to jittery allies. A lone wolf by temperament, MacArthur trusted his own instincts more than the collective judgment of the Joint Chiefs of Staff in Washington and was privately contemptuous of his commander in chief, the former captain in the Missouri National Guard.

During the first two months of fighting, U.S. and South Korean troops failed to halt the southward thrust of the North Korean army. The first contingents of U.S. troops thrown into battle in July came from an army that was a shadow of its 100-division World War II glory days. By 1950 the army fielded only ten divisions. The three doing occupation duty in Japan were woefully understrength, short on armor and artillery, poorly trained, and unevenly led. They were more at home in the pleasure houses of Japan than on the battlefield. Despite their best efforts, these troops were able to offer only limited resistance, especially with World War II bazooka projectiles that bounced off the heavy armor plating of enemy tanks. By the end of July, U.N. forces under Eighth Army commander General Walton Walker had been squeezed into the extreme southeastern corner of Korea, the so-called Pusan perimeter, an eighty-by-fifty-mile rectangle. There, bolstered by fresh troops, supplies, and upgraded equipment, including new and effective 3.5-inch bazookas, they managed to hold on. North Korean units not only faced greatly stiffened resistance but also suffered from overextended supply lines on which U.S. aircraft exacted a heavy toll. Their advance had run out of steam just short of victory.

MacArthur now struck against an overextended foe. He executed a massive amphibious landing of the sort perfected during the Pacific island campaigns against Japan. The target was the port city of Inchon, just 25 miles west of Seoul and 150 miles north of enemy lines. The Joint Chiefs of Staff had been profoundly skeptical. They feared the extensive tidal flats and tricky tides of Inchon harbor would disrupt the landing, but they finally let the implacable field commander proceed. MacArthur assembled an armada of 260 ships and a landing force of 70,000 men. At dawn on 15 September,

The Seesaw Peninsular War

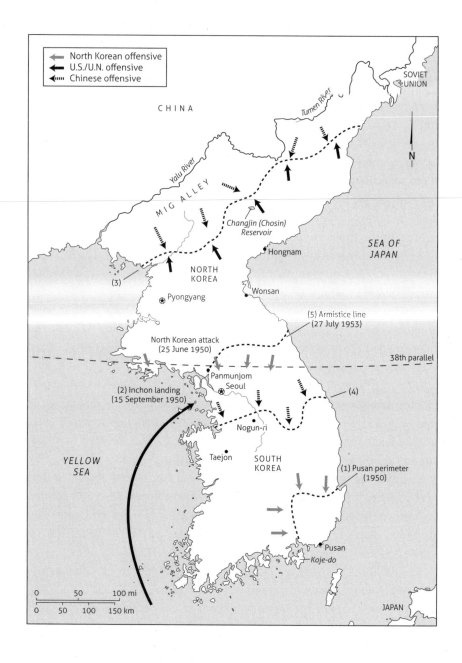

these forces carried out one of the most audacious and successful amphibious operations in military history, routing the enemy and swiftly liberating Seoul. The fortunes of war now shifted abruptly. North Korean troops in the south, cut off from reinforcements and supplies, began a desperate retreat, leaving scattered units behind to wage guerrilla war. Kim's sure bet had turned into a disaster. At this stage of the game MacArthur had proven the better gambler.

Or so it seemed. The general's very success now bred overconfidence. It was MacArthur's turn to grab for the brass ring of total victory. Rather than halt at the thirty-eighth parallel and end the war where it had started, he intended to push northward up to the Chinese border and exterminate the remnants of Kim's army and regime. MacArthur, with his self-professed mastery of the Asian mind, anticipated his offensive would unravel the Sino-Soviet alliance. "The Oriental follows a winner. If we win, the Chinese will not follow the USSR."[17] On 28 September, just thirteen days after the Inchon landing, South Korean troops crossed the thirty-eighth parallel, and other U.N. forces soon followed. On 19 October they took Pyongyang against only scattered resistance. They were joined the next day by U.S. forces. The way north to the Yalu River lay open.

This decision to strike north had the strong support of both Seoul and Washington. Syngman Rhee was eager to exploit this providential opportunity to reunify Korea under his leadership. The Truman administration was no less eager to take up the plans of a commander whose prestige was at its height and whose initiative had a strong political rationale. The enthusiasts of the march north argued that Kim Il Sung's invasion had invalidated the thirty-eighth parallel as an international boundary and that his aggression should not go unpunished. How could they forgo this irresistible solution to

(opposite)

Stages in the battle for Korea, 1950–1953. War began with the sudden North Korean offensive during summer 1950, which drove South Korean and U.S. forces into the Pusan perimeter (1) but failed to dislodge them. The second stage opened with MacArthur's surprise landing at Inchon (2) in mid-September. His forces in pursuit of fleeing North Koreans approached the Chinese border in October and November (3). The stunning Chinese intervention in late November forced UN forces south in disarray. In late January 1951 they managed to contain the Chinese advance (4). The final stage began in February with the hardening of the battle lines across the middle of the peninsula (5). That fighting front became the formal ceasefire line on the conclusion of the armistice agreement in July 1953.

the long-running dispute over Korea's political future? On 27 September the Joint Chiefs of Staff, with Truman's approval, gave its formal endorsement to MacArthur's military objective: "the destruction of the North Korean armed forces." But at the same time Washington wanted to avoid Soviet or Chinese intervention. MacArthur's instructions thus stipulated that U.S. forces were to stay away from the Soviet and Chinese border zones and that only South Korean troops were to deploy along the border with China defined by the Yalu and Tumen Rivers. To muddy matters, Secretary of Defense George Marshall in a follow-up message on 29 September seemed to give MacArthur a free hand: "We want you to feel unhampered tactically and strategically to proceed north of 38th parallel."[18]

At this very time, MacArthur's nemesis—a much more powerful enemy than he had thus far encountered—was moving into place. As Mao watched Kim Il Sung's plans implode (as he had feared might happen), he had good reason for alarm. An experienced military strategist, Mao was keenly aware of Korea's historic role as a foreign invasion route into China. He was also sensitive to the possibility of direct U.S. military pressure along China's border with North Korea. The three provinces comprising Northeast China (what the West called Manchuria) contained most of China's heavy industry, along with rich natural resources and fertile land, the foundations of plans to develop a modern socialist economy after two decades of devastating warfare. China's capital, Beijing, was less than 400 miles from the Korean border, about the distance from Los Angeles to San Francisco. MacArthur's advancing forces could threaten the very existence of the one-year-old government, the product of decades of struggle and sacrifice.

Whether as a nationalist or an internationalist, Mao had deeper concerns. He resented earlier U.S. interference in his country's affairs. Rather than bow before the U.S. threat, he boasted on several occasions that he would use the Korean crisis to "beat American arrogance." Mao also feared the domino effect of a successful U.S incursion. "If Korea were completely occupied by the Americans and the Korean revolutionary forces were substantially destroyed, the American invaders would be more rampant, and such a situation would be very unfavorable to the whole East." Such a development might well drown the hopes of communist revolutionaries in Vietnam, the Philippines, and throughout Asia. Checking the U.S. advance would, on the other hand, demonstrate loyalty to Stalin and the cause of international communism.[19]

Step by step, Mao prepared a response. Beginning in mid-July, he redeployed three Chinese armies from southern and central China to the

Northeast and established the Northeast Border Defense Army. (This redeployment came in the wake of Truman's decision on 27 June to interpose the Seventh Fleet in the Taiwan Strait, which had compelled Mao to cancel the invasion of Taiwan.) Even as the Korean People's Army was advancing south, he had foreseen the possibility of an American amphibious landing at Inchon and warned Kim Il Sung—but to no avail. While positioning himself for a collision, Mao also tried to avert it. Beijing began to issue warnings to the Americans and their partners privately, through third parties, notably India's ambassador to China, but also publicly. Premier Zhou Enlai, who coordinated the international signaling, made clear that China wanted a peaceful resolution of the crisis while warning flatly that "we will intervene."[20] Meanwhile, Mao regularly consulted with Stalin even as Kim Il Sung kept the Chinese leader at arm's length. Kim regarded Moscow as his patron. The willful young nationalist was disinclined to listen to Chinese advice any more than Stalin insisted he do.

In early October, as North Korean forces were disintegrating under the blows of MacArthur's offensive, Mao and his comrades had to decide whether China should act. On 1 October, Kim Il Sung, his regime facing imminent collapse, finally addressed a desperate appeal for help to Mao. Stalin, determined to stay on the sidelines, was counting on Beijing to rescue his hapless client. On 1 October, the Soviet leader sent Mao and Zhou Enlai a telegram urging China to send five to six divisions to Korea without making any reference to Soviet assistance. Uncharacteristically, Mao vacillated. The general sentiment among those close to him, including veteran generals, was to oppose intervention.

On 2 October Mao prepared two responses to Stalin. A draft not sent expressed resolve to turn back what it described as a counterrevolutionary tide dangerous to China and the entire region. But this draft also emphasized the importance of Soviet military assistance to the success of Chinese forces moving into Korea. The other version, which Mao actually sent, was equivocal and accurately reflected the doubts gripping most of his associates. This second message emphasized the risks of a Sino-American war, the inadequacy of Chinese military equipment, and the priority owed to domestic political consolidation and economic reconstruction. Mao indicated that he was deferring a final decision pending further consultation among party leaders and with the Kremlin. Stalin returned a thunderbolt. Revealing his hand, he indicated that from the outset he had taken into account the possibility of a wider war involving the United States, China, and even the USSR itself. He was not dismayed, however, because the balance of forces favored the socialist camp. "If war is inevitable, then let it be waged now, and not in a few years when Japanese militarism will be restored as an ally of the USA."[21]

On 5 October Mao took his stand with the Soviet leader (whether before or after reading Stalin's message is not clear). He presided that day over a meeting of the Politburo, the party's highest decision-making authority, which finally resolved to send troops to Korea. In carrying the day against skeptical colleagues, Mao observed that "all of what you have said is reasonable, but once another nation, one that is our neighbor, is in crisis, we'd feel sad if we stood idly by." Five days later, a delegation headed by Zhou Enlai reported from Moscow that Stalin had parried its plea for Soviet air cover. No such assistance was possible for at least two months. In the face of Stalin's equivocation, Mao once more wavered. The foe was formidable, his state still fragile.[22]

Meanwhile, Mao hastened preparations to send a Chinese expeditionary force into Korea. On 5 October he entrusted General Peng Dehuai with its command. Peng was a renowned veteran of the anti-Japanese and civil wars, a bluff soldier beloved by his troops, whose hardships he shared. Called to Beijing in early October to join the war council, he argued for intervention. China, he later recalled, had no choice but to confront the U.S. threat. "The tiger always eats people, and the time when it wants to eat depends on its appetite. It is impossible to make any concessions to a tiger."[23] Peng faced the tiger with an ill-prepared force. The army had been in the midst of demobilization when the Korean War broke out, and few of its units were near the Korean border. Only in late August did the command of Peng's army begin to take form and assume its organizational duties. When Peng took over in early October, his staff was still not fully assembled, and he had no experience working with the units now suddenly placed under his control. His situation was made more difficult by Mao's constant, detailed orders and advice, which tended to push the more cautious Peng in a more aggressive direction. His commanders were used to autonomy, and they would find coordination a challenge in a conventional war fought on a large scale in difficult terrain. They would, moreover, have to learn to deploy modern weapons and maintain the supply line on which they depended. Finally, relations with the North Korean commanders, fighting under Chinese direction, were bound to prove sensitive.

On 18 October Mao gave Peng the final order to move his troops into Korea. Though assembled from regular army units, his force advanced under the name Chinese People's Volunteers. Like Truman's labeling the

Korean War a "police action," this artful misnomer allowed Beijing to deny it was at war with the United States. It also suggested that the Chinese people were spontaneously discharging their "internationalist duty" to an imperiled fellow socialist state. On 19 October, as U.N. troops continued their final push, Chinese infantrymen crossed the Yalu River under cover of darkness and fanned out to take up concealed positions in the forested, snow-covered hills of northernmost Korea. Chinese forces numbering some 300,000 made their first contact with the enemy on the night of 26 October and then melted back into the hills pending further preparations for large-scale battles.

U.S. policymakers in Washington and Tokyo were unprepared for Chinese intervention. They had brushed aside Beijing's repeated warnings—what Acheson dismissed as "probably a Chinese Communist bluff." Intelligence officials as well as policymakers assumed that Moscow was still in control and would avoid massive Soviet or Chinese intervention unless resolved (unlikely as it seemed) on global war. With Truman's approval, the Joint Chiefs reassured MacArthur that he should continue as long as he felt his operation "offer[ed] a reasonable chance of success." On 15 October, one month after the triumph at Inchon, Truman had hastily arranged a conference with MacArthur on Wake Island in the mid-Pacific. In their hour and a half together, the general provided assurances that the war would soon be over. There was no risk of Chinese intervention. Any attempt to drive south would lead to "the greatest slaughter." Equally sanguine, the CIA predicted Chinese forces would remain small and directed toward establishing "a limited cordon sanitaire south of the Yalu River." Still overconfident, MacArthur made the fatal mistake of splitting his forces into two widely separated columns. The Eighth Army in the west and the X Corps in the east, comprising several marine divisions, advanced in bitter cold, with overnight temperatures plunging to 20 below zero.[24]

MacArthur soon discovered how badly his gamble had gone. On the night of 25 November, Chinese forces, now up to 450,000 (including support and supply), emerged from concealment and attacked both U.N. columns. The lightly armed Chinese armies prevailed by sheer force of numbers and dogged determination despite the staggering casualties they suffered in their advance. A Chinese officer later recalled how the first month of intense fighting and intense cold had turned units in his sector into "a giant field hospital for [their] wounded and severe frost-bite soldiers" and left them "virtually disabled and unable to fight a major engagement until the late spring of 1951."[25]

MacArthur's army was stunned. On the western flank, the Eighth Army rapidly disintegrated and fled south in disorder, suffering 11,000 casualties in just a few days. (To the tune of a popular song, the scornful marines mocked the infantrymen: "Hear the pitter-patter of tiny feet, It's the U.S. Army in full retreat.") Meanwhile, an epic battle took place in the east near the Changjin (in Japanese, Chosin) Reservoir. There the badly outnumbered First Marine Division, nourished in part on Tootsie Rolls, broke out of encirclement and managed an orderly withdrawal through a lethal rain of enemy fire to the ships awaiting them at the port of Hongnam. A correspondent attributed to First Marine Division commander Major General Oliver P. Smith the memorable phrase, "Retreat, hell—we're attacking in another direction!" Under heavy pressure, reeling U.N. forces abandoned Pyongyang on 5 December; Seoul fell for a second time on 4 January 1951.[26]

Panic gradually engulfed the U.N. side. Jolted from his post-Inchon euphoria, MacArthur at first in early November insisted on continuing his advance rather than face "the greatest defeat of the free world in recent times." By late November admitting that he was in "an entirely new war," he argued for a drastic response. He wanted to expand the war into China, use nuclear weapons, and employ Chiang Kai-shek's Chinese Nationalist troops. At a press conference in Washington on 30 November, a rattled president emphasized the high stakes—the prospect that aggression might "spread throughout Asia and Europe to this hemisphere. We are fighting in South Korea for our own national security and survival." He also acknowledged the possible use of nuclear weapons in Korea. As this stunning military reversal created consternation all around him, Truman several times avowed in his direct, homespun fashion that he was "unwilling to abandon the South Koreans to be murdered."[27]

The general's proposals for an expanded war and the president's nuclear comment provoked dismay in London. Aghast at the prospect of a general conflagration engulfing Europe, Prime Minister Clement Attlee rushed to Washington to meet with Truman, Acheson, and George C. Marshall, who had replaced the widely despised Louis Johnson as Secretary of Defense in September 1950. The Truman team sought to calm Attlee with disingenuous assurances that there was no active consideration of nuclear weapons. (In fact, the Pentagon maintained contingency plans for such use from the beginning of the conflict to the end.) Attlee returned home clinging to a fantasy long a favorite of British leaders. His dealings with the Americans proved that his country was "unequal in power but still equal in counsel."[28]

These Anglo-American strains reflected deeper tensions within the alliance. Attlee made the case not just for containing the conflict to the Korean peninsula but also for talking to the Chinese Communists as essential to any negotiated settlement. Britain had already in January 1950 extended formal diplomatic recognition to Mao's China. By late December, the Truman administration had grudgingly given up on the unification of Korea but still could not bear the thought of dealing with a regime that was "being directed by the Russians."[29] London's ability to influence Washington had declined since the Grand Alliance of World War II. As the British empire dissolved, the power gap between London and Washington continued to widen. The myth of the special relationship stayed alive because Truman did not want to go it alone in Korea. He needed Attlee and British collaboration as a symbol of international support and Cold War solidarity.

By late January 1951, the United Nations' immediate battlefield crisis had passed. Lieutenant General Matthew B. Ridgway, an experienced, self-effacing, and level-headed leader, had taken command of the Eighth Army in late December 1950 after General Walton Walker's death in a jeep accident. Ridgway assessed the situation, executed some tactical withdrawals to stabilize the front, and in late January launched small-scale offensives that restored confidence both in the field and in Washington. An intensifying air campaign against industrial sites and population centers also helped. Curtis LeMay's Strategic Air Command had proposed doing "a fire job," in a replay of the campaign against Japan five years earlier. U.S. aircraft set about doing just that following China's intervention. Two attacks on Pyongyang in early January 1951, executed without prior warning, burned out a third of the city and provided a taste of what awaited the rest of the enemy population.[30] On the diplomatic front the Truman administration sought to shore up its U.N. allies, prevailing upon the General Assembly on 1 February 1951 to brand China an aggressor state.

By this time the Chinese forces, like the North Korean army just five months earlier, had advanced beyond their supply lines and were suffering horribly during the unforgiving Korean winter from inadequate clothing, footwear, food, and shelter. Determined to persevere at whatever cost, Mao seemed almost impervious to the rapidly mounting toll, some 100,000 casualties during just the first four months of the war. At news of his eldest son Anying's death on 25 November 1950 during an air raid on Peng Dehuai's headquarters, Mao feigned indifference. "In war there are always sacrifices, it's really nothing," he said to a close comrade. To Peng Dehuai he said, "A simple soldier died, and one need not make a big deal out of this just because he was my son." But privately he grieved for a long time.[31]

When Peng requested a respite for his exhausted troops (first in December and again in January), Mao insisted that his field commander continue the offensive. Yet what Mao willed in Beijing was simply beyond the capacity of his troops on frozen Korean ground to deliver. Indeed, by the early spring U.N. forces had regained the initiative, recaptured Seoul on 14 March, and held it thereafter. Mao ordered a new offensive in April 1951, but his spent forces made no headway. Victory had eluded first the North Korean and then the U.N. forces; now the Chinese military tasted the same frustration.

A year of brutal but inconclusive combat extending from one end of the peninsula to the other had taught policymakers in Washington, London, Beijing, and Moscow the unstated rules that would thenceforth limit the fighting. Although none of them explicitly acknowledged this at the time, a standoff was virtually guaranteed. In May the Joint Chiefs instructed Ridgway's successor as Eighth Army commander, Lieutenant General James Van Fleet, that his mission was to halt any new communist offensive and pressure the enemy to come to the negotiating table. He would operate under constraints that included a prohibition against extending the air war into China, against employing nuclear weapons, and against introducing Chinese Nationalist forces from Taiwan. The Soviet Union, while serving as the armory for the Communist side, did not intervene directly in the war apart from providing substantial air support. And even there operations were restricted to northern North Korea, a short flight from secure bases in adjoining Chinese territory. To keep a low profile, Soviet pilots dressed in Chinese uniforms and avoided speaking Russian on their intercoms.

THE ANATOMY OF A STALEMATE

For the next two years, the Korean War consisted of an endless series of frustrating small and medium-sized battles and skirmishes. The fighting, costly in lives, did nothing to alter fundamentally the balance of forces or the territory each side controlled. It was reminiscent of the static but deadly trench warfare of World War I. James Brady, a marine on frontline duty in 1951–52, summed up this phase of the war to a fellow marine, "We never fight a real battle, we don't win or lose, yet guys get killed, we wrap them up and send them south somewhere. We eat some more, sleep some more, more of us get killed or lose a leg or go blind, and there's never a real battle and still the war goes on."[32]

Americans, proud of their wealth and industrial and technological superiority, initially expected a clear-cut victory in Korea as in the Philippines and against Japan. Their marked advantages persuaded most American military and civilian leaders that despite initial difficulties U.S. forces would ultimately prevail over this latest Asian enemy. Such hubris is a disease of empire. But their economic might was no guarantee of victory. After stunning MacArthur's command in November and December 1950, Chinese forces and their North Korean allies succeeded in maintaining a stalemate, something that neither Philippine insurgents nor Japanese imperial forces had been able to achieve. That Chinese forces were able to manage such a standoff signaled the emergence of a new power equation in eastern Asia.

The Chinese could not begin to match U.S. industrial capacity and advanced technology and thus the kind and quantity of military power the Americans could bring to bear on the ground, in the air, and on the seas. The country Mao took to war was a poor, basically agrarian society with little modern industry. Its people had been traumatized by three decades of intermittent civil war and an eight-year war of resistance against Japanese aggression. These wars had cost upward of 20 million lives and left much of China's economy and infrastructure in shambles. In 1950 the task of restoring the modest prewar levels of agricultural and industrial production had barely begun, and Beijing would have to wait three years before initiating its First Five-Year Plan, with an emphasis on heavy industry.

By contrast, the U.S. economy in the early 1950s accounted for almost 45 percent of total world industrial output, roughly twenty times larger than China's and four times greater than the Soviet Union's.[33] The USSR would serve as China's arsenal in the Korean War, but it lagged far behind the capacity of U.S. aircraft plants, shipyards, and motor vehicle factories. Truman, a fiscal conservative, had kept the military budget at peacetime levels in the late 1940s despite multiplying Cold War commitments. But once resolved on war in Korea, he nearly tripled military spending, enough to sustain forces in Korea while also upgrading the U.S. military in Europe. As in World War II, the economy demonstrated its capacity to mobilize war production rapidly.

With the exception of the ill-prepared and poorly equipped infantry first to deploy in July 1950, U.S. ground forces possessed an overwhelming superiority in firepower. They carried battle-tested m-1 rifles, carbines, Browning Automatic Rifles (BARS) that fired 500 rounds a minute, and .30-caliber machine guns. Their arsenal included a lethal array of more powerful weapons including bazookas, recoilless rifles, and mortars whose incendiary white phosphorus shells (nicknamed Willy Peter) could devastate enemy troop concentrations. Infantry received close support from massed artillery at the rear and from air force, marine, and navy fighters that owned the skies over the battlefields. Major firefights usually resulted in enemy dead carpeting the ground. Stacked like cord wood in freezing weather, they were sometimes used as defensive revetments. Field officers often called in napalm strikes on enemy positions, producing what one marine with a macabre aesthetic sense called "a spectacle of great beauty: orange flames and billowing black smoke against the snow."[34] Napalm (jellied gasoline), a fiendish weapon invented during World War II, incinerated or asphyxiated its victims, many of them peasants whose villages U.S. aircraft systematically attacked. U.S. air power also played an important role in inhibiting the flow of North Korean military supplies, which moved primarily by road and rail in the first months of the war.

U.S. troops enjoyed impressive logistical support that built on the achievements of World War II. During the bitterly cold Korean winters, troops from the land of plenty were warmly clothed, well shod (in insulated footwear the soldiers called Mickey Mouse boots), well fed, usually sheltered in solidly constructed bunkers, some equipped with wood stoves, and liberally supplied with cigarettes and even with beer. Units on the front lines were regularly rotated into reserve where they could rest, take hot showers, and eat hot meals including breakfasts of bacon and eggs, hash browns, biscuits, and coffee. Dependable mail service eased the loneliness of separation from loved ones back home. For U.S. servicemen hard time in-country was periodically broken by brief rest and recreation furloughs in Japan. (GIs in Korea referred to their R&R in Japan as I&I, for intoxication and intercourse.) In the huge U.S. naval base at Sasebo and elsewhere, for a small sum, wives and sweethearts back home could be forgotten in the company of obliging Japanese sex workers (panpan), who were often the main support of their families in a country still struggling to recover from the Pacific War.[35]

Medical care continued advances dating back to the Philippines War. In addition to fleets of trucks and hospital trains that carried wounded troops away from the battle lines, helicopters could now quickly medevac those who had suffered serious head, chest, or abdominal wounds from the battlefield to Mobile Army Surgical Hospitals. There trained surgeons, the real world prototypes of television's *M*A*S*H* comedy hit of the 1970s, provided treatment superior to that available just a few years earlier during World War II. Plentiful supplies of plasma and whole blood were instrumental in saving lives. These improvements brought the Korean War losses of the wounded down to 2.6 per thousand.[36]

Behind all this impressive firepower and sophisticated support, however, were reluctant soldiers, most draftees. Outbound on a troopship from San Francisco, William Childress, a soldier-poet, spoke of "bearing duffels / as heavy as our thoughts, we wound inward / like slaves in some gigantic pyramid, / selected by our Pharaoh for burial / against our wills." For many it was hard to see any great issue at stake to justify their sacrifice in an unknown land, especially once the war settled into stalemate. A sardonic 1952 Christmas ditty proclaimed: "Yuletide greetings from Korea, / Land of lice and diarrhea, / From mucky shores that we've half-mastered / MERRY CHRISTMAS YOU LUCKY BASTARD." Soldiers longed to return to the comforts and abundance of home, where an explosion of pent-up consumer spending was fueling a prosperity not seen since the 1920s. The minority who were veterans of World War II were especially disgruntled; they had already done their duty and now deserved a piece of the good times. One World War II vet spoke for many when he recalled his dislike of Truman's prolonged, inconclusive war. "I didn't want to be in Korea, but if I did have to be there, I wanted to fight to win and go home." To improve morale, the army decided in the summer of 1951 to follow the marines' practice of rotating troops home after a certain period of service. Front-line duty counted for more than rear or reserve service, so a tour of duty could run from a year up to eighteen months. A favorite topic of discussion among GIs was the number of points still needed to get that ticket home.[37]

Compounding the problem of morale was a corrosive racism. In part it was directed inward, the result of long-standing patterns of formal and informal segregation prevailing in the military that mirrored American society as a whole. By executive order 9981 in July 1948, President Truman had finally sought to do away with unequal treatment in the armed forces, but implementation of desegregation came slowly in a force that was disproportionately Southern and loath to change its ways. The Korean War forced the pace of change. Military necessity—the urgent need to replace combat losses—rather than a sense of justice led to the integration of combat units in the field. While commanders were divided on the wisdom of a color-blind policy, Korea in fact proved a breakthrough in the acceptance and promotion of that policy.

No less pronounced and debilitating were the soldiers' racist views of Asians. These views originated in domestic stereotypes and were reinforced by a half century's experience of asserting mastery over Asians. Most U.S. service personnel had a hard time distinguishing one group of Asians from another, and so they directed their condescension and contempt indiscriminately. One common pejorative dated back to the fighting in the Philippines. "Gook" was applied to Koreans, whether allies or enemies. Another that applied only to Chinese was "Chink," an epithet that dated back to the late nineteenth century and was still common in 1950s America.

Attitudes of superiority and condescension left American troops at best ambivalent toward their South Korean ally. Most of them regarded Republic of Korea troops assigned to their units, the so-called KATUSAS (Koreans Attached to the U.S. Army), as ineffective and brutish, and they described dismissively as "gook trains" the columns of wiry Korean oldsters and others unfit for combat who carried supplies on their backs to the front lines where trucks could not reach. American troops who, against regulations, routinely hired boys and men to do their chores, viewed Koreans as menials or worse. For sport, GIs would sometimes "take potshots at civilians working in rice paddies as they would roll by in a Jeep when no officer was around." At least the legions of dirty and ragged orphaned children evoked some sympathy. In "Letter Home," William Childress wrote:

Mother, they line the roads
like broken stalks,
children with bellies swollen,
and O, the flowers
of their faces, petals all torn,
and the flags
of their threadbare garments.
. . .
O, mother, wish me home!
With just one field of Kansas grain,
what I can do for them.[38]

While U.S. troops were assured during training that South Koreans were anticommunist and friendly to Americans, experience suggested a more complex reality. One U.S. infantryman accurately noted that "there were many South Koreans who didn't like Americans and didn't want us in their country, and they showed their feelings at every opportunity." American revulsion toward the dirt, squalor, and poverty of Korea was reciprocated by Korean distaste for the oversize and crude foreigners who were laying waste to their country in the name of defending it. Rape of Korean women by American troops was common. Poverty forced many women into prostitution as it did in Japan during the occupation and would later in Vietnam. Corporal Paul Tardiff recalled what he saw waking one night in July 1952: "A small group of Korean women, some with tiny babies tied to their backs or very small children clinging to their sides . . . digging our garbage out of the hole—and eating it." Little wonder that South Korean dependence upon Americans bred resentment as well as gratitude.[39]

The stalemate that developed on the Korean battlefield was rooted in more than weaknesses on the U.S. side. To be sure, Mao and his lieutenants had gone to war keenly aware of the resource and technology gulf that separated them from the enemy. Nonetheless, after mastering his initial doubts, Mao believed he could defeat the Americans. The key was to devise strategies to offset some of their inherent battlefield advantages. He had already waged protracted war against technologically superior foes, the Nationalists and the Japanese, and could draw lessons from that experience. He had an additional advantage: control of a large, veteran, and versatile army. It was skilled in irregular warfare, but it also had ample experience in large-unit conventional campaigning during the civil war. It was a thoroughly indoctrinated army whose commanders clearly understood the importance of political morale. Furthermore, Mao and his field commanders could be profligate with the lives of their peasant conscripts, routinely accepting casualty rates that no American leader would abide.

Chinese commanders found ways to offset potent U.S. military technology with skill, will, and mass. They emphasized stealth, surprise, and stamina. On the ground facing better-armed enemies, they burrowed into the hills and mountains, excavating networks of tunnels from which they emerged to attack at night when the enemy could not effectively bring air support into play. With only rudimentary equipment for field communications, officers resorted to time-tested means of directing their troops, employing whistles, bugles, horns, and cymbals that added a weird and often chilling cacophony to the din of battle. Chinese as well as North Korean infantry carried rifles, burp guns, hand grenades, mortars, and light machine guns most effective at short range. They compensated for their deficiency in firepower by attacking en masse, wave after wave, maintaining tight discipline even in the face of enemy cannonades. Thanks to well-organized recruitment and training, Peng's command was able to make up for heavy combat losses.

To maintain the flow of supplies in the face of a sustained enemy interdiction campaign, Peng implemented countermeasures including the extensive deployment of antiaircraft artillery, concealment, night transport, the use of decoys, and massive numbers of conscripted porters. The rising number of support aircraft flying out of fields on both sides of the border were an increasingly important part of the defensive effort. Already by 1951, they were inflicting losses not easily sustained by Americans and frustrating interdiction efforts aimed at rail lines and truck convoys. The combination of these strategies together with Chinese supply requirements that were relatively low (roughly a fifth the tonnage that U.S. units consumed) helped keep the war machine running with increasing ease.[40]

Field conditions were harsh for this army of peasant conscripts, especially during the early phase of involvement. Many were veterans of the just concluded Chinese civil war, including Nationalist soldiers whose units had been incorporated wholesale into Mao's army. Troops wore winter uniforms of quilted cotton. Most rank-and-file soldiers were shod in canvas shoes that provided almost no protection from subzero cold. Desperately trying to protect themselves, exhausted infantrymen coated their faces with pork fat and wrapped their feet in straw. Severe frostbite was extremely common. Medical services were basic. Simple wounds often proved fatal. Peng's army depended on a long and tenuous supply line that delivered a diet of mostly rice, beans, and corn. The six-to-eight-day food supply Chinese soldiers carried initially limited the length of their offensives since resupply under field conditions was uncertain at best.

By the spring of 1951 conditions began to improve. The supply system became more reliable; reinforcements raised the total force to around 1 million; old units had a chance to rest and replenish; better weapons arrived from the Soviet Union, including tanks, antiaircraft, and artillery; and the motley collection of arms carried into Korea gave way to standardized Soviet models. As battle lines stabilized, troops enjoyed the protection of tunnels and other well-prepared defensive works. Further lessening the pressure on Chinese troops, North Korean forces began to recover from the rout the previous year (reaching 340,000 men by the latter phase of the fighting). A decision to rotate Chinese units in and out of Korea to spread the combat experience resulted in shorter tours of duty from the fall of 1952 onward.

Under trying circumstances Chinese forces in Korea managed to maintain their morale. Since the soldiers were part of the People's Liberation Army, political education was an integral part of their training and daily routine. This contrasts sharply with the apolitical, hands-off approach of U.S. commanders. Political instructors were attached to every Chinese unit. Prior to every engagement they explained to rank-and-file soldiers why they were fighting. Their refrain was one of protecting family and fatherland against the American aggressors who were following in the footsteps of the hated Japanese. Traveling troupes moved from unit to unit performing patriotic songs, dances, and simple dramas to reinforce this message, and delivering comfort bags of toiletries, socks, and the like from home-front schoolchildren enlisted in the war effort. Yet, the substantial number of Chinese POWs who refused repatriation at the end of the war suggests the limits of political indoctrination, particularly when directed toward former Nationalist soldiers.

Unlike the Filipinos and the Japanese, who had fought alone, Mao had the additional advantage of going to war with the backing of a strong ally. He could supplement his own resources with critical military as well as political support from the Soviet Union. Equipment improved with the delivery in 1952 and 1953 of great quantities of Soviet war machines and matériel. By the end of the war Chinese and North Korean troops were better supplied than in the beginning, even though jet fighters, tanks, and artillery furnished by the Soviets never overcame the U.S. technological edge. In exchange for this support Chinese leaders had to assume a $2 billion loan. (They later bitterly resented Moscow's expectation of full repayment notwithstanding the huge human and material sacrifices China had made on behalf of the communist camp.)

Soviet air support was particularly important. In all some 72,000 Soviet personnel, including pilots and mechanics, served in Korea in conjunction with the air war.[41] In early November 1950, Soviet jet fighters shifted from the defense of Shanghai to bases in the Northeast. From there they began to engage U.S. bombers and fighters in combat that mainly took place over MIG Alley, a corridor just minutes south of the border. Soviet pilots flew MIG-15s, whose engines were reverse engineered from purchased British technology. They were faster and could fly higher than their primary opponents in the sky, the American F-86 Sabre jets. But the latter boasted greater maneuverability and superior avionics. Pilot training and equipment provided the Americans an early edge, especially against green, Soviet-trained Chinese pilots, who joined the fray for the first time in January 1951. After seeing many in their units prove easy pickings, Chinese airmen went back to school. They returned to action in September flying 100 to 150 MIGs and steadily improving their combat skills. As the number of Soviet and Chinese aircraft and the quality of the flying rose, so too did the losses among U.S. bombers. Morale among U.S. crews plummeted, and a syndrome known as "fear of flying" became epidemic, to the dismay of air force leaders.

The American and Chinese home fronts are another part of any explanation of the unexpected stalemate in Korea. While China's new leaders were able to mobilize their people, the American public grew more and more

Caught in the Maw of War

The sorrow of warriors, 28 August 1950. The loss of a comrade brings this moment of overwhelming grief and compassion between two U.S. Army soldiers on the battlefield in the Haktong-ni area. In the background, a corpsman dutifully attends to the casualty information form. (Courtesy of U.S. National Archives)

Refugees fleeing down the eastern coast of South Korea, early January 1951. As the war moved up and down the peninsula during its first year, it convulsed the entire Korean society, inflicting displacement, deprivation, injury, and death greater than combat losses. (Courtesy of U.S. National Archives)

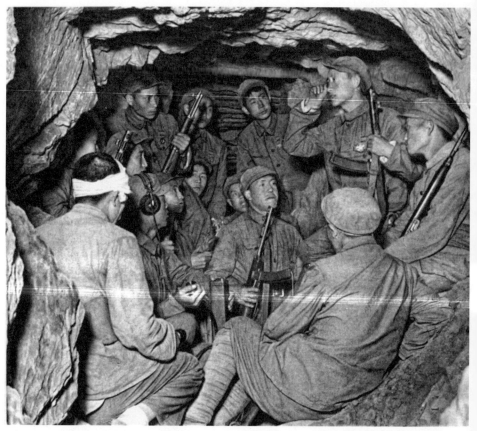

Chinese troops below ground during the stalemate war. A Chinese unit gathers to hear from a party cadre in the safety of a deeply dug bunker along the front line. (From *Guangrong de Zhongguo renmin zhiyuanjun* [1959])

disenchanted with this distant conflict. Here the relative U.S. weaknesses were marked from the outset. Post-Inchon euphoria aside, Americans were unenthusiastic about waging a far-off war in a little known country for abstract stakes according to unfamiliar rules that restricted the full exercise of American power. They thus shared the predominant view held by U.S. combat troops.

This tepid response was evident from the first months of the war. Truman set the tone with his initially hesitant reaction to the invasion of South Korea in June 1950. Once committed, he had to sell a symbolic war fought not because of Korea's intrinsic value, which in fact paled in comparison with that of Europe or Japan, but because communist aggression had made it a test of resolve. In waging his symbolic war, Truman sought to keep Congress quiet and avoid igniting a war fever among the public. Truman's mobilization of the economy was similarly half-hearted compared to the total mobilization of World War II. Not until mid-December, after the shock of Chinese intervention, did the president declare a state of emergency. To build popular support for the war and the huge defense buildup that accompanied it, the Truman administration hyped the threat of communist aggression and instituted press censorship in Korea to muzzle the handful of independent-minded reporters.

As the "police action" turned into a real war without a clear end in sight, Truman's domestic base of support eroded. Initially, a Gallup Poll taken in early July 1950 indicated that 81 percent of the public supported Truman's decision to aid South Korea. In mid-September, after the Inchon landing, 64 percent favored crossing the thirty-eighth parallel and fighting the enemy on its home turf. Surveys done in the wake of Chinese intervention (December 1950 to February 1951) revealed that public support for the war was softening, while a settlement with China and a return to a divided Korea was gaining significant backing. By early February 1951 Truman's own approval rating had sunk to 26 percent.[42]

A war in trouble had become by early 1951 a distinctly partisan issue. The Democrats had been able to maintain control of Congress during the midterm elections. But following the Chinese onslaught in late November, Republicans went on the offensive. Leading "isolationists" in the party stepped up their attack on Truman's policy of helter-skelter global intervention. Former president Herbert Hoover and Senator Robert Taft (R-Ohio) called for a more continentally oriented, go-it-alone approach. Reflecting this discontent, polling done in January 1951 revealed that Republicans favored simply pulling out of Korea more heavily than Democrats.

In April 1951, the deepening divisions over how to deal with a limited war gone wrong took a dramatic turn when the president fired his commander. The conflict between them had long been festering. Truman had had to put up with repeated acts of insubordination by MacArthur dating back to the start of the war, intensifying in the wake of Chinese intervention, and continuing into the early spring of 1951. At their only face-to-face meeting in October 1950 on Wake Island, a presidential public relations event that dismayed MacArthur, the general had shown ill-disguised contempt for Truman, behaving as if he, not Truman, were the commander in chief. The final provocation came on 5 April 1951, when Representative Joseph W. Martin Jr. (R-Mass.) read on the floor of the House a message he had received from MacArthur directly challenging Truman's limited war strategy and insisting that Asia was the primary battleground in the struggle against communism. "Here in Asia is where the Communist conspirators have elected to make their play for global conquest." He asserted, "If we lose the war to communism in Asia the fall of Europe is inevitable. . . . There is no substitute for victory."[43] This inspiring banality has resonated with jingoists ever since.

Even in the face of this latest provocation, Truman hesitated to confront what was not only an increasingly serious threat to his Europe-first strategy but also to the bedrock constitutional principle of civilian control of the military. It took the backing of Secretary of Defense George C. Marshall and the Joint Chiefs of Staff to get Truman to act. In the president's scheme of things, generals were objects of awe. Moreover, Truman, an avid reader, believed that history showed it unwise to interfere with the generals' conduct of war. But finally conscious of his responsibilities and backed by General Marshall, whom Truman practically venerated, the president decisively reasserted his authority as commander in chief. On 11 April, Truman recalled the obstreperous MacArthur and replaced him with General Matthew B. Ridgway.

This presidential stand made the war more than ever a political football and set the stage for an airing of strategic choices, none of them attractive. On his return home, the aggrieved general was accorded a hero's welcome that included ticker tape parades in San Francisco, Chicago, and New York and a rare opportunity to address a joint session of Congress. Even though he proved to be a meteor rather than a political star, his cause quickened Truman's critics and angered the public, of which only a quarter supported Truman's decision to fire MacArthur and fully two-thirds disapproved. Republican partisans asked how the United States, ever victorious in its foreign wars, could accept a stalemate in a local conflict against a ragtag coalition of Asian communists. These critics echoed MacArthur's argument that there was "no substitute for victory," whatever military force, including atomic weapons, was required. The Democratic failure of will in China, so the partisan argument went, was being repeated in Korea.[44]

The administration defended its limited war strategy, not only in public but against pressures from hawks in the Pentagon who favored escalation. In lengthy testimony before congressional committee hearings, Truman's senior aides managed to blunt the political attacks. Some of the most effective testimony came from the chairman of the Joint Chiefs of Staff, Omar Bradley, who warned that expanding the conflict in Korea would get the United States "in the wrong war, at the wrong place, at the wrong time and with the wrong enemy." The Cold War with its global span and nuclear risks required, so the administration line went, a patient, discriminating defense of the containment line. Stalemate was the Cold War substitute for victory.[45]

The controversy surrounding MacArthur's dismissal deepened public disillusionment as the realization began to sink in that Korea was not following the script of the other wars that had marked the ascent of the United States as a world power. Truman won the duel with MacArthur, but his presidency was fatally wounded. With his popularity at a nadir, in 1952 Truman chose to forgo another run for the White House. His political ordeal demonstrated just how difficult it was in a contentious democratic system to manage an overextended eastern Asian imperium that presented unsatisfactory choices and imposed unpopular sacrifices.

The unpopularity of the Korean War was reflected not only in Truman's sinking poll numbers, but also in American popular culture. During and after the conflict, Hollywood dutifully cranked out some ninety-one Korean War films by one count. The majority of these were low-budget, hastily shot productions based on patriotic World War II formulas, but these mostly mediocre films did poorly at the box office. Among the more realistic films was *Steel Helmet*, which chronicled the inglorious realities of infantrymen in combat. During the 1950s, World War II, the "good war," continued to prove the much bigger box office draw.[46]

The songs served up by Tin Pan Alley offer another barometer of lukewarm support. "Dear John," a hit 1953 duet sung by Jean Shepard and Ferlin Husky, provided a painful reminder of the emotional risk of overseas assignment. The song's title referred to the dreaded farewell letter from wife or sweetheart. Overjoyed to hear from his fiancée, a heartsick soldier opens up her letter to read, "Dear John, oh how I hate to write. / Dear John, I must let you know tonight / that my love for you has died away like grass upon the lawn. / And tonight I wed another, Dear John." Given the lawn's iconic status in 1950s American suburbia, dead grass was a perfect metaphor for a cold heart. Chicago bluesman J. B. Lenoir's "Korea Blues" (1951) lamented Uncle Sam's summons to fight in Korea and wondered whom his sweetheart was "gonna let lay down in my bed." "Weapon of Prayer," by the Louvin Brothers, a popular Southern gospel and bluegrass group, provided an uplifting antidote to the theme of betrayal. The song urged those on the home front to "trust and use the weapon of prayer," confident that in a fight against godless communists in Korea "the helpful Hand above" was once more on their side. "And against Him none on Earth prevail."[47]

War comics, a genre that flourished in the early 1950s, delivered the most positive view of the Korean War. These morality tales featured for their predominantly youthful audience individuals who manifested or acquired their manliness through violent deeds of individual heroism on a battlefield where good struggled against evil. In *Mutiny and Murder* from 1953, a Chinese-speaking American GI named Harry Baxter volunteers to infiltrate a prison camp for Chinese POWs in order to identify the Red prison boss. Baxter is body-painted to blend in with the other prisoners, but the wily boss sees through his disguise. "I thought you were spy when you did not squat as we do! No American can squat in our fashion even though he speaks our language." But our hero accomplishes his dangerous mission and hastens to wash off the goo that made him into a "gook." In *Only the Dead Are Free*, the hero Kim is the lone male survivor of a brutal Red attack on his peaceful Catholic village. He forms a guerrilla band and joins with U.S. forces to destroy a railroad bridge before the communists can transport the nuns and other captive women into slavery in Manchuria. Kim has the physique of a Korean Sylvester Stallone while his sickly yellow Chinese foe, Major Chu, sports a menacing Fu Manchu mustache.[48]

Wartime stereotyping, so pronounced in popular culture and the thinking of soldiers, did not affect Chinese Americans as it had Japanese Americans during the Pacific War. Fighting Red Chinese in Korea did not evoke a call for another internment of enemy aliens. Leftist Chinese Americans sympathetic to the new China were indeed regarded with official suspicion and some were hounded by the FBI. But leaders of Chinese American organizations, successful businessmen for the most part, continued to support the anticommunist regime on Taiwan, and thus helped to insulate the Chinese American community as a whole.

China's home front offers a study in contrast to the U.S. side. Fundamental to the difference was the simple fact that a war on China's doorstep created a demonstrable, direct strategic threat to a disciplined authoritarian party-state. A small group at the top, increasingly dominated by a bold and experienced leader, shaped a response in private, deliberately, and without second-guessing by outsiders. This contrasted dramatically with the relatively open, messy U.S. policy process. Mao and his colleagues kept securely under wraps whatever strategic differences they had, including over whether to intervene in the first place and whether to press the offensive into 1951. Peng Dehuai did not always agree with Mao's strategic judgments, but the commander of Chinese forces in Korea was no MacArthur; he quietly soldiered on after privately expressing his views to the commander in chief.

China's leaders set determinedly to work to mobilize limited domestic resources. This effort made heavy claims on available supplies, particularly in the Northeast adjacent to the war zone, and on the state budget. In 1950 roughly half of that budget went to the military and over half of military spending was occasioned by the crisis in Korea. By 1952, with the war stalemated and the Chinese economy recovering from the destruction incurred during more than a decade of foreign and civil war, the military's claim on the budget dropped to a third, with most going to support Chinese forces in Korea.[49]

Party leaders recognized that the war created opportunities as well as challenges on the home front. They had taken charge of a fractious and fractured society deeply penetrated by foreign institutions and values. Determined to consolidate their party-state, they took advantage of the Korean emergency to launch a domestic campaign of persuasion and compulsion. A primary objective was the urban population—important for promoting economic recovery but also worrisome as a hotbed of counterrevolutionary bourgeois sentiments. Nationwide campaigns employing propaganda and coercion, the domestic counterpart of the Chinese army's campaigns in Korea, targeted capitalists and venal officials as war profiteers. The campaigns also took aim at foreign and especially U.S. influence already under attack before the Korean crisis. The government shuttered Western educational and cultural institutions and expelled Western missionaries and businessmen. U.S.-educated university professors and other intellectuals were pressured to denounce their ties with American colleagues and friends.

Those who resisted were subjected to "thought-reform" or "brainwashing," an Orwellian process of psychological deconstruction and revolutionary rebirth that fixed Communist China's totalitarian image in the West.

The centerpiece of the effort to bring the home front fully behind the war effort was the nationwide campaign that unfolded under the slogan "Resist America, Aid Korea" (*kangmei yuanchao*). Launched in early November 1950 as the likelihood of a collision with the United States loomed, the campaign made its appeals to the public through official propaganda, public demonstrations, the collection of funds, and enlistment drives. The most controversial phase of the campaign came in the spring of 1952, prompted by charges that the United States was using germ warfare. The preponderance of evidence to date suggests that the charges were concocted (though precisely by whom is not clear). They were nonetheless endorsed by Western-trained scientists and North Korea's Soviet and Chinese allies, taken seriously even at the upper echelons of the Beijing leadership, and widely retailed all across China to highlight the country's victimization by a vicious and technologically sophisticated enemy. In northeastern cities such as Tianjin, thought to be under threat, party activists and municipal authorities organized residents to collect vermin, eliminate breeding grounds, and raise the level of sanitation.

The party-sponsored wartime message conveyed in popular media ranging from art posters and political cartoons to pamphlets, children's games, songs, stories, and film played less on Marxist-Leninist themes and more on a range of familiar patriotic notions. Films celebrated the exploits of the Chinese forces composed of vigorous young patriots unafraid of confronting Western imperialists. Children played war games in their schoolyards and sang anti-American ditties. Pity the child chosen to play Uncle Sam or an American GI in these games. On college campuses, large numbers of students stirred by patriotic feelings volunteered to fight in Korea. (Too valuable a human resource to expend on the battlefield, very few were accepted.) One of those students, later a leading U.S. specialist, has recalled how the Korea crisis "engendered intense anti-American feelings" at Tsinghua, a premier university in the capital, and turned her, a self-absorbed bookworm, into a true believer in the party program.[50] The most common rallying cry of the nationwide campaign was "Protect our families, defend the motherland." After the domestic bloodletting of the civil war, Chinese could now express their common patriotism in the face of the threat from "Meidi" (the common shorthand for "American imperialism"). Even ideologically correct public allusions to the capitalist bosses controlling U.S.

Popular Themes on the Home Front

"Always Glad to Loan My Neighbor a Shovel," 25 February 1951. This sketch by Herblock (pen name for Herbert Block), a leading cartoonist of the day, stresses Asian indifference to human life. It also depicts Mao as Stalin's dutiful if exhausted minion shoveling great scoops of Chinese troops into the cannon's mouth. Mao, as the less familiar figure to Herblock's audience, had to have an identifying label. ("Always Glad to Loan My Neighbor a Shovel"—A 1951 Herblock Cartoon, copyright by The Herb Block Foundation)

A grateful homeland, 1951. This poster by Zhang Biwu plays on the connection, commonplace in Chinese wartime propaganda, between front line and home. Here a proud family and fellow villagers see a volunteer off to war. One of the slogans surrounding the picture makes explicit that military service meant "protecting the home and defending the country." (Collection International Institute of Social History, Amsterdam)

policy behind the scenes tapped into images of arrogant, rapacious, big-nosed foreigners dating back a century.

The campaign's message also had an internationalist component, but this was less potent than nationalist themes. It extolled fraternal solidarity with socialist North Korea in part because of a shared commitment to the communist cause, but also in part because of a growing realization since the turn of the century that China's fate was tied up with other countries and peoples subjected to outside domination and exploitation. This approach ran up against widespread Chinese dislike of Koreans, who were seen as implicated in Japanese aggression because of their service in the Japanese army and police. So even as official propaganda glorified the battlefield solidarity of Chinese and North Korean troops as well as of the Chinese and Korean peoples, the reality was that on the communist side as on the U.N. side, the Koreans were looked down upon by their own allies.

ENDING THE WAR

Previous American wars in eastern Asia had ended with clear-cut victories followed by military occupation. The pledges of loyalty that Aguinaldo, Malvar, and other captured or surrendered Filipino nationalists tendered were the functional equivalent of the signatures on the Instrument of Surrender signed by Japanese officials aboard the USS *Missouri* on 2 September 1945. MacArthur, who had presided on that occasion as Supreme Commander Allied Powers, had hoped for a like victory in Korea, but before the end of the first year of fighting he was gone. Korea was a new kind of war for Americans operating on the frontiers of the American empire. It could not be won by force of arms without risking a regional or even a global conflict. Ultimately, Washington had to accept a diplomatic solution.

The first serious peace proposals had issued from Britain and from the nonaligned nations led by India in the wake of the Chinese intervention. They had promoted a cease-fire and a restoration of the status quo ante in early anticipation of the terms that would eventually end the war. Prime Minister Attlee also proposed during his visit to Washington in early December 1950 acknowledging Beijing's legitimate political claims by seating China in the United Nations and returning Taiwan to Beijing's control. Truman rejected the idea out of hand. He and Acheson were adamantly opposed to linking issues of China policy to the Korean question, a position they maintained throughout the war. They regarded the issues of U.N. representation and Taiwan's political future as nonnegotiable and were loath even to talk to a Chinese state they had labeled an international pariah—a rogue regime in today's parlance. In any case, both sides in late 1950 and early 1951 still believed they could ultimately prevail on the battlefield.

Lurking in the background as spoilers of any diplomatic initiative was a pair of stubborn U.S. clients. Even after the Chinese made clear their commitment to the survival of Kim Il Sung's government, South Korean president Syngman Rhee adhered to his goal of reunification and adamantly opposed any peace proposal that left Korea divided. Similarly, Chiang Kai-shek on Taiwan had his own claims as the supposed ruler of China to defend. He knew that he could count on a sympathetic hearing from Republican friends in Congress and an executive branch that by now wanted Taiwan as a strategic strong point in American, not Chinese, hands.

In late June 1951, with military stalemate clear, the Soviet Union launched a diplomatic initiative that finally got the belligerents talking to each other. Soviet U.N. ambassador Jacob Malik publicly proposed a cease-fire and armistice restoring the prewar line of division. Taking into account the failure of China's Fifth Offensive to achieve a military breakthrough, Moscow's minimal goal was to ensure that its North Korean client state survived without loss of territory. At the same time neither Stalin nor Mao was in a hurry to end a war that they both deemed a greater liability for the United States than for themselves. Just as Stalin had predicted, the fighting diverted Washington's attention from the central Cold War front in Europe, exacerbated tensions between the United States and its allies, particularly Britain and Canada, consumed American manpower, damaged America's reputation in the postcolonial world, and was increasingly unpopular in the United States itself. For China's leaders and their Soviet counterparts, the costs of continuing the war were acceptable. Not so North Korea, suffering under a rain of aerial destruction. By early 1952 Kim Il Sung had set aside any lingering hopes of reunifying Korea in the near future and begun pressing for a quick resolution of the negotiations. But after his monumental initial misjudgment, he no longer counted for much in communist councils.

While the Truman administration responded positively to the Soviet diplomatic overture, it was of two minds on how to proceed. Even as it publicly rebutted the strategy for victory promoted by MacArthur and his Republican sympathizers and contemplated negotiations, the administration toyed with carrying out the very measures that had triggered the break with MacArthur. In April 1951 and again in June, it seriously considered employing atomic weapons, including tactical nuclear weapons, expanding the war into Northeast China, where communist air bases were located, and lifting restrictions on bombing of North Korean targets such as dams and irrigation works. From within the administration, the Pentagon lobbied for escalation, while a strong current of public and political opinion wanted to exploit the U.S. advantage over the Soviet side in atomic bombs and long-range aircraft and denigrated compromise and concessions as a shameful and dangerous sign of national weakness. Republicans, still smarting over their loss in the 1948 presidential election and desperate to regain power, were quick to charge appeasement at any sign of flexibility on the part of the administration. Even Truman gave way to private bouts of frustrated anger, muttering to his diary about launching "all-out war" against China and the Soviet Union if that were the only way to end the fighting in Korea.[51] But as he well knew and as his successor was to learn, threats involving nuclear weapons were hollow. They frightened U.S. allies, failed to intimidate the enemy, ran up against a growing Soviet retaliatory capability, and on close examination offered scant help on the battlefield.

On 10 July 1951, military officers representing the warring sides sat down together for the first time to see if they could somehow end the stalemated war. Discussions were held at a neutral meeting site near the thirty-eighth parallel—first at Kaesong and later in the village of Panmunjom. The prospects were at first not encouraging. North Korean general Nam Il spoke for the communist side (though in fact Mao provided daily behind-the-scenes guidance), and Vice Admiral C. Turner Joy represented the U.N. side. In general, acrimony prevailed. Both sets of negotiators depended on intensified fighting to give them an advantage at the peace table. Both indulged in political posturing and vituperation. And both viewed their opposite numbers with profound hostility. Ridgway's characterization of the Communists as "treacherous savages" reflected the surly mood among the warrior-diplomats.[52]

Despite the poor atmospherics, the negotiating teams made headway toward an agreement. The U.N. side insisted on limiting the agenda to purely military issues, excluding from consideration China's standing demands on U.N. representation and the return of Taiwan. The first hurdle was to agree on an armistice line. The proposed U.N. boundary ran east from Pyongyang to Wonsan, incorporating much North Korean territory, while the Communists wanted to follow the thirty-eighth parallel. After a two-month suspension of the talks, the two sides agreed in November on a division following the battle line, with a four-kilometer-wide demilitarized zone (DMZ) separating the forces. The line started below the thirty-eighth parallel in the west, crossed it midway across the peninsula, and snaked north till it reached the Sea of Japan north of the thirty-eighth parallel. By December the negotiators had reached agreement on additional matters—

troop rotation, rehabilitation of airfields, establishment of a neutral-nations inspection commission to police the cease-fire, and convocation of an international conference after the armistice to address Korea's political future.

One sticking point—the disposition of prisoners of war—remained, and it would delay the conclusion of an armistice for another eighteen months. The Geneva Convention on Prisoners of War, which had come into force in October 1950, stipulated, "Prisoners of war shall be released and repatriated without delay after the cessation of active hostilities."[53] Rather than follow this unequivocal guideline, Truman took a stand on voluntary repatriation against the advice of Acheson, Ridgway, and key U.S. allies. He saw Korea as part of a contest between freedom and slavery and thus on principle could not countenance forcibly repatriating Communist POWs. The president proved as stubborn as a Missouri mule.

Awaiting resolution of the issue were prisoners from the U.N. side— some 12,000 by late 1951, including over 3,000 Americans. They were at first kept in harsh conditions in camps in northern North Korea run by the North Koreans. Prisoners were fed badly, provided almost no medical care, and subjected to unrelenting political indoctrination. Two out of five U.S. prisoners died. Death, one U.S. survivor recalled, "became an everyday occurrence for us."[54] Only when the Chinese took over the camps in late 1951 did conditions improve and the mortality rate sharply decline.

More contentious was the fate of prisoners in the hands of the U.N. side. By 1952 they totaled roughly 132,000 by U.N. count, most North Korean. These U.N. camps, run by U.S. forces, were badly understaffed, with poorly trained and often brutal guards. Dysentery, malaria, tuberculosis, and pneumonia took a heavy toll. Despite the rhetoric of free choice embodied in the principle of voluntary repatriation, the U.N. command had a vested interest in boosting the numbers of Communist prisoners who refused to go home. Chiang Kai-shek further politicized the situation by offering to welcome and resettle in Taiwan all Chinese POWs who refused repatriation. In addition to intense anticommunist political indoctrination, the camps were saturated with pro–Nationalist trustees, many of them ex-officers in Chiang Kai-shek's army. They beat up Chinese prisoners desiring to return home, had them forcibly tattooed with anticommunist slogans, and enforced discipline with the aid of goon squads. Beginning in mid-1951, Chinese and North Korean officers organized a militant resistance among pro-communist POWs in the main compound on Koje-do. They not only asserted control over their camp areas but also clashed repeatedly and violently with camp authorities. Communist prisoners armed with homemade weapons were no match for the heavily armed camp guards, who suppressed resistance with overwhelming force. Even so, the Communists maintained an organizational grip in the camps until the end.

Truman's insistence on voluntary repatriation together with Communist insistence on following the terms of the Geneva Convention created a prolonged diplomatic standoff. In an attempt to move talks ahead, the United Nations provided the Communist side on 1 April 1952 a reassuring estimate—that about 116,000 of their 132,000 POWs would likely choose to be repatriated. But when screening was done, only 70,000 of the North Korean and Chinese prisoners opted for repatriation. Coercion within the camps had sharply reduced the number of those who opted to return home. The Communist side was infuriated by what it considered a U.N. shell game. Efforts to find a compromise continued into the fall before negotiations were again suspended. In the absence of an agreement, U.N. commander General Mark Clark pressed for and received permission to intensify the air war over North Korea as a means of forcing Communist concessions. In late June 1952, the U.S. Air Force destroyed the Suiho hydroelectric plant on the Yalu River that supplied 90 percent of North Korea's power, and on 11 July it incinerated what remained of Pyongyang with a massive rain of napalm.

A break in the deadlock did not occur until two of the principal leaders exited the political stage. Truman was the first to go, handing the presidency and the deadlocked "police action" to Dwight D. Eisenhower. The general turned Republican politician was acutely aware of the war weariness of the American people. In a campaign speech on 24 October 1952, Eisenhower had promised that ending the war would be his first priority as president. He neither had nor offered any specific plan, only the Delphic utterance, "I shall go to Korea." He handily defeated Adlai Stevenson in the November election, and his party gained control of Congress. Three weeks after the election the president-elect was inspecting the front lines and chowing down with the troops in Korea. After he took office, Pentagon officials turned to dog-eared plans to increase military pressure on the Communists, to make them bend or crack on the POW issue. But the CIA countered with predictions that greater pressure would not make Beijing bend or break. Eisenhower and others in the administration hinted at the possible use of nuclear weapons in Korea. Secretary of State John Foster Dulles claimed he was ready for a showdown: "I don't think we can get much out of Korean settlement until we have shown—before all Asia—our clear superiority by giving the Chinese one hell of a licking."[55]

Stalin soon followed Truman off the stage, thus finally breaking the logjam. On 5 March 1953, he died in his Kremlin apartment. His successors, led first by Lavrentii Beria and then by Georgii Malenkov and Nikita Khrushchev, began to reshape Soviet foreign policy. Liberated from the atmosphere of terror created by the Boss, they sought a modus vivendi with the United States, including an end to the Korean War. To that end they were prepared to make concessions on the POW issue.

Mao for his part was in no haste and felt no obligation to follow the new Kremlin line. Stalin's death gave him a claim to greater revolutionary experience and seniority within the international communist movement. Mao was, moreover, confident that a show of determination on the battlefield would force concessions from the United States. He had at his disposal some 1.35 million men in the field in April 1952, backed by a North Korean army of 450,000. Their fortifications, logistics, and equipment were in the best state of readiness since the start of the war. And there is no evidence that the Chinese leadership was impressed by U.S. nuclear threats. Zhou Enlai observed, "Since Eisenhower took office, he has spouted a lot of hot air in an attempt to scare us." Only when Washington shifted toward the Chinese position on POWs in early June 1953 was Mao prepared to move to an agreement. When Rhee tried to obstruct that agreement, Chinese forces launched punishing attacks aimed specially at South Korean forces.[56]

Washington, Moscow, and Beijing finally all fell in behind third-party efforts, once more led by India, to devise a formula that bridged the gap over the POW issue. A repatriation commission made up of neutral nations was that bridge. It provided a relatively nonthreatening environment in which individual prisoners could make known their will absent the intimidation to which they were subjected within the camps. The first breakthrough came with an exchange of wounded and sick—684 U.N. soldiers and 6,670 Communist soldiers—in late April 1953. In August, as a result of the final agreement, the U.N. Command repatriated 76,000 North Koreans and Chinese and transferred 22,000 Communist prisoners to Indian custody pending final disposition of their cases. Of those screened by India, virtually all refused repatriation to their home country and wound up in South Korea or Taiwan. Those Chinese who did return home were generally treated as pariahs who had been contaminated by anticommunist propaganda during their captivity. The Communist side for its part repatriated 13,000 U.N. POWs; 359 from the U.N. side were transferred to Indian custody with almost all eventually choosing to go to North Korea or China. A couple of dozen Americans who chose to settle in China would eventually return to the United States to face courts-martial and disgrace.

Syngman Rhee had posed a final obstacle to peace in one more demonstration that clients were not the same as puppets. By 1953 his position was more secure than it had been at the outset of the war. He faced no significant political challenges at home, and Washington had no more compliant alternative to the old autocrat. Thanks to an intensified military training effort by U.S. advisors, Rhee had the support of a large, disciplined, and moderately well-equipped army that had taken on an increasing share of the fighting. He would now do what he could to disrupt an imminent cease-fire that would leave Korea divided and negate the huge sacrifices his country had endured. On 18 June 1953, Rhee arranged the breakout of more than 24,000 U.N.-held North Korean POWs. Most of them immediately melted into the general population. An angry, frustrated Eisenhower contemplated a coup to be carried out with the help of the U.S.-trained Korean military. Sensing danger, Rhee struck a bargain. He acquiesced to the armistice in exchange for the U.S. promise of a Mutual Security Treaty (concluded in 1954). Further reassuring Rhee was the continuing presence in South Korea of several tens of thousands of U.S. forces to guarantee the Demilitarized Zone that now separated North and South.

Late June and July 1953 witnessed the last spasms of violence as both sides launched attacks to gain slight territorial advantages. These futile offensives produced thousands of additional casualties. Exhausted, the combatants finally signed the armistice on 27 July. While it stopped the fighting, it did not bring true peace. The military commanders shifted the engines of war into neutral gear but remained ready to shift back to hostilities. An international conference convened in Geneva in April 1954 did nothing to alter the fragile peace. The conference delegates, including for the first time a Chinese team, made no progress on Korea's unification and instead quickly turned their attention to the more pressing issue of war in Indochina. Just as the thirty-eighth parallel, an imaginary line on a map, had evolved from a temporary demarcation in 1945 into an international boundary between two states that cleaved one nation, so the armistice of 1953 became a substitute for an elusive peace treaty that has yet to be achieved.

STORING UP TROUBLE

The Korean War, an armed wager repeatedly gone wrong, marked an important turning point in America's quest for informal empire in eastern Asia. For the first time, the United States had failed to work its will. An assertive China made the prime difference. The leaders in Beijing had managed to block a U.S. advance under way for half a century and frustrate rising U.S. aspirations to define the future of the region. Mao Zedong had learned that the United States was hardly what he dismissively called a "paper tiger," yet neither was it invincible. Total mobilization of resources by the apparently weaker side helped to offset U.S. technological and military superiority. So too had critical material and political support from the Soviet Union. Yet a far-flung and now embattled U.S. empire survived, its proponents unfazed despite the high cost of war, particularly to Korea and Koreans, despite China's demonstration of steely determination, and despite troubling changes in U.S. policy and domestic culture that made empire harder to manage and popularize.

Maintaining Korea's division, initiated and confirmed by diktat of outside powers, meant paying a painfully high price. A war raging up and down the peninsula devastated everything in its path. The U.S. Air Force, building on its World War II repertoire, inflicted the greater part of the devastation. Overall, U.N. planes dropped more ordnance than during the entire Pacific War, incinerated countless civilians as well as enemy combatants with nearly 10 million gallons of napalm, and obliterated most major northern cities. People on the peninsula lost 1.2 million homes, over 25,000 industrial plants, 9,000 schools, and well over 1,000 clinics and hospitals. In all, some 3 million Korean soldiers and civilians were killed, wounded, or missing. This amounted to 10 percent of the population. Of the approximately 3 million Chinese who served in Korea, a total of 152,000 died (including 4,000 missing in action). American service personnel who met their deaths in Korea came to 36,516. Other U.N. combatants suffered 4,141 dead. The Soviet Union—China and North Korea's invisible partner—suffered 299 deaths.[57]

For an even greater number of Koreans, the refugee experience defined the war. In the first weeks of the fighting, long lines of desperate civilians followed South Korean and U.S. forces retreating southward. The tragic tableau of ragged and hungry people—in all perhaps 6 to 7 million—trudging north and south with the fortunes of war, in summer heat and winter frost, quickly became a familiar sight. As social bonds dissolved amid chaos and destruction, many thousands of stick-thin children, orphaned or separated from their parents, joined the human tide.

Because North Korean soldiers, posing as refugees, sometimes infiltrated this human tide, wary U.S. soldiers often treated refugees as enemies rather than victims. In the first month of the war, the U.S. ambassador to Korea crisply described the standing practice: "If refugees do appear from north of U.S. lines they will receive warning shots, and if they persist in advancing they will be shot." One month into the war, near the South Korean village of Nogun-ri in central South Korea, U.S. forces killed hundreds of refugees who had taken shelter in a railroad tunnel. The falling bombs and rockets made it feel, a survivor later recalled, "like heaven crashed on us." Under orders, infantry joined the attack and later finished off any wounded amid the mass of dead. That same summer, in the village of Tanyang southeast of Seoul, American warplanes dropped napalm at the entrance to a cave sheltering refugees, killing 167 persons, the majority women. These were notorious but by no means atypical incidents to judge from the allegations received by the South Korean government of over sixty instances of large-scale killing of refugees by U.S. forces.[58]

The trauma visited on Korean society was pervasive. Villages were deeply and violently divided in their loyalties to one outside force or another, whether Japanese colonialism, Christianity, communism, or the U.S.-backed anticommunist dispensation. Political animosity created painful rifts within families tied to local police as well as local guerrillas. "It was a time of utter lawlessness," recalled a South Korean villager who had witnessed the brutalities of wartime as a child.[59] Families suffered an additional blow as able-bodied men were pressed into combat and older men into support services, while some women sank into beggary and prostitution. Both sides brutally mistreated civilians believed loyal to the enemy. Reprisal followed reprisal as population centers repeatedly changed hands. Amid the violence, social hierarchies based on age and family reputation collapsed. Rural folk crowded into squalid refugee encampments that sprang up on the periphery of southern cities. There stealth, cunning, and agility might spell the difference between life and death. Prostitution flourished, along with a black market supplied by goods stolen from U.S. Army warehouses.

Three years of war further hardened the mutual hostility between North and South Korea while also binding them closer to their great power patrons. Syngman Rhee ruled behind a U.S. protective shield until his ouster in a student-led uprising in April 1960. But the springtime promise of a democratic government in South Korea quickly faded. Waiting in the wings was the South Korean army, the most cohesive and disciplined institution in the south. This U.S.-trained force had by war's end grown to almost 600,000 (nearly two-thirds of the total U.N. force) and was the beneficiary of $1.5 billion a year in U.S. support. Its size and importance in a state constantly under threat gave it a growing voice in national life.[60]

In the North, Kim Il Sung clung to power, the ultimate survivor of the disastrous war that he had initiated. Chinese forces were entirely gone by October 1958, eight years after their dramatic appearance on the scene, but Beijing as well as Moscow continued to provide economic, military, and political assistance that bolstered Kim's position. Increasingly confident, the North Korean leader purged his rivals in the Korean Workers Party in the mid-1950s and basked in a cult of personality. This cult, which dwarfed the adulation accorded Stalin and Mao, continued undiminished even beyond Kim's death in 1994. Situated securely within the socialist bloc, Pyongyang embarked on a distinct development path that with the passing of time would separate the North ever more from the South while sustaining a belligerent nationalism that would continue to spawn tension and crises on the peninsula.

Koreans everywhere experienced the war in intensely personal terms—of individual suffering, loved ones killed or missing, families ripped asunder. In neither North nor South Korea could the generation that passed through the crucible of suffering and loss grieve and remember according to their own choosing. Pyongyang and Seoul decreed that personal memories be subordinated to official narratives. Both states were forged in the very same crucible of war; their diametrically opposed official memories of the war were embedded in their founding myths. A state-imposed orthodoxy denied ordinary Koreans the balm of recalling shared suffering in an unprecedented national tragedy.

In North Korea what was called the Fatherland Liberation War served as one of the two pillars of legitimacy for the regime of Kim Il Sung. He loomed large both as the patriot hero who had dared to reunify the country split by foreigners and as the anti-Japanese resistance fighter whose 1930s exploits were vastly exaggerated. Developing his own philosophy of *juche* or self-reliance, Kim posed as the true nationalist who charted his own path to a Korean communist paradise—this notwithstanding the reality of his country's dependence on Soviet and Chinese largesse. North Korea's state-controlled media, educational system, museums, and public monuments all celebrated the Great Leader and his ostensibly enormous contributions to the national struggle. Pyongyang's propaganda machine dismissed the authorities in Seoul as American lackeys. They had made the South into a de facto colony that was occupied by an American army and governed by an American proconsul in the guise of the U.S. ambassador. By enforcing strict control on the news media, North Korea kept its people ignorant about developments in the South and permitted no challenges to its ideological hegemony.

Under President Rhee and his military successors, the South Korean government, too, propounded a self-serving version of the war. In this version, North Korea, an illegitimate aggressor state ruled by a megalomaniac, was solely responsible for the war and continued to pose an imminent threat to South Korea's existence. The security threat posed by North Korean infiltrators and leftist sympathizers justified harsh measures of repression that belied the Cold War trope of South Korea as a free country. The Seoul government suppressed any mention of the atrocities committed by South Korean and U.S. forces during the war and persecuted South Koreans suspected of collaboration with North Korea during its brief occupation of the South (July–September 1950), including many who were simply trying to survive.

Not until the late 1980s did this straitjacket of anticommunist orthodoxy begin to loosen, allowing long-buried emotions associated with the war to surface, especially in literature and films. The anguish of divided families and personal trauma is superbly depicted in such works as Cho Chong-nae's ten-volume epic *T'aebaek Sanmaek* (T'aebaek Mountain Range), Yun Heung-gil's haunting story "The Rainy Spell," Ahn Jung-hyo's novel *The Silver Stallion*, and the film *Tae Guk Gi* (The Brotherhood of War).[61] With the advent of real democracy, a hitherto muzzled public opinion challenged the official narrative of the Korean War, the national security state it engendered, and the sanctity of the alliance with the United States. Anti-Americanism became one expression of a desired pan-Korean national identity.

The War Memorial erected in downtown Seoul in 1994 reflected the new view of the war as a "national calamity for both sides" and "a tragedy without comparison in world history." South Korea's Truth and Reconciliation Commission, established in 2005 during the presidency of Roh Mu-hyun, gave official sanction to the quest for literally unearthing the truth of wartime massacres and atrocities. The commission investigated hundreds of petitions from bereaved families alleging massacres of civilians by South Korean army and police forces. Mass graves containing the remains of many thousands of victims confirmed their chilling charges.[62]

For China, the Korean War also extracted a heavy price, in lives and scarce resources. But the war also offered significant gains. At home it gave the Communists a chance to harness popular nationalism to their broad revolutionary agenda and to demonstrate their impressive organizational capacity. The mobilization of hundreds of millions of people on a nation-wide scale would be repeated often in the following years as Mao pursued the goal of building a modern socialist state. Internationally, the Korean War bolstered China's standing as a regional power with its own revolutionary notion of Asia's future. For the first time, Chinese military forces, at great cost to be sure, had fought a coalition of modern Western armies to a standstill. China's performance gained the respect of the post-Stalin Soviet leadership, which greatly increased its development aid. China's achievement also won it recognition as a leader of the emerging third world. Its presence at the Geneva Conference in 1954 and the Afro-Asian Conference in Bandung, Indonesia, in April 1955—the third world's coming-out party—reflected its new status. Sooner or later Americans with eastern Asia dreams would have to come to terms with the reality of a Communist-dominated China with regional clout.

As in North Korea, an officially sanctioned orthodoxy weighed heavily in Chinese memories of the war. Patriotism was the hallmark of that orthodoxy after the war as it had been during the conflict. Posters and films depicted a glorious national achievement made possible by the party's leadership and the people's resolve and courage. The popular 1956 film *Shangganling* took its name from a bitterly contested position (also known as Samkumryung to Koreans and Heartbreak Ridge to Americans) that was the scene of a real battle in the fall of 1952. It celebrated a small unit of Chinese soldiers facing hordes of Americans. The heroic Chinese kept up their morale by singing about their "ancestral land," persevered against great odds, and ultimately forced the dispirited enemy to withdraw. Another popular film about the Korean War, *Heroic Sons and Daughters* (*Yingxiong ernu*) from 1964, based on a story by the famous writer Ba Jin, carried forward the familiar wartime themes of family sacrifice in patriotic service.[63]

Finally, for the United States, the human costs of war were relatively low. With no vulnerable civilians to get caught up in the fighting and with superior weaponry and wealth to shield its troops, the United States, as in earlier wars in eastern Asia, suffered only a fraction of the losses of its Asian foes. But its wealth and power were insufficient to maintain the momentum behind the U.S. quest for domination in eastern Asia that had crested with victory in the Pacific War.

The Korean conflict flashed a caution light for empire. Part, but only part, of the U.S. difficulty can be laid on a president who played a generally aloof but also a spasmodically disruptive role in Korean War policymaking.

After committing American troops to the defense of South Korea, he failed to provide guidance on initial war aims (even as Beijing issued ever more emphatic warnings), to rein in a repeatedly insubordinate MacArthur before considerable damage was done, to channel debates among his aides over how to bring a deadlocked war to a conclusion, to provide the public with a compelling sense of why the United States fought an inconclusive war, or to accept compulsory repatriation of prisoners after having earlier subscribed to an international convention stipulating precisely that.

But the faltering U.S. effort was more fundamentally the result of constraints accumulating during a supposedly golden age of Cold War omnipotence. The United States had assumed at midcentury an international position that posed profound difficulties for U.S. policymakers. An astonishing accumulation of Cold War commitments that virtually encircled the globe distracted U.S. leaders, forcing them to scramble from one trouble spot to another. Given the breadth of these commitments, policymakers never had enough resources, even after the huge boost in the military budget facilitated by the Korean War. Reform and expansion of the international-affairs apparatus that included a unified Department of Defense and the creation of new agencies such as the CIA and the National Security Agency meant for the president not just sources of support but also bureaucratic fiefdoms to keep under control.

This situation would get worse, not better, as decolonization accelerated during the 1950s and 1960s, as radical currents in the third world grew stronger, and as China persisted in its stout opposition to U.S. regional encroachment. Challenges in such diverse places as Iran, Guatemala, Suez, Cuba, Laos, and Lebanon all lay ahead. Adding to Washington's problems were restive transatlantic allies who wanted to keep the U.S. focus on the defense of Europe and were loath to support expensive and dangerous U.S. commitments to what they deemed peripheral zones. Nuclear strategy added another fresh layer of perplexity as the Soviets built up their arsenal, as delivery systems multiplied and became more sophisticated, and as the weapons they could deliver grew more powerful. Faced with the danger of a cataclysmic confrontation, leaders were under intense psychological pressure to keep wars on the periphery within manageable bounds.

Developments on the home front further undermined the U.S. position. The Korean War had made clear that the public had little taste for distant wars started for purposes not easily grasped and fought to inconclusive ends. This was reflected in a postwar impulse to think of Korea as an unpleasant episode best forgotten. Hollywood offered a distinctly unheroic version of a grim struggle by reluctant warriors determined to do their duty and return home alive. *The Bridges at Toko-ri* (1955) was one of the first films to capture this sour view. Based on James Michener's best-selling novel published just before the truce in Korea, it features a navy fighter pilot, a war-weary World War II veteran whose mission is to take out a fiercely defended bridge. The cause for which the pilot fights is dubious; his main preoccupation is survival and a reunion with his loving wife. In the end his plane is shot down, and he dies desperately resisting capture in what the film suggests is a pointless sacrifice. Another early and enduring Hollywood rendition of the Korean War was *Pork Chop Hill*. Released in 1959 and based on an account by the military historian S. L. A. Marshall, it played variations on the theme of futility as anxious American GIs battle for control of a barren hill in the closing days of the Korean War. Its grim scenes featured anxious men fighting dutifully with their minds fixed on the days remaining before they would return home.[64]

The passage of time has not added to the luster of "the forgotten war." The Korean War Memorial on the National Mall in Washington, D.C., completed in 1995, offered a fitting if perhaps unintended coda to this deeply unpopular conflict. Devoid of both the heroism of the Iwo Jima Memorial and the deeply affecting pathos of the Vietnam War Memorial, it depicts a group of nineteen grim-faced U.S. servicemen advancing to nowhere. Revelations some forty years after the fact about wartime atrocities perpetrated by U.S. troops cast an additional cloud over the war. The Associated Press team of Charles J. Hanley, Sang-hun Choe, and Martha Mendoza received a Pulitzer Prize in 2000 for their investigative reporting of the massacre of civilians at Nogun-ri in July 1950. A subsequent official Department of Defense inquiry, denying any deliberate killing of civilians as a matter of policy, whitewashed the incident as "a tragic and deeply regrettable accompaniment to war" in which jittery soldiers were responsible.[65]

Faced with a resurgent China, global distractions, and a lukewarm public, the U.S. policy establishment—officials and opinion leaders alike—was conflicted over what conclusions to draw from this first bout of limited war. On the surface, the mainstream response was to see in the stalemated Korean conflict a cautionary tale about getting bogged down in land wars in Asia. Generals as well as politicians joined the "never again" club, swearing to avoid committing U.S. troops in the future against enemies with inexhaustible manpower and without recourse to nuclear weapons. Better to stay offshore and exploit the comparative U.S. advantage in air and naval power. From its island bases in Japan, particularly Okinawa, in the Philippines, and on Taiwan, the United States could thus maintain its position of regional primacy and contain the further spread of communism. But in practice "never again" gave way to redoubled efforts to defend the stakes that American might and sacrifice had secured—even if this required more sacrifice on the Asian mainland. The half-century-old dream of regional dominance persisted.

Paradoxically, the prowess that China had demonstrated on the battle-field did not give U.S. policymakers pause. Rather, it deepened their fear of an expanding Sino-Soviet bloc and their hostility toward an oppressive state ruled by a fanatical despot. Like a fearful contagion, this morally and politically loathsome Asian mutant had to be isolated while pressure was applied to hasten its inevitable demise. To that end, the Truman administration clung to its nonrecognition stance, supported anticommunist guerrillas in Tibet and remnant Chinese Nationalist troops that had taken refuge in Burma across the Chinese border, while assisting Nationalist forces on Taiwan in carrying out commando raids along the China coast. The Truman team also banned U.S. trade with China and, in concert with its allies, established an export control regime intended to slow China's economic development.

The Eisenhower administration held views and followed a line of policy toward what was routinely called Red China that were strikingly similar to those of its predecessor. The president came to office already convinced that "the loss of China to the Communists [was] the greatest diplomatic defeat in this nation's history," and once there he characterized China's new masters as "completely reckless, arrogant, . . . and completely indifferent to human losses." Threatened by what Eisenhower perceived as these "Communistic brigands," the United States could not afford to go "slinking along in the shadows, hoping that the beast will finally be satiated and cease his predatory tactics before he finally devours us." Dulles indulged not only the commonplace contempt for the Communists but also a widely shared feeling of paternalism as old as the Pacific project. "We can look after the interests of Communist China a lot better than Mao Tse-tung can. . . . We've been friends of China for a hundred and fifty years and Mao Tse-tung is nothing but a puppet."[66]

Confrontations with Beijing over the Nationalist-controlled islands of Quemoy and Matsu lying right off the China coast intensified the feelings of hostility while also hardening support for Chiang Kai-shek. Beijing's shelling of the islands from late 1954 into early 1955 and again briefly in late summer 1958 worried Eisenhower. He feared that this might demoralize an ally and lead to the loss of Taiwan. That would in turn (as the president saw it) "doom the Philippines and eventually the remainder of the region." Eisenhower and Dulles responded by sending Chiang more economic aid, helping to modernize his armed forces, offering him a security treaty (signed in December 1954), and even rattling the nuclear saber on his behalf. Official U.S. propaganda converted Chiang's authoritarian and repressive government into Free China, the supposed nucleus of the entire country's liberation from communism. At the same time Eisenhower continued the hard-line Truman policy of isolating Mao's regime: no diplomatic contact, no place in the United Nations, no travel to China (with the handful of Americans who defied the prohibition losing their passports), and no trade.

The risks of another land war in Asia seemed more worrisome to Eisenhower's allies and fellow citizens than to his administration. Britain continued to follow its policy of greater diplomatic engagement with China and along with Japan objected to the U.S.-sponsored trade restrictions and increasingly evaded them. The U.S. public had similar reservations. Half or more of survey respondents during the Eisenhower years favored diplomatic and commercial contact with the mainland and visits by journalists (though not a seat for Beijing in the United Nations). Roughly half wanted to stand back from the 1954 Taiwan crisis and 91 percent of the informed public preferred to hand the 1958 crisis over to the United Nations.[67]

Increasing the likelihood that "never again" would yield to "once again" was the persistence of a Cold War culture with its set of sweeping principles and repressive practices. Cold War notions made it hard to accept geographical limits to U.S. action and interests. Indeed, proponents of freedom who agreed with MacArthur condemned Truman and the Democratic Party as weak-kneed. They made spirited claims that American ingenuity, resources, and pride could triumph even in the least promising environments. A powerful anticommunist hysteria buoyed policymakers who supported these claims while stifling skeptics. With constant reminders of the communist menace at home and abroad, public fear of communism became rampant. The reckless crusade of Senator Joseph R. McCarthy (R-Wis.) against "subversives" was but the most dramatic expression of this hysteria, which transcended partisan lines. Developing since the end of World War II, the Red Scare reached its apogee during the Korean War. In the pattern common to U.S. wars, fear of subversives penetrated the workplace, politics, civic organizations, schools, and the courts. The U.S. Communist Party was outlawed. Thousands of individuals with past links to the Communist Party or merely leftist causes that had once been respectable now fell under suspicion and lost their jobs. Anticommunism was a potent and indiscriminating weapon in domestic political battles that served to narrow significantly public discourse on a wide range of political issues, including health care, drug use, and immigration.

Taken together, fervently and insistently proclaimed Cold War principles helped to keep policy on a steady, familiar course. They rendered alternative policies implausible or dangerous and induced groupthink within the foreign policy establishment. They applied intense, relentless pressure on China specialists in government and the academy so that they swallowed their doubts, lay low, and even left the country. They made it difficult to differentiate Communists at home from those abroad and those abroad from one another. Whatever "never again" might suggest, this stifling anticommunist consensus banished any thoughts of abandoning eastern Asia as a dangerously exposed salient or a peripheral zone of scant interest and instead created pressure to tighten and defend the U.S. commitment to the region. Thus Washington persisted in backing regimes in the Philippines, in South Korea, in South Vietnam, and on Taiwan that could not have survived on their own. Carefully cultivated indigenous military establishments became one bulwark of stability, strongman governments the other. The overlapping array of authoritarian, right-wing clients and dependencies that Washington was pleased to call part of the Free World seemed the most effective, least costly means of holding at bay the specter of revolutionary wars and subversion haunting the official imagination.

This effort to consolidate the U.S. grip was strikingly evident in Japan, the centerpiece of the U.S. eastern Asia dominion. In a gesture of bipartisanship during the Truman presidency, John Foster Dulles, a leading Republican voice on foreign policy, agreed to serve as the point man in working out the formal terms of postoccupation ties. After extended talks, Prime Minister Yoshida Shigeru accepted a U.S.-drafted peace treaty, which was signed in San Francisco in September 1951 by Japan's former enemies—with two notable exceptions. (The Soviets withheld their signature, while Communist China was not even invited.) A secretly negotiated security treaty, formalized at the same time, maintained the U.S. position on what had become the anchor for an offshore island strategy. It guaranteed open-ended U.S. possession of military bases on Japanese soil and continued control over Okinawa as well as the right to intervene at will to suppress domestic disorder in Japan. The security treaty was a bitter pill for Yoshida, who had wanted to rid Japan of U.S. forces but learned that retention of U.S. bases was nonnegotiable. The best he could do in the face of intense U.S. pressure was to fend off U.S. demands that Japan begin rearmament regardless of what the U.S.-imposed peace constitution said. These formal documents clearly announced Japan's accommodation to U.S. Cold War requirements. The U.S. alliance turned out to be from the Japanese perspective a "gift from the Gods." U.S. military procurements during the Korean War helped revive their economy. Production and living standards continued their upward curve after the war, propelled by special access to the rich U.S. consumer market. At the same time the presence of U.S. forces—over a quarter of a million in 1953—provided security on the cheap in a tension-filled neighborhood.[68]

U.S. policymakers were equally active in Southeast Asia. The outbreak of fighting in Korea raised the strategic importance of the region and pushed the Truman administration deeply into a pair of proxy wars. One was fought to defend the flank of the U.S. imperial position. Washington was generous with the French battling Vietnam's Communists, though the returns on the investment proved deeply disappointing. The French abandoned the field in 1954, forcing hard choices on a string of U.S. presidents beginning with Eisenhower. The other proxy conflict sought to preserve U.S. influence at the point where the imperial enterprise had begun a half century earlier. In the Philippines, Washington faced another Communist-led insurgency with a familiar profile. The Huks had arisen from rural distress and became militarized in the 1940s opposing the Japanese invaders, local collaborators, and landowners from the Huk stronghold in central Luzon.[69] Sharpening postwar tensions with both landlords and the government of Manuel Roxas culminated in a decision in early 1950 by the Huks' Communist-dominated leadership to seize power.

The Truman administration at once rushed to the rescue of a panicked Manila government, now headed by President Elpidio Quirino. It was (Kennan told his boss, Dean Acheson) suffering from "immaturity and lack of political experience." Salvation obviously depended on U.S. action. Also hanging in the balance were invaluable air and naval bases. According to guidelines approved by Truman in November (just as the Korean War was underlining the importance of those bases), a takeover of the islands by a Soviet proxy would not just diminish U.S. international credibility but also "seriously jeopardize the entire structure of anticommunist defenses in Southeast Asia and the offshore island chain, including Japan."[70]

Washington quickly found in Ramon Magsaysay a Filipino face to put on the U.S. salvage mission. A man of modest origins who had worked his way into the established, elite-dominated system of political patronage, Magsaysay attracted the attention of Edward Lansdale as just the collaborator U.S. policy needed. Lansdale, a CIA operative quickly given fictional form by British novelist Graham Greene in *The Quiet American* (1955) and by American novelist William J. Lederer in *The Ugly American* (1958), became Magsaysay's main adviser and publicist. With U.S. backing, Magsaysay became defense minister in August 1950, and he won election as president in 1953. Stepped up U.S. military training, increased aid, and close supervision made his army a more effective instrument of rural pacification. A formal U.S. security guarantee bucked up Manila's morale. Magsaysay did his part by promising to take care of Huks who surrendered and to advance social welfare in the countryside. Finally, the capture of the Huks' Communist leaders and a campaign of psychological warfare demoralized and sowed dissension within the insurgency. By 1952, according to the recollections of Luis Taruc, one of the leading Huk commanders, Huk units had begun to act with such desperation that "the peasants' sympathy and loyalty began to turn into fear." Within a few years a movement that at its peak had boasted 11,000 to 15,000 combatants had virtually dissolved. The U.S. position was secure and U.S. officials had in the bargain derived important lessons from the Philippines as "a postcolonial laboratory for the creation of new counterinsurgency doctrines" (according to a leading historian of the islands).[71]

Despite Magsaysay's apparent success, the Philippines continued to suffer from familiar domestic woes and an uneasy, dependent relationship with the United States. The elites' death grip on the economy and the political system persisted, while entrenched local interests managed to frustrate Magsaysay's popular promise of land reform and thus perpetuated rural distress. Tension over the U.S. bases, which the U.S. military wanted to expand, provoked nationalist resentment. At the same time, incessant requests for more U.S. assistance to feed the political system collided with the Eisenhower administration's fiscal conservatism. By the time of Magsaysay's death in an airplane crash in 1957, his reputation had suffered. Dulles complained in May 1955 that he had "not proven himself a very shrewd or able politician." The United States had still not remade the Philippines to its liking. But it had gotten good value—secure bases and a Huk defeat—for the $2 billion in grants and loans provided between 1944 and 1958.[72]

To beef up this widening set of U.S. commitments in eastern Asia, the Eisenhower administration began proliferating formal treaty commitments in what amounted to a kind of pactomania. The government on Taiwan, having received a new lease on life from the Korean War, became linked to the United States via a Mutual Security Treaty in 1954. That same year Dulles midwifed the Southeast Asia Treaty Organization (SEATO) which along with the U.S.–South Korea, U.S.-Taiwan, and ANZUS (Australia, New Zealand, and the United States) treaties established a diplomatic bulwark that paralleled the string of U.S. bases in Asia. Although Eisenhower tried to contain increases in military spending and warned in his farewell address of the influence wielded by an increasingly powerful "military-industrial complex," his militarized policy in eastern Asia belied his words.

———

The indeterminate outcome of the Korean War had called into question control over the territorial expanse the United States had wrested in the western Pacific at the end of World War II. Americans thought they had "lost" China; in Chinese eyes China had finally "stood up." Mao Zedong's memorable phrase had more than a grain of truth. By their determination and skill at mobilizing their national resources and winning international support in the face of Washington's hostility, Chinese leaders had inflicted the first effective check on U.S. ambitions in the region.

Even so, those ambitions and the fundamental conceits behind them — that American will, ideals, and technology could triumph wherever they were brought to bear — survived largely intact. Leaders in Washington still believed they had it in their power to create a new Asia, and for that reason a wayward, hostile China had to be put in its place. They increasingly feared communist-inspired and assisted revolutionary wars in eastern Asia and elsewhere in the third world. They looked to reliable anticommunist nationalists, preferably ones who spoke English and had reassuring American connections, to keep the communists at bay. And despite their rhetoric about winning hearts and minds, they ultimately depended on aircraft carriers, bomber fleets, and mobile ground forces to make good on U.S. claims, eliminate wrongdoers, and protect American clients. The persistence of this nationalist can-do faith would bring further tragedy to Americans and to Asians and in Vietnam precipitate the final act in America's Pacific drama. In Korea the U.S. quest for dominion had faltered; the next battlefield would witness its collapse.

4 | **Vietnam,** 1965–1973

Early in the afternoon of 2 September 1945, the very day that Douglas MacArthur took Japan's formal surrender in Tokyo Bay, some half million Vietnamese crowded into Ba Dinh Square in central Hanoi. Flags, banners, lanterns, and flowers were everywhere. Those at the head of the liberation movement were intent on staging an impressive show. City folk and peasants from the nearby countryside arrived to hear Vietnam's independence declared by a physically unimpressive man wearing a faded jacket and rubber sandals. For nearly three decades he had lived a secretive existence abroad organizing resistance to French control of his country. He had operated under many aliases, including the well-known Nguyen Ai Quoc (literally Nguyen the Patriot). Recently he had taken the name that would stick, Ho Chi Minh.

Few in the crowd that day knew that Ho was Nguyen Ai Quoc, famed as an opponent of the French. But his message carried powerfully. The speaker began by declaring, "All men are created equal." By using this and other phrases from the American Declaration of Independence of 1776 and the French Declaration of the Rights of Man and the Citizen of 1791, Ho was making a calculated appeal for outside sympathy and support, but he was also appealing to a people weary of subjugation and poverty. He said nothing about the international communist movement with which he had long been closely affiliated or about a socialist future for Vietnam. Instead, he focused the crowd's attention on the crimes of the French: They had denied democratic rights. They had exploited and impoverished the economy. "They have built more prisons than schools. They have mercilessly massacred our patriots. They have drowned our uprisings in seas of blood." Ho concluded with the vow that the detested colonial era was over; there would be no turning back: "A people who have courageously opposed French enslavement for more than eighty years, a people who have resolutely sided with the Allies against the Fascists during these last years, such a people must be free, such a people must be independent." Early in his address Ho had looked up from his text to the great crowd before him and asked, "Do you hear me clearly, fellow countrymen?" The response came roaring back from men and women with tears in theirs eyes: "Yes, we can hear you."[1]

But Americans, approaching the apogee of their dominance in eastern Asia just at this moment, were not listening—with terrible results that would gradually manifest themselves over the following three decades. Their heads buzzed with old notions of an Asia developing under U.S. aegis, and they were now increasingly confident that they had an opportunity to direct the course of events. In Vietnam as earlier in the Philippines and South Korea, Americans would take the place of one colonial power and set to work with collaborators in yet another exercise in empire. U.S. policymakers would create and in time U.S. forces would sustain a client regime, inflicting in the process enormous destruction and suffering upon the peoples of Indochina—Laotians and Cambodians as well as Vietnamese. But a determined effort spanning two decades did not yield success. Nationalism had become a far more potent political force than it had been at the time of the pacification of the Philippines, and in places—notably Vietnam as well as China—it had given rise to a party-state distinctly at odds with U.S. ambitions. To be sure, American leaders had grasped the rising appeal of nationalism and championed self-determination as a universal principle during World Wars I and II and once more at the onset of the Cold War. But far from helping facilitate national self-determination, this professed support for independence movements was so blatantly violated by on-the-ground U.S. policy that it generated damaging charges of hypocrisy, not just in Vietnam but also among Cold War allies and even at home. The impulse toward domination was weakening. The U.S. failure in Vietnam coming on the heels of a frustrating war in Korea would precipitate a profound national crisis of confidence and a dramatic retreat from imperial pretensions in eastern Asia.

ON THE ORIGINS OF ANTAGONISM

During World War II and the early Cold War, a Vietnamese revolutionary movement and a rising American presence first made contact. What began as an effort at wartime cooperation soon turned distinctly hostile. Ho and his associates had made an unshakable commitment to an independent, united, and socialist Vietnam. Meanwhile, American elites came to see Vietnam, together with Japan, South Korea, and the Philippines, as part of what, by virtue of America's paramount power, should be a U.S.-dominated region. One side was no more willing to abandon its sacred struggle than the other was to assume a more modest regional role or beat a humiliating retreat.

World War II first brought to Washington's attention a land previously peripheral if not irrelevant to U.S. concerns. Franklin D. Roosevelt watched with alarm in 1940 and 1941 as Japanese forces moved into French Indo-china (consisting of Vietnam, Laos, and Cambodia). Later, with victory in the Pacific War increasingly likely, Roosevelt turned to the future of this French possession. He was initially guided by the principle of self-determination. He had included it prominently in the first formal statement of Allied war aims, the Atlantic Charter in August 1941, and reiterated it in both formal declarations and worldwide propaganda. The president was also guided by a conviction that the French had mishandled their colony. "After 100 years of French rule in Indochina, the inhabitants were worse off than they had been before," he declared privately.[2]

But a strong streak of condescension qualified Roosevelt's public stance in favor of independence and steadily eroded his distaste for French mis-rule. The Vietnamese were in his judgment not yet ready to handle their own affairs. Just like the Koreans, they would need time—twenty to thirty years of outside instruction and benevolent supervision—before they would be ready to stand on their own. Roosevelt was not prepared to serve as tutor. So after the Chinese government headed by Chiang Kai-shek declined the role, there was no alternative but the French. By granting colonialism a re-prieve, the president also removed a bone of contention with the British government. Prime Minister Winston Churchill had defiantly announced his attachment to the British empire, and he defended the French, making their colonial interests a stalking horse for his own. By early 1945, the prin-ciple of self-determination had given way to grudging U.S. acceptance of restored French control.

Following Roosevelt's death in April, the fate of Indochina fell to the State Department, which treated French colonial claims with deference, even sympathy. France under the leadership of Charles de Gaulle figured as an important prospective partner in settling postwar issues and in rehabili-tating a war-devastated Europe. A State Department analysis prepared in June 1945 noted an "increasingly strong" independence movement in Viet-nam and conceded that the Vietnamese like other colonial peoples ought to have "an opportunity to prepare themselves for increased participation in their own government with eventual self-government as the goal." But the authors of the report worried about instability in the meantime and recognized French sovereignty. While official U.S. observers in Vietnam were impressed by Ho, even the most sympathetic among them judged the forces that he represented "not politically mature" and thus easily manipulated by Japanese agents or other malign outside forces. At the very time Ho was formally declaring independence, the influential *New York Times* warned darkly of mounting disorder as "revolutionary groups" seized control and as "the natives" lashed out violently against French residents. Restoration of calm depended, so the educated public learned from these reports, on the arrival of foreign forces—Chinese, British, and French.[3]

The onset in the late 1940s of the Cold War rivalry with the Soviet Union and the civil war victory of Communist forces in China intensified the pro-French tilt of U.S. policy. Binding France into an anti-Soviet alliance took priority over decolonization, which as Washington saw it would create instability that communists were sure to exploit. U.S. diplomats reporting from Hanoi and Saigon in the late 1940s searched for evidence of Soviet machinations but reported they could find none. Some indicated that Ho was more a nationalist than a communist and enjoyed strong popular support, while the cause of the intransigent French was doomed. But pervasive Cold War fears smothered any doubts about backing the French and about seeing Indochina as part of the global anticommunist struggle.

Finally, in February 1950 Harry S. Truman concluded formally for the first time that Indochina was a strategic link in the worldwide containment line. Ho had become an agent of "communist aggression," and the anti-French resistance that he led constituted "only one phase of anticipated communist plans to seize all of Southeast Asia." To hold this aggressive force in check, Washington looked primarily to the French and to their implementation of an enlightened colonial policy of accommodating "legitimate nationalist aspirations." That meant above all recruiting noncommunist leaders who could provide an attractive alternative to Ho. Having decided that the monolithic communist threat had to be stemmed in the region, Truman's advisers recommended taking "all practicable measures," an approach that the president accepted. This recommendation would within several years make Washington the paymaster, arms supplier, and adviser to an embattled colonial regime with U.S. taxpayers footing two-thirds of the bill for the French struggle.[4]

Like Roosevelt, Truman was no friend of colonialism, but he too doubted Asians were ready to manage their own affairs. New nations swept up in great-power struggles could not be left to themselves. In the Cold War context, native impatience for independence threatened instability not just

harmful to their own welfare and development but also potentially dangerous to the broader anticommunist cause. Therefore, like Roosevelt, Truman
favored an enlightened tutelage—benevolent in its intentions and committed to ultimate independence—that was distinct from old-style colonialism. The French were not the best choice for tutors, U.S. officials conceded. Yet they hoped that once the French reestablished control over their
unruly subjects, they would honor their self-proclaimed mission to bring
civilization to the natives and prepare them for eventual independence.

The colonialism that U.S. policymakers had come awkwardly to embrace
clashed with the formidable nationalist spirit to which Ho had given voice
in September 1945. France's conquest of Indochina had in the course of
the nineteenth century provided the crucible for that nationalism. Scholar-
officials educated in the Confucian classics, dedicated to service in the imperial administration, and guided by a protonationalist faith had waged a
stubborn but ineffective resistance. Their only consolation was the thought
(as a famous southern patriot-poet had put it in 1861) that patriots had
"struggled for the king and for the land" and would "die fighting the enemy,
and return to our ancestors in glory rather than survive in submission to the
Occidentals."[5] Ho's father was from this educated class. Some uncertainty
surrounds the year of Ho's birth, though officially it is designated as 1890.
He grew up in a village in north-central Vietnam as the anti-French risings
that some scholar-officials had incited were sputtering out, while the imperial system they sought to rescue was falling into disrepute as a result of
the court's weak-kneed collaboration with the French.

The nationalism that took form in the early twentieth century blended
two strands from the Vietnamese historical experience. The dominant
strand was a tradition of resistance to China, which nationalists converted
into a stirring pageant of a patriotic people willing to sacrifice for their
country. The lesser strand in this emerging national self-conception drew
on the Vietnamese experience of southward expansion at the expense of
other ethnic groups. The notion of Vietnamese regional dominance was further encouraged by French favoritism in the effort to build a united colony
of Indochina. Vietnamese nationalists saw themselves as more advanced
than the Cambodians and the Laotians and thus their natural leaders.

As a young man, Ho was immersed in this emerging nationalism. Family
connections put him in personal contact with the two pioneering nationalists articulating alternative paths to independence, Phan Chu Trinh and
Phan Boi Chau. Trinh deplored Vietnam's decline. It had become a weak
and backward country whose people faced national extinction. He looked

for rescue and revival to the French, whom he wanted to play the role of "capable teacher" and "good mother who would treat us like her own children." Prompted by a similar faith, Ho had gone abroad in 1911 on his own quest for the sources of foreign strength the better to remedy Vietnam's weakness. That journey, which took him to Britain, the United States, and France, converted him to the alternative nationalist position of open resistance championed by Chau. The French, Chau had insisted, "are not our fathers, nor are they our brothers. How can they squat here, defecating on our heads? Are the men from Vietnam not ashamed of that situation?" His sojourn in France robbed Ho of any hope for an enlightened French colonial policy. He appealed in vain to the French Socialist Party and to the victorious powers meeting at the end of World War I in Paris to support modest steps toward independence. Desperate for political support and tired of living a hand-to-mouth existence within the Vietnamese expatriate community, Ho turned to the newly established international communist movement, which openly proclaimed its anti-imperialism. Only it, he concluded in 1920, would support resistance and revolution, the only path he saw open to Vietnam and other colonized countries.[6]

During the 1920s and 1930s Ho worked to undermine French control with the support of the Moscow-based Communist International (Comintern), dedicated to promoting revolution in the colonial world as well as in advanced capitalist countries. He operated clandestinely among Vietnamese communities in Thailand and China, returning periodically to a Moscow awash in political intrigue and determined to impose discipline over its sprawling international network. Ho had little taste for Marxist theorizing, kept a low profile, and so managed to avoid the Stalin-era purges of foreign communists. He channeled his energy into the education of a new generation of Vietnamese activists and the creation of an indigenous party organization. At last in 1930 he helped bring rival groups together to form the Indochinese Communist Party, so called on Comintern insistence. (In 1951 it relabeled itself the Vietnamese Workers' Party thereby narrowing its mandate to one country, and finally in 1976 assumed the name Vietnamese activists had preferred in 1930, the Vietnamese Communist Party.) Those interwar years completed Ho's international education and made him something of a cosmopolitan whose languages included Chinese, Russian, French, and English, and whose worlds included the Vietnamese society that he had grown up in, the French imperial milieu in Vietnam and elsewhere abroad, the Vietnamese expatriate communities in China, Southeast Asia, and France, the Comintern network spanning the Eurasian continent, and a fractious Chinese political scene dominated by the Nationalist and Communist Parties.

Ho's party survived the repeated blows of a vigilant French security service to emerge supple and effective, with a talented and dedicated leadership. Its survival and ultimate success depended on a broad and varied social appeal, attracting not just offspring of prominent families, intellectuals of modest means, and representatives from a minuscule working class but also recruits from the four-fifths of the Vietnamese population living on the land. The party assimilated peasants into the working class by a semantic sleight of hand shocking to orthodox European Marxists, who looked for the agents of change in the industrial centers of modern capitalism, not in a feudal countryside. But in Vietnam the countryside was essential to any hopes for liberation; urban centers were firmly under colonial control. A peasant rising in 1931 in Ho's home region in north-central Vietnam underlined the revolutionary potential of the countryside if the party addressed peasant demands for access to land and relief from taxes and debt.

In February 1941 Ho, by now a fifty-year-old veteran revolutionary, returned to Vietnam for the first time in thirty years. He saw an opportunity to strike a French administration thrown off balance by German conquest of metropolitan France and by the intrusion of Japanese forces. To exploit this opening, he arrived at the head of the Viet Minh (short for Viet Nam Doc Lap Dong Minh Hoi or Vietnamese Independence League), created and controlled behind the scenes by the Indochinese Communist Party. The Viet Minh, with its stress on patriotic struggle and sacrifice, proved a great success. It attracted a wide range of people—from poor and rich peasants to landlords to wealthy merchants to urban professionals. It raised its own army under the direction of Vo Nguyen Giap, a history teacher turned by his nationalism into a Marxist and by Ho into a military commander. Giap began with a motley, ill-armed force, formally established in late 1944. By early 1945 that force had helped expand the Viet Minh presence from the remote mountainous north into the populous Red River Delta, while an active program of grassroots organizing and propaganda raised the Viet Minh's political visibility and appeal. Famine that in 1944 had gripped the northern part of the country and eventually claimed 1 million lives facilitated that expansion. After the authorities failed to act, the Viet Minh demonstrated its concern for popular welfare and its organizational effectiveness by seizing grain hoards, blocking Japanese grain exports, and organizing famine relief.

The Japanese takeover of the French administration in early March 1945 and the collapse of the overall Japanese war effort in early August suddenly and unexpectedly put the prize of independence within reach. In a fever of popular excitement and in another demonstration of organizational skill, the Viet Minh hurriedly took control of Hanoi on 19 August and other cities within a week. On 2 September, when Ho proclaimed independence in Ba Dinh Square, he also inaugurated the new Vietnamese state (formally known as the Democratic Republic of Vietnam). Though the regime Ho headed was in fact dominated by Communists, he sought to disarm domestic and foreign critics by nominally disbanding his party and forming a governing coalition.

Declaring independence was one thing; making good on it another. Ho's preference was to ease the French out and avoid a costly armed conflict. From late 1945 into early 1946, Ho repeatedly appealed for support to President Truman and his secretary of state, citing the U.S. principle of self-determination and asking for a role in any international discussions of his country's future. He got no answer. He also sought to negotiate some transitional arrangement by which the French would gradually relinquish political control but retain their economic and cultural stakes. This calculated appeal to what Ho considered the self-interest of rational capitalists did not take into account French pride in colonial possessions or the outsized influence wielded by French settlers. They enjoyed privileged positions in Indochina that independence threatened. Confronted by the arrival of French forces bent on restoring the colonial status quo, Ho first temporized but then following armed clashes in late 1946 retreated into the countryside to resume the armed struggle.

The ensuing conflict followed a pattern that Americans would come to know twenty years later: Viet Minh guerrillas attacked French forces (a mix of North African, Foreign Legion, Vietnamese, and French soldiers), threatening communications lines and isolating French-controlled urban centers. The Viet Minh gradually expanded the scope of its operations and began fielding some conventional main-force units thanks to Chinese assistance that helped offset growing U.S. assistance to France.

The leader of the new Chinese state, Mao Zedong, played a critical role not only in building up the Viet Minh military but also in disarming Soviet doubts about Vietnam's place within the international Communist movement. Like some within Vietnam's Communist Party, Stalin had suspected that Ho was at heart a bourgeois nationalist and thus of doubtful loyalty. When Vietnamese appealed to Stalin to recognize "the importance of the anti-imperial struggle in our country, which is also a springboard for Southeast Asia," he ignored them.[7] The Chinese leader, on the other hand, developed an appreciation of Ho's leadership based on a decade of personal contact and Mao's own understanding of the difficulties faced by a vulnerable revolutionary movement. With the Communist victory secure in China in 1949, he promptly met with Ho, and together they took up Vietnam's cause with Stalin. In January 1950 Moscow joined Beijing in according Ho's government diplomatic recognition, and Stalin effectively delegated to Mao the task of supporting Asian revolutions. Chinese advisers and equipment began to cross the border in a buildup of the Viet Minh army. While Ho visited Moscow to curry favor, Vietnam's Communist Party issued statements praising the Soviet leader and announced policies meant to demonstrate its orthodoxy.

Viet Minh forces, bolstered by Chinese assistance, fought with such determination and success that by 1954 the French had lost their appetite for what they called a "dirty war." By then some 55,000 had died on the French side in a struggle that seemed distant to the French public and that was absorbing about 10 percent of the national budget. Coalition governments in Paris remained paralyzed on how precisely to resolve the deteriorating situation. The battle of Dienbienphu was the final blow to an already crumbling French empire in Southeast Asia. What French commanders intended as a decisive set-piece battle turned into a disaster. Viet Minh forces isolated the French garrison, and their Chinese-supplied artillery pounded it into surrender in early May.

French capitulation meant only a partial victory for Ho. The international conference convened in April in Geneva by the major powers on both sides of the Cold War divide would indeed liquidate the century-old French colonial enterprise in Vietnam as well as in Laos and Cambodia. But the Soviet and Chinese delegations also wanted to reduce international tensions, and in any case French forces might have more fight in them, especially against an overextended Viet Minh army. Ho accepted a compromise. While the Geneva accords concluded in July gave his government full control north of the seventeenth parallel, they stipulated that unification with the South would have to await national elections scheduled for 1956. Once more, Ho was willing to temporize—to see whether elections might in fact lead to national unity and whether the Americans would follow their French clients out the door.

In the face of some grumbling within the party, he convinced his senior colleagues to give priority to consolidating control in the North. There they would concentrate on creating a modern, powerful socialist state, pro-

Contested Colonial Ground

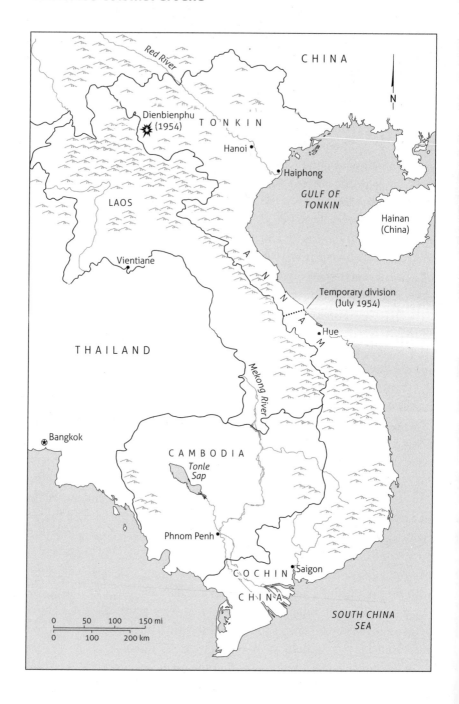

Planning the Dienbienphu campaign, late 1953. Flanking Ho Chi Minh (from the left): Le Duan, Pham Van Dong, Truong Chinh, and Vo Nguyen Giap. They would prove a stable leadership group that would press to victory the liberation struggle that Ho had begun. (From *Ho Chu Tich Song Mai Trong Su Nghiep Chung Ta* [1970])

(opposite)
French Indochina. Vietnam was the most restive portion of the French colony, with resistance strongest in the Red River Delta, the center of what the French designated as Tonkin. The most intense fighting of the French war, including the decisive Dienbienphu battle, took place in the north. Annam was the name given the narrow central coastal plain hemmed in by highlands and home to a fading imperial court in Hue. Cochin China was the longest occupied and most deeply French-influenced of the regions. The peace negotiated at Geneva drew a provisional line through Annam, leaving Saigon and Hanoi (each dominating populous river deltas) as the rival political centers.

Ngo Dinh Diem with village elders. Diem stood on one side of the deep social and political divide accentuated by the French colonial impact. His commitment to the social status quo as well as his Catholic faith set him sharply at odds with those who sought revolution. (Courtesy of U.S. Army Center of Military History)

moting industrialization (with Soviet and Chinese assistance), and collectivizing agriculture. These measures would enable Hanoi (so Ho argued to the party faithful) to better respond to the southern question no matter how developments unfolded. As further insurance, Hanoi preserved its southern political and military assets, bringing north an estimated 50,000 to 100,000 Viet Minh cadre and instructing some 15,000 of the stay-behinds to lie low and bury their weapons. Ho asked them to submit patiently to "the trials that they are going to endure for the sake of the interests of the whole country."[8]

CREEPING TOWARD WAR

Following the Geneva settlement, the Americans pursued the struggle that the French had abandoned. U.S. policymakers continued to worry about the fate of the Vietnamese if left to themselves. Against the communists—viewed as ruthless agents of a foreign force now entrenched in neighboring China—southern Vietnam would need protection and guidance. Americans officials felt a keen sense of entitlement as righteous representatives of a great power and superior civilization to save at least part of Vietnam and shape it into something better. Equally potent and more visible were Cold War concerns. Washington was intent on protecting a critical point along the Asian containment line and halting a string of reverses in Asia—the loss of China and the stalemate in Korea as well as the collapse of the French proxy in Vietnam. Another loss would have especially worrisome repercussions in a domestic politics suffused with fears of communism. With France's defeat formal empire had died in Vietnam, but this only served to reinforce America's motives for exercising informal control.

Informal empire no less than formal empire depended on enlisting the right kind of "natives." Washington could proceed only with the help of Vietnamese ready to resist Hanoi's claim to South Vietnam and amenable to U.S. guidance. The search began in 1954 with Ngo Dinh Diem, continued with the Saigon generals who overthrew him in 1963, and concluded with a regime dominated by Nguyen Van Thieu and Nguyen Cao Ky. Each in turn provided Washington a nominal partner in keeping Vietnam in the U.S. orbit. But none of the clients lived up to their assigned role. As Hanoi raised the pressure, John Kennedy and then Lyndon Johnson scrambled to shore up an embattled Saigon government. Guided by a loose but potent collection of justifications, fears, and assumptions, they inched toward and ultimately made a major commitment of U.S. forces.

Invariably, they proceeded like other empire builders, cautiously and with a clear sense of constraints. They understood the costs and risks of a commitment at a point on the containment line of limited intrinsic value, whether measured in economic output, critical raw materials, strategic location, or sentimental ties. Adding to their caution, policymakers carried in their heads a small voice warning against another Asian land war. Finally, they were constrained by their own repeated claim to fight for freedom and sensitive to charges of imperialism. They thus had to give Vietnamese collaborators some latitude in managing their own affairs. U.S. control exerted too directly might stir up opposition at home, further compromise collaborators in South Vietnam, and deepen resentment in a third world already suspicious of U.S. neocolonial intentions.

As the French position collapsed in early 1954, President Eisenhower began to lay a new foundation for U.S. involvement. He had considered sending U.S. air power to the rescue, but having just ended the war in Korea, he had no taste for a fresh Asian war in Vietnam. With the French beyond saving and Vietnam north of the seventeenth parallel lost, the Eisenhower administration acquiesced to the Geneva settlement, noting but not endorsing its arrangements. To forestall what his secretary of state, John Foster Dulles, described as the main danger of "subversion and disintegration," the president sought to evict the French and create a new nation to salvage Vietnam south of the seventeenth parallel.[9] After some indecision Washington settled on Ngo Dinh Diem, a staunch anticommunist and devout Catholic, as the father of this new Vietnam.

Born in Hue in 1901, Diem followed a family tradition of official service. He worked in the French-controlled bureaucracy during the 1920s, then broke with the foreigners in 1933 over demands for greater political autonomy, not independence. For the next two decades Diem represented a political middle way—best described as Confucian authoritarianism—between communism and French domination. During that time he remained a presence in court politics in Hue, flirted briefly with the Japanese occupation authorities, and rebuffed overtures from Ho Chi Minh to join his cause following the founding of the Democratic Republic of Vietnam. In 1950 with little support at home and fearful of Viet Minh assassins, Diem went into exile in the United States where he cultivated the overseas Vietnamese community and Americans looking for another friendly Asian leader like Syngman Rhee and Ramon Magsaysay. Diem attracted the attention of a distinguished group, heavily Catholic and dominated by liberal Democrats. They included Francis Cardinal Spellman, Massachusetts Senator John F. Kennedy, Supreme Court Justice William O. Douglas, and Montana Senator Mike Mansfield. Diem seemed just the ticket: an anticommunist nationalist who lost no love on the French and appreciated the prospect of U.S. backing.

Diem's moment came in June 1954. He returned to Saigon to form a government at the request of Bao Dai, the figurehead emperor who had abdicated in 1945 as the Viet Minh swept to power, then had second thoughts and agreed to a French invitation in 1949 to form a nominally independent Vietnamese state. Diem seemed to Bao Dai an attractive choice as prime minister. He was likely to appeal to the Americans while also curbing French attempts to salvage some influence in their former colony. By the fall of 1955 Diem had outmaneuvered the playboy-emperor, deposed him, and created his own state, the Republic of Vietnam.

The Eisenhower administration had by then swung four square behind Diem. Eisenhower himself had at first worried about doing anything carrying "any implication of colonialism" or even hinting of "objectionable paternalism." But on-the-ground U.S. action revealed no such hesitations. CIA operatives had assisted Diem from the time he landed in Saigon, while the U.S. military facilitated the flight of nearly 1 million Catholics from the Communist North to bolster his base of support in the South. To provide some security for this nascent state, Dulles began in late 1954 to put together an alliance, the Southeast Asia Treaty Organization (SEATO). Countries from the region (Thailand and the Philippines) plus France, Britain, Australia, and New Zealand joined the United States in a vaguely worded pledge to defend South Vietnam. A large and hyperactive U.S. establishment gradually grew up in Saigon, with the ambassador and the general in charge of the military advisory group running the "country team." Nominally devoted to nation building, their duties were in fact proconsular. They doled out funds to keep the economy afloat, trained and paid for an army supposed to be loyal to Diem, cultivated its French-trained officer corps, housed a CIA station with its own network of agents and contacts, and pressed advice and programs on the presidential palace all while keeping Washington up to date and squiring about visiting dignitaries. Eisenhower invested heavily in this new state with the expectation that it would prove a responsive and effective tool in the anticommunist struggle then increasingly being waged in the third world at a wide range of points from Iran and Indonesia to Cuba and Guatemala. By the late 1950s U.S. funding paid 85 percent of Diem's military budget, which itself amounted to two-thirds of all government spending, while also covering the cost of around 80 percent of the country's imports.[10]

Washington's reliance on Diem worked for a time. He suppressed two armed religious sects, quashed an urban mafia, and hunted down former Viet Minh. All the while he built up support among Catholics and the wealthy as well as U.S. officials. Diem relied heavily on his immediate family and family loyalists and cultivated a rigid self-certainty that baffled and frustrated some Americans who worked with him. At the same time, his evident success made him something of a miracle man to prominent cold warriors and the popular media. Senator Mansfield enthused, "Diem is not only the savior of his own country, but . . . of all Southeast Asia." South Vietnam "is our off-spring," Senator Kennedy flatly declared. "We presided at its birth, we gave assistance to its life, we have helped to shape its future."[11] The Eisenhower administration, impressed by Diem's achievements and keen to display its prize potentates who had seemingly stabilized the eastern Asia containment line, invited him as well as Syngman Rhee and Chiang Kai-shek for visits early in 1957. Diem began his victory lap in Washington with meetings with senior officials and an appearance before Congress. The two-week grand tour moved on to New York City and then other stops across the country.

The miracle ended in the early 1960s. A Hanoi-backed insurgency made alarming inroads in the countryside, while in 1963 simmering Buddhist discontent, fueled by Diem's preference for fellow Catholics, burst into urban protests. The Kennedy administration's response was to find a way to save its troubled client. The president had been worried from his first days in the White House about revolutionary threats to vulnerable third world societies such as Vietnam's, and he read with alarm Soviet leader Nikita Khrushchev's January 1961 declaration of support for wars of national liberation. Kennedy, therefore, publicly affirmed U.S. backing for the Saigon government and sent more advisers, more money, and better weapons. But he drew the line at U.S. troop deployments. He feared an overt military intervention would provoke an international and domestic uproar and prove the first step down a slippery slope. To one of his White House aides Kennedy explained, "The troops will march in; the bands will play; the crowds will cheer." But then what happens, he asked, when you wake up to discover that you need more? "It's like taking a drink. The effect wears off, and you have to take another."[12]

During 1963, with Diem's grip on both city and countryside slipping, Kennedy concluded that South Vietnam had to be saved even if it meant Diem had to go. The American leader could not abandon a client state without paying an exorbitant political price. He had by then suffered too many foreign policy setbacks. He had spectacularly failed to topple Cuba's Fidel

Castro in a covert operation in April 1961. Later that year he had acquiesced in the building of a wall sponsored by Khrushchev dividing Berlin. Once more he looked weak. Accentuating this impression, Kennedy had decided in mid-1961 to seek a deal neutralizing a Laos torn between communist and anticommunist armies. Kennedy's advisers had told him that Laos was not the place to take a military stand in the region. Vietnam offered more promising prospects. But even with South Vietnam's survival at stake, Kennedy seemed to waffle. He suggested publicly that the Vietnamese had to determine their own fate (with the implication that he might walk away), yet he also publicly pledged to defend the containment line. To do otherwise "would mean a collapse not only of South Viet-Nam, but Southeast Asia," he told a press conference.[13] Secretly he called for plans to withdraw U.S. advisers while also presiding over an ill-considered and awkwardly conducted attempt at overthrowing the Diem regime.

Diem bristled under U.S. pressure to reform his government, remove his influential brother Ngo Dinh Nhu, and generally pay closer attention to American guidance. Diem knew his patron might betray him but swore, "I will not permit myself or my country to be humiliated." One of his ranking officials, his anticolonial gall rising, told the U.S. ambassador to "cease the efforts of your CIA to make us a nation of 'boys.'" But if Diem would not fall in line, others would, a result Kennedy virtually guaranteed by signaling that new leadership would enjoy U.S. support where Diem might lose it. Diem's generals got the message and on 1 November seized power, killing both Diem and Nhu in the process.[14]

Diem's assassination, however, failed to resolve the crisis threatening South Vietnam. The new U.S.-backed military leaders engaged in a game of musical chairs as coup and countercoup absorbed Saigon's attention. Meanwhile, the threat from the insurgency worsened. Kennedy's assassination in late November dumped the defense of this deteriorating U.S. outpost into the lap of Lyndon Johnson. The new president began at once moving along a path already clearly marked out by his predecessors. A master politician, he understood the rules of the Cold War game at home and accepted as an article of faith the Cold War creed. He was in addition surrounded by former Kennedy advisers who had themselves already shown determination to hold on to South Vietnam. Secretary of Defense Robert McNamara—with his slicked-back hair, razor-sharp mind, and tireless work ethic—would prove especially influential.

Between November 1963 and July 1965 Johnson took the decisions leading to war. In his first review of Vietnam policy only a few days after Kennedy's assassination, Johnson emphatically endorsed his predecessors' support for a government in Saigon strong enough to hold Hanoi at bay. He would in the meantime concentrate his formidable political skills on getting congressional approval of his ambitious Great Society domestic program and getting elected in his own right. In early August 1964 an incident in the Gulf of Tonkin disrupted Johnson's plans. He took two apparent attacks on U.S. destroyers as a Hanoi-ordered provocation. As it turned out, the first reported attack came at the initiative of local commanders, while the second occurred only in the imagination of overanxious sonar operators. Despite high-level doubts about the second attack, the president decided to strike. He ordered the bombing of North Vietnam for the first time and secured congressional backing in the form of the Gulf of Tonkin resolution. Congressional leaders provided the open-ended endorsement of the use of force in the region that Johnson wanted. The Senate approved it 82 to 2 after less than ten hours of debate; the House agreed unanimously after forty minutes of contemplating the significance of the draft resolution supplied by the White House. The president intended the bombing and congressional backing as a message of determination to Hanoi. Showing the bravado to which he was prone in public, he boasted to a reporter after the air strikes, "I didn't just screw Ho Chi Minh, I cut his pecker off."[15] He also wanted to head off charges of weakness during the closing stage of his election campaign against a militantly anticommunist Barry Goldwater.

In February and March 1965 with a landslide victory behind him and Great Society legislation rolling forward, Johnson intensified pressure on Hanoi. He initiated a bombing campaign and sent the first U.S. combat units into South Vietnam to protect U.S. airbases. In June the U.S. commander in Vietnam, General William Westmoreland, asked for a major troop deployment to stem the continuing, potentially disastrous loss of rural control to insurgents. By July Johnson along with his civilian and military advisers had lined up in favor. After a pro forma meeting with congressional leaders, he announced at a low-key, noontime press conference that he was moving at once to raise troop levels to 125,000, with more to follow.

In making this string of fateful decisions the president heard out more or less gladly warnings against deeper involvement. In his immediate circle of advisers, Undersecretary of State George Ball offered the most forceful dissent. Drawing on his familiarity with the French defeat, he warned against committing U.S. troops to "a war they are ill-equipped to fight in a non-cooperative if not downright hostile countryside."[16] An impressive range of politicos close to Johnson raised their own warning flags, notably

Clark Clifford (an influential Democratic operator and personal adviser), Mike Mansfield (the Senate majority leader), Richard Russell (a prominent Democratic senator from Georgia and one-time Johnson mentor), and Vice President Hubert Humphrey. They were especially worried that Johnson would not be able to maintain public support over the long haul.

CIA and other government analysts also threw cold water on war talk. They expressed profound doubts that air power could cut the flow of northern supplies reaching the South or force Hanoi to accept U.S. terms. They also warned of the difficulties Americans would face in winning the hearts and minds of Vietnam's peasantry and in ruling what would at best be "an uneasy and costly colony." They also questioned the frequently invoked domino theory that the fall of Vietnam would set off a cascading collapse of neighboring states to communism. Finally, they pointed to "a congenital American disposition to underestimate Asian enemies." The conclusion in retrospect seems inescapable: the U.S. commitment unfolded despite, not because of, the information available to U.S. policymakers. The dreams of domination, doctrines of containment, and fears of policymakers trumped reality as the specialists so ably depicted it.[17]

Remarkably, Johnson himself came in 1964 and 1965 to share these doubts. On 21 June 1965, barely a month before making his major troop commitment, a troubled president rehearsed the reasons for caution in a secretly recorded telephone conversation with McNamara. The president anticipated virtually all the major reasons later cited by historians for the American defeat in South Vietnam. He thought Americans were already divided over the prospect of a distant war, especially one in Asia, and he predicted fighting would intensify those divisions. The enemy, in contrast, was in Johnson's estimation resolute—"I don't believe that they are *ever* going to quit." He was aware, even if he did not on this occasion say it, that Hanoi could expect backing from Beijing, thus imposing constraints on U.S. strategy. Finally, he grasped that there was no sure path to victory. The bureaucracy had failed to come up with "any . . . plan for victory—militarily or diplomatically." But at the end of this remarkable enumeration of dangers confronting him, Johnson reached an even more remarkable conclusion: "I don't think we can get out of there with our [SEATO] treaty like it is and with what all we've said. I think it would just lose us face in the world. I shudder to think what [other countries] would say." He had to stay the course—and so he did.[18]

Unlike the Americans with their recurrent, fundamental doubts, the Vietnamese revolutionaries were single-minded in their pursuit of national unity. The American attempt to perpetuate the temporary division imposed by the Geneva accord seemed nothing more than a more sophisticated and considerably better-funded version of the French colonial enterprise. Like their predecessors, the Americans were using as their base the rich Mekong Delta and its primary city, Saigon. Hanoi watched the Americans cultivate clients among the very groups favored under the old colonial regime—staunchly anticommunist Catholics and those who had found personal advancement in the French military or in the French administration. With good reason Hanoi described the government in the South as a puppet with its army bound to U.S. interests by patronage, training, and logistical support and its economy buoyed by ever more generous American spending. Saigon's survival was thus ultimately dependent on Washington's backing. But leaders in Hanoi had to think carefully about how to proceed. They were conscious of U.S. military power and knew full well that fighting the Americans would exact a price far exceeding the sacrifices required by the anti-French struggle. Repeatedly party leaders sought ways to head off a test of arms and win the South on the cheap.

Post-Geneva developments betrayed Ho's hopes for peaceful unification. With American blessings, Diem ruled out participation in the national elections. He also took careful aim at former Viet Minh activists. A campaign of repression resulted in the execution or imprisonment of many while others surrendered. The survivors, perhaps numbering only a tenth of those left behind in 1954, went underground or fled to remote rural refuges. One recalled that "by 1959 the situation in the South had passed into a stage the communists considered the darkest in their lives: almost all of their apparatus had been smashed, the population no longer dared to provide support, . . . and village chapters which previously had had one or two hundred members were now reduced to five or ten who had to flee into the jungle."[19] The surviving stay-behinds called in desperation for Hanoi to take action before the entire organization in the South was eliminated. Alarmed by news of Diem's repression and desperate to return, southern activists who had moved north as part of the Geneva separation of forces were so restive that the party had to make a concerted effort to settle them down.

With the prospects for peaceful unification fading, Hanoi gradually reconstituted the elements in the strategy that had accomplished the defeat of the French. Le Duan played a leading role. This native of central Vietnam was a genuine proletarian—a railway worker who had participated in the founding of Vietnam's Communist Party and spent a good part of the 1930s and early 1940s in French prisons. He was thereafter the guiding spirit behind the drive to win the South. During the war against France and right after the 1954 partition, he had headed the party's southern branch (known after 1951 as the Central Office for South Vietnam or cosvn). He had been critical of the party's 1954 decision to temporize in the South but had accepted party directives. Even after moving to Hanoi in 1957 to help Ho Chi Minh run the party, he remained focused on the South. In late 1958 he returned to assess conditions. His report in December proved the prelude to a gradual but major shift to a more active opposition to the U.S.-backed Diem regime. In January 1959 the Workers' Party Central Committee decided it was time for party members in the South to defend themselves militarily and to begin low-level political organizing. In May the orders to that effect went out. To strengthen the party organization, Hanoi began sending south former Viet Minh who had relocated north in 1954. Traveling down a rudimentary trail named in honor of Ho Chi Minh or by sea, the first 4,500 of these political and military veterans had returned by the end of 1960.

During 1960 the party leadership decided to seek the overthrow of the Diem regime. In a speech delivered in April, Le Duan (about to become formally the party's general secretary) announced that liberating the South was the task of all Vietnamese. His comment was part of the gradual eclipse of the building of socialism in the North by this new primary objective. In September 1960 he and his senior colleagues called for the creation of the National Liberation Front (NLF) as the instrument for their new offensive. Formally founded in December, this united-front organization looked and operated much like the Viet Minh. The new organization was headed by a noncommunist southerner, Nguyen Huu Tho, while behind the scenes Communist Party members called the shots. It recruited a wide range of social groups. Its founding manifesto made moderate demands and avoided references to class conflict and to eventual socialization of the economy. The NLF quickly elaborated its own multilevel political administration and fielded a military force consisting of irregulars (part-timers conducting guerrilla warfare within their immediate locale) as well as light infantry main force units operating either within a single region or throughout South Vietnam. The main force expanded rapidly—from 25,000 in 1961 to 70,000 in 1963.[20]

In the countryside the NLF quickly pushed out from former areas of influence. It renewed the old Viet Minh backing for land reform since neglected by a Diem regime dominated by the landlords. But its presence was also felt in the cities, where its agents gathered intelligence and encouraged anti-Diem demonstrations. In the Central Highlands the NLF also took the offensive. Just as ethnic minorities living in the northern mountains had played a critical role in the Viet Minh struggle against the French, so too would these highlanders within South Vietnam prove important in the fighting that was about to unfold. To secure its position in this strategic region adjoining the Ho Chi Minh Trail, the NLF promised autonomy to the local population (in the range of 1 million), which was angered by the Diem regime's policy of promoting ethnic Vietnamese settlement. The NLF soon had Diem on the defensive and the Americans alarmed.

In the course of 1963 Le Duan and those closest to him, Le Duc Tho and Nguyen Chi Thanh, went to work to win the South before the Americans became irrevocably committed. Early in the year Hanoi increased the number of cadres assigned to reinforce the NLF. Diem was in deepening trouble despite a major infusion of U.S. military advisers and equipment. An NLF squad's stunning victory in January against a large, well-armed, U.S.-advised Saigon force in what became known as the battle of Ap Bac was emblematic of this favorable trend. Impatient to move forward and eager to exploit strains between Diem and his impatient American patrons, Hanoi appears to have approached the South Vietnamese leader with some kind of political deal that would have neutralized the South while keeping him in power at least for the moment. (Washington's knowledge of these contacts likely added pressure to get rid of Diem.) In December, in the aftermath of his fall, the Communist leadership concluded privately that the prospects for the South were more favorable than ever. The Americans had created an ineffective "henchmen's army," while NLF forces had proved their skill and fighting spirit.[21] Hanoi now decided to widen the Ho Chi Minh Trail running through adjoining parts of Laos and Cambodia to accommodate heavier weapons and trucks. It also resolved to expand the North's own regular forces and to further increase aid to the NLF. All these measures were to be carried out in secret so as to give the Americans no excuse to retaliate.

As the Diem crisis moved toward a climax, leaders in Hanoi sought to gauge U.S. intentions. The situation was hard to read not least because they peered through a Marxist prism. They saw the United States as a capitalist power afflicted by disabling contradictions at home and abroad—the dangerous discontents of the "working masses," the jealousy of rival imperialists, and the upsurge in third world liberation movements. But the American ruling class was rational. They surely would not repeat the failed attempt by the French to block the Vietnamese revolution. As capitalists with a counting-house mentality, they were bound to make a cost-benefit calculation and recognize that losses incurred in trying to hold South Vietnam would exceed the gains. Ho himself thought he saw in the United States in the fall of 1963 a country that was "more practical and clear-sighted than other capitalist nations. They will not pour their resources into Vietnam endlessly." Perhaps indulging in wishful thinking, he predicted that they would learn. "Weariness, disappointment, the knowledge that they cannot achieve the goal which the French pursued to their own discredit" would eventually convince the Americans to disengage.[22]

To facilitate this outcome, Hanoi offered a diplomatic deal modeled on the 1954 Geneva settlement. The prime goal was to eliminate foreign (read U.S.) interference and leave Vietnamese to settle their own differences. Both before and after Diem's fall, the senior party leadership promoted a plan that would end the conflict over the South by setting up a neutral regime there. With neutralization in effect, Vietnamese could settle among themselves the issue of reunification—ultimately on its terms, Hanoi hoped. It had praised the 1961–62 international effort neutralizing Laos as a model that might be extended to Vietnam. The overtures to Diem in the latter part of 1963 probably reflected the priority Hanoi accorded some kind of neutralization scheme.

The Gulf of Tonkin incident in August 1964 proved a watershed, pushing Hanoi toward a pessimistic reading of U.S. intentions and toward preparation for a direct clash. Hanoi concluded that the air strikes against the North Vietnamese coast indicated that U.S. strategy was shifting from "special war" waged through puppet troops to "limited war" (also known as "local war") in which U.S. forces would directly enter the fray in the South. Rather than intimidating Hanoi as Johnson had desired, the U.S. show of force had prompted a top-level decision in September to make a major effort "to seek to win a decisive victory within the next few years" (in the words of an official Vietnamese history). Accordingly, the first of a string of combat units from the North set off on the six-week march down the Ho Chi Minh Trail. Early the next year, in response to U.S. bombing, the northern economy shifted to full wartime production, with facilities dispersed to make them harder to attack from the air. To support the war effort, the party launched a mass mobilization of a population estimated at roughly 20 million. Men (even veterans of the French war) were called up for an indefinite period of military service, while women were pressed to take the places of the men to keep the economy running. These measures had by the end of 1965 increased North Vietnam's army to 400,000 (up from 174,000 in 1963); enhanced that force's artillery, armor, and support capabilities; and brought the militia to 2 million. By then the party strategists could also count on some 346,000 NLF fighters (a combination of 92,000 in the main force, 80,000 in local units, and some 174,000 irregulars).[23]

Even as they prepared for war, Vietnam's Communist leaders continued to hold the door open to a neutralization agreement. They responded positively to proposals along those lines coming from French president Charles de Gaulle and U.N. secretary general U Thant, and they welcomed Soviet backing for a negotiated settlement. As late as April 1965, Premier Pham Van Dong was still holding out a settlement proposal based on the Geneva model.

By the time of the Gulf of Tonkin attack, Hanoi was well on its way to putting in place the last important element in its southern strategy. Lining up socialist-bloc allies was doubly important. Their support might deter Johnson while also sustaining the North materially through any prolonged conflict. Ever since the Geneva conference, China and the Soviet Union had resisted getting pulled into a struggle for South Vietnam, and even a war of words that broke out between Moscow and Beijing in 1959–60 did not disrupt their common aversion to seeing tensions rise in Southeast Asia. Both powers had kept up high-level contacts and provided economic assistance, with Chinese support constituting a third of all its foreign aid and outpacing Soviet contributions. In the summer of 1962, with the U.S. advisory role expanding in South Vietnam, Mao made the first substantial commitment of weaponry as part of a shift toward a more revolutionary stance at home and abroad, and Chinese military leaders began coordinating with their Vietnamese counterparts on how to handle any U.S. invasion of North Vietnam. In turn, Hanoi gingerly tilted toward Beijing in its ideological dispute with Moscow.

During the summer of 1964 Mao further increased his commitment, this time in response to signs of escalation by the Johnson administration. The Gulf of Tonkin bombing in August prompted Mao to observe that if the Americans were foolish enough to assault the North, "they will have to remember that the Chinese also have legs, and legs are used for walking."[24] While military staffs kept meeting, China boosted the flow of military equipment and promised to dispatch support troops across the border into northern Vietnamese territory. At the same time Chinese troops and aircraft took up positions to defend China's southern border against possible U.S. incursions. Beijing explicitly warned Washington in early 1965 that any expansion of the war carried the real risk of a Chinese retaliation. Chinese leaders did not say what might trigger such action or exactly what form retaliation would take. The Johnson administration took the message to heart; there would be no repeat of the Korean misadventure.

Mao's shift forced Moscow's hand. Inaction would have validated Chinese charges that the Soviets had abandoned the struggle against imperialism. Khrushchev's ouster in October 1964 by a group dominated by Leonid Brezhnev facilitated the shift to a more activist policy. The new leadership pledged assistance in November, sent Premier Alexei Kosygin to Hanoi to work out the details the following February (as the U.S. bombing campaign against the North began), and concluded a formal agreement in April (just as Johnson was moving toward a major troop commitment). Moscow's economic and military aid program included advanced weaponry not in the Chinese arsenal, notably surface-to-air missile systems (manned by Soviet personnel), advanced aircraft, and training for Vietnamese pilots. Grudgingly China agreed in early 1965 to let Soviet matériel bound for North Vietnam pass through China. Hanoi was now in the catbird seat, able to encourage its allies to outdo each other in support of Vietnam's national liberation struggle.

THE TEST OF ATTRITION

The war that began in 1965 was a continuation of the contest for southern Vietnam. Washington's conception of a separate state under U.S. sway was irreconcilable with Hanoi's commitment to an independent, united Vietnam (perhaps neutralist in the short term but ultimately a member of the socialist bloc). Washington on the other hand had to preserve its client in the name of containment and prestige. To resolve this fundamental contradiction, both parties took up arms with the goal of wearing down the resolve of the other. Each was thus committed to a strategy of attrition—but each for its own reason. Though possessed of a potent military, Johnson feared the consequences of an all-out war, especially worrisome in a nuclear age and a threat to the continued funding of his prized domestic programs. He counted instead on ever increasing pressure to eventually secure Hanoi's acceptance of a separate South Vietnamese state. Le Duan and his associates, for their part, were confident that the grinding approach that had worn down the French would work if patiently applied against the Americans. Small-unit operations, relentlessly carried out at favorable times and places and punctuated at the right moment by a major blow, were the only feasible option. "We were not strong enough to drive out a half-million American troops, but that wasn't our aim," Giap observed many years later. "Our intention was to break the will of the American Government to continue the war."[25]

The Johnson administration launched its war of attrition in February and March 1965 by unleashing U.S. air power against North Vietnam. Aircraft based in neighboring Thailand and on carriers offshore conducted the sustained bombing campaign, dubbed Rolling Thunder, meant to frighten the North's leaders if not effectively block supplies they were sending south. Johnson personally supervised the timing and targeting, hoping to avoid provoking Hanoi's allies but also to cause enough pain to push Hanoi to accept a negotiated settlement on U.S. terms. He limited targets at first to military installations and supply routes and sought to avoid civilian targets. But by 1967 the target list included industrial complexes, power grids, and transport networks where civilians were more likely to get hit. Paralleling Rolling Thunder was the aerial bombardment of Laos that had begun in late 1964 in an attempt to disrupt men and supplies moving down the Ho Chi Minh Trail while also supporting a CIA-backed army against a Hanoi-backed force. (The Laos bombing would continue until the end of the U.S. combat phase of the war in 1973.)

The ground facet of the U.S. attrition strategy took shape after Johnson agreed in July to Westmoreland's request for a major increase in the army and marines under his command. The total American force would steadily rise toward a maximum of slightly over half a million by late 1967. It would be supplemented by a significant South Korean force of nearly 50,000 attracted by a substantial U.S. subsidy. Considerably smaller contingents arrived under the flags of Australia, New Zealand, Thailand, and the Philippines. Westmoreland used these forces in "search and destroy" operations conducted across Vietnam's widely varied terrain—the scattered villages, canals, and great expanses of rice paddies in the Mekong Delta; the thick mangrove swamps of the deep south, the fertile and densely settled land squeezed between the highlands and the coast of the central provinces, the shadowed and quiet jungles and the plateaus heavy with large, saw-toothed grass found in the Central Highlands. Helicopter troop transport and logistical support as well as heavy air and artillery fire would help mobile U.S. forces wear down and eventually neutralize the enemy. Their main targets were northern units operating in the Central Highlands and along the seventeenth parallel dividing North from South. Their secondary concern was the NLF presence in the heavily populated Mekong Delta. There American forces were supposed to sweep through villages, round up suspects, and crush NLF military forces so that, as Westmoreland planned it, Saigon's provincial authorities could step into rural areas cleansed of guerrillas and provide long-term security and administration.

The U.S. force conducting this war of attrition required a massive logistical infrastructure spanning thousands of miles. Nearly 1 million men had to be moved in and out of the war zone each year. Those in-country at the height of the war were to be fed, clothed, and housed at levels of comfort known to no previous army but taken for granted in the postwar American society from which soldiers were drawn. The comforts of home became a substitute for soldiers who had scant political investment in the war and who grew more cynical from year to year about their mission. Excellent medical care in the field and rapid medical evacuation was also part of the package soldiers came to expect. The survival rate for the wounded jumped substantially from the Korean War level, itself an improvement on that of earlier wars.[26] A heavy reliance on firepower placed an especially heavy logistical burden met from sea and air bases in Guam, Okinawa, the Philippines, and Thailand as well as in South Vietnam itself. The flow had begun to quicken in 1961 and reached a flood during the years of direct U.S. military engagement from 1965 to 1972. Sustaining this rich man's war in all these different ways meant raising the "tooth to tail ratio" to a level unlike anything seen in any previous American war in Asia. For every man in a combat role, approximately six or seven served in some kind of support position.

The Americans serving in Vietnam went through strikingly similar stages of experience. The seasons of soldiering were familiar to virtually all Vietnam veterans. Of the total of nearly 27 million men eligible to serve between 1964 and 1973, only 8.6 million actually entered the military either through enlistment or the draft. At the next stage, boot camp, raw recruits were toughened, disciplined, given basic combat skills, and prepared psychologically to kill. The arrival in-country—something experienced by a total of over 3 million Americans over the course of the war—usually began with the glimpse of the calm, verdant Vietnamese countryside from an airplane window. Stepping onto the tarmac turned the servicemen instantly into FNGs ("fucking new guys")—without a weapon, without a unit, and without a clue about what was ahead of them. The first weeks and months provided newcomers, particularly the distinct minority assigned to combat units, that clue in a steady round of patrols, ambushes, sniper attacks, mine explosions, and base camp mortar attacks. The remainder of the year in Vietnam was devoted to coping with stress punctuated regularly by the loss of comrades and accentuated for those in the field by obsessive thoughts of survival. This long grinding time was broken by R&R in Hong Kong, Bangkok, or Saigon. For the lucky who survived unhurt to "get short," the day would come to report for processing to return home (including the unsettling surrender of the soldier's weapon), and the flight out aboard a plane of men cheering wildly over their escape back into "the World." The soldier's seasons formally ended with homecoming accompanied by indelible memories.

Hanoi countered the abundance of U.S. resources with an abundance of confidence and determination. The U.S. ruling elite, no matter how powerful, would sooner or later crack the way the French had. An analysis provided by Le Duan, Ho's heir apparent, made the point explicit in mid-1965 at the outset of the direct collision with the Americans. Peering through his Marxist prism, Duan perceived a United States beset by mass discontent at home over the costs of the war, by opposition from other capitalist countries resentful of U.S. dominance, and by resistance from the socialist world. He estimated that Washington might send as many as half a million troops. But they would be fighting far from home, on foreign ground where they would be regarded as "an old style colonial invader," in a climate to which they were not accustomed, and against indigenous forces backed by both North Vietnam as well as China and the Soviet Union.[27] The military task now was to bleed American forces until mounting pressure convinced Washington to liquidate its neocolonial adventure.

Hanoi's commander in the South, Nguyen Chi Thanh, had the task of inflicting the bleeding. Born in 1914 into a poor peasant family in central Vietnam near the old imperial capital of Hue, Thanh joined the Communist Party in 1937, became a member of the party's inner core in 1951, and in December 1963 took charge of military and political affairs in the South. He would direct operations for the first two years of the war. By late 1966 northern units together with NLF conventional forces under Thanh's command totaled some 200,000 troops.[28] Against them were arrayed a South Vietnamese army numbering half a million and U.S. forces rising toward their peak of half a million.

Thanh would fight his war, not the war the Americans wanted. Facing an enemy that was not just numerically but also technologically and logistically superior, Thanh's forces sought to avoid prolonged pitched battles in which American mobility and firepower could come into play. Instead, they relied on surprise, close-quarter combat, and quick and nimble disengagement to limit U.S. advantages. After attacking at a time and place of their own choosing, they could disappear into the jungle or move into the sanctuaries along the South Vietnamese border to train, treat the wounded, and resupply.

Thanh's northern troops were levied in the North, predominantly from the rural population. After basic training, units made the arduous trek down the Ho Chi Minh Trail and finally reached South Vietnam at one of several points—near the seventeenth parallel, in the Central Highlands, or in the Tay Ninh region just northwest of Saigon. They rested, trained some more, and finally went into action. Theirs was a daunting assignment: to face a foe with an overwhelming advantage in weaponry and to fight for the duration of the struggle (not just twelve months).

Maintaining morale was critical under these trying circumstances. Party-directed political work was the main tool wielded by North Vietnam's military to achieve that end. Political education began in basic training and continued in the field under the supervision of political officers assigned down to the company level. Adding to unit cohesion and fighting spirit were tight-knit three-man cells and regular meetings before and after operations. Moreover, soldiers went into battle confident that their commanders would do everything possible to recover the dead and wounded and that the party-state would take care of their families whether they lived or died.

Those who became "martyrs" could expect both symbolic and material recognition. Formal notification of death would trigger collective village rites to sanctify the "sacrifice," beginning with an officially sponsored ceremony of condolence. There the officer charged with the care of soldiers' families in the area would read a standard statement highlighting the deceased's place in a circle of obligation and loyalty: "The fatherland and people have lost a loyal and faithful child. His unit has lost a person united in will, a comrade-in-arms. His family has lost a loved one. All of the cadres and soldiers of the unit respectfully . . . ask to 'divide the sadness' with the family. They hope that the family will turn its grief into activity for the revolution." The ceremony set in place significant long-term benefits, including a larger rice ration, additional assistance for children and the elderly, special educational opportunities, preferential medical access, and a smoother road to party membership and government jobs. A captured northern soldier reflected the cumulative effects of this morale building in the field and back home when he flatly declared, "Even if I know that I would be killed in fighting, I wouldn't hesitate to keep on fighting because I fight for the just cause, and dying for the just cause, for the nation and for the people is glorious." Perhaps the bravado of a resentful captive, these remarks at least reflected the party's success at getting troops to internalize the defiant, self-sacrificing rhetoric of resistance.[29]

The other major part of Thanh's command consisted of NLF units, much expanded since the creation of the organization in 1960. In addition to their military task of disrupting operations by U.S. and Saigon forces, they also had the political one of supporting the NLF's organization in the country-side. Preserving bases scattered across the South was critical to the NLF's ability to recruit soldiers and organizers; to keep its units fed, manned, and well informed; and to maintain its political appeal and standing as a legitimate alternative government.

NLF fighters under Thanh's command had their own distinct sources of strength. They knew the land and the locals and thus had a vastly better shot at winning any contest for "hearts and minds." The home-court advantage was rooted in an emotional attachment to a particular place and the intimate local knowledge that went with it. Nguyen Van Be, a fighter in My Tho province (in the Mekong Delta) made poetry out of his love of nearby people and places: "Before me, flowers bloom in brilliant colors in front of someone's house, / A bamboo branch sways gracefully, reminding me of the native village I love. / Our unit stops to rest in an isolated area. / My shoes are still covered with dust gathered during the march. / I hurriedly compose this letter to you / And send you all my love." Their strong motivation gave NLF fighters an additional edge over both their U.S. and South Vietnamese foes, at best dutiful combatants. Personal grievances common to the countryside made recruits easier to attract and morale easier to maintain. Nguyen Tan Thanh, a poor peasant from Long An province in the Mekong Delta who became an officer in a main force unit, explained how social injustice had led him to embrace the NLF cause: "The rich oppressed the poor. The poor had nothing to eat, and they also had no freedom."[30]

Sustaining the war of attrition waged by northern and NLF forces depended heavily on Hanoi's keeping manpower and supplies moving south. To ensure that the North could play its supporting role, party strategists sought to counter the disruptive effects of the U.S. blows from the air. They improved anti-aircraft and civil defense systems, dispersed industry, offices, and population, and created overlapping transport routes tended by skilled repair teams. U.S. bombers quickly exhausted a limited list of industrial targets while their damage to the transport system was quickly repaired and after another attack repaired again. Anger over the aerial pounding and outrage over loss of family and friends raised rather than doused civilian morale. The Ho Chi Minh Trail—actually a system of roads running through thickly forested, inhospitable terrain—became ever more sophisticated and ever more important as the conduit for the goods and manpower needed in the South. With rest stations, supply depots, a wider path for motorized vehicles, and even double tracks at points, the trail could by 1967 move

20,000 soldiers a month, along with the supplies that they and units already deployed needed.

Absolutely critical to maintaining the war effort was allied support. By mid-1965 Chinese engineering and anti-aircraft units had begun to arrive to keep road and rail lines open, build airbases, and defend strategic targets against U.S. bombers. As in Korea, Chinese forces found themselves shaken by the foe's "overwhelming firepower" (as one soldier with an anti-aircraft unit recalled), but they also brought the old disciplined determination to their task. "I began to hate the American airplanes . . . and the furious air strikes that had minimized my world and my existence." Chinese forces would peak at 170,000. A total of 320,000 would serve in North Vietnam between June 1965 and March 1968; some 5,400 would be either killed or wounded. These forces freed northern forces to deploy south. At the same time Beijing provided a wide array of basic military equipment and provisions—from guns and ammunition to uniforms to basic foodstuffs and cloth to trucks and locomotives. Soviet-supplied air-to-ground missile batteries and fighter aircraft added to the gauntlet that took the lives of thousands of U.S. fliers, destroyed hundreds of their aircraft, and forced the Americans to spend approximately ten dollars for every dollar of damage inflicted.[31]

Hanoi waged its war of attrition on a second, international front in a campaign of public diplomacy and propaganda that the Johnson administration could not match. Hanoi sought with some success to drive a wedge between Washington and its allies, generate popular condemnation around the world, and encourage American groups pressing for peace. One consistent theme was American brutality. The U.S. bombing campaign provided shocking images of dead, maimed, and stunned civilians North and South. Scenes of burning villages and weeping villagers that U.S. patrols left in their wake provided added evidence for the indictment against a superpower bully. Hanoi invited sympathetic foreign visitors to vouch for its claim of massive, indiscriminate destruction inflicted by U.S. bombs. Rounding out this international outreach, diplomats representing Hanoi and the NLF regularly extended peace terms meant to put the Americans on the defensive. This campaign helped turned public opinion in Europe, Japan, the third world, and even the United States against the American war. The resulting public demonstrations, condemnation in international meetings, and public investigations into U.S. war crimes created a climate of increasing anti-Americanism and put pressure on foreign leaders aligned with Washington.

By 1967 the U.S. war was not going well. Even as the air campaign widened, technologically outmatched northern air defenses managed to inflict significant losses on U.S. aircraft, and doubts deepened in Washington about the campaign's effectiveness in either breaking Hanoi's will or hampering support for the NLF. McNamara and intelligence analysts in the CIA were among the leading doubters. At the same time Thanh's forces were demonstrating that they could withstand a formidable military machine. U.S. combat units were unbeatable, but they were also unable to sweep the enemy from the field. Despite heavy losses, both North Vietnam and the NLF maintained combat-ready forces that could inflict and absorb casualties, recuperate, and come back for more.

The unsettling truth for U.S. forces became apparent during their first major encounter with northern troops in November 1965. Elements of the Seventh Cavalry Division conducting one of Westmoreland's search-and-destroy missions in the Ia Drang valley in the remote Central Highlands came under attack. What followed was three days of close-quarter fighting by fragmented units on both sides amid a rain of U.S. napalm, B-52 strikes, and heavy artillery. By the time northern forces broke off contact, the Americans had lost 305 killed and at least as many wounded (in all roughly 40 percent of those engaged in the battle). American military leaders claimed 3,561 enemy deaths, but because the enemy carried away its dead, the claim was like most body counts at best an educated guess. Westmoreland publicly hailed Ia Drang as "an unprecedented victory," citing the favorable ratio of enemy to U.S. dead. But privately McNamara questioned this rosy assessment. Arriving in Vietnam shortly after the battle, he reported to the president not only that the North was increasing its forces in the South but also that Ia Drang revealed "the increased willingness of the Communist forces to stand and fight, even in large-scale engagements." McNamara now told the president that it would take more U.S. forces than earlier estimated, perhaps as many as 600,000 men, to realize the objective of saving South Vietnam. Even then, he warned, success was not assured, and still more forces might be required. An officer on the ground put sardonically the prospects taking shape after less than a year of direct U.S. engagement: "If there is a God, and he is very kind to us, and given a million men and five years and a miracle in making the South Vietnamese people like us, we stand an outside chance of a stalemate."[32]

During 1966 and 1967 Westmoreland's war of attrition failed to destroy the enemy, but it did visit devastation across South Vietnam. Derided by his critics as "General Waste-more-men," the more fitting moniker might have been "Waste-more-land" for the way his forces administered the modern equivalent of a scorched-earth strategy. Increasingly, U.S. forces declared great expanses of the countryside free-fire zones into which aircraft and long-range artillery could pour ordnance without constraint and helicopter gunships could fire at anything that moved. B-52 bombers could blanket large expanses of the ground with terrifying effects. A hardened cadre recalled, "People pissed and shat in their pants. You would see them come out of their bunkers shaking so badly it looked as if they had gone crazy." The countryside was also heavily defoliated by herbicides (Agent Orange was the most notorious) to deprive enemy units of cover. Defoliation missions, which had begun in 1962, continued throughout the war. Raw numbers hint at the destruction wrought by U.S. operations over the course of the war. All Indochina absorbed approximately 15 million tons of explosives (three times all of World War II). About 4 million tons took the form of bombs dropped on South Vietnam along with 400,000 tons of napalm and 19 million gallons of herbicides. Destruction administered so indiscriminately, pervasively, and at a distance took civilian lives on a massive scale and raises the question of war crimes as a defining facet of the U.S. war.[33]

While the enemy's determination and skill partially explains this resort to attrition through indiscriminate destruction, the failure of the Saigon government to play the pacification role Westmoreland had assigned left U.S. strategists with little option but to exploit their advantage in brute force. The team of Nguyen Van Thieu and Nguyen Cao Ky had taken charge in mid-1965 and brought a stability to Saigon politics not known since Diem's overthrow. Though Ky the air force pilot was the more colorful figure, the reserved Thieu would emerge as the dominant partner after his election as president in 1967. He epitomized the Vietnamese collaborator. He came from a prosperous landlord family, got his military training from the French, and converted to Catholicism. These credentials helped him rise to prominence under Diem, whom Thieu in turn helped overthrow. Despite substantial U.S. assistance, the Saigon government failed to create an effective fighting force that could hold and pacify areas cleared by U.S. troops. It could not offer a credible nationalist alternative to the NLF. It failed to administer effectively areas under its control. And it undermined pacification programs, including the Phoenix program of targeting NLF members for assassination or capture and interrogation. A probing official CIA history concludes, "In practice, the generals [in control in Saigon] held at arm's length not only the peasantry but their own peasant-based pacification cadres, treating them just as another instrument of bureaucratic control."[34] All the while Thieu faced a rise of war weariness among the urban population and a stream of refugees flocking to the safety of cities from the nightmarish, random violence of the countryside. While this rural exodus deprived NLF cadres of their base of support, it also overwhelmed the limited capacity of the Saigon government to supply basic needs.

Without Saigon to secure the land U.S. forces cleared, American units had good reason to make heavy use of the firepower available to them. They wanted to minimize casualties in the endless round of their frustrating operations, and so hit suspected targets hard. Better still, to make sure there was no enemy to encounter, they randomly pounded the countryside with artillery and bombs. What could not be made secure for Saigon could at least be made too dangerous for the enemy. Finally, Westmoreland and his subordinates knew all too well that the favored measure of progress, territory under Saigon's control, would not show the desired progress, so they made much of "body count." U.S. commanders estimated the number of enemy dead with an eye not to accuracy but to their own career advancement. Thus the strategy of attrition had turned into a steady rain of destruction on Vietnam's land and people.

Nowhere was the failure of Westmoreland's strategy clearer than in the "hearts and minds" contest against the NLF in the southern countryside. There American forces were culturally clueless in operations rife with potential for misunderstanding and overreaction. The U.S. unit that entered two hamlets of Son My village in Quang Ngai province along the central coastal plain on 16 March 1968 offered an extreme example of the failing of the hearts and minds strategy. The men who participated that day in the massacre to be known as My Lai had suffered a steady loss of comrades to mines and snipers in the name of a cause they could not grasp and in an environment in which friend blended with foe. They were poorly led from their platoon leader right up the chain of command. They operated on poor intelligence. The massacre that followed was probably unique in its sustained violence: the rape and killing of some 500 villagers; the destruction of livestock and houses; and the poisoning of wells. One soldier recalled the terrible day simply: "We went on through the village and there was killing and more killing."[35]

But anecdotal evidence in memoirs, oral histories, and letters home point to a pervasive pattern of wanton violence. Sometimes it occurred in small-scale encounters. Tired, frightened, dispirited troops lashed out indiscriminately and covered questionable killings with the "gook" rule. "If it's dead, it's a gook." Sometimes the disregard for Vietnamese life was the result of commanders, intent on securing high body count, actively encouraging heedless use of firepower. Operation Speedy Express, conducted during the spring of 1969 in the Mekong Delta, stands out as a clear instance of responsibility for war crimes resting high up the chain of command.[36]

Americans in Vietnam had unwittingly revived the strategy U.S. forces had applied to the most resistant parts of the Philippines over a half century earlier. But there was one difference: the technology of war and the wealth of the warriors had increased many times over. The capacity for greater violence could be measured in the rising level of bloodshed in eastern Asia—in the urban infernos of World War II and in the devastation inflicted during the Korean War. Vietnam served up the most potent cocktail of military technology to date—the infantryman's automatic weapons, the long-range artillery, the supporting fighter aircraft, the massive loads of the strategic bombers, and the tons of chemicals. Only nuclear weapons remained out of bounds.

Adverse trends were also evident on the U.S. home front. The war suffered a broad, inexorable decline in public support. Opinion surveys done in mid-1965 revealed roughly a third of the respondents either doubtful or undecided about making a major commitment. The two-thirds behind Johnson began defecting almost at once. The decline continued at a steady pace, driven by daily headlines of casualties and costs without measurable success reinforced by disturbing images broadcast from the battlefield to the large audience attracted to newly expanded evening television news. By mid-1967 the public was split evenly over whether the war was a mistake, and "hawks" favoring escalation began rapidly losing ground to "doves" who wanted out. Public support continued to dwindle.

Paralleling this trend was the rise of a broad-based antiwar movement. It began to take form in March and April 1965 in response to the beginning of the bombing campaign and the dispatch of the first combat units. College campuses were suddenly alive with lectures and debates on the war called "teach-ins." A march in Washington in mid-April organized by the Students for a Democratic Society brought onto the public stage a minority already intensely antiwar and convinced that ending the war was linked to effecting profound changes at home. Speaking before a crowd of around 20,000, the president of the activist organization, Paul Potter, made the link explicit: "What we must do is begin to build a democratic and humane society in which Vietnams are unthinkable, in which human life and initiative are precious." That same spring the noted international affairs specialist Hans Morgenthau attacked the Johnson administration from a different direction. Already a critic of deepening U.S. involvement during the Kennedy

Waging War in a Foreign Land

Marine patrol, December 1965. This unit is walking along the dikes of rice fields in the northern part of South Vietnam. Small patrols fanned out across difficult terrain in a trying climate in a tedious search for an elusive enemy—an exercise with a striking similarity to the earlier fighting in the Philippines. (Courtesy of U.S. National Archives)

Leading away a suspected "Viet Cong," August 1965. A marine takes in hand a villager during a patrol near the Da Nang airbase. Distinguishing ordinary civilians from enemy fighters was a daily challenge for U.S. forces. The result was a distant and often tense relationship with the rural population, as in the Philippines decades earlier. The steady loss of comrades fed the fear and anger that could dehumanize Vietnamese and thus facilitate indiscriminate violence. (Courtesy of U.S. National Archives)

NLF fighters, date unknown. Members of a unit that had received special recognition project an air of professional nonchalance and combat readiness in this posed scene. The inclusion of the woman offers a reminder that women made up a substantial part of the NLF. Despite the lack of information about the identity of this group, their location, or the date, this photo gives a face to an enemy the Americans found elusive. (Photograph by Van Phuong)

years, he lamented "the crusading moralism" behind Johnson's call to arms. His administration was acting on a mistaken assessment of conditions in Vietnam and in the Communist bloc and in general "deluding" itself. This academic champion of realism would within a few months declare the U.S. course of brutality and destruction comparable to Hitler's Germany and a sign of "psychopathology" among policymakers.[37]

By 1967 the protest movement had expanded from campuses to the broader society. Women's and antinuclear groups, civil rights and black power advocates, union members, people of faith, representatives of professional organizations, and the first veterans swelled the numbers attending rallies. A quarter of a million showed up to protest in New York and San Francisco in April. The following October saw in Washington, D.C., alone around 100,000 on the streets. The currents of opposition to the war both drew upon and intensified the ferment that marked the decade—from civil rights and gay rights to feminism, environmentalism, and ethnic identity movements. The call for social and cultural liberation made it a bad time to be fighting a distant, deadlocked war. Spreading disenchantment made it difficult for Johnson to speak in open public venues where crowds chanted, "Hey, hey, LBJ, how many kids did you kill today?" The president lashed back privately, "I don't give a damn about those little pinkos on the campuses; they're just waving their diapers and bellyaching because they don't want to fight."[38] But he was powerless to reverse the loss of public support.

The foreign policy establishment—influential Americans including those serving in Congress and the executive—joined the rumblings of discontent. Doubts expressed confidentially to Johnson in early and mid-1965 broke into the open in early 1966, when Senator J. William Fulbright (D-Ark.) made his Senate Foreign Relations Committee a forum for debate. Skeptics got equal time alongside administration defenders in hearings that made criticism of the war politically respectable. By then Johnson's inner circle was dissolving. His national security adviser, McGeorge Bundy, quietly exited in February 1966. McNamara, the principal architect of the war, had entered a prolonged period of anguish. He pressed for bombing halts to get peace talks going and finally, tormented and frustrated, left the Pentagon in early 1968.

Media coverage—both in the press and on television—was if anything a lagging indicator of public and establishment disenchantment. During the first several years of fighting, press and television reports coming out of Washington and from the field overwhelmingly reflected the official version of the conflict retailed in military briefings, presidential press conferences and speeches, detailed white papers, and propaganda films. The media focused on U.S. soldiers, and it gave short shrift to the role of Vietnamese, the Vietnam context, antiwar demonstrations, and statements by critics. Only in the course of 1967, with public opinion clearly shifting, did newspapers and television begin to pay more attention to the opposition and tone down hostile commentary. Critical to this shift was the discovery of disarray at the top of the Johnson administration and within Congress as well as the pessimism expressed by soldiers interviewed in the field. Whatever the source, the tide of discontent began to overwhelm the once potent official version of how the war was going.

In late January 1968 Hanoi struck a blow that it hoped would cause the collapse of an already fragile U.S. position. That blow was the Tet offensive (so named because it was launched during the Tet or lunar new year holiday). In Hanoi the general staff and senior party leaders had started exploring in April 1967 a way to break the stalemate on the battlefield with a knockout punch similar to the one administered at Dienbienphu. Following the death in July of Nguyen Chi Thanh, who had returned to Hanoi to join in the consultations, Le Duan took charge of the planning with the assistance of Giap's most senior deputy, Van Tien Dung. The plan that emerged incorporated a favorite concept within the army and the party—that the war would build toward a general military offensive accompanied by a "general uprising" in urban centers. The loss of those strongholds would cause the collapse of the Saigon government and force the United States (in Le Duan's words) "to accept that it has failed militarily and that it has become isolated politically." Even so, the plan proved controversial. Giap thought it premature and thereafter had nothing to do with it. Ho directly questioned its riskiness within meetings of the top leadership. Le Duan persisted, securing a final decision on the offensive in mid-January. The party's southern office, now led by Pham Hung, had already alerted NLF loyalists to a looming big operation that would give them a chance "to avenge evil done to our families, to pay our debt to the Fatherland, to display our loyalty to the country, affection for the people and love for our families."[39]

The Tet gamble began with a feint meant to draw U.S. forces away from the main points of assault. Northern troops laid siege to an isolated U.S. marine position at Khe Sanh in northern South Vietnam. Sensing a decisive set-piece battle in the making, Westmoreland shifted about half of U.S. combat forces at his disposal to Khe Sanh. Then on 31 January amid the lunar new year celebrations, the trap sprang shut. The NLF threw its full resources—political as well as military—into an assault that was supplemented at a few points by North Vietnamese forces. The initial gains were spectacular. Provincial capitals, smaller cities, and towns all over the South fell to the offensive; Hue was taken; and Saigon became a battleground with the U.S. embassy under siege.

Nevertheless, the gamble failed within South Vietnam. The "general uprising" in the urban centers failed to materialize. South Vietnamese and U.S. forces quickly rallied, repelled a second and third enemy offensive later in the year, retook population centers, and moved into rural areas long off limits. The NLF suffered heavily. Tran Van Tra, then in command of its forces, later lamented, "Many infrastructures were lost and many comrades were lost, especially in the areas adjacent to cities and the highly populated areas which were important strategically." In many areas the NLF was virtually eliminated as an effective fighting force. The loss of land and population to Saigon damaged NLF prestige, reduced its resources, and forced northerners to take up the slack. Noncommunist southerners in the NLF and in its Provisional Revolutionary Government (created in June 1969) began to sense a slide into irrelevance. Rather than marking the beginning of the end of the war as Le Duan had hoped, Tet inaugurated what would prove to be the bloodiest two years of fighting. The test of battlefield attrition would continue, pitting increasingly impatient and dispirited U.S. troops against a stubborn Northern army once again commanded by Giap and a determined people with a remarkable capacity to "perceive victory in a retreat" (as one North Vietnamese doctor serving in the South put it).[40]

In the United States Tet shocked an already weakened Johnson administration. The administration had invited trouble by launching in late 1967 a publicity campaign intended to shore up support. Westmoreland had returned stateside to announce "a light at the end of the tunnel." Not only did Tet give the lie to this forced optimism but it also prompted Westmoreland to ask for another 200,000 troops with no assurances of breaking the enemy. Commentators spoke of a "credibility gap," and Johnson's advisers were cool to the request for more troops. A group of influential Johnson foreign policy consultants known collectively as the "wise men" told the president they no longer supported the war. Secretary of State Dean Rusk, the staunchest of cold warriors in Johnson's inner circle, called for peace talks. McNamara's successor as secretary of defense, Clark Clifford, opposed sending more troops and urged instead getting South Vietnamese forces to do better and do more. Presidential primaries revealed serious electoral discontent, with Senator Eugene McCarthy (D-Minn.) posing a direct challenge to Johnson in New Hampshire voting. The redoubtable Walter Cronkite, an icon of the TV news, looked into the camera and questioned the wisdom of continuing the conflict.

Finally, Tet dealt a body blow to Johnson himself. The difficulties that the president had himself foreseen in mid-1965 had all come to pass. The public had turned on him. Isolated in his White House bunker, Johnson had lost the popular acclaim and public political contact that was his life-blood. The military could not deliver as long as Saigon failed to exploit the opening created by U.S. operations. The war costs were pushing the federal budget into deficit, weakening the dollar internationally, and draining money and support from his Great Society programs. The loss of U.S. lives weighed heavily on the president. He had had vivid nightmares about the dangers facing American soldiers and fliers ("his boys"), and he monitored the casualty lists carefully, dolefully. His advisers were beginning to tell him to look for an exit from Vietnam. At the end of March Johnson announced that he would not run for reelection and instead concentrate on drawing Hanoi into a negotiated settlement. To get those talks started, he had at once to limit bombing of North Vietnam to the area just north of the seventeenth parallel dividing the two Vietnams. In May 1968 negotiations opened that brought U.S. and North Vietnamese representatives together in Paris along with their respective clients, the Saigon government and the NLF. But Hanoi's demand for a full and unconditional end to U.S. bombing frustrated Johnson's hopes for making progress toward a settlement in these four-sided talks.

Even as Johnson sought a way out, the political temperature at home continued to climb, with a distant war only one of a collection of divisive, emotional issues. Campuses were wracked by protests. Following the assassination of Martin Luther King Jr., outraged blacks torched inner cities across the country (including Washington). In the year before his murder King had taken a strong public stand against the war, while Senator Robert Kennedy (D-N.Y.) began tentatively exploiting the antiwar theme before also falling victim to an assassin's bullet. Johnson's heir apparent, Vice President Hubert Humphrey, won the Democratic Party presidential nomination at the Chicago convention, but Johnson would not let him appeal to the antiwar element within a deeply divided party. Outside the convention hall protesters provoked a police riot, televised to the nation and tailor-made for the law and order campaign of Republican nominee Richard Nixon. In late October, on the eve of the vote, Johnson sought to expedite talks by agreeing to Hanoi's demand for a full end to the bombing—but too late to help Humphrey. In a country now sharply polarized, Nixon won the

November election narrowly. The author of the war, exhausted, dishonored, and bitter, would retire to his beloved Texas Hill Country ranch. After suffering a massive heart attack, he would die in January 1973 just as his successor finally managed to end the U.S. phase of the fighting.

EXHAUSTION AND PEACE

By 1968 a war that neither side had wanted had become the war that neither side could escape. Hanoi and Washington continued to exchange blows for another four years like a pair of punch-drunk fighters, each straining for a knockout but each steadily weakening. Finally in January 1973 they had had enough and reached an agreement that ended the direct U.S. combat role in the war but left a well-armed Saigon government in place. Another two and a half years would pass before the outcome that Washington feared and Hanoi dreamed about: the fall of South Vietnam to the North.

Nixon had good reasons for getting the war out of the way. He faced on the battlefield a stalemate humiliating to the world's mightiest military. Outsiders could not secure by themselves what indigenous forces could not help provide—political vision, social sacrifice, and ultimately a modicum of territorial administration and security. Paradoxically, by making up what the client lacked and by exercising vigilant supervision outsiders made local nonperformance all the more likely. The fighting would continue to consume lives and resources, poison U.S. political life, and sow foreign policy discord. The war was, moreover, an obstacle and a distraction to realizing Nixon's vision for a new U.S. foreign policy. He had accumulated an unusual level of foreign policy insight during the 1950s as Eisenhower's vice president and during the 1960s as he prepared for a second try at the presidency after his defeat by Kennedy. He was determined to set aside orthodox notions of the Cold War as a test between good and evil in which diplomacy constituted surrender. He wanted instead to seek détente with the Soviet Union and to explore opening relations with China.

But the Vietnam War hogtied Nixon from the moment he stepped into the Oval Office. He was constrained by the rigid anticommunism that had been a feature of his worldview going back to the late 1940s. The anticommunist consensus had pushed Nixon to argue strongly within the Eisenhower administration for shoring up the faltering French in 1953 and 1954 on the grounds that the fall of Indochina would topple dominoes within the region and beyond. After Geneva, Nixon had warmly supported Diem. And he continued to press through the Kennedy and Johnson years for a resolute stand in South Vietnam. He was now ironically saddled with a failed war policy that he himself had supported and that Democrats had shaped to fend off attacks by the likes of himself.

Nixon faced an additional problem: admitting defeat was difficult. He had demonstrated early in his political career a ruthlessness in dealing with those insufficiently anticommunist. How could he himself now engage in serious give and take with the old enemy? He moreover feared what it might mean for the United States to seem "a pitiful helpless giant" (as he phrased it in a 1970 speech). The commitments of a panicked America full of self-doubt would become suspect, its leadership questioned, and its security compromised. He insisted to his aides that he would not be the "first president to lose a war." He rejected "an elegant bug-out." He wanted instead "a peace we can be proud of." His principal foreign policy adviser, Henry Kissinger, explained on the eve of entering the White House why Vietnam remained an important test: "However fashionable it is to ridicule the terms 'credibility' or 'prestige,' they are not empty phrases; other nations can gear their actions to ours only if they can count on our steadiness." This Harvard professor with roots in an Old World tradition of statecraft and a New World determination to make his name was equally against cutting and running.[41]

What emerged during Nixon's first year in the White House was a three-pronged strategy to produce a negotiated, orderly American disengagement while preserving South Vietnam as a noncommunist entity. Nixon's exit strategy gave primacy to building up Saigon's army so that it would be able to hold Hanoi's forces at bay and allow American troops to withdraw. This policy of Vietnamization had first emerged as part of the Johnson administration's post-Tet reappraisal. Nixon made the policy his own in the form of what came to be called the Nixon doctrine. In the course of 1968 South Vietnam's army had already grown from 685,000 to 801,000. The next year it surpassed 1 million. A massive arms infusion made it one of the best-equipped armies in the world backed by a substantial air force (the world's fourth largest by 1973). This buildup provided the justification for a steady U.S. troop pullout. Nixon entered office with 543,000 Americans in-country. In July 1969 the first batch came out, and others followed on a regular basis. By late 1971 U.S. forces were down to 175,000 even as the pressure mounted to train a rapidly expanding South Vietnamese force, introduce a new stock of U.S.-supplied weaponry, and help with rural pacification—all while maintaining a combat capability and a large support infrastructure.

Nixon also adopted Johnson's policy of negotiations as the second element in his exit strategy. The private meetings that had begun in Paris in the latter part of 1968 continued, and in August 1969 Kissinger began parallel but intermittent secret talks with a North Vietnamese delegation. To push Hanoi toward compromise, Nixon sought to make clear to Moscow and Beijing that progress on bilateral relations with the United States depended on Hanoi's taking a more accommodating stance in the Paris talks. If diplomatic pressure did not work, he calculated that occasional unleashing of the considerable military power at his disposal would induce Hanoi to be reasonable. He could punish Hanoi from the air and at points on the ground where it did not expect him to strike, and he could make Hanoi and its allies fearful of what this unpredictable leader with his finger playing nervously on the nuclear trigger might do. Nixon's dependence on this "madman strategy" grew as U.S. troop levels declined, Hanoi held firm, and the 1972 reelection campaign approached, with an unpopular war that the president had promised to end still in progress.

Pacifying the home front was the third and final part of Nixon's strategy. Public pressure to liquidate the war had grown intense by the time Nixon entered the White House. While a minority was outspoken in its criticism, the broader public response was to descend into a slough of despondency over a war gone bad and discomfort over the deep social divisions at home that the war was spawning. The new president had to win time so that he could strengthen Saigon and maneuver Hanoi into an acceptable deal. Nixon repeatedly invoked the backing of the "silent majority" of Americans—those "squares" who shared his patriotic values and insisted on victory even as they tired of the war. He reassured them with a steady drawdown in the U.S. combat presence. That trend meant not only fewer casualties but also fewer recruits to fill out the ranks. The institution of a draft lottery in 1970 helped deflate the antiwar movement, especially on college campuses. (The draft ended entirely in 1973.) To frustrate the most determined opponents of the war, Nixon followed Johnson in waging a largely covert campaign against prominent critics. Government agencies—the FBI, the National Security Agency, the CIA, the IRS, and military intelligence—spied upon, provoked, harassed, audited, entrapped, and slandered opponents. What subterfuge did not accomplish, taking dissidents into court might. Defending themselves against broad government charges consumed their attention and exhausted their funds.

To Nixon's considerable frustration and growing anger, a northern negotiating team headed by Xuan Thuy and supervised by Politburo member Le

Duc Tho refused to budge. Tho proved a formidable adversary sitting opposite Kissinger. Tho's early party career resembled that of the leader with whom he would work closely. Like Le Duan, he had been present at the creation of the party and became familiar with the insides of French prisons. During the French war he had become Le Duan's deputy in the southern operations. In 1963 he assumed oversight of the increasingly important policy toward the South. In managing the Paris talks, Tho had good reason to think time on his side. Nixon had begun unilaterally pulling out U.S. forces, and opinion polls and large and noisy demonstrations in late 1969 and 1970 indicated a continued decline in U.S. public support. The Communist leadership held firm to demands that American forces unilaterally withdraw and that the Thieu "puppet" regime make way for a coalition government.

But Le Duan and his senior colleagues labored under their own set of problems that made it difficult to sustain the war effort. The collapse of the NLF as a result of the Tet offensive forced North Vietnamese regulars in the South to bear the brunt of even more of the fighting. Heavy northern casualties created a steady demand for replacements, and increasingly recruits marched down the Ho Chi Minh Trail knowing that they were not likely to survive. They were (as the saying had it) "born in the north to die in the south." North Vietnam's population was by mid-1969 showing signs of war weariness. Draft dodging became more frequent, with children of senior party leaders using their family connections to stay out of harm's way, even escaping abroad to study. No less a headache were the growing tensions with Beijing. Chinese leaders were deeply suspicious of Hanoi's ties to Moscow. They worried about the prospect of a Soviet client on their doorstep, and they opposed Hanoi's decision in 1968 to open talks with Johnson as an expression of Soviet-style capitulation in the global revolutionary struggle. As an expression of disapproval, Chinese troops began leaving North Vietnam (a withdrawal they completed by July 1970). Vietnamese leaders countered with references to poor advice from Chinese military advisors during the French war and to the betrayal of Vietnamese interests at Geneva in 1954 and insisted that they would chart their own course. Pham Van Dong was clear on this point at a meeting with Mao Zedong in November 1968: "Ultimately, it is we who make the decisions based on the actual situation in Vietnam and on how we understand the rules of the war."[42]

Stubborn but weakened, Hanoi and Washington traded blows between 1969 and 1972 and grudgingly made the concessions necessary to a peace agreement. Nixon struck the first blow. In March 1969 he ordered a secret campaign of bombing in Cambodia. His targets were North Vietnamese supply lines and rest areas. (Conducted under the code name Menu, the campaign would continue until August 1973.) Nixon backed this move with tough talk: he professed limited patience and threatened unspecified action if Hanoi did not start making its own concessions. But Hanoi held firm, and Moscow and Beijing showed no signs of putting meaningful pressure on their ally. Moreover, the honeymoon Nixon had enjoyed on the home front came to an end. With peace talks going nowhere, antiwar demonstrators took to the streets in October and again in November 1969. The turnout was massive with the October event attracting a couple of million protesters in hundreds of cities.

In 1970 Nixon tried once more to push Hanoi toward concessions, but without result. In April he ordered U.S. forces backed by South Vietnamese troops into Cambodia. The objective was to deny the enemy a transport route and rest area—but also to convince Hanoi that Nixon the "madman" was ready to escalate the conflict in unpredictable ways. The invasion, which continued into June, proved disruptive but not permanently damaging, and Le Duan even interpreted it as a positive development. Nixon had helped to create an Indochina-wide revolutionary front that now included notably the Kampuchean (Cambodian) Communist Party, also known as the Khmer Rouge. The result was to spread thin an ever-diminishing U.S. force, deepen the difficulties facing Vietnamization, and intensify antiwar sentiment within U.S. society and the U.S. military.

Nixon did indeed face an eruption of antiwar activity whose intensity shook the White House. A hundred thousand protesters converged on Washington on 8 May, and 1–2 million students demonstrated around the country, closing hundreds of colleges. Fueling the anger was the death of four students after the Ohio National Guard fired into a crowd on the campus of Kent State University on 4 May 1970. The Cambodian operation intensified congressional pressure to end the war, cut funding, and limit presidential war-making power. In June the Senate repealed the Gulf of Tonkin resolution. The Senate was by then also contemplating measures to cut off funding for U.S. operations in Cambodia by 30 June and to withdraw all American forces from Vietnam by the end of 1971. This congressional activism threatened Nixon's ability to pursue his Vietnam strategy not to mention control foreign policy. The "imperial" powers of the presidency that McKinley had begun to accumulate were coming under threat.

Nixon was now ready to make his first major concession. Up to this point he had held to the Johnson position of linking any U.S. troop withdrawals to

North Vietnamese forces leaving South Vietnam. Through Kissinger, Nixon now indicated that he would accept a cease-fire in-place and the continued presence of Communist forces in the South even as Vietnamization went forward and U.S. troops pulled out. He thus effectively agreed to Hanoi's insistence on a unilateral U.S. withdrawal, leaving Saigon to face remaining Northern forces. But for Hanoi this concession was not enough. The Americans would have to abandon their puppet; the Thieu regime could not be a party to the postwar political process.

In the course of 1971 Nixon made his third try at pushing Hanoi toward terms that he could accept—and he endured his third failure. In February Nixon made another of his unexpected moves on the battlefield, this time to demonstrate how Vietnamization had made South Vietnam's army a more effective force. Two of its best divisions, backed by heavy U.S. air, artillery, and logistical support, advanced into southern Laos with the aim of disrupting the Ho Chi Minh Trail. By April the North Vietnamese army had routed them. Nixon fulminated in private that he would not "go out whimpering." He swore, "We're gonna hit 'em, bomb the livin' bejesus out of 'em." This first real test of Vietnamization had proved a disaster. Saigon government forces were still beset by corruption, poor leadership, and low morale. Meanwhile U.S. popular support continued to decline. Polls that year revealed that 71 percent of Americans believed getting involved in Vietnam had been a mistake, and 65 percent pronounced the war effort "morally wrong." Bombing was unlikely to break the negotiations logjam. Hanoi was still adamant on the removal of the Thieu government, and that was a concession Nixon was not prepared to make.[43]

It was finally Hanoi's turn to apply pressure. In late March 1972 party leaders set in motion a major offensive to break the southern army. Hanoi threw virtually all its combat resources into the assault (fourteen divisions and twenty-six independent regiments, leaving only a training division in Hanoi and two divisions in Laos in reserve). Northern units attacked at four separate points: across the demilitarized zone, toward Hue, across the Central Highlands, and toward Saigon. With only about 50,000 U.S. troops still in Vietnam, the prospects for success looked bright. Instead the offensive turned into a costly defeat. Giap's failure to concentrate his force and to launch all the attacks simultaneously allowed Saigon's army to brace for the onslaught and deal with it piecemeal. Finally, northern forces were not yet skilled in combined armor-artillery-infantry operations, so the attacks were not well coordinated.

The offensive had agitated the president, prompting loose talk of using nuclear weapons. He vowed "for once we've got to use the maximum power of this country against a shit-asshole country to win the war."[44] To help turn back the enemy attack, Nixon ordered American bombers into action in April and then intensified the attack in Operation Linebacker I, which lasted from May to October. In some of the most intense bombing of the war, U.S. aircraft (including B-52 bombers from Guam and Thailand) not only hammered exposed northern units but also hit Hanoi and mined the usually busy Haiphong harbor. Much of the reconstruction in the North made possible by the bombing restrictions Johnson had imposed in 1968 was turned to rubble.

Finally, the leaders in Hanoi blinked and agreed to a concession. At the Paris talks in August, Le Duc Tho dropped demands for Thieu's removal even while insisting upon U.S. war reparations to speed reconstruction. The calculations behind this concession were complex. The offensive had failed to break the stalemate. "We have not yet established [battlefield] predominance over the enemy." Moreover, Nixon seemed particularly vulnerable with the approach of the election. Now was the time to exploit the "sharp contradictions between the U.S. people and Nixon, and between the Republican Party and the Democratic Party regarding the Vietnam problem." With American forces finally out of the way, Hanoi would find it easier to eliminate the Saigon puppets.[45]

Perhaps most important of all, leaders in Hanoi had begun to worry that their allies might apply pressure for another compromise settlement as they had at Geneva in 1954. While Mao came to accept the wisdom of his ally's 1968 decision to open negotiations with the United States, he also made a decision to open his own diplomatic line to Washington. Nixon's visit to China earlier in the year (February 1972) signaled a shift in China's policy. Also roiling the relationship was Beijing's resentment about Soviet influence over the Vietnamese Communists and rivalry over predominance in Cambodia, whose Communists sought Chinese patronage to offset longtime Vietnamese dominance. Nixon's diplomatic overtures to Moscow were also creating problems. In May, even as U.S. bombers pummeled the North in retaliation for the spring offensive, the Brezhnev leadership went ahead with plans to host a summit meeting with Nixon and in the process revealed the importance it attached to détente. Workaday tensions in the relationship with the Vietnamese made the shift in Soviet policy easier. Despite aid contributions that had come to equal Chinese support, Soviet representatives complained that the Vietnamese were prickly, mistrustful, secretive, and single-minded in their preoccupation with their war.

A Long War with Many Fronts

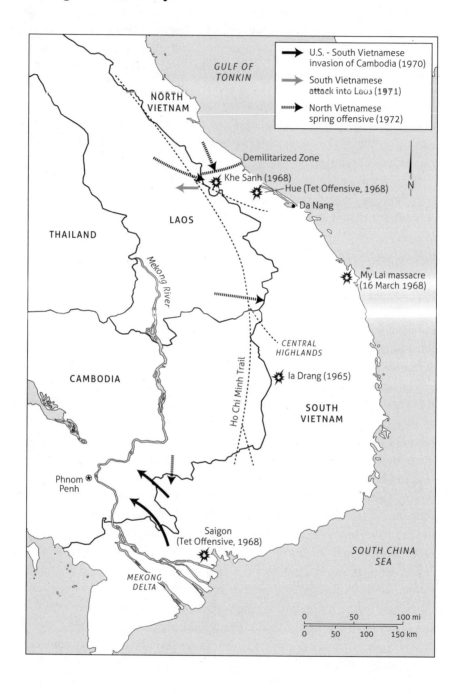

With the Thieu issue resolved, the U.S. and North Vietnamese delegations meeting secretly in Paris were able to produce in October a draft peace agreement incorporating the key concessions made by the two sides. Washington would get its POWs back as soon as it completed a total troop withdrawal, while Hanoi and Saigon troops would effect a cease-fire in-place. To facilitate a peaceful resolution of the differences among Vietnamese after the cease-fire, the agreement created a tripartite electoral commission consisting of the Saigon regime, the NLF-sponsored Provisional Revolutionary Government, and representatives from neutral countries. Responding to the breakthrough, Nixon ended the Linebacker I bombing campaign and kept air strikes below the twentieth parallel.

Rather than lead to a quick peace, the October agreement immediately hit a roadblock in Saigon. Thieu withheld his endorsement. He objected vehemently to a deal that Kissinger and Le Duc Tho had negotiated behind his back and that would likely set the stage for a Communist political or military takeover of his country. He was adamant that all northern forces leave, and he rejected the NLF as a legitimate political player in the postwar peace process. Thieu, who had placed obstacles in the way when Johnson had sought to get talks going in 1968, was now making trouble for Nixon.

Kissinger flew to Saigon but failed to change Thieu's mind. Nixon himself tried to assuage Thieu's sense of betrayal, offering assurances of continued assistance and "swift and severe retaliatory reaction" to any act of aggression by Hanoi. But he also warned in increasingly sharp language that a failure to cooperate now would further fray on the home front already tattered popular and congressional goodwill, on which Thieu's country depended. Privately Nixon and Kissinger admitted that they had placed the Saigon government in an exposed position that would likely lead to its collapse. Nixon rationalized this outcome in his typically crude way: "We cannot keep this child sucking at the tit when the child is four years old."

(opposite)
The struggle for South Vietnam, 1959–1972. Each region and each year had its own story. Critical to Hanoi was creating and expanding the supply line to the South known as the Ho Chi Minh Trail, building up NLF strength from 1960 onward (heavily spent down during the 1968 Tet offensive), and raising the offensive capability of northern forces (first tested in spring 1972). Washington countered first by dramatically raising U.S. troop levels between 1965 and 1967 and then trying to score a breakthrough during the Nixon years with incursions into Cambodia in 1970, into Laos in 1971, and by intense bombing all across Indochina.

But he also did not want a blowup with Saigon to become an election issue, even though his reelection prospects were bright against the strongly anti-war Democratic challenger, George McGovern.[46]

Neither assurances nor threats swayed Thieu, so Nixon turned to Hanoi, demanding a long list of concessions that might make the agreement more palatable in Saigon while demonstrating his own toughness as a negotiator. Le Duc Tho angrily refused. Boxed in by unyielding Vietnamese—ally as well as enemy—Nixon went into madman mode one last time. He ordered air strikes against Hanoi. The bombing between 18 and 29 December (code-named Linebacker II but popularly referred to as the Christmas bombing) was the heaviest of the war, indeed the heaviest in the history of warfare. The price for this exercise in muscle-flexing was the loss of fifteen strategic B-52 bombers along with other aircraft, a groundswell of domestic and international condemnation, and several thousand civilian deaths.[47]

In January the foes returned to the negotiating table to accept a settlement that was in essence the same as the one formulated in October. This time Nixon browbeat Thieu into accepting the accord. On 27 January representatives of Washington, Saigon, Hanoi, and the NLF's provisional government gathered in Paris to sign the final agreement. Nixon followed up on 1 February with a secret pledge to Hanoi of aid in the range of $3.25 billion. This payment served, depending on one's point of view, as war reparations or as an inducement for Hanoi to play nice with the Thieu regime.

Mutual exhaustion had paved the way for peace. By the time Americans and Vietnamese released their death grip on each other, the war had inflicted incredible damage. Taken by itself, the period between Nixon's inauguration and the January 1973 peace accords saw almost half a million northern and NLF soldiers die, accompanied to the grave by over 100,000 South Vietnamese combatants. Americans had paid for four more years of fighting with the death of nearly 21,000 of their troops and with the accentuation of already deep social divisions and political bitterness. The strains of fighting a war emptied of meaning inflicted on the U.S. Army between 1970 and 1972 what one military historian has characterized as "a collective nervous breakdown." Morale, discipline, and combat effectiveness all hit the skids.[48]

The war was on the verge of destroying another presidency. Trapped in the Vietnam maze, the Nixon White House had grown more and more isolated and paranoid. Nixon saw himself as a strong leader required by a U.S. public that was in general "like helpless children."[49] He bristled at anyone who got in his way and met opposition with intrigue and deception. He blamed his mounting troubles on the "liberal" (but in fact mainstream) media, Jews, blacks, Democratic loyalists, an unreliable bureaucracy, and a spineless eastern establishment, and he unleashed his secret operatives ("the plumbers") to get the dirt on his enemies. Their burglary of Democratic Party offices in the Watergate complex in June 1972 and the subsequent White House attempt at a cover-up became a national scandal. By early 1973 (in the immediate aftermath of the Vietnam peace agreement) scrutiny from Congress and the media distracted Nixon from shoring up his fragile Vietnamese client.

An accidental president handled the final phase of the Vietnam conflict. When the scandal-plagued vice president Spiro Agnew resigned in October 1973, Nixon appointed House Minority Leader Gerald Ford (R-Mich.) to succeed him. Less than a year later, in August 1974, Nixon resigned under threat of congressional impeachment, and Ford stepped into the Oval Office with Kissinger, still secretary of state, at his side. They had little room for maneuver in the face of intense public aversion to continued involvement in Vietnam and a rising congressional impulse to curtail presidential powers. In May 1973, when the Cambodia bombing became public, Congress had intervened to cut operations off. In November the passage of the War Powers Act required of the president a prompt accounting for the use of U.S. forces abroad.

On paper at least, the prospects for Thieu's U.S.-trained and equipped army looked promising. U.S. aid had continued after the Paris settlement. It totaled $3.3 billion in 1973 and 1974; an additional $1 billion took the form of equipment transferred from late 1972 to 1973. This aid created a major military machine with the world's fourth-largest army and air force.[50] But Congress was tiring of its role as paymaster. A vote in September 1974 cut aid for the next year in half (from $1.4 billion to $700 million). Adding to Saigon's difficulties, the economy suffered from high inflation and widespread unemployment. Food was in short supply. The social disruption caused by the war and continuing hardship gave rise to pervasive social unrest. Urban centers, swollen with refugees from the devastated countryside, were deeply infected by war weariness. The songs of Trinh Cong Son, a draft dodger, conveyed a fatigue and fatalism that proved popular among a broad swathe of the population despite the efforts of government censors. After the bloodshed of the Tet Offensive, he had asked with characteristic sadness: "Which corpse is my love / Lying in that trench, / In the burning fields, / Among those potato vines?" Presiding over this dispirited society was a regime riddled with corruption, suffering from low morale, hobbled by factionalism and mistrust at the top, and habituated to the Americans' carrying the war. Looking back, Vice President Ky recognized the disabling dependence on outsiders: "Thieu always worried about America. He believed that the Americans could do everything."[51]

In contrast, North Vietnam's army was formidable. It had corrected the problems that had hobbled its 1972 offensive, recovered from its losses, and raised manpower to 400,000. From the Defense Ministry in Hanoi, Giap oversaw the planning over the course of 1974 for a fresh offensive under the command of Van Tien Dung. The leaders at the top were increasingly confident that "the Americans would not come back even if you offered them candy" (as Pham Van Dong joked in December). Addressing his troops, Dung recited a snatch of verse to remind them of the long struggle that they could bring to consummation. "For thirty years our land has taken up the gun, yet still the disk of our moon is split in two." In early March 1975 those troops set about ending that division in an offensive emphasizing flexibility, speed, and surprise. By attempting to defend all his scattered strong points, Thieu had put himself in a passive position and vulnerable to piecemeal defeat. The first North Vietnamese thrust—across the Central Highlands— panicked Saigon forces, and additional northern units pushed across the seventeenth parallel to link up with the leading attack force. With the Saigon government thrown into confusion and already fragile morale cracking, the southern defense quickly fell—Hue on 28 March, Danang two days later, and Saigon one month later. After fifty-five days the spring offensive named in Ho Chi Minh's honor had brought to a sudden end a war that the strategists in Hanoi had expected would last well into the next year.[52]

As Hanoi's forces closed in around Saigon in April, Nixon's earlier assurances of support proved empty. Kissinger still worried that the fall of a dependent would undermine U.S. credibility and prestige. But Congress made clear that it was pointless to provide more aid to a failed army, and 78 percent of the public agreed. As a result, President Ford would not approve any last-minute bombing campaign or even emergency supplies, and he failed to give high priority to an orderly evacuation of Vietnamese now in danger because of their collaboration with the United States. In the disorganized scramble to get out, many struggled for a place on overcrowded helicopters and small boats. As the Saigon debacle moved to a conclusion, Ford proclaimed emphatically in lines he had inserted himself into a speech in New Orleans that Vietnam was "a war that is finished as far as America is concerned." His largely college audience voiced approval.[53]

PAINFUL LEGACIES OF A LONG WAR

Not surprisingly, Vietnam's long colonial war against the French and then the Americans had profound, enduring effects. Americans had to come to terms with a resounding defeat. That lost war hovered in the American consciousness, much misunderstood and always discordant. The end of the fighting confronted a shaken, decimated, and impoverished Vietnam with a tricky set of postcolonial challenges. Vietnamese would have to rebuild, but the question of what blueprint to follow was only gradually resolved. Even the bystanders, Cambodia and Laos, would eventually suffer severe collateral damage. The war's legacy was perhaps heaviest of all for Cambodia, culminating in a catastrophic reign of brutality and death.

For Americans, the fact of defeat was demoralizing in multiple ways. In broad, popular terms, the depressing outcome challenged a national mythology that incorporated righteous violence as a central strand, took victory as confirmation of national virtue, and celebrated the international rewards and respect that went with military success. Defeat also traumatized a generation of military leaders. Their weaponry, which could pulverize southern Vietnam and pound the northern part at will, could not deliver victory, and their institution had in the attempt suffered serious damage. The officer corps thus carried into the postwar a determination to avoid another war of pointless sacrifice. Policymakers for their part had one after another fallen prey to the siren call of intervention in Vietnam and then failed to cut their losses once disaster was staring them in the face. This double failure—of policy and arms—threw the American state into crisis. The consensus that had united the foreign policy public and supplied the public's understanding of the Cold War cracked; the imperial president came under congressional assault; and public trust in elected officials and by extension in the democratic process plummeted. Instead of triumph and vindication, Americans had suffered a stunning loss of reputation as an enlightened international leader. Through the late 1960s critics around the world had accused Washington of folly at best and criminal misconduct at worst. Allies became alienated while antipathy deepened in the third world. Vietnam left Americans as isolated internationally as they had been at any time in recent memory.

Along with pervasive demoralization went an almost studied and certainly dysfunctional determination to avoid a searching consideration of what had gone wrong. Why was victory so far beyond the reach of American forces and why in the first place had Americans taken on a task so far beyond their means? These questions were a potentially rich source of lessons and of insights. But Americans managed to evade a critical post-mortem mainly by writing the Vietnamese out of the story. A war remembered only in terms of one side is more a nationalist psychodrama than an instructive history.

Veterans suggested one way of sidestepping the hard questions. Beginning in the late 1970s, they broke the willed national amnesia about Vietnam by telling their personal stories. While those accounts were often haunted by the peripheral presence of Vietnamese, the American warriors held center stage. Tales of soldiering proved attractive to Hollywood as well as to the reading public. A string of films appearing from the late 1970s to the 1990s celebrated the toughness, courage, and sacrifice of a generation of ordinary Americans caught in a dirty war. The memorials to the war that began to appear in the 1980s, largely on the initiative of veterans, kept the focus on the travails of citizen-soldiers. They were, according to President Ronald Reagan in a Veterans Day speech, "gentle heroes" who had fought for "a noble cause."[54]

The debate over how to properly depict the soldiers' travails proved revealingly controversial. The nature of this war ruled out the stirring heroic images and patriotic celebration familiar from representations of earlier conflicts, epitomized by the tribute to the marines who took Iwo Jima during the Pacific War. The most notable of the Vietnam memorials, standing at the very heart of official American memory—on the National Mall in Washington—took a fresh direction with its stark, abstract qualities. Critics demanded a more conventional, representational rendering of the war. What they got in monuments both on the Mall and at sites across the country was not heroic but rather strikingly grim images (much like Hollywood's) of soldiers beset by danger, clinging to their wounded comrades, and anxiously scanning the sky for rescue.

The theme of victimization took especially fervent form in claims that Americans missing in action (MIA) were still held in cruel captivity by treacherous communists abetted by duplicitous U.S. officials. The National League of Families of American Prisoners and Missing in Southeast Asia was the vocal champion of this view. Consisting mainly of angry, frustrated parents and siblings of MIAs, the league demanded a "full accounting" for their loved ones. Though logic and evidence was against them, they clung to their position sustained by revenge fantasies, conspiracy theories, and political and popular sympathy. Even though the incidence of the missing during the Vietnam War was but a quarter of that for World War II and the Korean War (in real numbers at most some 2,500 men), MIAs proved a volatile symbol in a country suffering from wounded national pride. A 1991 survey revealed the popular sympathy for the league's view. Two-thirds believed U.S. combatants were still held hostage in Indochina, and half were convinced their government was doing little to save them. Little wonder *Rambo* proved such a popular film, with its boldly developed themes of rescue and revenge. The league's widely accepted charges of betrayal intimidated a succession of administrations from Nixon onward and obstructed steps toward diplomatic ties with Vietnam. Only as the search for remains got under way in the mid-1980s and the list of missing fell by a third could leaders in Hanoi and Washington move gingerly toward better relations. Even so, full diplomatic relations did not come until 1995. By then export-oriented corporations and veterans seeking closure had offset league opposition and given cover to President Bill Clinton's decision to turn the page, at least diplomatically.[55]

Career army officers seeking to redeem the lost war by drawing practical lessons from it found an alternative way to avoid hard questions. In constructing military might-have-beens, these revisionists have mixed selected pieces of evidence to suggest that victory was in the American grasp. A sophisticated counterinsurgency strategy, according to one version, would have served better than a strategy of attrition at securing control of the countryside and bringing an effective end to the guerrilla threat to the South Vietnamese government. An alternative angle suggests that a more robust use of military power—heavy bombing of North Vietnam at the very outset of the war or greater conventional military pressure along the seventeenth parallel and the Ho Chi Minh Trail—would have stopped Hanoi. A better decision-making process is the focus of a third point of view encapsulated in the prudential rules laid down by Secretary of Defense Caspar Weinberger and by Colin Powell while head of the Joint Chiefs of Staff. Had civilian leaders weighed their choices more deliberately and listened more carefully to military leaders, and had military leaders spoken more forthrightly, then the war effort would have had a far higher chance of success. Tellingly, while military intellectuals debated the lessons of the past, practical military planning simply ignored Vietnam and prepared for a conventional war fought by high-tech, mobile U.S. forces.[56]

Finally, Americans preoccupied with recuperating nationalist fervor and presidential power have tried their hand at making the war retrospectively right by identifying scapegoats on whom to place responsibility for defeat. Participants in this blame game have demonstrated striking enterprise in finding weak points in the American war effort: a defeatist media, pusillanimous political leaders, a traitorous antiwar movement, or even a soft and self-absorbed public. The usual remedy applied by those who drew up this inventory of U.S. defects has been to give the president more power to start and wage wars. To that end, the White House had to control the media and head off defeatist reporting, to extol the virtues of a professional military (free from the bother of citizen-soldiers), and to vilify dissent as weak kneed and unpatriotic. The prescription of restored presidential authority and martial national pride makes sense so long as it ignores the role of the Vietnamese. But would a more authoritarian, militaristic America plagued by fewer doubts and less division have overcome the Vietnamese advantages? The remedies these scapegoat theories have suggested are as unsound as the history supporting them is dangerously ethnocentric, not to mention willfully tendentious.

These various ways of dealing with the Vietnam War have replicated the fatal flaw inherent in the U.S. decision for war and in its conduct. They erased the Vietnamese from the picture or at best gave them bit parts in an American drama. This meant expunging a half century and more of nationalist ferment, rural tensions, and Communist organizing that taken together had created the formidable obstacle facing U.S. forces and U.S. ambitions. None has grappled seriously with a war in which Vietnamese fought with greater determination than Americans could ever muster, got backing from allies far more helpful than the Americans could find, and developed popular engagement in villages and cities in which even the best-intentioned Americans would remain outsiders. How exactly would counterinsurgency, more decisive use of conventional military power, better decision making, or a stronger president have overcome the range of advantages on the side of the Vietnamese revolution? Neglecting the enemy and for that matter the U.S.-aligned Vietnamese is an odd approach for making sense of any war. It has led to poorly drawn lessons. It has kept the price paid overwhelmingly by Vietnamese soldiers and civilians out of the postwar American consciousness. And it has helped to obscure the imperial dimensions of the conflict. Americans had sought to impose their will on Vietnam as a territory and a people, applying the full range of tools at their disposal—and failed. The age of empire was over in Asia, but someone forgot to tell the U.S. public and the policy establishment. Americans looking back have still not absorbed the message.

While Americans wrestled with how to make the Vietnam War come out right at least as they replayed it in their minds, the Vietnamese got on with their revolution. They had absorbed staggering losses buoyed by confidence in the righteousness of their cause and the inevitability of their victory. From the run-up to the American war to April 1975, some 3.3 million had died, most of them civilians (approximately 2 million). Another 1.5 million were wounded or missing, and 2 million suffered from exposure to chemicals, notably Agent Orange. When victory finally came, the Vietnamese, unlike the Americans, had no postmortems to conduct or regrets to express. Le Duan's victory speech in Hanoi emphasized the sense of national triumph and gratification: "In the four thousand years of our nation's history, the last hundred years were the hardest and fiercest period of struggle against foreign aggression, but they were at the same time the period of our most glorious victories." Some two decades later Giap conceded in a meeting with Robert McNamara that the war might have been a tragedy for the United States, but for Vietnam it had been "a noble cause" for which "our people sacrificed tremendously." The Americans, not the Vietnamese, needed to reflect and draw lessons.[57]

The myth of the just struggle against the Americans as well as the French would dominate public memory, promoted by the party-state's control of cultural life and unblemished by any of the misgivings about the war that weigh on American memory. In war museums and memorials Vietnamese have depicted their sacrifice in ways dramatically divergent from the Americans. The message repeatedly conveyed is of community solidarity, popular defiance, and courage in a heroic if costly patriotic war. To be sure, Vietnamese veterans would eventually challenge the neat, simple official version of the war. Bao Ninh was one of those voices. His powerful novel *The Sorrow of War* summoned up a vision of "barbarous fighting," of "broken bodies, bodies blown apart, bodies vaporised," of veterans with "horrible, poisonous nightmares," of a peace that was "painful, bitter and sad," of the triumph of justice but also "cruelty, death and inhuman violence." While he and other veterans set the propriety of their struggle beyond question, they also wanted room in the heroic version of the war for the personal suffering, sacrifice, and disillusionment of their generation and attention paid to the difficult postwar adjustment that they had had to endure.

Most Vietnamese could not afford to linger on the past either in triumph or in anguish. They faced the immediate challenge of overcoming massive death and destruction inflicted over some three decades of conflict. The fighting had left many maimed. Combatants and noncombatants alike — on the order of several million — suffered from the widespread wartime application of herbicide through either direct environmental exposure or genetic transmission. Political passions and the violence they inspired had

At Last a Reckoning

Monument at the My Lai memorial, Son My village, Quang Ngai province. The central figure of a woman with a dead child in her arms and other victims at her feet conveys grief for the hundreds killed by U.S. forces. But this statue at the site of the 1968 massacre also signifies the militant defiance and mutual support so prominently featured in the orthodox version of the anti-U.S. war sponsored by the Vietnamese state. (Photograph by Sandy Pham)

Vietnam Veterans Memorial, Washington, D.C. Maya Lin, while still a Yale undergraduate, won the design competition with a proposal that avoided conventional
patriotic references to a war most Americans had come to regard as a mistake. Instead,
the names of the individual dead marched in row after row across dark marble slabs at
eye level. Here, as Lin's proposal described it, was "a quiet place, meant for personal
reflection and private reckoning." This invitation to connect personally with the fallen
has attracted many visitors and personal tributes placed at the base of the memorial.
(Courtesy of Prints and Photographs Division, Library of Congress)

disrupted families and divided communities. Some on the Saigon side had fled abroad as the war ended; many ethnic Chinese followed during a time of Sino-Vietnamese tension in 1979–80. There was no bloodbath in Vietnam (as many U.S. supporters of the war had predicted), but the flight of the boat people and the rounding up of Saigon loyalists for long-term "reeducation" in prison-like camps under harsh conditions revealed the serious tensions left for resolution in the postwar. Those setting about building their lives and communities did so in what had become one of the poorest countries in the world. Vietnam's overall income per person had stayed essentially flat for decades while growth rates in much of the rest of eastern Asia had shot upward.

Finding a way out of poverty led Vietnamese in time into a psychodrama quite different from the one Americans contended with. For leaders in Hanoi the war was over but the revolution in whose name they had fought and demanded sacrifice still gripped their imagination. Territorial unity was not the culmination of the revolution. The postwar task as Le Duan and others who had risen with Ho Chi Minh understood it was to create a modern, socialist nation dominated politically, economically, and culturally by the Communist Party. A generation that had directed the decades-long war effort now wanted to mobilize the public in a fresh struggle. They wanted to expunge the deep imprint of the French and Americans on the South and to remake southern society, politics, and economy with the socialist North serving as the template. Vietnamese could at last realize Ho's dream (as he had put it in 1969 at the end of his life): "The American invaders defeated, we will rebuild our land ten times more beautiful."[58]

This confident vision of the future quickly proved wanting in what was to prove a troubled peace. The attempt to recast the South in the northern image miscarried. Hanoi's handling of political unification alienated southerners who had accepted wartime promises of postwar autonomy for their region. The detention of the defeated Saigon elite (up to 300,000 former government officials, military officers, and U.S. employees) alienated and eliminated a talented group from the reconstruction effort. Highlanders, who during the war had suffered displacement and heavy loss of life (somewhere in the range of a third of their population), found promises of autonomy betrayed by a policy of forced assimilation and the official promotion of Vietnamese settlements. The Central Highlands simmered with anger and spasms of violence. Finally, a socialist economy imposed on the South in 1978 proved a poor fit for a region with a history of strong entrepreneurship and vigorous foreign trade and an independent and land-hungry peasantry. Steps to abolish private enterprise, nationalize industry, and impose central planning led to plunging production in the southern countryside as well as in the city. Peasants resisted collectivized agriculture, sabotaging crops and killing livestock. By 1979 Vietnam's economy was suffering from food shortages, collapsing agricultural collectives, high unemployment, and the flight of merchants and entrepreneurs of Chinese descent. International tensions aggravated an already difficult situation. Military intervention in Cambodia to oust the Pol Pot regime was followed by a limited Chinese invasion which had the country back on a war footing by early 1979. An embattled leadership in Hanoi clung to the Soviet Union as a source of economic assistance and as a counterweight to a jealous China and a vengeful United States.

By the mid-1980s a new and younger party leadership directed reconstruction along fresh and ultimately fruitful lines. Nguyen Van Linh's election to head the party in 1986 marked the beginning of the real postwar. He brought to his tenure as party general secretary (a post he held until 1991) a fresh perspective based on his long experience working for the party in the South during the war and immediately after, when he had resisted Hanoi's rigidly orthodox postwar economic policies. Once party leader, Linh adopted economic reforms known as *doi moi* (literally, renovation) that gradually put less reliance on state planning and more on market forces. Vietnam's economic performance improved dramatically. At the same time cultural and political life became more open (though still firmly under party supervision). Linh subordinated foreign policy to his domestic reform agenda. He ended the costly involvement in Cambodia, reached an accommodation with China, and improved relations with the United States as well as his neighbors. Linh's policies marked the consummation of the Vietnamese revolution. After roughly a century of struggle the country was not just independent and united but also at peace and increasingly prosperous (if not actually socialist).

Cambodia began a bystander to the Vietnam War and ended up unexpectedly its leading victim, with the worst consequences in the postwar period. While the principals in the conflict called it quits in 1975, Cambodia was by then heading into one of the more horrific genocidal spasms in a century distinguished for mass, systematic killing. The Vietnam War did much to make this genocide possible, and thus Cambodia's ordeal has to be counted among the major legacies (and moral costs) of the war.

In the early 1960s Cambodia began to feel the effects of the escalating war next door. Hanoi was the first to encroach, using eastern Cambodian territory for supply lines supporting the NLF and then for sanctuary for northern units operating in the South. The U.S. response was initially low key, limited to covert operations and "hot pursuit" by U.S. forces across the border. To insulate Cambodia from deeper involvement, its ruler, Prince Norodom Sihanouk, sought to maintain the appearance of neutrality. Hanoi and Beijing expressed their appreciation of his quiet acceptance of a North Vietnamese military presence by putting a leash on his domestic foe, the Cambodian Communist Party. Nixon's decision in March 1969 to begin bombing brought the full fury of modern warfare to the Cambodian countryside—and accelerated the downward spiral into catastrophic violence. In March 1970 even the pretense of neutrality fell by the wayside when Lon Nol, one of Sihanouk's anticommunist generals, seized power confident of U.S. backing. Nixon at once exploited this promising development by ordering support for Lon Nol's government and an attack against sanctuaries in Cambodia used by North Vietnamese forces and the NLF. Hanoi and Beijing responded by unleashing the Cambodian Communists. Their forces went on the offensive, exploiting rural anger over the U.S. bombing to win popular support. In 1975, shortly before the fall of Saigon, the Khmer Rouge seized the capital, Phnom Penh.

The stage was now set for genocide. Pol Pot, the party leader, dreamed of building a new society inspired by a rural utopian strain of Marxism. But he was also in the grip of a nationalist xenophobia that told him alien forces would seek to undermine the revolution. The new regime moved quickly to head off any challenge. It targeted privileged urbanites tainted by foreign influences, Vietnamese residents who symbolized the long-term threat from a historical enemy, Communist Party leaders suspected of ties to Hanoi, and ethnic groups that resisted integration into the new society. Already before the Communist takeover, some half million had died in the fighting; under Khmer Rouge rule between 1975 and 1978 at least another 1.5 million Cambodians would die from disease, overwork, starvation, and executions. In less than a decade Cambodia lost at least a fifth of its 8 million people.

The nightmare began to end in late 1978 with Hanoi's decision to overthrow Pol Pot. This decision followed a long string of provocations, including the persecution of Vietnamese in Cambodia, cross-border attacks into disputed territory, and a close alignment with China against Vietnam. Vietnamese units accompanied by Cambodian Communist defectors swept the Pol Pot regime from power and put one of those defectors, Hun Sen, in charge. But to keep him there Vietnamese troops had to remain in occupation and contain an anti-Vietnamese coalition that included the remnants of Pol Pot's forces and that enjoyed the backing of Beijing and Washington. (For both the Carter and the Reagan administrations the impulse to even the score with Vietnam overrode any aversion to a genocidal regime.) The Vietnamese occupation came to an end in 1989, followed in 1991 by a U.N.-sponsored process of disarmament, economic recovery, and national reconciliation with Hun Sen still the dominant political figure. After some three decades of fighting and upheaval including three deadly rounds of civil war, peace had at last come to Cambodia.

Laos, the smallest in population and economy of the Indochina states, may have been a backwater of the Vietnam War, but it, too, suffered massive destruction. Laotians had fallen to fighting each other during the last years of French control, and the warfare continued intermittently for twenty years. One by one outsiders got involved — the Soviets, the Chinese, the Thais but above all the North Vietnamese and the Americans. The fighting reached its greatest intensity from 1965 onward, especially in the eastern part of the country through which the Ho Chi Minh Trail ran. By the time peace came in early 1973, Laos had lost tens of thousands of combatants and even more civilians (a total perhaps in the range of a quarter of a million from a population of about 3 million). The land had been subjected to over 2 million tons of U.S. bombs (dropped from 1964 onward), considerable amounts dangerously unexploded. A cease-fire agreement in early 1973 not only brought an end to the largely covert U.S. presence but also opened the way to the consolidation of a pro-Hanoi Communist regime. Frightened Laotians, especially from the Hmong ethnic group that had fought with the French and then shifted allegiance to the Americans, fled the country. Those in Thai refugee camps faced pressure to return home and political resistance to acceptance in the United States. Ultimately some 200,000 were allowed entry. Hmong who stayed behind in Laos mounted some resistance and suffered brutal repression.[59]

The Americans who had sought to determine the future of Vietnam had had impressive advantages. Their advanced military technology, their logistical sophistication, and their lavish funding were all far beyond the capacity of their Vietnamese adversaries. The executive branch of the U.S. government was stronger than ever, with great latitude to make ambitious overseas commitments and with a wide array of tools to sustain any distant initiatives. The half century of foreign wars that had greatly enhanced presidential power had also rendered the Congress, the media, and the public deferential. Backed by the resources of an incomparably rich country, Washington could spend profligately to preserve its position in South Vietnam. Expenditures between Kennedy's arrival in the White House in 1961 and the fall of Saigon in 1975 came to $826.8 billion in 2001 dollars (twice the cost of the Korean War).

Those Americans suffered from one fatal flaw. They manifested colonial attitudes rooted in the previous century—a missionary confidence in the United States as a transformative force in the world and a conviction of cultural superiority over Asians seen as alternately barbaric and childlike. These attitudes had smoothed the way for Americans—politicians, the informed public, the military, and the media—into a war that no one particularly wanted. And once Vietnam became a new battle front in the quest for an informal Asian empire, what amounted to a fundamental misreading of the situation convinced them that they could not fail. They were blind to the way nationalism had over half a century captured the imagination of educated Vietnamese. They failed to see the legitimacy the Communist Party had won and effectively exploited to overwhelm its fragmented domestic opposition and wear down clueless if powerful Americans. They could scarcely imagine the way villages became long-term assets to the nationalist cause, nor could they devise a counter to the NLF's rural appeal. They did not reckon on the sacrifices that Hanoi's allies in Beijing and Moscow would make in sustaining the struggle. Perhaps most striking of all, American leaders put aside what they had learned in Korea—the unpopularity that a limited war could generate at home. In the end the faith of Americans in their own righteousness and the potency of their technology and material resources was not enough to avert defeat.

Just as the victory in the Philippines had set the U.S. imperial project in eastern Asia in motion, the defeat in Vietnam would mark its end. But this reverse did not in fact shake the basic convictions that had inspired the push into Asia in the first place. Americans continued to cherish a nationalism in which they saw themselves as world-shapers and denigrated or ignored anyone standing in their way. So Washington would embark on a new project in another seemingly troubled and vulnerable region. There, in a repeat of a familiar imperial scenario, Americans would seek to tame alien forces and reshape other societies. For all too familiar reasons, the new crusade in the Middle East was by the 1970s already well under way and would unfold along disturbingly familiar lines.

Conclusion

EMPIRE AND AFTERMATH

William McKinley's determination to take the Philippines set in motion an imperial project in eastern Asia that became one of the main facets of U.S. global policy. Control of this advanced outpost unleashed ambitions and nourished anxieties that entangled Americans more and more deeply in the affairs of countries all along the western periphery of the Pacific. At each strong point in their advance, Americans encountered resistance. They prevailed decisively by force of arms in the Philippines and later against Japan. But after these two successful expeditionary wars, American arms began to run into difficulties in Korea, and those difficulties were compounded in Vietnam. After some seven decades, the U.S. drive began to draw to a close.

These claims about a sustained, cumulative, and ultimately failed U.S. advance raise a set of fundamental questions. Is *empire* a label that fits the evidence presented in the four preceding chapters? Why did the U.S. project ultimately fail? How did eastern Asia fare in the wake of the U.S. retreat? And what insights regarding our current entanglement in the Middle East and Central Asia can be derived from the eastern Asia regional enterprise? We offer our own views on these points keenly aware that there is ample room and lots of good reasons for spirited debate given the practical significance and immediacy of the history treated here.

EARMARKS OF EMPIRE

From start to finish the U.S. undertaking was marked by features that most observers would automatically associate with empire were any other country under consideration. However exceptional their outlook, unique their methods, deep their hesitations, and intense their debates, Americans embraced empire in a prolonged, often violent struggle to control a wide swath of eastern Asia. The evidence for empire is plainly visible in the features identified in the historically based definition provided in the introduction. The American empire was at its most fundamental level about the command of territory. The Philippines, Japan, South Korea, and Vietnam all came under U.S. control by the exercise of military power. They remained in a subordinate position for periods ranging from seven years in the case of Japan to at least four decades for the Philippines.

Of these features, the regional context is the most easily overlooked Americans operated in a turbulent eastern Asia defined by the making and unmaking of empire. The conduct of British, French, Dutch, Spanish, and Japanese empire builders demonstrated that conquering and exercising control over others was integral to earning great-power status. Americans acted accordingly. They wrested the Philippines from Spain's faltering empire even as they worried about the possible breakup of China, and they proceeded to demonstrate their efficiency in the exercise of mastery over other peoples. They marked time in eastern Asia following the pacification of the Philippines, concentrating instead on fastening control over the Caribbean and Central America. Eastern Asia reclaimed center stage in the 1930s as Japanese ambitions directed at China and European colonies aroused American opposition. Rising tensions exploded in a war that not only destroyed Japan's empire but also fatally weakened the Europeans' grip on their colonial possessions. These outcomes of the Pacific War created fresh opportunities that Americans were quick to seize. Their dramatic postwar advance expanded the zone of U.S. control to its broadest extent. But even as the old rival empires passed from the scene, U.S. leaders feared the rise of a fresh imperial threat. They worried that an Asia in the throes of decolonization, from British India to divided Korea, would fall into the clutches of a new empire masterminded by Moscow.

The world of Asian empire which Americans boldly entered offered more than models to emulate and a spur to action. It harbored a little noticed and initially embryonic danger that over time would prove Washington's nemesis. In the shadow of empire, anti-imperial politics took form and gained strength. The typhoon-force winds of nationalism would lash against the structures of authority erected during decades or even centuries of foreign domination and eventually destroy them from one end of eastern Asia to the other. In the Philippines, a nationalist revolt against Spain would transform itself into dogged resistance to U.S. rule. For Emilio Aguinaldo and like-minded Filipinos, *empire* meant hated domination no matter who exercised it. By the middle of the twentieth century, those nationalist sentiments had grown considerably more powerful and widespread in China, Korea, and Vietnam. Through bitter struggle, political activists had gained experience in political organization and popular mobilization essential to driving the foreigners out.

Faced with weakening European authority, Japan's sudden capitulation, and impatient nationalists, Americans were conflicted over how to proceed. They not only advertised themselves as, but also believed themselves to be, champions of freedom. They spoke passionately of self-determination and an end to colonial empires. But they would deal only with moderate nationalists who stood foursquare against communism. Otherwise, they preferred to prop up decrepit and discredited European colonial regimes such as France's in Indochina rather than come to terms with nationalist revolutionaries. They recoiled at accusations that Americans were essentially no different than the long line of foreign colonialists whom they sought to displace in the name of freedom.

Imperial rivalry, emulation, and anti-imperial resistance provided the context for the U.S. imperial project. Ideology provided the inspiration. Like other empire builders, Americans needed a compelling reason to act as they did. Their embrace of empire was inspired and sustained by a potent self-image as a unique people destined by geography, history, and moral character to guide politically immature and easily misled Asians to a better future. They exulted in their elevated standing in the world and celebrated each success as confirmation of greater achievements to come. Such an ideological self-conception was first evident in the Philippines. Americans landed on the shores of Manila Bay confident of their right, even their presumptive obligation, to direct the destiny of the peoples of the western Pacific and advance the cause of civilization. This conceit was strong enough to sustain American decision makers, politicians, generals, and proconsuls across three-quarters of a century as they played variations of the Philippine experiment in occupied Japan and South Korea and in the new nation of South Vietnam.

This self-conception proved a double-edged sword. U.S. policymakers imagined themselves acting quite differently from other powers with a baleful record of brutality and rapacity. Precisely because America's motives were supposedly selfless and its cause just, the natural conclusion was that victory was guaranteed. But this strong sense of exceptionalism and destiny could become a source of anxiety and misapprehension if the expected victory was delayed or denied. Rather than explaining reverses in terms of inherent American limits in the face of capable, determined enemies fighting on home ground, U.S. jingoists tended to look for deficiencies within the American body politic. The scapegoats varied—from meddling politicians, to traitorous protesters, to a biased media, to a morally flabby public.

If ideology sounded the summons to empire, its realization depended on the tools and techniques applied by empire builders over the ages. The U.S. military was the prime instrument. The wars it waged marked the progress of American conquest, pacification, and rule. Quashing Philippine insurgents and destroying the Japanese war machine convinced U.S. leaders that American arms sustained by unmatched industrial and logistical capacity could handle any situation. The illusion that the U.S. possessed an invincible military that could secure the imperial realm was punctured in Korea when Peng Dehuai's troops checked Americans poised to secure their third major triumph on the eastern Asian battlefield. Seven and a half years of fighting in Vietnam shattered the illusion. The definitive failure of military prowess spelled the end of dominion. The United States was far from being the pitiful giant of Richard Nixon's fears, but after Vietnam it could no longer assume that it could work its will in the region by force of arms whenever it chose to do so.

This mixed military record carried a lot of symbolic weight. Achieving mastery over other lands and peoples dramatically demonstrated command of an advanced technology and, by implication, confirmed American claims to civilizational superiority. But determined foes—whether using conventional or unconventional warfare—led U.S. commanders to resort repeatedly to indiscriminate violence. Bomb tonnage provides a gauge of the rising capacity and will to deal out general destruction. Korea absorbed more than twice what U.S. aircraft had dropped on Japan, and Indochina as a whole an astonishing fifty times more.[1] These tactics undermined the conqueror's claim to represent enlightened progress. The dogged persistence of enemies in what seemed like suicidal resistance also forced the "civilizers" to consider what price they were prepared to pay to maintain their claim and intensified doubts among domestic critics about the propriety of the imperial project itself. Filipino insurgents, imperial Japanese warriors on Pacific islands, Chinese and North Korean soldiers in Korea, and Vietnamese guerrillas and regular soldiers momentarily put in question but hardly purged the American tendency to associate modern military technology with dominance and superiority.

Though U.S. military prowess ultimately failed to secure the political objectives to which it was harnessed, it inflicted high human and material costs on those who resisted. Destruction was visited upon one country after another, leaving masses of dead and maimed noncombatants as well as enemy soldiers. Less well-armed Asian foes—Filipinos, Japanese, Koreans, Chinese, and Vietnamese—suffered much higher casualty rates than the Americans. Losses among vulnerable civilian populations were even higher—nowhere more so in percentage terms than in the Philippines at the outset of the U.S. project. Combatant and civilian deaths together total nearly 9 million, while U.S. deaths in the four wars are estimated at a third of a million. Moreover, those whose homelands became the battlegrounds suffered widespread economic destruction and deep social trauma while the U.S. economy flourished. Even the conflict that did the most damage in the United States, the Vietnam War, inflicted psychic and political rather than material harm and on nothing like the scale of personal trauma and social disruption that Asians experienced. The breathtaking destruction inflicted by American firepower, whether in victory or defeat, gave the lie to the rhetoric of uplift and civilization. Dominion came at a high price, but Americans paid little of it.

While military power was essential to gaining and in extremity maintaining empire, it was by itself insufficient. Undercutting resistance and instituting a low-cost, sustainable administration required civil action on a broad front, as Elwell Otis, William Howard Taft, Arthur MacArthur, and Adna Chaffee had first demonstrated in the Philippines. It meant negotiating collaborative bargains with local elites. It also meant promoting hygiene, running schools, apprehending subversives, and constructing bureaucracies. It was no small matter to tackle these measures in the right sequence, to keep all the parts running smoothly together, and to avoid the conflicts common to any complex enterprise. Already in the Philippines, Taft and the generals who made his proconsular authority possible had proven that they were fast learners. They showed themselves adept at creating the garrisons, training the police, installing the minor functionaries, and manipulating the political system—all essential to low-cost, long-term control.

Establishing and maintaining that kind of control required above all else enlisting collaborators. The rewards of collaboration with the likes of Pedro Paterno, Syngman Rhee, Yoshida Shigeru, Ramon Magsaysay, Ngo Dinh Diem, and Nguyen Van Thieu were multiple. Important in any imperial effort, collaboration was doubly so in an informal empire in an age of nationalism. It put a native face between American proconsuls and populations suspicious of outsiders and thus helped defuse possible resistance. Collaborative arrangements also helped to make empire more palatable in the United States, especially among those who took seriously principles of self-determination and freedom. Agents of empire, however jealous of their prerogatives, knew how to turn the necessity of collaboration into a virtue. Knowledgeable locals could help in destroying and demoralizing the resistance, and they could be the good pupils Americans wanted to teach the lessons of political and cultural modernity. Americans had demonstrated in the Philippines how recruited agents could serve as eyes and ears, staff the bureaucracy, and collect the taxes. And, like other empire builders before them, Americans repeatedly returned to this mechanism of control as they extended their sway into postwar Japan and South Korea and later South Vietnam. But collaboration also carried risks. By definition it depended on a quid pro quo with local elites. The price U.S. proconsuls paid for services rendered included involvement in troublesome local quarrels, making concessions inimical to U.S. values or preferences, and bolstering the career of leaders who might develop minds of their own.

Of these local helpers, none were more important than the military men. "Native" forces played an important role in the Philippines as an instrument of pacification, just as they had been part of the toolkit of every empire. Local militaries that were U.S. trained and supplied became important auxiliaries to U.S. forces operating in Korea and Vietnam. This "nativization" of coercive control also helps explain the military's rising prominence in South Korea and its dominance in post-Diem South Vietnam. Japan was the exception to this pattern of Americans' raising the profile of the local forces. Of the four cases treated here, it predictably spent the least time in a tight U.S. orbit, and its armed forces played the least prominent role in politics.

Over the long haul, the Asian project contributed significantly to important trends within the United States. The society that builds empire changes itself in the process of seeking to control others. Imperial conquest, defense, and management of far-flung, usually vulnerable, and often unruly client states contributed to the aggrandizement of the executive branch. What Arthur Schlesinger called in 1973 the "imperial presidency" has come to refer to the steady expansion of White House capabilities. Presidents disposed of secret funds, struck international bargains, and waged foreign wars—all with barely a nod to Congress and with the general acquiescence of the highest courts in the land. With the multiplication of functions and rise in authority came a steady increase in staff, duplicating in the White House the expertise once the monopoly of major executive departments. All the new machinery of government required yet more machinery to control it. In the process the presidency came to command and presidents to expect a deference quite at odds with what the Constitution defined as a three-way division of power among coequal branches of government. The presidency also took on a symbolic role in American life, with the president and his family becoming celebrated embodiments of the country akin to royalty.

A powerful presidency was tailor-made for empire, indeed provided its institutional basis. The president along with his close aides made and managed the U.S. Asian enterprise. The dozen or so men who made the key decisions over a seventy-five-year period were all in the executive branch—from McKinley and Taft to Nixon and Kissinger. They decided which territories to take and what forces to deploy. They formulated the response to the crises that regularly broke out on the broad imperial frontier. And they laid down the law in the lands they had claimed. At each step presidents relied heavily on their powers as commanders in chief, no surprise given the inherently coercive nature of the imperial project, and this regular exercise of armed might helped spawn a regional network of bases whose garrisons stood ready to do the president's bidding. No less essential to the enterprise was an increasingly elaborate secret apparatus devoted to gathering intelligence and carrying out covert operations. At home presidents and their agents formulated a rich array of public justifications for an Asian commitment, while deploying against critics the considerable administrative power of executive agencies (from the IRS to the FBI) and the full symbolic power invested in the president.

During the prolonged imbroglio in eastern Asia, the president came to exercise authority that the authors of the Constitution could hardly have imagined in a republic and comparable only to the untrammeled power wielded by the tyrannical monarchs they loathed. One man acting under the protean concept of national security could proceed unhindered with the help of secret appropriations, executive agreements, and handy euphemisms like "police action." This concentration of power not only failed to preserve America's primacy in Asia, but it was also partially responsible for the undoing of that dominance. It was precisely the discretionary powers accumulated in the Oval Office over decades that facilitated the fatal and fateful commitments in Korea and Vietnam. Given the latitude to overreach, presidents felt no compunction to exercise self-restraint and, therefore, suffered the consequences of their hubris.

The impact of empire at home can also be measured in social and cultural terms that call to mind the experience of other empires, such as Rome,

Tang China, and Britain, culturally altered by intruding into the lives of others. The Americans who went abroad to pacify and rule were exposed to a wider world that they otherwise would not have known. In the process they contributed to the distinctly more cosmopolitan outlook that arose in the United States, particularly from the 1940s onward. Perhaps even more important, peoples from lands impacted by U.S. wars and subject to U.S. rule made the American population more ethnically diverse, with U.S. metropolitan centers the focal point of this influx from the imperial periphery.

A sweeping immigration revision passed in 1965 made possible a significant Asian influx. In 1900 those defined by the census as Asian had amounted to 114,000 (a small fraction of 1 percent of the total population), and the numbers did not change dramatically for over six decades. Immigration restrictions had meant no American sanctuary for the war-wracked inhabitants of the Philippines, China, Japan, or Korea. In 1965 Congress dramatically changed the situation when it overturned the restrictions, and in 1977 it gave special consideration to those fleeing Indochina. The result was a significant uptick in migration. The 1990 census registered the result. It recorded some 5.7 million individuals (a bit over 2 percent of the total U.S. population) identified specifically with the countries touched by America's Asian wars. Chinese and Filipinos each accounted for about a quarter of that group, with Japanese, Koreans, and the various peoples of Indochina (including Saigon loyalists, ethnic Chinese, Cambodians, and Hmong from Laos) each amounting to roughly a seventh. Reflecting their recent rise, roughly two-thirds of all Asian Americans were foreign born.[2]

CAUSES OF COLLAPSE

Between 1950 and 1973 the air gradually escaped from an overinflated imperial enterprise. The American public was tolerant of empire at bargain-basement prices. But when the costs started to rise, support began to fall. Occupants of the imperial presidency and custodians of imperial dreams had to recognize the limits imposed by popular frustrations over Asian misadventures. Eisenhower hastened to wind up the Korean conflict, and he and his lieutenants concluded that they had to avoid another land war in Asia. Johnson and his advisers fully understood the perils in making the 1965 troop commitment in Vietnam. By 1968, with their fears realized and their political base fast dissolving, they too sought a way out. Both impatient public and chastened leaders confronted a region undergoing profound changes. Even as the U.S. drive gathered force, Asians were marshaling the resolve and resources to limit the advance and frustrate the intruders. It took quite a while, but eventually Americans got the point.

Richard Nixon took office facing an anomalous situation. Prolonged fighting had given wide currency to the views of an antiwar minority and undermined public support. Twice in his long political career he had seen the electorate make clear its distaste for distant, inconclusive conflicts. And twice Republicans had benefited electorally—Eisenhower in 1952 and Nixon himself in 1968. Though Nixon had supported the decision to make a major commitment in Vietnam, he had also watched the tide of opinion shift decisively against that decision as its opponents took to the streets and policymakers had to face up to the receding prospect of victory.

Nixon's response was to accept and regularize the now apparent limits on the eastern Asian project. His policy of Vietnamization aimed at liquidating the Vietnam War, but more broadly he sought to accommodate U.S. policy to a transformed world in which the United States had suffered a relative decline and in which the Asian Cold War made little sense. He announced a lowered U.S. profile in July 1969. At a press conference during a visit to Guam, he enunciated what became known as the Nixon doctrine: that security "will be handled by, and the responsibility for it taken by, the Asian nations themselves." While promising to honor U.S. treaty commitments, provide a nuclear shield, and continue aid programs, he professed a determination to avoid another Vietnam in which the United States carried the major burden. Asia had changed, Nixon stressed. A growing sense of national and regional pride ruled out foreign dictation and foreign-controlled dependencies.[3]

Nixon's commitment to a diminished U.S. role was also evident in his accommodation of Mao Zedong's China. This involved reversing a two-decades-old policy of isolating and containing China that Nixon himself had fully supported. To U.S. cold warriors the Chinese revolution seemed like a fearful contagion, and China's leaders international outlaws whose sway over the world's most populous country was a standing rebuke to U.S. interests and ideals. Questioning these views was taboo until the surfacing of Sino-Soviet tensions prompted some specialists in government and out to suggest more flexibility. The ferment associated with the Vietnam War created an opening for skeptical political and intellectual leaders such as Senator J. William Fulbright (D-Ark.) to go public. Secretary of State Dean Rusk, firmly attached to a rigid China policy, stood in the way of any meaningful change, leaving Kennedy to brood ineffectually over growing Chinese might and limiting Johnson to signaling Beijing that he did not want a direct confrontation over Vietnam. Nixon by contrast was ready from the time he entered the White House to overturn what had become an out-dated, even dangerous orthodoxy.

The hard-line U.S. policy toward China that prevailed from the end of the Korean War through Nixon's assumption of the presidency had been premised on a dubious and wishful assumption, namely, that the Communist government in China was a passing phenomenon that should not be validated by U.S. diplomatic recognition and trade. Powerful domestic U.S. lobbies had straitjacketed any discussion of U.S. China policy and ballyhooed Taiwan under Chiang Kai-shek's dictatorship as Free China, a viable anticommunist alternative to the dreaded and despised Red China of Mao Zedong. Yet China had outlived the prophets of its imminent demise, such as John Foster Dulles, and a devastating famine had not shaken the foundations of Communist rule. Moreover, by the late 1960s Beijing's sharp break with Moscow had buried the notion of world communism as a unitary threat to American interests. Washington was finally ready to talk.

Nixon found Beijing responsive to his overtures. Its soured relations with Moscow deteriorated further as a result of border clashes in March 1969. Mao became deeply worried by the Soviet threat. Nixon's opening to Beijing, consummated in the course of 1971 and 1972, had the immediate effect of applying pressure on Hanoi to accept a compromise peace. But it had far broader implications. It finally brought the United States to terms with China's revolution. Nixon had concluded that the United States would have to learn to live with rather than convert or destroy Communist China. A close aide recalled Nixon explaining in July 1971 as his opening to Beijing gathered momentum: "In 25 years you can't have a quarter of the people of the world isolated and have any chance of peace."[4] The choice of words was revealing. Nixon sought concord, not confrontation.

Nixon's bold stroke had some decided regional implications. One immediate result was to put Taiwan's close security relationship with the United States in limbo. In the Shanghai communiqué, issued at the end of his visit to China in February 1972, Nixon accepted Taiwan as a part of China (as Beijing claimed) while getting Mao to agree that its future was to be settled peacefully. As part of the bargain, Nixon promised that the United States would "progressively reduce its forces on Taiwan as the tension in the area diminishes." Tokyo was almost as shocked as the Nationalist government on Taiwan. For two decades the Liberal Democratic Party had bowed to U.S. pressure to keep its distance from China and had stood by the U.S. security treaty and U.S. military action in Vietnam despite significant popular protest. Nixon repaid this loyalty by giving Japanese leaders no prior warning of his reversal of China policy. He had in addition earlier advanced the discomfiting proposition that Japan should play a larger military role in the region. This notion was congruent with his Guam doctrine, his decision to return control of Okinawa to Tokyo's jurisdiction, and his sense of the broader role that Japan could play as a rising economic superpower. What Nixon had in mind was a Japan less dependent on the United States and better able to replace the United States as (in his words) "the major counter-force to China."[5]

Vietnam and China were two important pieces in the president's larger scheme. The liquidation of an unpopular war and the dramatic opening of relations with China was in turn linked to a policy of détente with the Soviet Union. Talking to Moscow was yet another way to put Hanoi in an awkward position while also exploiting the breach between the two Communist giants. But more broadly, Nixon's strategic adjustment helped exorcise the Cold War fears that had prompted the Korean and Vietnam interventions in the first place. The communist empire—dissolved into its constituent parts and amenable to negotiation and compromise—no longer provided a justification for a robust, vigilant U.S. presence in Asia.

To be sure, none of Nixon's initiatives were original. Johnson had set Vietnamization in motion. The domestic proponents of opening diplomatic ties to Beijing had become more vocal during the 1960s, and Nixon himself had gingerly moved toward that position in public in 1967. Better relations with the Soviet Union had become a major U.S. policy preoccupation following the traumatic Cuban missile crisis in 1962. Nixon's contribution was not simply to turn these policy impulses into reality. He got his Vietnam peace; he opened relations with China; and he secured the arms control agreements that were at the heart of his Soviet policy, while also extending cooperation into economic and cultural areas. His real achievement was to assemble those pieces into a coherent package and provide an underlying rationale.

In comments delivered in July 1971, just days before Kissinger's secret breakthrough meetings in Beijing, Nixon offered a remarkable review of his thinking. He called for turning the Cold War from an ideological contest to the death into a competition between great powers, each with core interests and each with a readiness to compromise on issues outside that core. He stressed the way a five-power world—in which a revived Europe and Japan as well as China and the Soviet Union occupied a place alongside the United States—had undercut American dominance. In this new international context, Nixon argued, the husbanding of U.S. national resources became of prime importance. This meant notably a government program of revitalizing American society in areas as diverse as the environment, education, health care, and moral commitment. Poignantly and in language hard to imagine at any earlier points in the drive into Asia, Nixon concluded with a sobering lesson he drew from history: great civilizations fall as well as rise. The task of American statecraft was to delay that time of decline for a power that had, he suggested, passed its apogee.[6]

Nixon's initiatives contributed to an ongoing transformation of client states into allies (with the exception of South Vietnam, which would disappear from the map). As Asian states aligned with the United States grew more confident, sensitive issues once largely a matter for Americans to decide became the subject of negotiations and compromise. The day of the diktat was over. Japan had quickly moved beyond the direct control of its occupation patron in the 1950s, while remaining a docile junior partner in a security alliance imposed at the end of the occupation. In the 1960s, South Korea also began to secure greater autonomy, though like Japan, it remained constrained by its reliance on U.S. military support against a perennially hostile and unpredictable North Korea. No longer could Washington sweep under the rug problems arising from continued U.S. military presence, trade disputes, and differences over regional problems. They became the stuff of serious diplomacy with ample give and take. Relations with eastern Asia generally, and not just China, were becoming "normal." None of these changes removed the United States from a position of great influence in eastern Asia; rather they transformed and may actually have strengthened the long-term position of the United States in eastern Asia as a post-imperial power.

The post-imperial relationships were most complicated by the military residue from decades of involvement. Nixon's peace agreement with Hanoi eliminated one strong point. U.S. bases in the Philippines, the oldest in the regional network, were the next to go. President Jimmy Carter had thought them important enough to ignore the authoritarian excesses of the Ferdinand Marcos regime and conclude a half-billion-dollar-a-year lease renewal. But in 1991 disagreement over renewal of the lease, tension over the continued U.S. military presence, and physical damage from a volcanic eruption led Manila and Washington to agree to close U.S. facilities. Bases created after World War II in South Korea, the Japanese home islands, and above all Okinawa had become the hub of U.S. military activity, and as such they evoked recurrent controversy and inter-allied tensions. With the end of the Japanese occupation went a grand bargain. Tokyo got the guarantee of a U.S. security umbrella and in return left Washington in possession of its bases while also secretly agreeing to cover the U.S. costs and to turn a blind eye to U.S. nuclear weapons brought into this nuclear-averse country. Calming South Korean president Syngman Rhee while ending the Korea War had elicited a second security treaty (formalized in 1954) and the perpetuation of a U.S. military presence. The Nationalists on Taiwan got similar formal assurances in 1954 after the Korean War made the island too important to lose, and with the security treaty went yet another point from which the U.S. military operated.

In Japan these military ties proved a mixed blessing. U.S. forces extended a nuclear umbrella over Japan, thus keeping nuclear weapons out of the hands of Japan's Self-Defense Forces (developed in the 1950s) and providing Japan's anticommunist neighbors assurances against a repeat of the militarist nightmare. The classic 1953 film *Ugetsu* by Mizoguchi Kenji captured the spirit of the new Japan integrated into the postwar U.S. order. Though set in the sixteenth century, the film had its protagonists emerging from a brutal bout of fighting and conceding that "the war drove us mad with ambition." Now chastened and resolved to settle for a modest place in the world, they made their new watchword "Pull yourself together and work hard." These notions, uttered just as the occupation was ending, reflected the postwar rejection of the warrior tradition and the embrace of a U.S. security guarantee that facilitated economic growth and an unprecedented degree of domestic prosperity.

But this intimate relationship with the U.S. military also generated controversy. The renewal of the security arrangements in 1960 sparked sharp political opposition, particularly among Japanese students and leftist unions, and repeated rounds of street violence. The sprawling U.S. military presence in some thirty-eight bases occupying nearly a fifth of the main island on Okinawa became a perennial irritant in local politics and the cause of popular outrage over crimes including rapes, numerous traffic accidents, and drunken brawling committed by U.S. servicemen with virtual impunity. Nixon's return of Okinawa to Japanese control in 1972 resolved one complaint but left the base issue to fester, with nationalists on the island attacking both Tokyo and Washington for ignoring their interests. Finally, the presence of nuclear weapons in U.S. bases became public knowledge and the source of additional criticism in a country with a profound nuclear allergy.

The U.S. presence in South Korea was no less problematic. While Chinese troops completed their pullout from the North in late 1958, the Americans stayed on—and became a lightning rod for growing tensions in the South Korean–U.S. relationship and the target of repeated rounds of protest. Like the Japanese, Koreans grew angry when troops guilty of criminal behavior were shielded from legal consequences. Behind this anger was resentment over the U.S. impact on the country's affairs. The Americans were guilty of backing a conservative establishment and a dictatorship by a military that they had trained, of tolerating its brutal repression of left-wing and democratic protesters, and of imposing and then perpetuating the division of their country. South Korea's transition to genuine democracy in the late 1980s did not diminish anti-American sentiment. A 2002 survey found that 36 percent of South Koreans viewed the United States unfavorably compared to only 13 percent with a favorable view. Young people were especially insistent on a more equal relationship with the United States.[7]

Fanning this rising anti-American sentiment was an increasingly strong belief that unification and the reduction of tensions on the peninsula depended on diminishing the U.S. presence while also building stronger trade, educational, and cultural ties with South Korea's neighbors, including North Korea. The presidencies of Kim Dae-jung and Roh Mu-hyun (1997–2009) put national reconciliation at the top of the agenda, exacerbating tensions with Washington, where Cold War views of Korea persisted. North Korea's reluctance to reciprocate South Korean overtures and its successful drive to develop nuclear weapons in the face of U.S. and regional hostility have frustrated but not killed the quest for national reconciliation on the Korean peninsula.

Despite this divergence between peninsular priorities and U.S. preferences, Washington continues to view developments in a rich and strategically sensitive Northeast Asia largely through the prism of conventional military power and interstate conflict. Now some six decades after U.S. forces pushed deep into Northeast Asia, American leaders still cling to their bases and the old security treaties. They follow anxiously developments that threaten the status quo, whether the fall of their long-time allies in Japan's Liberal Democratic Party, anti-base demonstrations on Okinawa, or outbursts of anti-American sentiment in South Korea and the attendant calls for more restrictive status-of-forces agreements. Barack Obama no less than George W. Bush has fixated on North Korea's nuclear ambitions, while also attributing sweeping significance to the alliance with Japan. That alliance was, Obama claimed while in Tokyo in November 2009, "a foundation for security and prosperity not just for our two countries but for the Asia Pacific region" and a vehicle that has "helped us become the world's two largest economies."[8] His remarks suggest that the United States, though an ocean away, is not just a regional stakeholder but one whose self-proclaimed good intentions and robust capabilities justify its continuing role as the dominant power in enforcing regional security, a role that it claims to perform self-lessly in the general interest rather than its own national interests.

For now at least, this U.S. policy goes virtually unchallenged at home for familiar reasons. What might regional actors do if left without the "adult" supervision provided by Uncle Sam? What would a retreat mean symboli-cally to U.S. global prestige and to the already much diminished dreams of an American century in Asia? Finally, why retreat from a region that allows such full scope to the one element of U.S. global power—the capacity to project military force—that remains unrivaled and on which the U.S. gov-ernment lavishes abundant resources?

Behind the shifts and tensions that marked the U.S. regional role was an eastern Asia in fundamental transformation. Even as Americans fought for an expanding empire, Asian tolerance of outside control declined and strong nationalist commitments to state building gathered force. Already at the very outset Asian elites, including those that admired aspects of Ameri-can society and culture, were entertaining dreams for the Pacific and their place in it that were distinctly at odds with the U.S. visions. In both Japan and China "wealth and power" figured prominently as prime goals, and the state figured as the indispensable agent for realizing them. Their statist political cultures stressed not open political debate but rather broad accep-tance of an official sociopolitical orthodoxy, and their prescriptions defined society not as a collection of competing self-interested units or atomistic individuals but rather as a mutually dependent, tightly linked, hierarchi-cally arranged organism. In other words, neither country was ready to ac-cept Americans' self-serving notions of uplift or civilization. The struggle already under way in eastern Asia put a premium on centralizing and mobi-lizing power, not dispersing it. A prime reason for this insistence on cen-tralized power was to accumulate the state capacity to resist the incursions of imperial powers, be they Britain, France, Russia, or the United States. These differences—whether strategic or cultural in origin—would unfold inexorably and fatefully.

Already in the 1860s Japanese leaders had embarked on their state building project. The Meiji restoration had as its prime goal a powerful, modern state that could regain its autonomy from intrusive foreigners and safeguard its security from outside threats. By the turn of the century Japan was on its way to becoming a great power, a dominant force in China, and a threat to U.S. influence. Japan's defeat in the Pacific War eliminated its dreams of military power but not of making itself an economically advanced country with strong indigenous cultural roots.

The nationalist currents at work in Japan were by the 1880s also present in the colonial Philippines. There nationalism provided the first regional demonstration of its anti-imperial potential. What a new political class began against Spain, they continued against the Americans. In the resulting conflict, American empire builders were lucky. A divided elite in a still poorly integrated land enjoyed only limited popular support, had no international patron to turn to, and thus gradually succumbed to U.S. pressure. While Americans triumphed, they also got a small taste of the opposition they might encounter as they pushed deeper into the region.

By the early decades of the twentieth century, with the heyday of the U.S. drive yet to come, Asian nationalism took a radical turn. Japan's shift, which some have described as fascist, involved a militarization of polity and society with the emperor presiding as the sacred symbol of the country and an economy that harnessed large-scale modern industry to the state's expansionist goals. China took the alternative revolutionary path influenced by Soviet doctrine and example, Soviet agents, and Soviet financial support. After its advent to power in 1949 the Communist Party effected changes as sweeping as those earlier in Japan, but they unfolded even more rapidly. Success came at a price in human suffering caused by misguided and brutally repressive policies. At least 30 million died as a result of the early 1950s campaign against "counterrevolutionaries," the Great Leap Forward experiment in the late 1950s, and the Cultural Revolution a decade later.

The rise of China as a powerful, determined, and skillful regional power significantly altered the regional landscape to the distinct disadvantage of U.S. pretensions. A country that had loomed large in American eyes as a passive victim of colonial depredations and then a weak ally in opposition to Japan emerged in 1950 a formidable foe of empire. Starting that year, the new regime in Beijing invested scarce resources in the Viet Minh struggle against U.S.-supported French colonial rule. The Chinese forces that crossed the Yalu River into Korea later that same year delivered a blow that did indeed (as Mao Zedong wished) give "arrogant" Americans pause. China's new international prominence was confirmed at the 1954 Geneva conference liquidating France's position in Indochina and again in the early 1960s as Beijing acquired its own nuclear capability and renewed its commitment to the Vietnamese comrades headed toward a showdown with the United States. Beijing helped Hanoi administer a spectacular and, as it turned out, definitive defeat to lingering notions of a U.S.-dominated Asia. Nixon's normalization policy represented a painful and belated U.S. recognition that China was a major player in an emerging Asian order antipathetic to American control.

ASIA AFTER EMPIRE

The retreat of the Americans was a critical moment in the history of eastern Asia. Having exhausted themselves against local resistance, they scaled back their ambitions and thus widened the possibilities for the rise of a stronger, more autonomous region. As it emerged as a new center of international power and influence, it constrained the exercise of U.S. global leadership, offered compelling alternatives to U.S.-championed social, political, and economic models, and caused considerable heartburn within a U.S. foreign policy establishment thrown on the defensive.

Fundamental to these dramatic changes were economic gains. In 1955, with the American occupiers gone, savvy Japanese government technocrats embarked on a state-guided, market-driven, export-oriented development program. Backed by the dominant Liberal Democratic Party and big business, they built on a foundation of state capacity developed earlier in the pursuit of empire and the conduct of the Pacific War. By 1968 Japan's had become the world's third-largest economy and had entered a stage of mass consumption unimaginable amid the rubble of 1945. By then South Korea had begun to tap the potential of the Japanese strategy. General Park Chung Hee, whose military career began in the service of the Japanese empire and continued under the U.S. occupation, took power in a coup in 1961. He and his fellow officers reacted against the incompetence and corruption of their predecessors, Syngman Rhee and Chang Myon. The country seemed to Park politically adrift and economically stagnant. "I felt, honestly speaking, as if I had been given a pilfered household or a bankrupt firm to manage," he wrote.[9] He created a garrison state guaranteeing social stability and gave his economic technocrats free rein. Park was assassinated in 1979, but state planning continued, pushing the South's economy rapidly forward.

The U.S. contribution to these successes was considerable. The destruction the U.S. military machine had inflicted on Japan and then Korea was partially offset by U.S. military spending on wars elsewhere in eastern Asia in what amounted to a kind of military Keynesian effect. The Korean War turned occupied Japan into a logistical support base and helped propel a damaged Japanese economy toward prewar levels of output. The U.S. military commitment in Vietnam provided an even greater stimulus. On top of the war-related impact, U.S. aid programs hastened the recovery of Japan in the late 1940s and South Korea after the 1953 armistice. Total U.S. assistance and procurement programs benefited Japan to the tune of about $4.5 billion (1945–72), while South Korea gained roughly $12.6 billion (1946–76).[10] More indirect but no less important, U.S. postwar policy created an environment conducive to the two countries' export strategies. The U.S.-sponsored international free trade regime, currency stability based on the dollar, and special access to the United States as the largest single consumer market were all critical contributions.

The two Communist powers that had done the most to frustrate U.S. regional ambitions soon joined the march to greater prosperity. China's Deng Xiaoping presided in the late 1970s over a dramatic shift toward a state-guided market mechanism and international trade. Reforms implemented by a still dominant Communist Party ignited an unprecedented pace of economic growth. By the end of the century personal income had quadrupled and the country was on its way to becoming the world's second-largest economy behind the United States. Both Taiwan with its own strong state sector and Hong Kong with its venerable free-trade orientation and close ties to the Canton region were drawn more and more tightly into the orbit of China's massive, burgeoning economy. In the mid-1980s, Vietnam under Nguyen Van Linh made a successful turn toward greater reliance on market forces and export industries—guided at each step by the Communist Party. Once more, reform yielded a rapid rate of growth.

In this advance of the Asian economies, two were distinct laggards. The Philippines, though the country longest and most firmly under the U.S. sway, became the poor cousin in a prospering Asian family as a result of the continuing dominance of self-interested regional elites. Development woes fed discontents among landless peasants and an urban underclass but also among intellectuals and the political Left. The result has been repeated rounds of serious armed conflict—first in the 1920s, again in the 1940s and early 1950s (the Huks), and most recently following the creation of the New People's Army in 1969. North Korea was an even greater laggard—a specimen of high Stalinism preserved in amber by the ruling Kim family. Support from Moscow and Beijing had helped Pyongyang rebuild after the Korean War and triple its per capita gross domestic product (GDP) between 1953 and 1973. The economy then ran into trouble. Problems rooted in its rigid and inefficient operation were compounded by the loss of outside support after the collapse of the Soviet Union and by the impatience of Deng's reform-minded China. By 1998 North Korea's per capita GDP had declined to less than half of its 1973 peak, and the country was in the grip of recurrent food crises.[11]

Growing prosperity in much of the region was accompanied by a distinct political liberalization. While Americans might hail this development, they had if anything impeded it by bolstering authoritarians. U.S. cold warriors had much preferred the stability and predictability of dictatorship to the uncertainty that would attend any democratic openings. Japan's Liberal Democratic Party, the preferred U.S. partner, maintained its hammerlock on power for nearly four decades. (It finally lost an election in 1993 and, after rallying, suffered a second defeat in 2009.) South Korea's U.S.-trained military ran the country from 1961 until the late 1980s. Not until 1992 was the first civilian leader elected. On Taiwan the old U.S. ally, the Nationalist Party, waited until the 1980s before gradually loosening its iron grip by ending the decades-old state of emergency, opening the political system to rival parties (even those calling for Taiwan's independence), and holding the first democratic elections. This regionwide liberalization extended even to China and Vietnam. In both, younger, reform minded leaders broadened the parameters for legitimate discussion, conceded more oversight to the national legislature, and tolerated the existence of some public interest groups within a system still dominated by the party-state. In politics as in economics, the Philippines and North Korea remained in a state of arrested development. The Philippines fell under the fifteen-year dictatorship of Ferdinand Marcos, a strongman generously backed by Washington virtually until his overthrow in 1986 and the return of the old elite to its accustomed role. Kim Il Sung was intent on creating a communist dynasty. On his death in 1994 power passed to his son, Kim Jung Il.

A region charting its own economic and political course posed a double challenge to the United States. First, economic success diminished U.S. clout even as it altered the global landscape. By 1998 China, Japan, and South Korea accounted for a fifth of world production.[12] No less significant, the means by which countries in the region had forged ahead served as a standing rebuke to Americans still dreaming of a region developing along U.S. economic and political lines. States, not some hidden hand, were the ultimate arbiter of an efficient economy. Champions of this "illiberal" development path had little patience with American hectoring over violation of free-market norms and human rights. Putting a premium on state power dedicated to the societal and national good within the context of order and consensus had worked for them. They rejected U.S. criticisms as at best paternalistic and at worst a strategy for weakening an increasingly successful and self-confident region.

The second prong of the eastern Asian challenge was a growing impetus toward regional autonomy that had steadily limited U.S. influence. Trade and investment were more and more concentrated within the region, while environmental and other transnational problems called for regular consultation and coordination. The Asia-Pacific Economic Cooperation forum, of which the United States is a member, floundered while the Association of Southeast Asian Nations (ASEAN) became the core of an evolving set of regional links with a large and dynamic Chinese economy supplying considerable impetus to informal integration and with the Americans on the outside looking in. Regionally based economic organizations provided an alternative to U.S.-sponsored global institutions such as the International Monetary Fund and the World Bank, while local aid donors began to eclipse U.S. assistance programs. The only part of the U.S. shadow that did not shrink was its military arm, a reminder of a defunct, violent imperial project as well as a sign of the American desire to preserve a shred of past glories.

The gap between the United States and an increasingly dynamic, integrated region became dramatically evident in the 1970s and 1980s. A Japanese export drive put pressure on a U.S. economy suffering from stagnant growth and high inflation. Competitive, high-quality Japanese products combined with American consumers' low savings and their runaway preference for imports to create persistent trade deficits and turn once prosperous industrial areas into rust belts. To protect the dollar, Nixon was forced in 1971 to break its fixed link to gold and thus end the U.S. currency's special postwar role as the single point of reference for international trade and investment.

Tensions roiled the U.S.-Japan relationship in a way that suggested to some a return to the 1930s. Pundits asked with amazement and alarm whether Japan had taken away the U.S. position as "number one." The media bristled as Japanese investors took control of such national icons as Rockefeller Center and Columbia Pictures. Politicians showed their outrage by literally smashing Japanese-made cars. Cartoonists depicted Japan as a fierce samurai warrior or a giant sumo wrestler to convey their fear of an overwhelming economic juggernaut. Americans sought salvation by demanding that the Japanese lower trade barriers, save less, and spend more. Resentful of U.S. demands for reform of a system that had brought them prosperity, Japanese blamed the Americans for their own woes. The U.S. economy and society seemed unproductive and conducive to crime and social breakdown. A popular literary genre sprang up urging Japanese to learn to "say no" to the exigent and arrogant Americans and instead follow a course true to their own values and interests. Japanese cartoonists showed their small, vulnerable country confronted by a towering and imperious America.[13]

By the 1990s, when a Japanese economy turned stagnant seemed to eliminate one threat, Americans were already fixating on China as the new danger. Nixon's trip to Beijing had inaugurated an era of good feeling, with the U.S. public suddenly discovering that the Chinese were an "intelligent," "artistic," "progressive," and "practical" people.[14] Deng's embrace of the free market reinforced this positive view. But even then some in Congress, the media, and think tanks were unhappy about consorting with Chinese totalitarians. When President Jimmy Carter established diplomatic relations with China at the expense of an old ally on Taiwan, Congress quickly countered with the Taiwan Relations Act. Passed in April 1979, it maintained de facto diplomatic ties and promised the island whatever arms it needed to resist a Communist takeover. Others turned the spotlight on the mainland's transgressions and pressed for greater political and religious freedom, the liberation of Tibet, and an end to Beijing's draconian population-control policy. The Tiananmen repression in June 1989 turned murmurs of discontent into cries of outrage. Nowhere else around the world was the revulsion against "the butchers of Beijing" more strongly felt.

No matter what critics might say about the frustratingly durable and deeply irritating Communists, their diplomatic influence and economic success made them impossible for Washington to ignore and dangerous to challenge. Ronald Reagan, who made a political career by talking of freedom's advance and the evils of communism, had in 1979 described the Communist regime as "founded on violence and propaganda, and destructive of the humane tradition of the Chinese people themselves," and he had promised in his 1980 presidential campaign to reestablish official ties with the Nationalist government on Taiwan. But once in the White House, he backpedaled to the position Nixon had staked out and sought to appease Beijing on arms sales to Taiwan. During a 1984 trip to China, Reagan discovered that it was in fact only a "so-called Communist country." George H. W. Bush dutifully signaled displeasure following the 1989 repression while quietly working to protect good relations. Bill Clinton continued the game, attacking the coddling of Beijing as presidential candidate. Once elected, however, he put trade promotion over human rights and opened China's way to membership in the World Trade Organization. He adopted the cheery view that an open, growing economy and greater use of cell phones and the Internet guaranteed that "the genie of freedom will not go back into the bottle." George W. Bush was his father's son at least on China policy, treating Beijing as an ally in his struggle against terrorism and North Korea's nuclear program.[15]

As the Chinese economy continued humming along and Beijing began throwing its international weight around more and more, commentators made dark predictions of a rising regional hegemon that "is seeking to re-place the United States as the dominant power in Asia," not realizing that they were merely acknowledging a fait accompli. The critics clung to that piece of Cold War wishful thinking about China's inevitable failure. An increasingly self-confident Chinese government brushed aside its critics, while Chinese commentators, including a growing and vocal number of young urban Chinese on the Internet ("netizens"), gave voice to a strong current of nationalism. They appealed to their government to assume the defiant "say no" position popular earlier in Japan and reacted to U.S. af-fronts (as in the bombing of the Chinese embassy in Belgrade) by proclaim-ing, "The Chinese race will not be insulted," and dismissing the United States as a "paper tiger" (a phrase from the Mao era). There was an element of truth in the label. Americans had become deeply dependent on China supplying cheap goods and holding a ballooning U.S. debt. American cor-porations wanted to protect their foothold in a major market. And Wash-ington needed help with a range of issues, from combating terrorism to cli-mate change to containing North Korea and Iran. A century had produced a tectonic shift in China's relationship to the United States.[16]

TRY, TRY AGAIN?

Both the violent rise and the long, painful decline of the American Pacific project offer a cautionary tale applicable to the U.S. entanglement in the Middle East and Afghanistan. There is perhaps good and certainly long-standing resistance to the drawing of historical parallels. Some two millennia ago a Chinese politician-philosopher vented his hostility toward busybody scholars: "Those who use the past to criticize the present should be put to death, together with their relatives." But without historical per-spective we flounder in mid-ocean, the shore from which we came already out of sight, the land we seek well beyond the horizon. Consider the problems now plaguing the contemporary U.S. commitments: a strong dislike of the United States felt across the Islamic world; a flourishing transnational religious ideology playing on that dislike; the U.S. military campaigning in not one but two countries; an even broader pattern of U.S. covert activities; Americans at home and abroad frightened by shadowy forces; and a U.S. political leadership guided by an unwavering faith in its own good intentions and power to shape events. Maybe a bit of historical perspective would help.

The most obvious point suggested by the eastern Asia experience is the need to consider the way a regional commitment can develop out of a long string of seemingly separate but accumulating decisions. Regional ambitions snowball, and their gathering momentum makes them hard to slow down or reverse. The armed entanglement in eastern Asia began with McKinley's decision to take the Philippines, a step whose ever widening circle of consequences he did not foresee. (The anti-imperialists who opposed him were much more prescient.) It ended in Vietnam with defeat, retreat, exhaustion, and demoralization. A chain of imperial logic connected the Philippines War to the Pacific War, the Pacific War to Korea, and the Korean War to Vietnam. To see each of the Asian wars in isolation is to miss what U.S. policymakers themselves viewed as America's Pacific destiny. This mélange of imperial, commercial, religious, and cultural ambitions was leavened by the conceit of America's mission to uplift and democratize the peoples of eastern Asia and secure them against internal and external foes.

By extension, we should see the occupations of Iraq and Afghanistan and the broad and open-ended battle against "terrorism" as part of a history that long antedates September 11, 2001. A string of U.S. interventions and declarations incrementally raised the stakes in the Middle East beginning in the late 1940s and the 1950s even as the Asian drive was running into trouble. Backing for the new state of Israel in 1948, the overthrow of the Mossadeqh government in Iran in 1953 in favor of a client regime, and the Eisenhower doctrine in 1957 on using U.S. military power to shape the region were the first steps toward entanglement. Growing dependence on regional oil supplies, unconditional support for Israel in its wars with neighbors, and the containment or subversion of Soviet-aligned governments pushed the process steadily ahead. The first major crisis erupted with the Iranian revolution in 1979 and the taking of U.S. embassy hostages. The American sense of humiliation and antagonism spurred deeper U.S. involvement, including backing for Saddam Hussein's Iraq in its eight-year war with Iran (1980–88) and substantial military assistance to the Islamist mujahideen insurgency against the Soviet-supported Communist government in Afghanistan beginning in 1978 and continuing for the next decade. Soon afterward, the collapse of the Soviet Union in 1991 removed a strategic competitor in the region and gave the United States greater latitude to apply pressure against any noncompliant regime. Today the drive has arrived at a point comparable to the late 1940s in eastern Asia. Washington now claims regional dominance backed by an assemblage of client governments, a vast system of military bases, and an annual transfer of billions in economic and military aid. And that claim has in turn, inevitably, made enemies and aroused critics within the region and doubts at home.

The Middle East drive was, like its Asian predecessor, fueled by a strong sense of national mission and pride. At no point has this been clearer than during the initiatives of the George W. Bush administration and its public supporters. They claimed that their country had the capacity, will, and virtue to dominate—to create its own reality in a world imagined as fundamentally malleable and receptive. This outlook was married to an impatience for results and resistance to careful calculations and second thoughts. What the sociologist C. Wright Mills once called "crackpot realism" guided policymakers toward a massive misreading of the region.[17] They also did not count on a restive electorate—ignorant to be sure, trusting without doubt, but patient only to a point. Even the sleepwalking media began to stir, despite the best efforts of the administration to manage it. The administration's views and approach were products of the Cold War experience of those surrounding Bush, notably Vice President Dick Cheney, Secretary of Defense Donald Rumsfeld, and their neoconservative policy advisers. They were going to correct the errors of the past, restore presidential power, reject the moral appeasement represented by Nixon's détente, and erase the humiliation of the Vietnam defeat. Their sense of wrongs to right if the nation were to get back on its destined path provided energy and direction all too familiar from the earlier adventure in eastern Asia.

As earlier in Asia, dreams of dominance rested on a sense of superiority over the region's peoples, whose histories and outlooks were not taken seriously. As a result, now no less than in the Asian enterprise, it is American ignorance that makes the enemy appear inscrutable. Its resistance to American attempts to impose a neocolonial order is interpreted as proof of its malevolence and fanaticism. The case of the mounting challenge from political Islam is especially telling. American leaders have responded with a mix of anger, anxiety, and bewilderment. This response assumes good

U.S. intentions and ignores the ways the direct U.S. role in the region and its sustained efforts to prop up friendly (though developmentally troubled) secular regimes has fed powerful Islamic intellectual and political currents dating back to the era of decolonization. Hardly aware of their own history of involvement in the region, it is no surprise that American leaders know virtually nothing of Islamic politics. By the 1960s Egypt's Sayyid Qutb and Iran's Ruhollah Khomeini—two leading voices of the postwar Islamist resurgence—began developing a critique of failed secular leadership and secular ideologies in the region. That critique has gained transnational appeal, spreading across the Muslim world in tandem with the developing U.S. project. That project, with its support for repressive regimes, close association with an expansionist Israel, reliance on covert operations, and resort to destructive military blows has helped to make the United States an important target and provided a spur to those bent on countering U.S. control. That most Americans, ignorant of the past, fixated on the present, and convinced of their own national virtue, cannot see a long-developing, fundamental contradiction does not make it untrue.

Finally, the U.S. experience in eastern Asia provides a reminder that every territorial drive so far from home eventually falters and collapses. Only those deluded by myths of U.S. exceptionalism—and oblivious to the regional perspective—can think otherwise. What by now should be a familiar combination of factors will fall into place to frustrate and even undercut the current U.S. project. Previous empires offer abundant examples of grand initiatives conducted far from home bogging down in difficult and unfamiliar terrain. Americans, with their strong anti-imperial tradition, should have been especially sensitive to this truth. Yet they did not absorb it at the end of the failed Asian project. The push into the Middle East, which has created its own regional backlash and its own quagmire for the United States, offers a belated second chance to recognize the odds against any state, however powerful, seeking to secure and sustain dominion. With the Middle East drive now in its sixth decade, are Iraq and Afghanistan equivalent to Vietnam? Or are they more like Korea, with additional conflicts in the offing before U.S. leaders decide to abandon mission impossible? Is dominance, as the Asia campaign suggests, so difficult to renounce that persisting is more likely even as costs rise and support falls? Has the United States reached a point in the unfolding tragedy where, like Macbeth, one president after another can only say, "I am in blood stepped in so far that, should I wade no more, returning were as tedious as to go o'er?"

The important role played by national myths stands out in this juxtaposition of two protracted regional entanglements. Such myths arise with empire and help sustain it through hard times. An imagined glorious past foreshadowing an even more glorious future with only some evil ogre standing in the way—a fairy tale that simultaneously delights and inspires dread—can galvanize elites and stir popular enthusiasm for the bloody deeds of conquest and the imperious exercise of foreign rule. Even after empire dies, such tales of duty and destiny linger in the national imagination, conjuring up new ogres and inspiring fresh adventures.

Myths enshrouded every step of the tumultuous and often violent U.S. involvement in eastern Asia. Eager empire builders stripped the Philippines of its own history and turned it instead into a backdrop in the unfolding of a grand U.S. transpacific drama. The ugly truth of an overtly colonial enterprise imposed by force, attended by heavy loss of life, and resisted by an angry minority at home made the American war in the Philippines a struggle better forgotten than celebrated. The fairy tales revived in the official and popular mind following Pearl Harbor. The ensuing conflict waged all the way across the Pacific became part of the larger narrative of World War II as the "good war" fought by the "greatest generation," and the occupation at war's end became prime evidence for U.S. efficacy and enlightenment that could be replicated at will anywhere else. Korea, with all its political messiness and military disappointments, fell victim, like the Philippines, to amnesia. The members of the "never again club" that emerged after the Korean armistice swore to avoid another land war in Asia, but their resolve lasted only until Vietnam and the rest of Indochina were about to escape the U.S. orbit. The fairy tales that Americans in Vietnam told themselves assumed a striking variety of forms. Terrorized peasants, magically toppling dominoes, a menacing Chinese dragon, and a United States about to become a pitiful helpless giant figured prominently in them.

The current Middle Eastern project demonstrates the persistence of fairy tales. Were McKinley revived by a kiss from the Fairy Princess of Empire, he would surely applaud the recent claims to U.S. policy advancing the cause of "the West," a term he would quickly recognize as a synonym for his commitment to "civilization." He would read with approval, as have ranking policymakers in our time, such experts as Bernard Lewis and Fouad Ajami, who argue for transforming, or at least holding at bay, a flawed Islamic civilization that has failed to come to terms with the modern world.[18] Similarly, Truman and Kennedy could understand why policymakers might feel that Iran today, like China in their time, poses a danger to the region as well as to U.S. prestige. The refrains of injured innocence that played out in the wake of Pearl Harbor echo in the post-9/11 fury against murderous and treacherous enemies. The spirit of fanatic Japanese was reincarnated in wild-eyed mullahs, shifty tribal chieftains, and hate-filled terrorists. The inspiring story of a prostrated Japan risen under U.S. auspices—like Lazarus revived from the dead—has proven so appealing that the architects of the Iraq War fervently embraced it. Self-styled realist elites preferred to indulge in magical thinking than learn hard lessons from history. Eisenhower and Johnson would immediately recognize the return of their dominoes as Dick Cheney, Paul Wolfowitz, and George W. Bush imagined the outcome of an intervention in Iraq setting off a cascade of happy consequences in the region and beyond. The champions of vulnerable clients such as Rhee and Diem would appreciate the arguments that patrons of Hamid Karzai make today, the need to hide U.S. intervention behind a local face, and the frustrating effort to train effective and responsive indigenous forces.

Only someone beguiled by a fairy-tale mentality could miss the empire that is written all over the revival of "counterinsurgency" doctrine. General David Petraeus, who led the pacification effort in both Iraq and Afghanistan, and his brain trust of younger officers have been its foremost champions. Outfitted with graduate degrees and determined "to avoid repeating the mistakes of the Vietnam War," they set to work codifying their doctrine in a new field manual.[19] They turned to distinctly colonial sources for instruction: French officers drawing lessons in the early 1960s from their own failed wars in Indochina and Algeria and from U.S. marine and British ideas on pacification based on operations a century earlier. The resulting formulation frankly confronted the classic challenge of empire builders: how to operate in a strange land, how to overwhelm the recalcitrant with superior technology and firepower, and how to attract collaborators to share the burden and give local color to foreign intervention.

This vogue of counterinsurgency generated considerable controversy, especially in the sources it drew on, the claims it advanced about success in Iraq, and the relevance it argued for Afghanistan. One commentator with military expertise dismissed it as "a new dogmatism" constructed from a "narrow selection of history and theory." Another saw in it "one questionable proposition" built on another, yielding in turn prescriptions "of little or no use" and amounting to "a kind of malpractice." Yet a third was scathing in his evaluation of an approach "so buoyed by illusions, caulked in ambiguous language and encrusted with moral claims, analogies and political theories that it can seem futile to present an alternative."[20]

The tacit colonial mindset that goes with counterinsurgency is strikingly evident in the case of the Petraeus acolytes. After contributing to the new Army counterinsurgency handbook, Major John Nagl got a chance to convert theory to practice in a Sunni area of Iraq. A December 2003 interview revealed that he had brought to the job a set of views familiar to generations of empire builders. He was guided, he insisted, by a benevolent impulse to liberate Iraqis. "What we want for them is the right to make their own decisions, to live their own lives." But "these clowns"—Nagl's good-natured term for the locals—were not ready and needed his help to transcend their recent political experience, which had left them twisted. But before uplift had to come obedience. Drawing on another favorite bit of colonial wisdom, he stressed the importance of force as the language the natives understood best. Neighborhoods from which his troops took fire had to understand that they risked retaliation and that their actions would endanger whole families. The takeaway lesson he wanted to convey: "You need to turn in the bad guys." The hearts and minds strategy thus turned on the threat of destruction during what Nagl called the "behavior-modification phase. I want their minds right now." Their hearts would come later with generous spending on schools and clinics. Nagl conceded few Arab-speaking Americans were on hand to give him a sense of local sentiment and psychology, and he seemed little concerned by the alienating effects of collective punishments, humiliating roundups, and building demolitions carried out by his troops. As he and other champions of counterinsurgency may have at some level understood, colonial enterprises are ultimately not about the aspirations of the benighted subject peoples but about imposing the will of self-professed enlightened foreigners.[21]

These fairy tales associated with empire have had a profoundly damaging effect. A world framed by American preoccupations leaves little space for the preferences of subjugated peoples. Culturally blind and historically obtuse, it takes no account of the local costs, it cannot tolerate a vision of the future apart from one Americans desire, it depends on compromised collaborators, and it ignores the influence of regional powers. As a result, while Americans remain in denial about the imperial nature of their project, political movements and regional powers mobilize to impede their way. At home, these fairy tales entice the United States with the sugar plum promises of empire and away from foundational national values.

Critics of imperial initiatives were most vocal at the beginning of the eastern Asian drive in the Philippines and at the end during the Vietnam conflict. At those points, they were especially eloquent and insistent on the damage done by distant wars for territorial control. Indeed, they were right to fear the growth and consequent abuse of presidential power, the lasting political divisions and popular disenchantments arising from foreign adventures, the recurrent violation of civil liberties, and the steady erosion of constitutional provisions and republican values as one national emergency followed another. Fundamentally, empire raises for the American system the question of power that so preoccupied the national founders, who believed they were launching a great experiment but one that history told them was fragile. Profoundly fearing the tendency of the powerful to abuse their position, they framed the constitutional system to serve as a check on this malign prospect. Otherwise, the arrogance of the mighty would prevail. The plain-spoken John Adams mordantly expressed this instinctive fear characteristic of an entire generation: "Power always thinks it has a great Soul and vast Views, beyond the comprehension of the Weak; and that it is doing God's Service when it is violating all his Laws."[22]

Taking empire seriously as a historical phenomenon offers a means of returning fairy tales to the nursery. If a definition of insanity is doing the same thing over and over and expecting a different result, then accepting empire as something as American as apple pie may be a step toward sanity. At least it offers a learning opportunity. Some who find what the past suggests unpalatable may resolve not to do empire. Others convinced that empire is defensible or unavoidable may find insights on how to proceed in a more sustainable way and to confront the real costs and risks. Either way, a wider, more historical field of vision can yield rich, practical rewards.

Notes

Chapter 1

1. Grayson quote from press interview of 5 August 1899, published in 1900 and reproduced in *Documentary Sources of Philippine History*, ed. Gregorio F. Zaide and Sonia M. Zaide, 12 vols. (Metro Manila: National Book Store, 1990), 10:75–76. On his return to the United States later in 1899, Grayson took citizenship and settled in San Francisco. Biographical information in Benito J. Legarda Jr. and Ina Bulatao, *The Opening Actions of the Philippine-American War, February 4–5, 1899* (Makati City, Philippines: Bookmark, 2001), 162. Filipino and American versions of this incident disagree on whether Philippine forces provoked that first shot, where along the lines just outside Manila the collision occurred, and whether any Filipinos were killed in the exchange. There is general agreement that the Americans shot first.

2. *Speeches and Addresses of William McKinley from March 1, 1897, to May 30, 1900* (New York: Doubleday & McClure, 1900), 192.

3. Josiah Strong, *Our Country: Its Possible Future and Present Crisis* (New York: American Home Missionary Society, 1885), 165.

4. Data from Walter L. Williams, "United States Indian Policy and the Debate over Philippine Annexation: Implications for the Origins of American Imperialism," *Journal of American History* 66 (March 1980): 828.

5. The phrase appears in a letter by John Hay (then U.S. ambassador in London) to Theodore Roosevelt, 27 July 1898, in William Roscoe Thayer, *The Life and Letters of John Hay*, 2 vols. (Boston: Houghton Mifflin, 1915), 2:337.

6. Phrase quoted in Walter LaFeber, *The American Search for Opportunity, 1865–1913* (Cambridge, U.K.: Cambridge University Press, 1993), 175.

7. Instructions in U.S. Department of State, *Papers Relating to the Foreign Relations of the United States, 1898* (Washington, D.C.: Government Printing Office, 1901), 935, 937–38.

8. The quotes are drawn from McKinley's most elaborate, though distinctly after-the-fact, account of how he reached his decision. See James Rusling, "Interview with President William McKinley [21 November 1899]," *Christian Advocate* 178 (22 January 1903): 137–38 (also available at George Mason University's "History Matters" website at http://historymatters.gmu.edu/d/5575/ [accessed 25 November 2004]). General Rusling's record of McKinley's remarks appeared in print over three years after the meeting, which itself came a year after his decision to take the Philippines and ten months into the war there. Another witness to the interview, James M. Buckley, confirmed in an editorial note published along with Rusling's record that it was "substantially correct." For additional insight, see Ephraim K. Smith, "'A Question from Which We Could Not Escape': William McKinley and the Decision to Acquire the Philippine Islands," *Diplomatic History* 9 (October 1985): 369–70 (on McKinley's interview of 19 November 1898).

9. The October and December rounds of speech making are in *Speeches and Addresses of William McKinley from March 1, 1897, to May 30, 1900*, 85–156, 158–84. Quotes from 114, 161.

10. Ernest R. May, "The Structure of Public Opinion," in May, *American Imperialism: A Speculative Essay* (New York: Atheneum, 1968), chap. 2, suggests a plausible way to think about this important but difficult topic.

11. Quote from *Speeches and Addresses of William McKinley from March 1, 1897, to May 30, 1900*, 193.

12. On Cortelyou's role and the small but growing White House staff, see Lewis L. Gould, *The Modern American Presidency*, 2nd ed. (Lawrence: University Press of Kansas, 2009), chap. 1.

13. José Rizal, "The Philippines a Century Hence," *La Solidaridad* (Barcelona newspaper), 1889–90, reproduced in *Documentary Sources of Philippine History*, 8:68.

14. Bonifacio quoted in Reynaldo Clemeña Ileto, *Pasyon and Revolution: Popular Movements in the Philippines, 1840–1910* (Quezon City, Philippines: Ateneo de Manila University Press, 1979), 105; and statement of principles by Emilio Jacinto from *Documentary Sources of Philippine History*, 8:194–95.

15. Phrase from Glenn Anthony May, "Warfare by *Pulong*: Bonifacio, Aguinaldo, and the Philippine Revolution against Spain," *Philippine Studies*, vol. 55, no. 4 (2007): 463.

16. See the examples in *The Philippine Insurrection against the United States: A Compilation of Documents with Notes and Introduction by John R. M. Taylor*, 5 vols. (Pasay City, Philippines: Eugenio Lopez Foundation, 1971–73), 4:634, 5:637.

17. Mabini, open letter to Filipino patriots, April 1898, reproduced in *Documentary Sources of Philippine History*, 9:110–11.

18. Paterno on "one blood" and the Paterno-Aguinaldo exchange, both quoted in Resil B. Mojares, *Brains of the Nation: Pedro Paterno, T. H. Pardo de Tavera, Isabelo de los Reyes, and the Production of Modern Knowledge* (Quezon City, Philippines: Ateneo de Manila University Press, 2006), 16, 19.

19. Paterno, manifesto to the Filipino people, 31 May 1898, in *Documentary Sources of Philippine History*, 9:174.

20. Aguinaldo to Felipe Agoncillo, 26 August 1898, in *The Philippine Insurrection against the United States*, 3:325.

21. Interview with Emilio Vergara by Glenn A. May in May, "Private Presher and Sergeant Vergara," in *Reappraising an Empire: New Perspectives on Philippine-American History*, ed. Peter W. Stanley (Cambridge, Mass.: Harvard University Press, 1984), 53.

22. Pratt quote from *The Philippine Insurrection against the United States*, 1:476–77; and Dewey quote from *Documentary Sources of Philippine History*, 9:278.

23. Aguinaldo to McKinley, 10 June 1898, in *Documentary Sources of Philippine History*, 9:231, 232.

24. The record of these meetings is in *The Philippine Insurrection against the United States*, addendum to vol. 5, pp. 105–29. Quotes from 114 ("savages") and 126 ("substantial harmony").

25. *Documentary Sources of Philippine History*, 10:80–81.

26. This estimate is based on Angus Maddison, *The World Economy: Historical Statistics*

(Paris: Development Centre of the Organisation for Economic Co-operation and Development, 2003), 82 and 160 (population 1900) and 85 and 170 (GDP 1902).

27. This paragraph draws on Kyle Roy Ward, *In the Shadow of Glory: The Thirteenth Minnesota in the Spanish-American and Philippine-American Wars, 1898 to 1899* (St. Cloud, Minn.: North Star Press of St. Cloud, 2000).

28. Data from U.S. Bureau of the Census, *Historical Statistics of the United States: Colonial Times to 1970* (Washington, D.C.: U.S. Government Printing Office, 1975), 1140.

29. Quotes from Ward, *In the Shadow of Glory*, 123 (Kurtz) and 131 (Bowe).

30. Kreps diary entries for March 1899 and Combs letter to parents in Bedford, Iowa, 2 May 1899, both in *America at War: The Philippines, 1898–1913*, ed. A. B. Feuer (Westport, Conn.: Praeger, 2002), 103, 104, 107, 140; and Paul A. Kramer, "The Darkness That Enters the Home: The Gender Politics of Prostitution during the Philippine-American War," in *Haunted by Empire: Geographies of Intimacy in North American History*, ed. Ann Laura Stoler (Durham, N.C.: Duke University Press, 2006), 370 ("harlotry").

31. Quotes in Ward, *In the Shadow of Glory*, 138, 139.

32. Emilio Vergara quoted in May, "Private Presher and Sergeant Vergara," 54.

33. Troop numbers from Willard B. Gatewood Jr., *Black Americans and the White Man's Burden, 1898–1903* (Urbana: University of Illinois Press, 1975), 263.

34. Quotes from *"Smoked Yankees" and the Struggle for Empire: Letters from Negro Soldiers, 1898–1902*, ed. Willard B. Gatewood Jr. (Urbana: University of Illinois Press, 1971), 248, 257, 280.

35. All quotes from James G. Crawford, "The Warriors of Civilization: U.S. Soldiers, American Culture, and the Conquest of the Philippines, 1898–1902" (Ph.D. diss., University of North Carolina at Chapel Hill, 2002), 55–57, 109–10; except for Sara Bunnett, ed., *Manila Envelopes: Oregon Volunteer Lt. George F. Telfer's Spanish-American War Letters* (Portland: Oregon Historical Society Press, 1987), 29 ("quick of thought"); and Sean McEnroe, "Painting the Philippines with an American Brush: Visions of Race and National Mission among the Oregon Volunteers in the Philippine Wars of 1898 and 1899," *Oregon Historical Quarterly* 104 (Spring 2003): 28 ("lazy").

36. Crawford, "The Warriors of Civilization," 156; McEnroe, "Painting the Philippines with an American Brush," 34–53; *Manila Envelopes*, 151 (Telfer letter of 7 April 1899); and Frank Harper, *Just Outside of Manila: Letters from Members of the First Colorado Regiment in the Spanish-American and Philippine-American Wars* (Denver: Colorado Historical Society, 1991), 63–64, 66, 69, 74, 76, 80, 89 (racial slurs in letters of Corporal Selman Watson), 95 (Private Edwin Segerstrom's letter of 13 June 1899 on bravery).

37. For an example of the usage, see *Manila Envelopes*, 158 (letter of 7 May 1899). On the origins and evolution of a term, see David Roediger, "Gook: The Short History of an Americanism," in Roediger, *Towards the Abolition of Whiteness: Essays on Race, Politics, and Working Class History* (London: Verso, 1994), 117–20.

38. Kreps diary entry in *America at War*, 106.

39. Quotes from May, "Private Presher and Sergeant Vergara," 43 (description), 313 n. 11 (verse).

40. Quotes from McKinley's instructions to Major General Wesley Merritt, 19 May 1898, and to Major General Elwell Otis, 21 December 1898, both in *A Compilation of the Messages and Papers of the Presidents, 1789–1904*, ed. James D. Richardson and George Raywood Devitt, rev. ed., 10 vols. ([New York]: Bureau of National Literature and Art, 1904), 10:344 ("beneficent purpose") and 10:356–57 (December instructions).

41. *Documentary Sources of Philippine History*, 10:89 (proclamation of 4 April 1899) and 10:268 (first commission's private views, 31 January 1900).

42. McKinley's instructions to the Second Philippine Commission, 7 April 1900, in *A Compilation of the Messages and Papers*, 10:219; and Taft quoted in Glenn A. May, *Social Engineering in the Philippines: The Aims, Execution, and Impact of American Colonial Policy, 1900–1913* (Westport, Conn.: Greenwood, 1980), 10.

43. Quote from Anti-Imperialist League platform in Carl Schurz, *The Policy of Imperialism*, Liberty Tract No. 4 (Chicago: American Anti-Imperialist League, 1899), 1.

44. Benjamin R. Tillman, "Causes of Southern Opposition to Imperialism," *North American Review* 171 (October 1900): 444; Carnegie's views originally published in the *North American Review*, August 1898, and reprinted in Andrew Carnegie, *The Gospel of Wealth* (New York: Century, 1901), 157; and Twain, "To the Person Sitting in Darkness," February 1901, reproduced in *Mark Twain's Weapons of Satire: Anti-Imperialist Writings on the Philippine-American War*, ed. Jim Zwick (Syracuse, N.Y.: Syracuse University Press, 1992), 28, 33–34.

45. Quotes from *The Philippine Insurrection against the United States*, 4:201 (Mabini to Apacible, 18 March 1899), and 4:68–69 (Mabini's response to the first Philippines commission, 15 April 1899).

46. Quotes from Mojares, *Brains of the Nation*, 25 (Mabini on Paterno and Buencamino); and from *The Philippine Insurrection against the United States*, 4:91 (Aguinaldo on tasks of the new government), 4:246–56 (Buencamino's memorial, 20 August 1899).

47. Negros' views in May 1899 quoted in John A. Larkin, *Sugar and the Origins of Modern Philippine Society* (Quezon City, Philippines: New Day, 2001), 120.

48. Federal Party leader Trinidad H. Pardo de Taverra to MacArthur, quoted in May, *Social Engineering in the Philippines*, 84; and Vicente Lukban, appeal to the Philippine people, 4 February 1901, in *The Philippine Insurrection against the United States*, 5:677.

49. Quotes from *The Philippine Insurrection against the United States*, 5:140 (Aguinaldo's proclamation to the Filipino people, 19 April 1901); 5:317 (Trías announcement, March 1901); and Resil B. Mojares, *The War against the Americans: Resistance and Collaboration in Cebu, 1899–1906* (Quezon City, Philippines: Ateneo de Manila University Press, 1999), 144 (Maxilom reflection from January 1902). Aguinaldo would go on to advocate for the interests of soldiers who had fought under him. He collaborated with the Japanese during their World War II occupation of his homeland and lived to see the Philippines gain independence from the United States in 1946. He died in 1964 at age ninety-four.

50. Quote from Taft's inaugural address as governor, 4 July 1901, in *Documentary Sources of Philippine History*, 10:385.

51. Quoted in Reynaldo C. Ileto, "The Philippine-American War: Friendship and For-
getting," in *Vestiges of War: The Philippine-American War and the Aftermath of an
Imperial Dream, 1899–1999*, ed. Angel Velasco Shaw and Luis H. Francia (New York:
New York University Press, 2002), 13.

52. General Order 100 is available from the Avalon Project at the Yale Law School:
http://www.yale.edu/lawweb/avalon/lieber.htm (accessed 9 January 2005); Chaffee quoted in Michael H. Hunt, "The Forgotten Occupation: Peking, 1900–1901,"
Pacific Historical Review 48 (November 1979): 529.

53. Chaffee quoted in Alfred W. McCoy, *Policing America's Empire: The United States,
the Philippines, and the Rise of the Surveillance State* (Madison: University of Wisconsin Press, 2009), 84; Smith quoted in Glenn Anthony May, "Was the Philippine-
American War a 'Total War'?" in *Anticipating Total War*, ed. Manfred F. Boemeke
(Cambridge, U.K.: Cambridge University Press; and Washington, D.C.: German Historical Institute, 1999), 445.

54. Malvar, manifesto, 13 July 1901 in *The Philippine Insurrection against the United
States*, 5:347–48.

55. Quotes from Theodore Roosevelt, *The Strenuous Life* (New York: Century, 1902), 330
("cause of civilization" and "uplifting mankind"), 371 ("Apache reservation"), and
389 ("corrupt syndicate").

56. Roosevelt to Harvard president Charles William Eliot, 4 April 1904, in *The Letters of
Theodore Roosevelt*, ed. Elting E. Morison et al., 8 vols. (Cambridge, Mass.: Harvard
University Press, 1951–54), 4:769 ("actual betterment"), 4:770 ("despotism and an-
archy").

57. U.S. Bureau of the Census, *Census of the Philippine Islands Taken under the Direction
of the Philippine Commission in the Year 1903*, 4 vols. (Washington, D.C.: U.S. Government Printing Office, 1905), 2:14; Philippines Census Office, *Census of the Philippine
Islands Taken under the Direction of the Philippine Legislature in the Year 1918*, 4 vols.
(Manila: Bureau of Printing, 1920–21), 4:15.

58. Data on U.S. losses in the Philippine from Brian McAllister Linn, *Guardians of Empire: The U.S. Army and the Pacific, 1902–1940* (Chapel Hill: University of North Carolina Press, 1997), 16. Linn notes that 2,911 were wounded while "several thousand"
died from disease once back in United States. For other wars, see Department of
Defense figures in "Principal Wars in which the United States Participated," available at http://siadapp.dmdc.osd.mil/personnel/CASUALTY/castop.htm (accessed
12 July 2007).

   The Philippine war costs are conventionally put at $400 million direct and $600
million indirect (equivalent to about $10.5 billion in 2000 dollars), but neither the
source for these figures nor the method by which they were calculated is clear.

59. Brian McAllister Linn, "The Impact of the Philippine Wars (1898–1913) on the U.S.
Army," in *Colonial Crucible: Empire in the Making of the Modern American State*, ed.
Alfred W. McCoy and Francisco A. Scarano (Madison: University of Wisconsin Press,
2009), 466.

60. May, "Was the Philippine-American War a 'Total War'?" 437, sets total combatant
losses at "at least 20,000." The estimate of three-quarters of a million appears in the

most painstaking review of the total population losses: Ken De Bevoise, *Agents of Apocalypse: Epidemic Disease in the Colonial Philippines* (Princeton, N.J.: Princeton University Press, 1995), 13.

61. Electoral data from Bonifacio S. Salamanca, *The Filipino Reaction to American Rule, 1901–1913* (Hamden, Conn.: Shoe String, 1968), 66.

62. Quote from Yasuo Wakatsuki, "Japanese Emigration to the United States, 1866–1914: A Monograph," *Perspectives in American History* 12 (1979): 433.

63. Quotes from Akira Iriye, *Pacific Estrangement: Japanese and American Expansion, 1897–1911* (Cambridge, Mass.: Harvard University Press, 1972), 35 (Inagaki), 76 (Kotoku).

64. Quotes from Michael H. Hunt, *The Making of a Special Relationship: The United States and China to 1914* (New York: Columbia University Press, 1983), 45–47.

65. "The Development of Imperialism and the Future of the Twentieth Century World," quoted in Rebecca E. Karl, *Staging the World: Chinese Nationalism at the Turn of the Twentieth Century* (Durham, N.C.: Duke University Press, 2002), 64. Ellipses as they appear in Karl.

66. Liang quotes from Chang-fang Chen, "Barbarian Paradise: Chinese Views of the United States, 1784–1911" (Ph.D. diss., Indiana University, 1985), 259; and from Hunt, *The Making of a Special Relationship*, 264.

67. Zhang Binglin quoted in Michael H. Hunt, *The Genesis of Chinese Communist Foreign Policy* (New York: Columbia University Press, 1996), 115.

68. Quoted in Hunt, *The Genesis of Chinese Communist Foreign Policy*, 95.

Chapter 2

1. Gordon W. Prange with David M. Goldstein and Katherine V. Dillon, *God's Samurai: Lead Pilot at Pearl Harbor* (Washington, D.C.: Brassey's, 1990), 33–35.

2. Paul Joseph Travers, *Eyewitness to Infamy: An Oral History of Pearl Harbor* (Lanham, N.Y.: Madison, 1991), 48–49 (Gaynos quote), 83 (Jenkins quote), 15 (U.S. losses).

3. *The Public Papers and Addresses of Franklin D. Roosevelt, 1941,* comp. Samuel I. Rosenman (New York: Harper, 1950), 514.

4. Major General William P. Duvall quoted in Brian McAllister Linn, "Cerberus' Dilemma: The US Army and Internal Security in the Pacific, 1902–1940," in *Guardians of Empire: The Armed Forces of the Colonial Powers, c. 1700–1964,* ed. David Killingray and David Omissi (Manchester, U.K.: Manchester University Press, 1999), 127.

5. Roosevelt to the British diplomat Cecil Spring-Rice, 19 March and 3 June 1904, in *The Letters of Theodore Roosevelt,* ed. Elting E. Morison et al., 8 vols. (Cambridge, Mass.: Harvard University Press, 1951–54), 4:760 (dynamic Japan) and 4:830 ("paramount interest").

6. Roosevelt to Taft, 21 August 1907, on Achilles' heel in *Letters of Theodore Roosevelt,* 5:762.

7. California legislator quoted in Roger Daniels, *The Politics of Prejudice: The Anti-Japanese Movement in California and the Struggle for Japanese Exclusion,* 2nd ed. (Berkeley: University of California Press, 1977), 47.

8. Roosevelt to President Taft, 22 December 1910, in *Letters of Theodore Roosevelt,* 7:189.

9. *The Public Papers and Addresses of Franklin D. Roosevelt, 1937*, comp. Samuel I. Rosenman (New York: Macmillan, 1941), 407.

10. George H. Gallup, *The Gallup Poll: Public Opinion, 1935–1971*, 3 vols. (New York: Random House, 1972), 135 (*Good Earth*), 72 and 159 (support for China).

11. Quote from *Japan's Decision for War: Records of the 1941 Policy Conferences*, ed. and trans. Nobutaka Ike (Stanford, Calif.: Stanford University Press, 1967), 10.

12. Hull memo of conversation, 27 November 1941 in U.S. Department of State, *Foreign Relations of the United States* [hereafter *FRUS*]: *Japan, 1931–1941*, 2 vols. (Washington, D.C.: U.S. Government Printing Office, 1943), 2:772; Roosevelt on "Prussians of the East," quoted in Ross T. McIntire, *White House Physician* (New York: G. P. Putnam's Sons, 1946), 109; and Roosevelt to Ambassador in Tokyo Joseph C. Grew on "five continents," 21 January 1941, in *FRUS, 1941*, vol. 4 (Washington, D.C.: U.S. Government Printing Office, 1956), 8.

13. Henry R. Luce, "The American Century," *Life*, 17 February 1941, 65; Gallup, *The Gallup Poll*, 306–7; and Gallup Poll #1941–0254, 27 November–2 December 1941 from the iPOLL Databank, Roper Center for Public Opinion Research, University of Connecticut, http://www.ropercenter.uconn.edu.libproxy.lib.unc.edu/data_access/ipoll/ipoll.html (accessed 24 January 2011).

14. Quotes from Noriko Kawamura, "Emperor Hirohito and Japan's Decision to Go to War with the United States: Reexamined," *Diplomatic History* 31 (January 2007), 59 (emperor); and from *Japan's Decision for War*, 139 (Nagano), 238 (Tojo in early November), 283 (Tojo in early December).

15. Paul Bairoch, "International Industrialization Levels from 1750 to 1980," *Journal of European Economic History* 11 (Fall 1982): 299 (relative industrial capacity); Richard Overy, *Why the Allies Won* (New York: W. W. Norton, 1997), 190 (U.S. production of key commodities); Angus Maddison, *The World Economy: Historical Statistics* (Paris: Development Centre of the Organisation for Economic Co-operation and Development, 2003), 82, 162 (population).

16. Overy, *Why the Allies Won*, 331.

17. Quote from Mark A. Stoler, "The 'Pacific-First' Alternative in American World War II Strategy," *International History Review* 2 (July 1980): 434.

18. Richard B. Frank, *Guadalcanal: The Definitive Account of the Landmark Battle* (New York: Penguin, 1992), 527 (quotes), 613–14 (casualties).

19. Quote from E. B. Sledge, *With the Old Breed: At Peleliu and Okinawa* (New York: Oxford University Press, 1990), 59.

20. Sledge, *With the Old Breed*, 34, 121.

21. David M. Kennedy, *Freedom from Fear: The American People in Depression and War, 1929–1945* (New York: Oxford University Press, 1999), 561 (marine on Guadalcanal); Gavan Daws, *Prisoners of the Japanese* (New York: William Morrow, 1994), 22 (list of insults; italics in original).

22. Daws, *Prisoners of the Japanese*, 71.

23. Quotes from *Japan at War: An Oral History*, comp. Haruko Taya Cook and Theodore Cook (New York: New Press, 1992), 383 (U.S. fleet and bombardment).

24. *Japan at War*, 291 (surrender quote and death data).

25. Itabashi diary entry for 3 January 1945, in *Leaves from an Autumn of Emergencies:*

Selections from the Wartime Diaries of Ordinary Japanese, ed. and trans. Samuel Hideo Yamashita (Honolulu: University of Hawai'i Press, 2005), 66.

26. Overy, *Why the Allies Won*, 61 (merchant marine tonnage).

27. Diary entry of a schoolgirl, Maeda Shoko, 2 April 1945, in *Leaves from an Autumn of Emergencies*, 225; Araki in *Japan at War*, 324–25.

28. Tamura diary entries, 1 August 1944 and 10 March 1945, in *Leaves from an Autumn of Emergencies*, 89, 122; and Takahashi diary entries, 8 June 1942, 10 June 1943, 18 July and 19 October 1944, in *Leaves from an Autumn of Emergencies*, 165, 170, 174, 176.

29. The theme song "Bei ei gekimetsu!" from this film released in 1944 is available at http://rasiel.web.infoseek.co.jp/en/beieigekimetsu.htm (accessed 13 August 2009); Tamura diary entry, 10 March 1945, and Takahashi diary entry, 9 August 1945, both in *Leaves from an Autumn of Emergencies*, 122 and 187.

30. Maria Rosa Henson, *Comfort Woman: A Filipina's Story of Prostitution and Slavery under the Japanese Military* (Lanham, Md.: Rowman and Littlefield, 1999), 36.

31. *The Words and Music of World War II*, compact disc (New York: Sony Music Entertainment, 1991, 2001), disc 2, track 2.

32. Ronald Takaki, *Strangers from a Different Shore* (New York: Penguin, 1990), 370 (quoting *Time*, 22 December 1941), 371 (signs).

33. Data from William M. Tuttle Jr., *"Daddy's Gone to War": The Second World War in the Lives of American Children* (New York: Oxford University Press, 1993), 31.

34. Data from Judith A. Bellefaire, *The Women's Army Corps: A Commemoration of World War II Service* (U.S. Army Center of Military History publication 72-15), unpaginated, available at: http://www.history.army.mil/brochures/WAC/wac.htm (accessed 7 July 2008).

35. David H. Price, *Anthropological Intelligence: The Deployment and Neglect of American Anthropology in the Second World War* (Durham, N.C.: Duke University Press, 2008), 184; and Reischauer in mid-1942 quoted in Richard H. Minear, "Cross-Cultural Perception and World War II: American Japanists and Their Images of Japan," *International Studies Quarterly* 24 (December 1980): 562.

36. Price, *Anthropological Intelligence*, 32.

37. Kurihara interview in Dorothy S. Thomas and Richard S. Nishimoto, *Japanese-American Evacuation and Resettlement during World War II*, vol. 1, *The Spoilage* (Berkeley: University of California Press, 1946), 369; Takaki, *Strangers from a Different Shore*, 399 (numbers who served); and National Park Service, U.S. Department of the Interior, *Japanese-Americans in World War II*, 30 (those assigned to Asia and the Pacific), available at http://www.nps.gov/history/nhl/themes/JPNAmericanTS.pdf (accessed 3 March 2011).

38. Quote from Mark Clodfelter, *Beneficial Bombing: The Progressive Foundations of American Air Power, 1917–1945* (Lincoln: University of Nebraska Press, 2010), 187; and figures on destruction from Mark Selden, "A Forgotten Holocaust: U.S. Bombing Strategy, the Destruction of Japanese Cities, and the American Way of War from the Pacific War to Iraq," in *Bombing Civilians: A Twentieth-Century History*, ed. Yuki Tanaka and Marilyn B. Young (New York: New Press, 2009), 83, 85.

39. Data from Ronald H. Spector, *Eagle against the Sun: The American War with Japan* (New York: Free Press, 1985), 532, 540.

40. For the projected size of the U.S. invasion force, see Barton J. Bernstein, "Reconsidering Truman's Claim of 'half a million American lives' Saved by the Atomic Bomb: The Construction and Deconstruction of a Myth," *Journal of Strategic Studies* 22 (March 1999): 62.

41. Bernstein, "Reconsidering Truman's Claim," 64–65.

42. Quote from Harry S. Truman, *Memoirs: Year of Decisions* (Garden City, N.Y.: Doubleday, 1955), 419; and Bernstein's judgment in "Reconsidering Truman's Claim," 75.

43. Truman diary entry at the Truman Presidential Museum and Library, http://www.trumanlibrary.org/whistlestop/study_collections/bomb/large/documents/index.php?pagenumber=4&documentid=4&documentdate=1945-07-17&studycollectionid=abomb&groupid= (accessed 14 May 2005); and the Potsdam Proclamation, 26 July 1945, at the Avalon Project, http://avalon.law.yale.edu/20th_century/decade17.asp (accessed 26 January 2011).

44. Quote from *Widows of Hiroshima: The Life Stories of Nineteen Peasant Wives*, ed. Mikio Kanda and trans. Taeko Midorikawa (New York: St. Martin's, 1989), 40.

45. Remarks recorded by Secretary of Commerce Henry A. Wallace, in *The Price of Vision: The Diary of Henry A. Wallace, 1942–1946*, ed. John M. Blum (Boston: Houghton Mifflin, 1973), 474. This paragraph follows the interpretation advanced by Tsuyoshi Hasegawa in *Racing the Enemy: Stalin, Truman, and the Surrender of Japan* (Cambridge, Mass.: Harvard University Press, 2005): that it was Soviet entry into the war, more than the atomic bombing of Hiroshima, that finally broke the impasse in Japanese decision-making circles by puncturing the illusion of a Soviet-brokered negotiated end to the war.

46. Emperor's radio address quoted in John W. Dower, *Embracing Defeat: Japan in the Wake of World War II* (New York: W. W. Norton, 1999), 36; Takahashi diary entries for 14 and 15 August 1945, in *Leaves from an Autumn of Emergencies*, 188, 189.

47. Paul Fussell, "'Thank God for the atom bomb': Hiroshima—A Soldier's View," *New Republic*, 22 and 29 August 1981, 29 and Micheal Clodfelter, *Warfare and Armed Conflicts: A Statistical Encyclopedia of Casualty and Other Figures, 1494–2007*, 3rd ed. (Jefferson, N.C.: McFarland, 2008), 561 (Japanese noncombatant losses), 563 (U.S. and Japanese combat losses).

48. Luce, "The American Century," 65.

49. Quotes from Sodei Rinjiro, *Dear General MacArthur: Letters from the Japanese during the American Occupation*, ed. John Junkerman and trans. Shizue Matsuda (Lanham, Md.: Rowman & Littlefield, 2001), 108 (abuse of power and money), 279 (former military leaders), 22 (son in Burma).

50. Quotes from Saburo Ienaga, *The Pacific War: World War II and the Japanese, 1931–1945*, trans. Frank Baldwin (New York: Pantheon, 1978), 255–56.

51. Quote from John W. Dower, "The Bombed: Hiroshima and Nagasaki in Japanese Memory," *Diplomatic History* 19 (Spring 1995): 295.

52. Poll results in Steven R. Weisman, "Japanese Think They Owe Apology and Are Owed One, Poll Shows," *New York Times*, 8 December 1991, 26; Kappa Senoh, *A Boy Called H: A Childhood in Wartime Japan*, trans. John Bester (Tokyo: Kodansha International, 1999), 341.

53. Paul W. Tibbets Jr., speech of 8 June 1994, quoted in extenso in Martin Harwit, *An*

Exhibit Denied: Lobbying the History of the "Enola Gay" (New York: Springer-Verlag, 1996), 289; *Wall Street Journal*, 29 August 1994, quoted in Richard H. Kohn, "History and the Culture Wars: The Case of the Smithsonian Institution's *Enola Gay* Exhibit," *Journal of American History* 82 (December 1995): 1054; Buchanan quote from Edward T. Linenthal, "Anatomy of a Controversy," in *History Wars: The "Enola Gay" and Other Battles for the American Past*, ed. Linenthal and Tom Engelhardt (New York: Henry Holt, 1996), 59; Ford quoted in a partial transcript of the hearings of the Senate Committee on Rules and Administration, in "History after the *Enola Gay* Controversy," in *Journal of American History* 82 (December 1995): 1042, 1041.

54. *Pearl Harbor* (2001, dir. Michael Bay, 183 min.); *Tora! Tora! Tora!* (1970, dir. Richard Fleischer with Kinji Fukusaku and Toshio Masuda, 144 min.).

55. Quote from Walter LaFeber, *The Clash: A History of U.S.-Japan Relations* (New York: W. W. Norton, 1997), 221.

56. Lyrics from "Better World" at http://www.woodyguthrie.org/Lyrics/Better_World/htm (accessed 6 September 2008); and Kathleen E. R. Smith, *God Bless America: Tin Pan Alley Goes to War* (Lexington: University Press of Kentucky, 2003), 12 ("it's our Pacific").

57. Harold R. Isaacs, *No Peace for Asia* (Cambridge, Mass.: MIT Press, 1967 [1947]), 1, 3.

Chapter 3

1. Quote from William Dannenmaier, *We Were Innocents: An Infantryman in Korea* (Urbana: University of Illinois Press, 1999), 181–82. Walter G. Hermes, *Truce Tent and Fighting Front* (Washington, D.C.: U.S. Army Center of Military History, 2005), 489–90, describes the signing ceremony.

2. This divergence emerges clearly in "Communications between Mao and Stalin: Seven Telegrams, January 1949" (trans. Song Dat), *Chinese Historians* 7 (Spring–Fall 1994): 163–72.

3. John V. A. MacMurray to Secretary of State Frank B. Kellogg, 16 November 1926, in U.S. Department of State, *Foreign Relations of the United States* [hereafter *FRUS*], vol. 1 (Washington, D.C.: U.S. Government Printing Office, 1941), 899.

4. FDR comments reported by Anthony Eden, March 1943, quoted in Walter LaFeber, "Roosevelt, Churchill, and Indochina, 1942–45," *American Historical Review* 80 (December 1975): 1280.

5. Thomas G. Paterson, "If Europe, Why Not China? The Containment Doctrine, 1947–49," *Prologue* 13 (Spring 1981): 23–24 (Truman quote and details of U.S. aid).

6. Truman remarks, 11 March 1948, in *Public Papers of the Presidents* [hereafter PPP]: *Harry S. Truman, 1948* (Washington, D.C.: U.S. Government Printing Office, 1964), 181; and Acheson's characterization from public letter to Truman, 30 July 1949, in U.S. Department of State, *United States Relations with China with Special Reference to the Period 1944–1949* (Washington, D.C.: U.S. Government Printing Office, 1949), xvi.

7. On public opinion on aid for the Nationalists, see George H. Gallup, *The Gallup Poll: Public Opinion, 1935–1971*, 3 vols. (New York: Random House, 1972), 818 (May 1949), 853 (August 1949); and on nonrecognition of the Communists, *The Gallup Poll: Public Opinion, 1935–1971*, 831 (June 1949), 868 (October 1949), 881 (November 1949), 915 (May 1950).

8. Lives lost from Kim Dong-choon, *The Unending Korean War: A Social History* (Larkspur, Calif.: Tamal Vista, 2009), 150–51, 189.

9. Charles Armstrong, *The North Korean Revolution, 1945–1950* (Ithaca, N.Y.: Cornell University Pres, 2003), 77; Robert A. Scalapino and Chong-Sik Lee, *Communism in Korea*, part 1, *The Movement* (Berkeley: University of California Press, 1972), 349 n. 66 (refugee figures).

10. Quoted phrases from National Security Council report on Korea, 2 April 1948, *FRUS, 1948*, vol. 6 (Washington, D.C.: U.S. Government Printing Office, 1974), 1169 ("*casus belli*"), 1166 ("immaturity").

11. Data for 1950 in Angus Maddison, *The World Economy: Historical Statistics* (Paris: Development Centre of the Organisation for Economic Co-operation and Development, 2003), 153 (population North and South), 174 (GDP for South), 178 (GDP for North).

12. Shen Zhihua, "Sino-Soviet Relations and the Origins of the Korean War: Stalin's Strategic Goals in the Far East," *Journal of Cold War Studies* 2 (Spring 2000): 50 (Politburo decision, 24 September 1949), 63 (recollections of Foreign Ministry official Mikhail Kapitsa).

13. Quote from Anatolii V. Torkunov, *Zagadochnaia voina: Koreiskii konflikt, 1950–1953 godov* [The enigmatic war: The Korean conflict, 1950–1953] (Moscow: ROSSPEN, 2000), 70.

14. Details on these killings can be found in Bruce Cumings, "The South Korean Massacre at Taejon: New Evidence on U.S. Responsibility and Coverup," posted 23 July 2008, at http://japanfocus.org/-Bruce-Cumings/2826; Charles J. Hanley and Jae-soon Chang, "Summer of Terror: At Least 100,000 Said Executed by Korean Ally of U.S. in 1950," posted 3 July 2008, at http://japanfocus.org/-Charles-J-Hanley/2827 (both accessed 4 August 2008); and Kobayashi Akira, "The Unknown Korean War: The Truth and Reconciliation Commission of Korea and Excavation of the Remains of Mass-murdered Victims" (trans. Nobuka Adachi), posted 3 May 2010 at http://japanfocus.org/-Kobayashi-Akira/3351 (accessed 3 May 2010).

15. Stalin message to Czech president Klement Gottwald, 27 August 1950, Cold War International History Project Korean War collection, http://www.wilsoncenter.org/index.cfm?topic_id=1409&fuseaction=va2.document&identifier=E4474099-B4AD-4067-B4A88B9C7643B3BE&sort=Collection&item=The%20Korean%20War (accessed 9 December 2010).

16. Data from Micheal Clodfelter, *Warfare and Armed Conflicts: A Statistical Reference to Casualty and Other Figures, 1500–2007*, 3rd ed. (Jefferson, N.C.: McFarland, 2008), 708.

17. Quote from late August 1950 in James I. Matray, "Truman's Plan for Victory: National Self-Determination and the Thirty-Eighth Parallel Decision in Korea," *Journal of American History* 66 (September 1979): 326.

18. Quotes from *FRUS, 1950*, vol. 7 (Washington, D.C.: U.S. Government Printing Office, 1976), 781 (Joint Chiefs of Staff, directive to MacArthur, 27 September 1950) and 826 (Marshall to MacArthur, 29 September 1950).

19. Quotes from *Chinese Communist Foreign Policy and the Cold War in Asia: New Documentary Evidence, 1944–1950*, ed. and trans. Shuguang Zhang and Jian Chen (Chi-

cago: Imprint, 1996), 162 (Mao on dominoes in telegram to Stalin, drafted 2 October 1950 but not sent); and Chen Jian, *China's Road to the Korean War: The Making of the Sino-American Confrontation* (New York: Columbia University Press, 1994), 271 n. 57 ("beat American arrogance").

20. Minutes of Zhou conversation with Indian Ambassador K. M. Pannikar, 3 October 1950, in *Chinese Communist Foreign Policy and the Cold War in Asia*, 164.

21. Stalin's response to Mao quoted at length in Stalin to Kim Il Sung, 8 October 1950, in Kathryn Weathersby, "New Evidence on the Korean War," *Cold War International History Project Bulletin* 6-7 (Winter 1995/1996), 116.

22. This reconstruction follows Shen Zhihua, "The Discrepancy between the Russian and Chinese Versions of Mao's 2 October 1950 Message to Stalin on Chinese Entry into the Korean War" (trans. Chen Jian), *Cold War International History Project Bulletin*, nos. 8–9 (Winter 1996–97): 237–42; quote from 241.

23. Marshal Peng Dehuai, "My Story of the Korean War," in *Mao's Generals Remember Korea*, ed. and trans. Xiaobing Li, Allan R. Millett, and Bin Yu (Lawrence: University Press of Kansas, 2001), 31.

24. Quotes from *FRUS, 1950*, 7:869 (Acheson comment to the British U.N. delegation, 4 October); 953 (MacArthur remarks to Truman, 15 October); 1025 (CIA director Walter B. Smith memo of 1 November 1950).

25. Former captain Wang Xuedong quoted in *Voices from the Korean War: Personal Stories of American, Korean, and Chinese Soldiers*, ed. Richard Peters and Xiaobing Li (Lexington: University Press of Kentucky, 2004), 124.

26. Quotes from Martin Russ, *Breakout: The Chosin Reservoir Campaign, Korea 1950* (New York: Penguin, 2000), 335 (marine scorn), 355 (General Smith).

27. *FRUS, 1950*, 7:1109 (MacArthur to the Joint Chiefs of Staff, 9 November 1950), 1237 (MacArthur to the Joint Chiefs of Staff, 28 November 1950); *PPP: Harry S. Truman, 1950* (Washington, D.C.: Government Printing Office, 1965) 724, 727 (Truman press conference, 30 November 1950); *FRUS, 1951*, vol. 7 (Washington, D.C.: U.S. Government Printing Office, 1983), 69 (Truman remarks to senior advisers, 12 January 1951).

28. Attlee to Foreign Secretary Ernest Bevan, 10 December 1950, quoted in Ra Jong-yil, "Special Relationship at War: The Anglo-American Relationship during the Korean War," *Journal of Strategic Studies* 7 (September 1984): 312.

29. Acheson quoted in David McLean, "American Nationalism, the China Myth, and the Truman Doctrine: The Question of Accommodation with Peking, 1949–50," *Diplomatic History* 10 (Winter 1986): 41.

30. Conrad C. Crane, *American Airpower Strategy in Korea, 1950–1953* (Lawrence: University Press of Kansas, 2000), 32 ("fire job"), 63 (Pyongyang attack).

31. Mao quotes from Ye Zilong, *Huiyilu* [Reminiscences] (Beijing: Zhongyang wenxian, 2000), 197 ("always sacrifices"); and Li Min, *Wode fuqin Mao Zedong* [My father Mao Zedong] (Shenyang: Liaoning renmin, 2001), 148 ("a simple soldier").

32. James Brady, *The Coldest War: A Memoir of Korea* (New York: Orion, 1990), 191.

33. Data from Paul Bairoch, "International Industrialization Levels from 1750 to 1980," *Journal of European Economic History* 11 (Fall 1982): 275, 284.

34. Russ, *Breakout*, 318.

35. Treatment here of living conditions for U.S. servicemen comes from Rudolph

Stephens, *Old Ugly Hill: A G.I.'s Fourteen Months in the Korean Trenches, 1952–1953* (Jefferson, N.C.: McFarland, 1995), 54, 63–82; Dannenmaier, *We Were Innocents*, 191; and Sarah Kovner, "Base Cultures: Sex Workers and Servicemen in Occupied Japan," *Journal of Asian Studies* 68 (August 2009): 786, 794–99.

36. Data from U.S. Bureau of the Census, *Historical Statistics of the United States: Colonial Times to 1970* (Washington, D.C.: U.S. Government Printing Office, 1975), 1140.

37. William Childress, "Korea Bound, 1952," in *War, Literature & the Arts* 9 (Spring–Summer 1997): 53; "Yuletide Greetings," in *We Will Not Be Strangers: Korean War Letters between a M.A.S.H. Surgeon and His Wife*, ed. Dorothy G. Horwitz (Urbana: University of Illinois Press, 1997), 165; reflections of Army Sergeant James Hart in *Voices from the Korean War*, 241.

38. Brady, *The Coldest War*, 19 ("gook trains"); Stephens, *Old Ugly Hill*, 167 ("potshots"); and William Childress, "Letter Home," in *War, Literature, & the Arts* 9 (Spring–Summer 1997): 54 (poem).

39. Dannenmaier, *We Were Innocents*, 159 ("showed their feelings"); and Linda Granfield, *I Remember Korea: Veterans Tell Their Stories, 1950–53* (New York: Clarion, 2003), 95 ("digging our garbage").

40. Tonnage estimates in Eduard Mark, *Aerial Interdiction: Air Power and the Land Battle in Three Wars* (Washington, D.C.: Center of Air Force History, 1994), 307.

41. Clodfelter, *Warfare and Armed Conflicts*, 709.

42. On support for Truman's decision to intervene, Gallup Poll, 9–14 July 1950 (USGALLUP.50-458.QK09A) from the iPOLL Databank, Roper Center for Public Opinion Research, University of Connecticut, http://www.ropercenter.uconn.edu .libproxy.lib.unc.edu/data_access/ipoll/ipoll.html (accessed 22 September 2010). For later popular reactions, see *The Gallup Poll: Public Opinion, 1935–1971*, 943 (mid-September 1950 on crossing the thirty-eighth parallel), 970 (early February 1951 on Truman's overall performance). The trends in opinion from December 1950 through February 1951 are the same in Gallup and National Opinion Research Center polling (both available in the iPoll Databank), though at important points the percentages reported vary quite considerably.

43. MacArthur to Martin, 20 March 1951, in *FRUS, 1951*, 7:299.

44. *The Gallup Poll: Public Opinion, 1935–1971*, 981 (mid-April 1951 on Truman's firing of MacArthur); Burton I. Kaufman, *The Korean War: Challenges in Crisis, Credibility, and Command*, 2nd ed. (New York: McGraw-Hill, 1997), 100 (MacArthur phrase).

45. Quote from Kaufman, *The Korean War*, 107 (Bradley).

46. Film count from Robert J. Lentz, *Korean War Filmography* (Jefferson, N.C.: McFarland, 2003), 2–3; *Steel Helmet* (1951, dir. Samuel Fuller, 84 min.).

47. "Dear John" lyrics from http://lyricsplayground.com/alpha/songs/a/adearjohn letter.shtml (accessed 14 June 2011); "Korea Blues" from http://www.lyricsbay/ Korea_blues_lyrics_jb_lenoir.html (accessed 25 March 2011); "Weapon of Prayer" from http://www.atomicplatters.com/more.php?id=129_0_1_0_M (accessed 10 March 2010).

48. These comics are available online at http://www.authentichistory.com/1946-1960/ 2-Korea/4-comicsindex.html (accessed 14 June 2011).

49. Chinese budget data from Yang Kuisong, "Mao Zedong and the Indochina Wars," in

Behind the Bamboo Curtain: China, Vietnam, and the World beyond Asia, ed. Priscilla Roberts (Washington, D.C.: Woodrow Wilson Center Press; and Stanford, Calif.: Stanford University Press, 2006), 92 n. 9.

50. Quote from Zi Zhongyun's autobiography (in collaboration with Steven I. Levine), tentatively titled "Becoming Myself Again: A Chinese Woman's Odyssey."

51. Diary entry for 27 January 1952, quoted in Rosemary Foot, *The Wrong War: American Policy and the Dimensions of the Korean Conflict, 1950–1953* (Ithaca, N.Y.: Cornell University Press, 1985), 176.

52. Ridgway report to the Joint Chiefs of Staff, 7 August 1951, in *FRUS, 1951*, 7:788.

53. Quote from Article 118 of the convention available at University of Minnesota Human Rights Library, http://www1.umn.edu/humanrts/instree/y3gctpw.htm (accessed 9 December 2010).

54. Quote from Wadie J. Rountree in *Voices from the Korean War*, 224. POW figures here and in the paragraphs that follow come from Steven Hugh Lee, *The Korean War* (Harlow, U.K.: Longman, 2001), 78–80, 86–87, 95–96.

55. The still classified CIA estimate (NIE-80 of 3 April 1950) summarized in Clayton D. Laurie, "A New President, a Better CIA, and an Old War: Eisenhower and Intelligence Reporting on Korea, 1953," *Studies in Intelligence* 54 (December 2010): 7 (available at https://www.cia.gov/library/center-for-the-study-of-intelligence/csi-publications/csi-studies/studies/vol.-54-no.-4/a-new-president-a-better-cia-and-an-old-war.html); and Dulles comment to speechwriter Emmet J. Hughes, quoted in Foot, *Wrong War*, 212.

56. Shen Zhihua, "Chinese and Soviet Strategy on Ending the Korean War," ed. and trans. Steven I. Levine (ms.), originally published in *Shijie zhishi* [World Affairs], no. 2 (2001): 16 (data), 19 (Zhou quote).

57. Data on destruction from the air from Clodfelter, *Warfare and Armed Conflicts*, 708 (bombs and napalm); and from Crane, *American Airpower Strategy*, 168 (postwar U.S. assessment that of twenty-two major cities eighteen were at least half destroyed and ten were 80 to 100 percent gone). Data on Korean human and material losses from B. C. Koh, "The War's Impact on the Korean Peninsula," in *A Revolutionary War*, ed. William J. Williams (Chicago: Imprint, 1993), 245–46. Chinese losses calculated from military archives in Xu Yan, "The Chinese Forces and Their Casualties in the Korean War: Facts and Statistics" (trans. Li Xiaobing), *Chinese Historians* 6 (Fall 1993): 54, 56. Loss of U.S., other U.N. (except South Korean), and Soviet combatants from Clodfelter, *Warfare and Armed Conflicts*, 709–10.

58. Ambassador John J. Muccio to Assistant Secretary of State Dean Rusk, 25 July 1950, quoted in Associated Press report, 29 May 2006, in *The Independent* (online edition), 30 May 2008, at http://www.independent.co.uk/news/world/politics/1950-letter-shows-us-approved-of-killing-Korean-War-refugees (accessed 25 March 2011). Survivor quote from Charles J. Hanley, Sang-hun Choe, and Martha Mendoza, *The Bridge at No Gun Ri: A Hidden Nightmare from the Korean War* (New York: Henry Holt, 2001), 122. On the village of Tanyang, see Choe Sang-hun, "Korean War's Lost Chapter: South Korea Says U.S. Killed Hundreds of Civilians," *International Herald Tribune* (online edition), 2 August 2008 (accessed 4 August 2008).

59. Choi Jae-sang quoted in Choe Sang-hun, "A Korean Village Torn Apart from within Mends Itself," *New York Times* (online edition), 21 February 2008.

60. Data from Lee, *The Korean War*, 105.

61. The ten volumes that comprise *T'aebaek Mountain Range* were published in Korean in 1983–86; Yun Heung-gil, "The Rainy Spell," in *The Rainy Spell and Other Korean Stories*, ed. and trans. Suh Ji-moon, rev. ed. (Armonk, N.Y.: M. E. Sharpe, 1998); Ahn Jung-hyo, *The Silver Stallion* (New York: Soho, 1990); *Tae Guk Gi: The Brotherhood of War* (2004, dir. Kang Je-gyu, 140 min.).

62. Sheila Miyoshi Jager and Jiyul Kim, "The Korean War after the Cold War: Commemorating the Armistice Agreement in South Korea," in *Ruptured Histories: War, Memory, and the Post–Cold War in Asia*, ed. Sheila Miyoshi Jager and Rana Mitter (Cambridge, Mass.: Harvard University Press, 2007), 242, 245 (War Memorial quotes); and Choe Sang-hun, "Korean War's Lost Chapter."

63. *Shangganling* (1956, dir. Lin Shan and Sha Meng, 124 min.; DVD release with English subtitles December 2007); *Yingxiongernu* (1964, dir. Wu Zhaodi, 117 min.).

64. *The Bridges at Toko-ri* (1955, dir. Mark Robson, 102 min.); and *Pork Chop Hill* (1959, dir. Lewis Milestone, 97 min.).

65. U.S. Department of the Army Inspector General, *No Gun Ri Review* (January 2001), 192, available at http://www.army.mil/nogunri (accessed 8 March 2011).

66. Blanche Wiesen Cook, *The Declassified Eisenhower: A Divided Legacy* (Garden City, N.Y.: Doubleday, 1981), 108 (Eisenhower to members of Congress on the loss of China, 19 June 1951); *The Eisenhower Diaries*, ed. Robert H. Ferrell (New York: W. W. Norton, 1981), 296 (Eisenhower entry for 26 March 1955 on character of Chinese Communists); *The Churchill-Eisenhower Correspondence, 1953–1955*, ed. Peter G. Boyle (Chapel Hill: University of North Carolina Press, 1990), 206 (Eisenhower to Churchill, 29 March 1955 on "brigands"); and Ronald W. Pruessen, *John Foster Dulles: The Road to Power* (New York: Free Press, 1982), 487 (Dulles interview, 15 May 1951).

67. *The Churchill-Eisenhower Correspondence*, 204 (Eisenhower to Churchill on the importance of Taiwan, 29 March 1955); *The Gallup Poll: Public Opinion, 1935–1971*, 1226, 1329, 1471, 1495, 1542 (on contact with China), 1169, 1254, 1259, 1335, 1337–38, 1365, 1471, 1542, 1569–70, 1610 (on China's U.N. seat), 1273, 1333–34, 1569 (on Taiwan crises).

68. Troop levels for 1953 in Roger Dingman, "The Dagger and the Gift: The Impact of the Korean War on Japan," *Journal of American–East Asian Relations* 1 (Spring 1993): 50.

69. "Huks" was a popular shorthand for the wartime People's Anti-Japanese Army (in Tagalog, Hukbo ng Bayan Laban sa Hapon or Hukbalahap) and for the postwar People's Liberation Army (Hukbong Mapagpalaya ng Bayan, or HMB).

70. Kennan memo to Secretary of State Acheson, 6 January 1950, in *FRUS, 1950*, vol. 1 (Washington, D.C.: U.S. Government Printing Office, 1977), 131; "The Position of the United States with Respect to the Philippines" (NSC 84/2), 9 November 1950, in *FRUS, 1950*, vol. 6 (Washington, D.C.: U.S. Government Printing Office, 1976), 1516 (defensive line).

71. Luis Taruc, *He Who Rides the Tiger: The Story of an Asian Guerrilla Leader* (New York: Praeger, 1967), 160; Benedict J. Kerkvliet, *The Huk Rebellion: A Study of Peasant Re-*

volt in the Philippines (Berkeley: University of California Press, 1977), 210 (Huk figures); Alfred W. McCoy's estimate in *Policing America's Empire: The United States, the Philippines, and the Rise of the Surveillance State* (Madison: University of Wisconsin Press, 2009), 379.

72. Nick Cullather, *Illusions of Influence: The Political Economy of United States–Philippines Relations, 1942–1960* (Stanford, Calif.: Stanford University Press, 1994), 119 (Dulles quote), 176 (total aid).

Chapter 4

1. Address in *Ho Chi Minh: Selected Writings (1920–1969)* (Hanoi: Foreign Languages Publishing House, 1973), 53–56. Ho's exchange with the crowd is vividly recalled in Vo Nguyen Giap's memoir (prepared with the assistance of Huu Mai), *Unforgettable Days*, 3rd ed. (Hanoi: The Gioi, 1994), 29. For other eyewitness accounts, see the on-camera interview with Tran Duy Hung in *Vietnam: A Television History*, part 1, "Roots of a War (1945–1953)" (1983, written and produced by Judith Vecchione for WGBH Boston, 60 min.), 34:00–35:40; Archimedes L. A. Patti, *Why Viet Nam? Prelude to America's Albatross* (Berkeley: University of California Press, 1980), 250; and Tran Trung Thanh recollections in David G. Marr, *Vietnam 1945: The Quest for Power* (Berkeley: University of California Press, 1995), 532.

2. Roosevelt comment to Soviet premier Joseph Stalin at the Tehran conference, 28 November 1943, in minutes by Roosevelt's interpreter Charles E. Bohlen, in U.S. Department of State, *Foreign Relations of the United States* [hereafter *FRUS*]: *The Conferences at Cairo and Tehran, 1943* (Washington, D.C.: U.S. Government Printing Office, 1961), 485.

3. State Department policy paper on postwar Asia, 22 June 1945, in *FRUS, 1945*, vol. 6 (Washington, D.C.: U.S. Government Printing Office, 1969): 567, 569. On the reaction of U.S. officials in Vietnam and in Washington, see Mark Philip Bradley, *Imagining Vietnam and America: The Making of Postcolonial Vietnam, 1919–1950* (Chapel Hill: University of North Carolina Press, 2000), 134–45. Phrase "not politically mature," 136. References to Vietnam appear in dispatches published in the *New York Times* (online edition), 3, 4, 9, 11, 22, and 30 September 1945.

4. National Security Council report 64, "The Position of the United States with Respect to Indochina," 27 February 1950, in *FRUS, 1950*, vol. 6 (Washington, D.C.: U.S. Government Printing Office, 1976): 745–47.

5. Nguyen Dinh Chieu's elegy to righteous resistance in *Patterns of Vietnamese Response to Foreign Intervention, 1858–1900*, trans. Truong Buu Lam (New Haven, Conn.: Southeast Asia Studies, Yale University, 1967), 70–71.

6. Quotes from Chau and Phan, both writing in 1907, in *Colonialism Experienced: Vietnamese Writings on Colonialism, 1900–1931*, ed. and trans. Truong Buu Lam (Ann Arbor: University of Michigan Press, 2000), 107, 139.

7. Christopher E. Goscha, "Courting Diplomatic Disaster? The Difficult Integration of Vietnam into the Internationalist Communist Movement (1945–1950)," *Journal of Vietnamese Studies* 1 (February–August 2006): 68.

8. Ho report to the Communist Party Central Committee, 15 July 1954, in *Ho Chi Minh: Selected Writings (1920–1969)*, 179.

9. Dulles remarks at National Security Council meeting, 22 July 1954, in *FRUS, 1952–1954*, vol. 13, pt. 2 (Washington, D.C.: U.S. Government Printing Office, 1982), 1869.

10. David L. Anderson, *Trapped by Success: The Eisenhower Administration and Vietnam, 1953–1961* (New York: Columbia University Press, 1991), 36 (Eisenhower quote), 154 (aid data).

11. Quotes from Seth Jacobs, *America's Miracle Man in Vietnam: Ngo Dinh Diem, Religion, Race, and U.S. Intervention in Southeast Asia, 1950–1957* (Durham, N.C.: Duke University Press, 2004), 249 (Mansfield), 242 (Kennedy).

12. Kennedy's comment on sending troops in Arthur M. Schlesinger Jr., *A Thousand Days: John F. Kennedy in the White House* (New York: Houghton Mifflin, 1965), 547.

13. Kennedy, press conference comment, 17 July 1963, in *Public Papers of the Presidents of the United States* [hereafter *PPP*]: *John F. Kennedy, 1963* (Washington, D.C.: U.S. Government Printing Office, 1964), 569.

14. Quotes from Philip E. Catton, *Diem's Final Failure: Prelude to America's War in Vietnam* (Lawrence: University Press of Kansas, 2002), 193.

15. Quote from Fredrik Logevall, *Choosing War: The Lost Chance for Peace and the Escalation of War in Vietnam* (Berkeley: University of California Press, 1999), 205.

16. Ball to Johnson, memo on "A Compromise Solution in Vietnam," 1 July 1965, in U.S. Department of Defense, *United States–Vietnam Relations, 1945–1967* [Pentagon Papers], 12 books (Washington, D.C.: U.S. Government Printing Office, 1971), 4:616.

17. Quotes from Harold P. Ford, "Unpopular Pessimism: Why CIA Analysts Were So Doubtful about Vietnam," *Studies in Intelligence* (1997) available online at https://www.cia.gov/library/center-for-the-study-of-intelligence/csi-publications/csi-studies/studies/97unclass/vietnam.html (accessed 26 March 2008).

18. Transcript of Johnson comments to McNamara, 21 June 1965, in *Reaching for Glory: Lyndon Johnson's Secret White House Tapes, 1964–1965*, ed. Michael Beschloss (New York: Simon & Schuster, 2001), 365–66.

19. Quote from Jeffrey Race, *War Comes to Long An: Revolutionary Conflict in a Vietnamese Province* (Berkeley: University of California Press, 1972), 110.

20. Data from Military History Institute of Vietnam, *Victory in Vietnam: The Official History of the People's Army of Vietnam, 1954–1975*, trans. Merle L. Pribbenow (Lawrence: University Press of Kansas, 2002), 459 n. 41.

21. Phrase from Communist Party Central Committee, Resolution 9 on strategy toward the South, December 1963, in *Vietnam: A History in Documents*, ed. Gareth Porter (New York: New American Library, 1981), 256.

22. Ho remarks reported in Mieczyslaw Maneli, *War of the Vanquished*, trans. Maria de Görgey (New York: Harper and Row, 1971), 154–55.

23. Military History Institute of Vietnam, *Victory in Vietnam*, 137 (quote) and 94, 156, 164 (data).

24. Quoted in Chen Jian, *Mao's China and the Cold War* (Chapel Hill: University of North Carolina Press, 2001), 213.

25. Giap remarks in Stanley Karnow, "Giap Remembers," *New York Times Magazine* (online edition), 24 June 1990.

26. Casualty rates in Micheal Clodfelter, *Vietnam in Military Statistics: A History of the Indochina Wars, 1772–1991* (Jefferson, N.C.: McFarland, 1995), 240.

27. Quote from Le Duan speech to a cadre conference, 6–8 July 1965, in *Vietnam: The Definitive Documentation of Human Decisions*, ed. Gareth Porter, 2 vols. (Stanfordville, N.Y.: Earl M. Coleman, 1979), 2:383.

28. Military History Institute of Vietnam, *Victory in Vietnam*, 211.

29. Ceremonial statement quoted in Shaun Kingsley Malarney, "'The Fatherland Remembers Your Sacrifice': Commemorating War Dead in North Vietnam," in *The Country of Memory: Remaking the Past in Late Socialist Vietnam*, ed. Hue-Tam Ho Tai (Berkeley: University of California Press, 2001), 57; and transcript of interview with K-11 in *A Vietnam War Reader: A Documentary History from American and Vietnamese Perspectives*, ed. Michael H. Hunt (Chapel Hill: University of North Carolina Press, 2010), 155.

30. Quotes from David W. P. Elliott and Mai Elliott, *Documents of an Elite Viet Cong Delta Unit: The Demolition Platoon of the 514th Battalion*, part 5, *Personal Letters* (Rand memorandum RM-5852-ISA ARPA, May 1969), 7 (Be); and from David Chanoff and Doan Van Toai, *Portrait of the Enemy* (New York: Random House, 1986), 43 (Thanh).

31. Zhao Shufen quoted in *Voices from the Vietnam War: Stories from American, Asian, and Russian Veterans*, ed. Li Xiaobing (Lexington: University Press of Kentucky, 2010), 81; data on Chinese troops from Xiaoming Zhang, "The Vietnam War, 1964–1969: A Chinese Perspective," *Journal of Military History* 60 (October 1997): 759.

32. Westmoreland quoted in "The Valleys of Death," *Time*, 26 November 1965, 33; McNamara report to Johnson, 30 November 1965, in *FRUS, 1964–1968*, vol. 3 (Washington, D.C.: U.S. Government Printing Office, 1996): 592; and comments of an unidentified officer to journalist Clyde Pettit, quoted in Randall Bennett Woods, *Fulbright: A Biography* (Cambridge, U.K.: Cambridge University Press, 1995), 393.

33. Quote from Trinh Duc in Chanoff and Toai, *Portrait of the Enemy*, 111; data from James P. Harrison, "History's Heaviest Bombing," in *The Vietnam War: Vietnamese and American Perspectives*, ed. Jayne S. Werner and Luu Doan Huynh (Armonk, N.Y.: M. E. Sharpe, 1993), 131.

34. The judgment is Thomas L. Ahern Jr.'s in Ahern, *CIA and Rural Pacification in South Vietnam* (Washington, D.C.: Center for the Study of Intelligence, August 2001), 412. This is one of the six volumes in Ahern's classified study of CIA operations in Vietnam, available at the National Security Archives, http://www.gwu.edu/~nsarchiv/NSAEBB/NSAEBB284/index.htm (accessed 26 November 2009).

35. The testimony of rifleman Herbert L. Carter, 6 November 1969, in James S. Olson and Randy Roberts, *My Lai: A Brief History with Documents* (Boston: Bedford, 1998), 81.

36. Details on Operation Speedy Express (first uncovered by Kevin Buckley of *Newsweek*) in Ronald H. Spector, *After Tet: The Bloodiest Year in Vietnam* (New York: Free Press, 1993), 221; and Nick Turse, "A My Lai a Month," *The Nation*, 1 December 2008, 13–20.

37. Potter speech, 17 April 1965, in *A Vietnam War Reader*, 165; Jennifer W. See, "A Prophet without Honor: Hans Morgenthau and the War in Vietnam, 1955–1965," *Pacific Historical Review* 70 (August 2001): 437 ("crusading" and "deluding"), 442 ("psychopathology").

38. Johnson quoted in Joseph A. Fry, *Debating Vietnam: Fulbright, Stennis, and Their Senate Hearings* (Lanham, Md.: Rowman & Littlefield, 2006), 87.

39. Le Duan quoted in Merle L. Pribbenow II, "General Vo Nguyen Giap and the Mysterious Evolution of the Plan for the 1968 Tet Offensive," *Journal of Vietnamese Studies* 3 (Summer 2008): 13; and directive from Province Party Standing Committee to district and local party committees in South Vietnam, 1 November 1967, in *Vietnam: The Definitive Documentation*, 2:477.

40. Tran Van Tra, *Vietnam: History of the Bulwark B-2 Theatre*, vol. 5, *Concluding the 30-Years War*, trans. Foreign Broadcast Information Service (Fort Leavenworth, Kan.: Combat Studies Institute, U.S. Army Command and General Staff College, 1983), 39; Tran Dang Thuy Tram, *Last Night I Dreamed of Peace: The Diary of Dang Thuy Tram*, trans. Andrew X. Pham (New York: Harmony, 2007), 30.

41. Nixon's "helpless giant" phrase from his speech on the Cambodian invasion, 30 April 1970, in *PPP: Richard Nixon, 1970* (Washington, D.C.: U.S. Government Printing Office, 1971), 409; Nixon on peace to "be proud of" in speech of 14 May 1969, in *PPP: Richard Nixon, 1969* (Washington, D.C.: U.S. Government Printing Office, 1971), 374; Nixon remarks on losing a war and a "bug-out" at a Camp David meeting, 27 September 1969, in *FRUS, 1969–1976*, vol. 1 (Washington, D.C.: U.S. Government Printing Office, 2003), 109; and Henry Kissinger, "The Viet Nam Negotiations," *Foreign Affairs* 47 (January 1969): 219.

42. Pham Van Dong comments, 17 November 1968, in *77 Conversations between Chinese and Foreign Leaders on the Wars in Indochina, 1964–1977*, ed. Odd Arne Westad et al. (Washington, D.C.: Cold War International History Project working paper, 1998), 154.

43. Nixon comment from transcript of taped conversation with Kissinger in the Oval Office, 2 June 1971, in *The Vietnam War Files: Uncovering the Secret History of Nixon-Era Strategy*, ed. Jeffrey P. Kimball (Lawrence: University Press of Kansas, 2004), 165; public opinion survey of April 1971 on mistaken involvement and survey of October 1971 on immoral war effort, both by Louis Harris & Associates from the iPOLL Databank, Roper Center for Public Opinion Research, University of Connecticut, available at http://www.ropercenter.uconn.edu.libproxy.lib.unc.edu/ipoll .html (accessed 8 January 2010).

44. Transcript of Nixon taped comments in Oval Office to Kissinger, Chief of Staff H. R. Haldeman, Treasury Secretary John Connally, and Kissinger aide Alexander Haig, 4 May 1972, in *The Vietnam War Files*, 221.

45. Guidance to Le Duc Tho and Xuan Thuy, in Luu Van Loi and Nguyen Anh Vu, *Le Duc Tho–Kissinger Negotiations in Paris* (Hanoi: The Gioi, 1996), 254–55 (22 July on internal contradictions) and 279 (mid-August on battlefield predominance). The mid-August item may be either a direct quote or a paraphrase.

46. Nixon message to Thieu, 14 November 1972, reproduced in Nguyen Tien Hung and Jerrold L. Schecter, *The Palace File* (New York: Harper and Row, 1986), 386; Nixon comments to Kissinger, 6 October 1972, in draft transcript of tape no. 793-6 produced by the Presidential Recordings Program, Miller Center of Public Affairs at the University of Virginia, available at http://tapes.millercenter.virginia.edu/clips/ 1972-10-06%20-%20nixon%20on%20thieu.swf (accessed 24 January 2009).

47. Data from Marshall L. Michel III, *The Eleven Days of Christmas: America's Last Vietnam Battle* (San Francisco: Encounter, 2002), 239–40.

48. Casualties for 1969 to January 1973 from Micheal Clodfelter, *Warfare and Armed*

Conflicts: A Statistical Encyclopedia of Casualty and Other Figures, 1494–2007, 3rd ed. (Jefferson, N.C.: McFarland, 2008), 763; and "breakdown" characterization from Ronald H. Spector, "The Vietnam War and the Army's Self-Image," in *Second Indochina War Symposium*, ed. John Schlight (Washington, D.C.: U.S. Army Center of Military History, 1986), 170.

49. Nixon comment in entry for 27 June 1972, in H. R. Haldeman, *The Haldeman Diaries: Inside the Nixon White House* (New York: G. P. Putnam's, 1994), 476.

50. Data from T. Christopher Jespersen, "Kissinger, Ford, and Congress: The Very Bitter End in Vietnam," *Pacific Historical Review* 71 (August 2002): 443.

51. "A Song for the Corpses," translated in John C. Schafer, "The Trinh Cong Son Phenomenon," *Journal of Asian Studies* 66 (August 2007): 614; Ky quote from interview conducted by Michael Charlton in Charlton and Anthony Moncrieff, *Many Reasons Why: The American Involvement in Vietnam* (New York: Hill and Wang, 1978), 216.

52. Dong quoted in Tran Van Tra, *Vietnam: History of the Bulwark B-2 Theatre*, 5:125; Van Tien Dung, *Our Great Spring Victory: An Account of the Liberation of South Vietnam* (New York: Monthly Review Press, 1977), 29.

53. Jespersen, "Kissinger, Ford, and Congress," 456 n. 41 (polling data); Ford address at Tulane University, 23 April 1975, *PPP: Gerald D. Ford, 1975*, book 1 (Washington, D.C.: U.S. Government Printing Office, 1977), 569.

54. President Ronald Reagan, remarks at the Vietnam Veterans Memorial, 11 November 1988, in *PPP: Ronald Reagan, 1988–89*, book 2 (Washington, D.C.: U.S. Government Printing Office, 1991), 1495.

55. MIA and polling data from Michael J. Allen, *Until the Last Man Comes Home: POWs, MIAs, and the Unending Vietnam War* (Chapel Hill: University of North Carolina Press, 2009), 2. The Vietnam-relevant Rambo films consist of *First Blood* (1982, dir. Ted Kotcheff, 96 min.) and *Rambo: First Blood Part II* (1985, dir. George P. Cosmatos, 96 min.).

56. The first view was articulated by Andrew F. Krepinevich Jr., *The Army and Vietnam* (Baltimore: Johns Hopkins University Press, 1986). The second is closely associated with Harry G. Summers, *On Strategy: A Critical Analysis of the Vietnam War* (Novato, Calif.: Presidio, 1982). The third gets its most elaborate development by an officer from a post-Vietnam generation in H. R. McMaster, *Dereliction of Duty: Lyndon Johnson, Robert McNamara, the Joint Chiefs of Staff, and the Lies That Led to Vietnam* (New York: HarperCollins, 1997).

57. Losses for 1959–75 from Luu Doan Huynh, "Commentary: A Vietnamese Scholar's Perspective on the Communist Big Powers and Vietnam," in *Behind the Bamboo Curtain: China, Vietnam, and the World beyond Asia*, ed. Priscilla Roberts (Washington, D.C.: Woodrow Wilson Center Press; and Stanford, Calif.: Stanford University Press, 2006), 443; Le Duan speech, 15 May 1975, in *Le Duan: Selected Writings (1960–1975)* (Hanoi: The Gioi, 1994), 539; Giap comments from transcript translated by Pham Sanh Chau, in Robert S. McNamara et al., *Argument without End: In Search of Answers to the Vietnam Tragedy* (New York: Public Affairs, 1999), 24.

58. From Ho Chi Minh's testament published following his death in September 1969, in *Ho Chi Minh: Selected Writings (1920–1969)*, 361.

59. Clodfelter, *Warfare and Armed Conflicts*, 660 (total population), 662 (total dead and bomb tonnage); and "Southeast Asian American Data 2006 American Community Study" (Hmong in the United States), available at http://www.hmongstudies.org/ SEA2006ACS.html (accessed 22 March 2011).

Conclusion

1. Marilyn B. Young, "Bombing Civilians from the Twentieth to the Twenty-First Centuries," in *Bombing Civilians: A Twentieth-Century History*, ed. Yuki Tanaka and Young (New York: New Press, 2009), 157.
2. U.S. Bureau of the Census, *We the Americans: Asians* (Washington, D.C.: U.S. Government Printing Office, 1993), 1–3; U.S. Department of Commerce and Labor, *Statistical Abstracts of the United States, 1910* (Washington, D.C.: U.S. Government Printing Office, 1911), 45.
3. Nixon comment at his 25 July 1969 press conference, in *Public Papers of the Presidents of the United States* [hereafter *PPP*]*: Richard Nixon, 1969* (Washington, D.C.: U.S. Government Printing Office, 1971), 549.
4. Nixon quoted in H. R. Haldeman, *The Haldeman Diaries: Inside the Nixon White House* (New York: G. P. Putnam's Sons, 1994), 322.
5. Shanghai communiqué, 27 February 1972, reproduced in Robert S. Ross, *Negotiating Cooperation: The United States and China, 1969–1989* (Stanford, Calif.: Stanford University Press, 1995), 269; Nixon phrase from February 1970, quoted in Liang Pan, "Whither Japan's Military Potential? The Nixon Administration's Stance on Japanese Defense Power," *Diplomatic History* 31 (January 2007): 115.
6. Remarks to Midwestern news media executives meeting in Kansas City, 6 July 1971, in *PPP: Richard Nixon, 1971* (Washington, D.C.: U.S. Government Printing Office, 1972), 802–12.
7. Polling data in Charles K. Armstrong, "South Korea and the United States: Is the Love Affair Over?" available on the History News Network at http://hnn.us/ articles/12241.html (accessed 7 June 2005).
8. Remarks in Tokyo, 13 and 14 November 2009, available at http://www.whitehouse .gov/the-press-office/remarks-president-barack-obama-and-prime-minister-yukio-hatoyama-japan-joint-press and http://www.whitehouse.gov/the-press-office/ remarks-president-barack-obama-suntory-hall (both accessed 14 May 2010).
9. Park Chung Hee, *To Build a Nation* (Washington, D.C.: Acropolis, 1971), 105.
10. Estimates in Richard Stubbs, *Rethinking Asia's Economic Miracle: The Political Economy of War, Prosperity, and Crisis* (New York: Palgrave Macmillan, 2005), 105 (for South Korea), 68 and 128 (for Japan).
11. Data from Angus Maddison, *The World Economy: A Millennial Perspective* (Paris: Development Centre of the Organisation for Economic Co-operation and Development, 2001), 306.
12. Data from Maddison, *The World Economy*, 130.
13. The most widely read announcement of Japan's ascent was Ezra F. Vogel, *Japan as Number One: Lessons for America* (Cambridge, Mass.: Harvard University Press, 1979). Politician Ishihara Shintaro and Sony founder Morita Akio originated the

"say no" genre in 1989. Ishihara's views alone appear in translation as *The Japan That Can Say No* (New York: Simon & Schuster, 1991).

14. Survey findings in "Mainland Chinese Have Risen in Favor in U.S., Poll Finds," *New York Times* (online edition), 12 March 1972.

15. Reagan quoted in James Mann, *About Face: A History of America's Curious Relationship with China, from Nixon to Clinton* (New York: Alfred A. Knopf, 1999), 144 (1979 comment) and 147 (1984 comment); and Clinton's "genie" remark at the School of Advanced International Studies, Washington, D.C., 8 March 2000, in *PPP: William J. Clinton, 2000–2001* (Washington, D.C.: U.S. Government Printing Office, 2001), book 1:407.

16. The quote on the China threat is from Richard Bernstein and Ross H. Munro, "The Coming Conflict with China," *Foreign Affairs* 76 (March–April 1997): 19. The authors drew from their experience as Beijing correspondents for *Time* magazine and Toronto's *Globe and Mail*, respectively. Predictions of a looming China crisis became a genre in its own right. Notable examples include Nicholas D. Kristof and Sheryl WuDunn, *China Wakes: The Struggle for the Soul of a Rising Power* (New York: Vintage, 1995), laying out the frustrations of a pair of *New York Times* reporters; Ted Galen Carpenter, *America's Coming War with China: A Collision Course over Taiwan* (New York: Palgrave Macmillan, 2005), reflecting the hostility of Carpenter's home base at the Cato Institute; and James Mann, *The China Fantasy: How Our Leaders Explain Away Chinese Repression* (New York: Viking, 2007), also from the pen of a journalist with experience reporting from China in the late 1980s. "Netizens" quote from Peter H. Gries, *China's New Nationalism: Pride, Politics, and Diplomacy* (Berkeley: University of California Press, 2004), 106. The most notable of the "say no" rebukes to the United States is the best-selling Song Qiang et al., *Zhongguo keyi shuo bu* [The China that can say no] (Beijing: Zhonghuo gongshang lianhe, 1996).

17. This phrase appears in C. Wright Mills, *The Power Elite* (New York: Oxford University Press, 1956), 313.

18. The most widely read book in the Lewis corpus is *What Went Wrong? Western Impact and Middle Eastern Response* (Oxford: Oxford University Press, 2002). Ajami has often appeared in the print and broadcast media. His *The Arab Predicament: Arab Political Thought and Practice since 1967*, 2nd ed. (Cambridge, U.K.: Cambridge University Press, 1992), made an influential argument about a dysfunctional region and its failure to adjust to a dominant, dynamic, liberal West.

19. Quote from Nathaniel C. Fick and John A. Nagl, "The U.S. Army * Marine Corps Counterinsurgency Field Manual: Afghanistan Edition," *Foreign Policy* 170 (January–February 2009): 43.

20. Gian P. Gentile, "The Selective Use of History in the Development of American Counterinsurgency Doctrine," *Army History*, no. 72 (Summer 2009): 21 ("narrow selection"); Edward N. Luttwak, "Dead End: Counterinsurgency Warfare as Military Malpractice," *Harper's Magazine*, February 2007, 35 ("questionable proposition"), 42 ("little or no use" and "malpractice"); and Rory Stewart, "The Irresistible Illusion," *London Review of Books*, 9 July 2009, 6 ("buoyed by illusions").

21. Nagl quoted in Peter Maass, "Professor Nagl's War," *New York Times Magazine*,

11 January 2004, 25 ("clowns"), 30 ("own decisions"), 31 ("bad guys"), 49 ("their minds").

22. Adams to Jefferson, 2 February 1816, in *The Adams-Jefferson Letters: The Complete Correspondence between Thomas Jefferson and Abigail and John Adams*, ed. Lester J. Cappon, 2 vols. (Chapel Hill: University of North Carolina Press, 1959), 2:463.

Guide to the Historical Literature

In light of the extraordinary accumulation of scholarship relevant to U.S. policy and eastern Asia over the decades treated here, this guide is necessarily selective. It bypasses polemical works and omits memoirs, oral histories, collections of documents, and fiction, and it focuses instead on the scholarly books (and some articles) most pertinent to our concerns and helpful to readers wishing to explore further.

Introduction

This study in broadest terms involves bringing together two distinct bodies of literature—histories of U.S. involvement in eastern Asia and the more conceptual and sometimes more argumentative works treating empire in the abstract or in relation to the United States.

U.S. involvement in the eastern, maritime fringes of Asia is treated in a notably broad-gauge fashion in Warren I. Cohen, ed., *Pacific Passage: The Study of American–East Asian Relations on the Eve of the Twenty-first Century* (New York: Columbia University Press, 1996), a good guide to the scholarship; Philip West, Steven I. Levine, and Jackie Hiltz, eds., *America's Wars in Asia: A Cultural Approach to History and Memory* (Armonk, N.Y.: M. E. Sharpe, 1998), notable for the range of themes it explores; and Yuki Tanaka and Marilyn B. Young, eds., *Bombing Civilians: A Twentieth-Century History*, ed. (New York: New Press, 2009), which highlights an increasingly prominent feature of the U.S. drive. Of the various syntheses putting the U.S. role in broad context, none makes the case for a sustained, coherent American drive in the region or takes up the imperial theme. For help in following the military campaigns that defined the course of U.S. Asian empire, see the map collection maintained by the History Department of the U.S. Military Academy: http://www.dean.usma.edu/history/web03/atlases/Atlases TableOfContents.html.

The notion of an American empire has enjoyed a surge of interest over the last decade, beginning with a run of polemical works. Max Boot, *Savage Wars of Peace: Small Wars and the Rise of American Power* (New York: Basic, 2002); and Niall Ferguson, *Colossus: The Price of America's Empire* (New York: Penguin, 2004), both championed an American imperial calling. For the response by critics of empire of varying political shades, see Patrick J. Buchanan, *A Republic, Not an Empire: Reclaiming America's Destiny* (Washington, D.C.: Regnery, 1999); Andrew J. Bacevich, *American Empire: The Realities and Consequences of U.S. Diplomacy* (Cambridge, Mass.: Harvard University Press, 2002); and Chalmers A. Johnson's trilogy: *Blowback: The Costs and Consequences of American Empire* (New York: Metropolitan, 2000); *The Sorrows of Empire: Militarism, Secrecy, and the End of the Republic* (New York: Metropolitan, 2004); and *Dismantling the Empire: America's Last Best Hope* (New York: Metropolitan, 2010).

For works on empire in a more scholarly vein, see Charles Maier, *Among Empires:*

American Ascendancy and Its Predecessors (Cambridge, Mass.: Harvard University Press, 2006), a learned comparison of empires that stresses their shared dynamic qualities but that withholds judgment on how the United States fits in; Frank A. Ninkovich, *The United States and Imperialism* (Malden, Mass.: Blackwell, 2001), which explores the mindset behind empire; Philip S. Golub, *Power, Profit and Prestige: A History of American Imperial Expansion* (London: Pluto, 2010), which argues for the long-standing constraints imposed by "an imperial cosmology"; Richard H. Immerman, *Empire for Liberty: A History of American Imperialism from Benjamin Franklin to Paul Wolfowitz* (Princeton, N.J.: Princeton University Press, 2010), which is helpful on changing conceptions of empire; and Alfred W. McCoy and Francisco A. Scarano, eds., *Colonial Crucible: Empire in the Making of the Modern American State* (Madison: University of Wisconsin Press, 2009), notably the opening discussion by McCoy and Ian Tyrell's conclusion. For help in bringing some conceptual clarity to a tricky term, see Robin W. Winks, "The American Struggle with Imperialism: How Words Frighten," in *The American Identity: Fusion and Fragmentation*, ed. Rob Kroes (Amsterdam: Amerika Instituut, Universiteit van Amsterdam, 1980), 143–77; Stephen Howe, *Empire: A Very Short Introduction* (Oxford, U.K.: Oxford University Press, 2002); and Jürgen Osterhammel, *Colonialism: A Theoretical Overview*, 2nd ed. (Princeton, N.J.: Markus Wiener, 2005).

Historians of the British empire have important things to say pertinent to the U.S. case. Ronald Robinson's "Non-European Foundations of European Imperialism: Sketch for a Theory of Collaboration," in *Studies in the Theory of Imperialism*, ed. Roger Owen and Bob Sutcliffe (London: Longman, 1972), 117–40, is a seminal study. More recent works of note include Patrick Karl O'Brien and Armand Cleese, eds., *Two Hegemonies: Britain, 1846–1914, and the United States, 1941–2001,* (Aldershot, U.K.: Ashgate, 2002), particularly the essays by O'Brien, "The Pax Britannica and American Hegemony," and John M. Hobson, "Two Hegemonies or One?"; David Cannadine, "'Big Tent' Historiography: Transatlantic Obstacles and Opportunities in Writing the History of Empire," *Common Knowledge* 11 (Fall 2005): 375–92; Bernard Porter, *Empire and Superempire: Britain, America and the World* (New Haven, Conn.: Yale University Press, 2006); and A. G. Hopkins, "Capitalism, Nationalism and the New American Empire," *Journal of Imperial and Commonwealth History* 35 (March 2007): 95–117.

The Philippines, 1899–1902

The conflict in Vietnam, which turned out to be the last phase in the U.S. Pacific crusade, directed scholarly attention back to the long-neglected first phase in the Philippines. For general works written under the shadow of the Vietnam War, see Richard E. Welch Jr., *Response to Imperialism: The United States and the Philippine-American War, 1899–1902* (Chapel Hill: University of North Carolina Press, 1979); and Stuart C. Miller, *"Benevolent Assimilation": The American Conquest of the Philippines, 1899–1903* (New Haven, Conn.: Yale University Press, 1982). Synthetic treatments have continued to appear, notably Stanley Karnow, *In Our Image: America's Empire in the Philippines* (New York: Random House, 1989); H. W. Brands, *Bound to Empire: The United States and the Philippines* (New York: Oxford University Press, 1992); and David J. Silbey, *A War of Frontier and Empire: The Philippine-American War, 1899–1902* (New York: Hill and Wang, 2007). Recurrent in all these general accounts are charged questions about whether parallels with Vietnam make sense, whether American forces lived up to the standards of civilized warfare, and whether U.S. colonial policy was genuinely benevolent.

The U.S. imperial impulse that inspired the Philippines initiative is treated in a large literature. For guidance, see Joseph A. Fry, "Imperialism, American Style, 1890–1916," in *American Foreign Relations Reconsidered, 1890–1993*, ed. Gordon Martel (London: Routledge, 1994), 52–70; and Fry, "From Open Door to World Systems: Economic Interpretations of Late Nineteenth Century American Foreign Relations," *Pacific Historical Review* 65 (May 1996): 277–303. Notable broad interpretations published since the last Fry review include Kristin L. Hoganson, *Fighting for American Manhood: How Gender Politics Provoked the Spanish-American and Philippine-American Wars* (New Haven, Conn.: Yale University Press, 1998); and Paul A. Kramer, *The Blood of Government: Race, Empire, the United States, and the Philippines* (Chapel Hill: University of North Carolina Press, 2006). The documentary *Savage Acts: Wars, Fairs and Empire* (1995, dir. Pennee Bender, Joshua Brown, and Andrea Ades Vasquez, 30 min.), uses cartoons and other contemporary materials to highlight the racial preoccupations behind the American imperial drive.

William McKinley's pivotal role in the Philippine-American War has given historians fits. His correspondence tends toward the perfunctory; his public addresses were carefully calculated; and his comments to colleagues rarely confessional. No personal diary has turned up; an assassin's bullet eliminated the possibility of a memoir. For two considered but divergent appraisals on why he embarked on an imperial path, see Lewis L. Gould, *The Spanish-American War and President McKinley* (Lawrence: University Press of Kansas, 1982); and John L. Offner, *An Unwanted War: The Diplomacy of the United States and Spain over Cuba, 1895–1898* (Chapel Hill: University of North Carolina Press, 1992).

Military studies of the Philippine-American War have developed in two directions. One has been to examine its conduct with an eye to refuting charges of brutality aimed at the U.S. Army. Notable examples include John Morgan Gates, *Schoolbooks and Krags: The United States Army in the Philippines, 1898–1902* (Westport, Conn.: Greenwood, 1973); and Brian McAllister Linn, *The Philippine War, 1899–1902* (Lawrence: University Press of Kansas, 2000), a careful campaign history. The alternative concern has been with the ordinary men who waged the war. See James G. Crawford, "The Warriors of Civilization: U.S. Soldiers, American Culture, and the Conquest of the Philippines, 1898–1902" (Ph.D. diss., University of North Carolina at Chapel Hill, 2003); Kyle Roy Ward, *In the Shadow of Glory: The Thirteenth Minnesota in the Spanish-American and Philippine-American Wars, 1898 to 1899* (St. Cloud, Minn.: North Star Press of St. Cloud, 2000); Willard B. Gatewood Jr., *Black Americans and the White Man's Burden, 1898–1903* (Urbana: University of Illinois Press, 1975), chap. 10; and Glenn A. May, "Private Presher and Sergeant Vergara," in *Reappraising an Empire: New Perspectives on Philippine-American History*, ed. Peter W. Stanley (Cambridge, Mass.: Harvard University Press, 1984), 35–57.

In giving McKinley's domestic critics their due, Robert L. Beisner took the lead—first in *Twelve against Empire: The Anti-Imperialists, 1898–1900* (Chicago: University of Chicago Press, 1968), published in a revised edition in 1986, and second in a critical examination of the Vietnam and Philippines parallels, "1898 and 1968: The Anti-Imperialists and the Doves," *Political Science Quarterly* 85 (1970): 186–216. Other reappraisals followed, including E. Berkeley Tompkins, *Anti-Imperialism in the United States: The Great Debate, 1890–1920* (Philadelphia: University of Pennsylvania Press, 1970); Judith Papachristou, "American Women and Foreign Policy, 1989–1905," *Diplomatic History* 14 (Fall 1990): 493–509; Kristin Hoganson, "'As Badly off as the Filipinos': U.S. Women's Suffragists and the Imperial Issue at the Turn of the Twentieth Century," *Journal of Women's History* 13 (Summer 2001): 9–33; and Eric T. L. Love, *Race over Empire: Racism and U.S. Imperialism, 1865–1900* (Chapel Hill: University of North Carolina Press, 2004).

In developing the Philippine side of the conflict, Glenn A. May stands out for the substantial body of fresh and thoughtful work that he has done. See "The Unfathomable Other: Historical Studies of U.S.-Philippines Relations," in *Pacific Passage: The Study of American-East Asian Relations on the Eve of the Twenty-first Century*, ed. Warren I. Cohen (New York: Columbia University Press, 1996), 279–312; "Why the United States Won the Philippine-American War, 1899–1902," *Pacific Historical Review* 52 (November 1983): 353–77; and "Was the Philippine-American War a 'Total War'?" in *Anticipating Total War: The German and American Experiences, 1871–1914*, ed. Manfred F. Boemeke et al. (Cambridge, U.K.: Cambridge University Press; and Washington, D.C.: German Historical Institute, 1999), 437–57. These essays build on three major monographs (noted below) and reflect May's interpretive versatility and resistance to easy answers, also nicely showcased in his collected writings, *A Past Recovered* (Quezon City, Philippines: New Day, 1987).

Philippine nationalism has attracted special scholarly attention—and ignited controversy. Milagros Camayon Guerrero, "Luzon at War: Contradictions in Philippine Society, 1898–1902" (Ph.D. diss., University of Michigan, 1977), first drew attention to the division within nationalist ranks between proponents of genuine social change embodied by Bonifacio and those such as Aguinaldo supporting a revolution with limited political goals. For further elaboration of this theme, see Reynaldo Clemeña Ileto, *Pasyon and Revolution: Popular Movements in the Philippines, 1840–1910* (Quezon City, Philippines: Ateneo de Manila University Press, 1979); Peter Stanley, *A Nation in the Making: The Philippines and the United States, 1899–1921* (Cambridge, Mass.: Harvard University Press, 1974), which stresses the bargain elite Filipino collaborators struck with American proconsuls; and most recently Glenn May's sharply revisionist *Inventing a Hero: The Posthumous Re-creation of Andres Bonifacio* (Madison: University of Wisconsin, Center for Southeast Asian Studies, 1996). For a lavish and engaging biopic on the leading voice and enduring symbol of Philippines nationalism, see *Jose Rizal* (1998, dir. Marilou Diaz-Abaya, 178 min.).

Regional studies have provided additional perspective on the role of Philippine elites as well as on the variegated nature of the resistance to U.S. control. Particularly helpful are May, *Battle for Batangas: A Philippine Province at War* (New Haven, Conn.: Yale University Press, 1991); Norman G. Owen, "Winding Down the War in Albay, 1900–1903," *Pacific Historical Review* 48 (November 1979): 557–89; and Andrew J. Birtle, "The U.S. Army's Pacification of Marinduque, Philippine Islands, April 1900–April 1901," *Journal of Military History* 61 (April 1997): 255–82. See also John A. Larkin, *The Pampangans: Colonial Society in a Philippine Province* (Berkeley: University of California Press, 1972), particularly chaps. 5 and 6; William Henry Scott, *Ilocano Responses to American Aggression, 1900–1901* (Quezon City, Philippines: New Day, 1986); and Resil B. Mojares, *The*

War against the Americans: Resistance and Collaboration in Cebu, 1899–1906 (Quezon City, Philippines: Ateneo de Manila University Press, 1999).

The consequences for the Philippines of the U.S. takeover have increasingly pre-occupied scholars. The horrific demographic impact of the war are the subject of Glenn May, "150,000 Missing Filipinos: A Demographic Crisis in Batangas, 1887–1903," published in 1985 and reproduced in May's *A Past Recovered* (Quezon City, Philippines: New Day, 1987); and Ken De Bevoise, *Agents of Apocalypse: Epidemic Disease in the Colonial Philippines* (Princeton, N.J.: Princeton University Press, 1995). For assessments of U.S. colonial practice and the grip regional elites maintained, see Glenn A. May, *Social Engineering in the Philippines: The Aims, Execution, and Impact of American Colonial Policy, 1900–1913* (Westport, Conn.: Greenwood, 1980); Norman G. Owen, *Compadre Colonialism: Studies on the Philippines under American Rule* (Ann Arbor: University of Michigan Center for South and Southeast Asian Studies, 1971), especially the essays by Owen on the economy and by Michael Cullinane on local government; Bonifacio S. Salamanca, *The Filipino Reaction to American Rule, 1901–1913* (Hamden, Conn.: Shoe String, 1968), a pioneering work that still repays attention; Paul D. Hutchcroft, "Colonial Masters, National Politics, and Provincial Lords: Central Authority and Local Autonomy in the American Philippines, 1900–1913," *Journal of Asian Studies* 59 (May 2000): 277–306; and Julian Go and Anne L. Foster, eds., *The American Colonial State in the Philippines: Global Perspectives* (Durham, N.C.: Duke University Press, 2003). Reynaldo Ileto, *Knowing America's Colony: A Hundred Years from the Philippine War* (Philippine Studies Occasional Papers Series, no. 13, Honolulu: Center for Philippine Studies, University of Hawai'i at Manoa, 1999), is notable for its searching critique of the well-established social history approach represented by the works of May, Owen, and McCoy.

On Asian reactions to the U.S. seizure of the Philippines, Rebecca E. Karl, *Staging the World: Chinese Nationalism at the Turn of the Twentieth Century* (Durham, N.C.: Duke University Press, 2002); Shunsuke Kamei, "The Sacred Land of Liberty: Images of America in Nineteenth Century Japan," in *Mutual Images: Essays in American-Japanese Relations*, ed. Akira Iriye (Cambridge, Mass.: Harvard University Press, 1975), 55–72; and Akira Iriye, *Pacific Estrangement: Japanese and American Expansion, 1897–1911* (Cambridge, Mass.: Harvard University Press, 1972), are especially helpful.

Japan, 1941–1945

The controversies long surrounding World War II in the Pacific have calmed down if not disappeared. The passage of time has helped. So too has much good scholarship offering a more dispassionate, diverse, and fine-grained perspective.

A variety of reviews provide a convenient entrée to the scholarship. On the U.S. side of the war, see Michael A. Barnhart, "Driven by Domestics: American Relations with Japan and Korea, 1900–1945," in *Pacific Passage: The Study of American–East Asian Relations on the Eve of the Twenty-first Century*, ed. Warren I. Cohen (New York: Columbia University Press, 1996), 190–212; Michael A. Barnhart, "The Origins of the Second World War in Asia and the Pacific: Synthesis Impossible," in *Paths to Power: The Historiography of American Foreign Relations to 1941*, ed. Michael J. Hogan (Cambridge, U.K.: Cambridge University Press, 2000), 268–95; and J. Samuel Walker, "The Decision to Use the Bomb: A Historiographical Update," in *America in the World: The Historiography of American Foreign Relations since 1941*, ed. Michael J. Hogan (Cambridge, U.K.: Cambridge University Press, 1995), 206–33. The literature on the Japanese side has received more recent treatment in the collection edited by William M. Tsutsui, *A Companion to Japanese History* (Malden, Mass.: Blackwell, 2007). See in particular chap. 13 ("The Japanese Empire" by Y. Tak Matsusaka), chap. 14 ("The Fifteen-Year War" by W. Miles Fletcher III), and chap. 15 ("The Occupation" by Mark Metzler). Yukiko Koshiro surveys Japan in assessments in "Japan's World and World War II," *Diplomatic History* 25 (Summer 2001): 425–41.

For engaging and authoritative overviews of the war, see Ronald H. Spector, *Eagle against the Sun: The American War with Japan* (New York: Free Press, 1985), an older survey that has withstood the test of time; and Mark D. Roehrs and William A. Renzi, *World War II in the Pacific* (Armonk, N.Y.: M. E. Sharpe, 2004), which has the virtue of including recent scholarship and being concise. The single most influential interpretive account is John Dower's *War without Mercy: Race and Power in the Pacific War* (New York: Pantheon, 1986), with its claims about the war's intense racial dimensions. James B. Wood, *Japanese Military Strategy in the Pacific War: Was Defeat Inevitable?* (Lanham, Md.: Rowman & Littlefield, 2007), offers a compelling counterfactual analysis. Gerhard L. Weinberg, *A World at Arms: A Global History of World War II*, 2nd ed. (New York: Cambridge University Press, 2005); and Richard Overy, *Why the Allies Won* (New York: W. W. Norton, 1997), set the Pacific War in context.

The road to Pearl Harbor and war was an early and sharply contentious topic among historians. Perhaps more than anyone James B. Crowley, in his *Japan's Quest for Autonomy: National Security and Foreign Policy, 1930–1938* (Princeton, N.J.: Princeton University Press, 1966), let the revisionist cat loose among the historian-pigeons. "A New Deal for Japan and Asia," in *Modern East Asia*, ed. James B. Crowley (New York: Harcourt, Brace and World, 1970), 235–64, sharpened and broadened his case for seeing prewar Japanese policymakers on their own terms and in their particular contexts rather than caricaturing and condemning them. This effort is carried forward in Ian Nish, *Japanese Foreign Policy in the Interwar Period* (Westport, Conn: Praeger, 2002), which sticks close to the main policy developments and personalities; W. (William) G. Beasley, *Japanese Imperialism 1894–1945* (Oxford, U.K.: Oxford University Press, 1987), which is valuable for its attention to the phases in the making of an empire; and Wm. Miles Fletcher III, *The Search for a New Order: Intellectuals and Fascism in Prewar Japan* (Chapel Hill: University of North Carolina Press, 1982), a pioneering treatment of the intellectual foundations of Japanese expansion.

For the continuing controversy over the emperor's war guilt (as well as his role in peacemaking), see Stephen S. Large, *Emperor Hirohito and Showa Japan: A Political Biography* (London: Routledge, 1992); Peter Wetzler, *Hirohito and War: Imperial Tradition and Military Decision Making in Prewar Japan* (Honolulu: University of Hawai'i Press, 1998); and Herbert P. Bix, *Hirohito and the Making of Modern Japan* (New York: HarperCollins, 2000).

On the U.S. road to war, Franklin D. Roosevelt's role roiled scholarly waters until Roberta Wohlstetter, *Pearl Harbor: Warning and Decision* (Stanford, Calif.: Stanford University Press, 1962), came along. This classic study of an intelligence failure had a calming effect, as did later works by Gordon W. Prange with David M. Goldstein and

Katherine V. Dillon, *At Dawn We Slept: The Untold Story of Pearl Harbor* (New York: McGraw-Hill, 1981); Jonathan G. Utley, *Going to War with Japan, 1937–1941* (New York: Fordham University Press, 2005 [1985]); Waldo Heinrichs, *Threshold of War: Franklin D. Roosevelt and American Entry into World War II* (New York: Oxford University Press, 1988); and Edward S. Miller, *Bankrupting the Enemy: The U.S. Financial Siege of Japan before Pearl Harbor* (Annapolis, Md.: Naval Institute Press, 2007).

The big battles and the experience of those who fought them have attracted considerable attention over the last decade. Notable works include Donald L. Miller, *D-days in the Pacific* (New York: Simon & Schuster, 2005); Richard B. Frank, *Guadalcanal: The Definitive Account of the Landmark Battle* (New York: Penguin, 1992); Thomas W. Zeiler, *Unconditional Defeat: Japan, America, and the End of World War II* (Wilmington, Del.: SR, 2004); Conrad C. Crane, *Bombs, Cities, and Civilians: American Airpower Strategy in World War II* (Lawrence: University Press of Kansas, 1993); Craig M. Cameron, *American Samurai: Myth, Imagination, and the Conduct of Battle in the First Marine Division, 1941–1951* (Cambridge, U.K.: Cambridge University Press, 1994); Peter Schrijvers, *Bloody Pacific: American Soldiers at War with Japan* (Basingstoke, U.K.: Palgrave Macmillan, 2010); Edward J. Drea, *Japan's Imperial Army: Its Rise and Fall, 1853–1945* (Lawrence: University Press of Kansas, 2009), chaps. 11–12; Yoshimi Yoshiaki, *Comfort Women: Sexual Slavery in the Japanese Military during World War II*, trans. Suzanne O'Brien (New York: Columbia University Press, 2000); and Tanaka Yuki, *Hidden Horrors: Japanese War Crimes in World War II* (Boulder, Colo.: Westview, 1996). Visually dramatic evocations can be found in *Victory in the Pacific* (2005, dir. Austin Hoyt, 120 min.), a PBS documentary supplemented by a website that includes maps, oral history, and specialist comment (at http://www.pbs.org/wgbh/amex/pacific/); *Letters from Iwo Jima* (2006, dir. Clint Eastwood, 141 min.), a thoughtful attempt to re-create the Japanese soldiers' perspective and a fascinating counterpoint to John Wayne's performance in the 1949 *Sands of Iwo Jima*; and two films from the late 1950s directed by Ichikawa Kon: *The Burmese Harp* (1957, 116 min.) and *Fires on the Plain* (1959, 108 min.).

The impact of the war on the home front is the subject of deft surveys by Allan M. Winkler, *Home Front U.S.A.: America during World War II*, 2nd ed. (Wheeling, Ill.: H. Davidson, 2000); and Thomas R. H. Havens, *Valley of Darkness: The Japanese People and World War Two* (New York: W. W. Norton, 1978). The roundup of Japanese Americans has attracted considerable attention, including most recently Greg Robinson, *By Order of the President: FDR and the Internment of Japanese Americans* (Cambridge, Mass.: Harvard University Press, 2001); Brian Masaru Hayashi, *Democratizing the Enemy: The Japanese American Internment* (Princeton, N.J.: Princeton University Press, 2004); and Erik Muller, *American Inquisition: The Hunt for Japanese Disloyalty in World War II* (Chapel Hill: University of North Carolina Press, 2007). Paul A. C. Koistinen, *Arsenal of World War II: The Political Economy of American Warfare, 1940–1945* (Lawrence: University Press of Kansas, 2004), explores the dimensions of an extraordinary economic mobilization. Special insights on Japan's home front can found in Gregory J. Kasza, "War and Welfare Policy in Japan," *Journal of Asian Studies* 61 (May 2002): 417–35; Barak Kushner, *The Thought War: Japanese Imperial Propaganda* (Honolulu: University of Hawai'i Press, 2006); and David C. Earhart, *Certain Victory: Images of World War II in the Japanese Media* (Armonk, N.Y.: M. E. Sharpe, 2008).

The end of the war and the atomic bomb became highly contentious issues with the publication of Gar Alperovitz's landmark *Atomic Diplomacy, Hiroshima and Potsdam: The Use of the Atomic Bomb and the American Confrontation with Soviet Power* (New York: Simon and Schuster, 1965). The latest works in a long-running, multifaceted, and increasingly nuanced debate include J. Samuel Walker, *Prompt and Utter Destruction: Truman and the Use of the Atomic Bombs against Japan* (Chapel Hill: University of North Carolina Press, 1997), a level-headed assessment; Richard B. Frank, *Downfall: The End of the Imperial Japanese Empire* (New York: Random House, 1999), thoroughly researched and balanced; Tsuyoshi Hasegawa, *Racing the Enemy: Stalin, Truman, and the Surrender of Japan* (Cambridge, Mass.: Harvard University Press, 2005), notable for its use of imperial archives; and Yukiko Koshiro, "Eurasian Eclipse: Japan's End Game in World War II," *American Historical Review* 109 (April 2004): 417–44, which focuses on the wide variety of schemes hatched by desperate Japanese policymakers. Ronald H. Spector, *In the Ruins of Empire: The Japanese Surrender and the Battle for Postwar Asia* (New York: Random House, 2007), traces the regional ramifications of Japan's total collapse.

The U.S. occupation of Japan poses the puzzle of how two countries so bitterly at odds in wartime could shift so quickly to a cooperative relationship. Answers emerge in John W. Dower, *Embracing Defeat: Japan in the Wake of World War II* (New York: W. W. Norton, 1999), a prize-winning study that stresses the role of conservative elites; Yukiko Koshiro, *Trans-Pacific Racisms and the U.S. Occupation of Japan* (New York: Columbia University Press, 1999), which explores comparable forms of racial thinking; and Naoko Shibusawa, *America's Geisha Ally: Reimagining the Japanese Enemy* (Cambridge, Mass.: Harvard University Press, 2006), with its stress on gender and racial notions critical to turning an enemy into an ally. A long career integral to the story of American empire in Asia is the subject of Michael Schaller's compact, critical *Douglas MacArthur: The Far Eastern General* (New York: Oxford University Press, 1989); and Richard B. Frank's more recent picture of a flawed visionary in *MacArthur* (New York: Palgrave Macmillan, 2007). The war crimes trials—first treated in Richard H. Minear's critical *Victor's Justice: The Tokyo War Crimes Trial* (Princeton, N.J.: Princeton University Press, 1971)—has received more recent, balanced attention in Yuma Totani, *The Tokyo War Crimes Trial: The Pursuit of Justice in the Wake of World War II* (Cambridge, Mass.: Harvard University Asia Center, 2008).

Memory and representation of the Pacific War are topics on which historians have lavished attention over the last decade and a half. Unusually rich treatments can be found in Michael J. Hogan, ed., *Hiroshima in History and Memory* (Cambridge, U.K.: Cambridge University Press, 1996), especially the essays by John W. Dower, Paul Boyer, and J. Samuel Walker; Emily S. Rosenberg, *A Date Which Will Live: Pearl Harbor in American Memory* (Durham, N.C.: Duke University Press, 2003); and Franziska Seraphim, *War Memory and Social Politics in Japan, 1945–2005* (Cambridge, Mass.: Harvard University Asia Center, 2006).

Korea, 1950–1953

Paradoxically, what is best-remembered as the "Forgotten War" has attracted considerable attention from historians. Drawing on sources in a variety of languages, their work offers insights on a rich array of topics from multiple perspectives, including political and cultural as well as military history. The opportunities for researchers vary greatly from country to country, with the United States and Britain the most open and North Korea firmly locked down. Post-Soviet Russia, postauthoritarian South Korea, and reform-era China stand somewhere between the two extremes.

Overviews and orientations have begun to reflect the broadening of coverage, the expansion of sources, and the loosening of the straitjacket of Cold War assumptions. Steven Hugh Lee, *The Korean War* (Harlow, U.K.: Longman, 2001), is the most succinct, broadly cast, and up-to-date overview. William Stueck's *Rethinking the Korean War: A New Diplomatic and Strategic History* (Princeton, N.J.: Princeton University Press, 2002), as well as his "In Search of Essences: Labeling the Korean War," in *Remembering the "Forgotten War": The Korean War through Literature and Art*, ed. Philip West and Suh Ji-moon (Armonk, N.Y.: M. E. Sharpe, 2001), 187–202, grapples with some key interpretive issues in a way readers will find helpful. Peter Lowe's concise two-volume treatment— *The Origins of the Korean War*, 2nd ed. (London: Longman, 1997) and *The Korean War* (New York: St. Martin's, 2000)—is strongest on diplomacy and politics. Allan R. Millett has under way a fuller account richest on the U.S. military role. *The War for Korea, 1945–1950: A House Burning* (Lawrence: University Press of Kansas, 2005), and *The War for Korea, 1950–1951: They Came from the North* (Lawrence: University Press of Kansas, 2010), are to be followed by a third, final volume. Millett has also prepared the most up-to-date assessment of the Korean War scholarship, archives, and websites—to be found as one section of his *The Korean War* (Washington, D.C.: Potomac, 2007).

Establishing the context in which the Korean War erupted is like peeling an onion; one tightly wrapped layer follows another. At the outermost is the work on U.S. policy and the origins of the Cold War. The place to begin is with the general treatments by Melvyn P. Leffler: his detailed policy reconstruction in *A Preponderance of Power: National Security, the Truman Administration and the Cold War, 1945–52* (Stanford, Calif.: Stanford University Press, 1992), and his shorter and more interpretively explicit *The Specter of Communism: The United States and the Origins of the Cold War, 1917–1953* (New York: Hill and Wang, 1994).

A closely related second layer of work deals with U.S. cold warriors' increasing pre-occupation with containment in Asia. Notable works here include Marc S. Gallicchio, *The Scramble for Asia: U.S. Military Power in the Aftermath of the Pacific War* (Lanham, Md.: Rowman & Littlefield, 2008); Steven Hugh Lee, *Outposts of Empire: Korea, Vietnam, and the Origins of the Cold War in Asia, 1949–1954* (Montreal: McGill-Queen's University Press, 1995); Gordon H. Chang, *Friends and Enemies: The United States, China, and the Soviet Union, 1948–1972* (Stanford, Calif.: Stanford University Press, 1990); Nancy Bern-kopf Tucker, *Patterns in the Dust: Chinese-American Relations and the Recognition Controversy, 1949–1950* (New York: Columbia University Press, 1983); and Simei Qing, *From Allies to Enemies: Visions of Modernity, Identity, and U.S.-China Diplomacy, 1945–1960* (Cambridge, Mass.: Harvard University Press, 2007). Zi Zhongyun, *No Exit? The Origin and Evolution of U.S. Policy toward China, 1945–1950*, trans. Zhang Ciyun and Jia Yanli (Norwalk, Conn.: EastBridge, 2002), stands out as a perceptive, pathbreaking Chinese treatment. Michael H. Hunt and Steven I. Levine, "The Revolutionary Challenge to Early

U.S. Cold War Policy in Asia," in *The Great Powers in East Asia, 1953–1960*, ed. Warren I. Cohen and Akira Iriye (New York: Columbia University Press, 1990), 13–34, highlights the importance of postwar ferment in the region.

Japan, where U.S. Cold War concerns sharply redirected occupation policy, constitutes a third layer of work. The place to start is John W. Dower, *Empire and Aftermath: Yoshida Shigeru and the Japanese Experience, 1878–1954* (Cambridge, Mass.: Council on East Asian Studies, Harvard University, 1979), as well as Dower, *Embracing Defeat: Japan in the Wake of World War II* (New York: W. W Norton, 1999); and Michael Schaller, *The American Occupation of Japan: The Origins of the Cold War in Asia* (New York: Oxford University Press, 1985).

The turbulent process of decolonization in Southeast Asia in the 1940s and 1950s has been the subject of a fourth layer of scholarship. General works include Anne L. Foster, *Projections of Power: The United States and Europe in Colonial Southeast Asia, 1919–1941* (Durham, N.C.: Duke University Press, 2010); and Robert J. McMahon, *The Limits of Empire: The United States and Southeast Asia since World War II* (New York: Columbia University Press, 1999). For more specialized, country-specific studies, see Benedict J. Kerkvliet's classic "moral economy" interpretation, *The Huk Rebellion: A Study of Peasant Revolt in the Philippines* (Berkeley: University of California Press, 1977); Nick Cullather, *Illusions of Influence: The Political Economy of United States–Philippines Relations, 1942–1960* (Stanford, Calif.: Stanford University Press, 1994), trenchant on negotiating collaboration; Robert J. McMahon's pioneering *Colonialism and Cold War: The United States and the Struggle for Indonesian Independence, 1945–49* (Ithaca, N.Y.: Cornell University Press, 1981); Frances Gouda and Thijs Brocades Zaalberg, *American Visions of the Netherlands East Indies/Indonesia: U.S. Foreign Policy and Indonesian Nationalism, 1920–1949* (Amsterdam: Amsterdam University Press, 2002), a richly researched account; and Richard Stubbs, *Hearts and Minds in Guerrilla Warfare: The Malayan Emergency, 1948–1960* (Singapore: Eastern Universities Press, 2004 [1889]), a careful treatment of a much cited but generally misunderstood case. The literature on the challenge to French control of Indochina is treated below in relation to chapter 4.

Yet a fifth layer is made up of work on the collapse of China's Nationalist government and the triumph of the Communists. Items from a large literature worth attention include Hsi-sheng Chi, *Nationalist China at War: Military Defeats and Political Collapse, 1937–1945* (Ann Arbor: University of Michigan Press, 1982); Odd Arne Westad, *Decisive Encounters: The Chinese Civil War, 1946–1950* (Stanford, Calif.: Stanford University Press, 2003); Steven I. Levine, *Anvil of Victory: The Communist Revolution in Manchuria, 1945–1948* (New York: Columbia University Press, 1987); Niu Jun, *From Yan'an to the World: The Origin and Development of Chinese Communist Foreign Policy*, ed. and trans. Steven I. Levine (Norwalk, Conn.: EastBridge, 2005); Michael H. Hunt, *The Genesis of Chinese Communist Foreign Policy* (New York: Columbia University Press, 1996); and Chen Jian, *Mao's China and the Cold War* (Chapel Hill: University of North Carolina Press, 2001), chaps. 1–4.

Finally, the innermost layer deals with developments in Korea before June 1950. An elaborately developed and controversial argument for the war originating in civil conflict can be found in Bruce Cumings, *The Origins of the Korean War*, vol. 1, *Liberation and the Emergence of Separate Regimes, 1945–1947* (Princeton, N.J.: Princeton University Press, 1981), and vol. 2, *The Roaring of the Cataract, 1947–1950* (Princeton, N.J.: Princeton University Press, 1990). For studies focusing on the North Korean regime, see Charles K. Armstrong, *The North Korean Revolution, 1945–1950* (Ithaca, N.Y.: Cornell University Press, 2003); A. N. Lankov, *From Stalin to Kim Il Sung: The Formation of North Korea, 1945–1960* (New Brunswick, N.J.: Rutgers University Press, 2002); and Dae-Sook Suh, *Kim Il Sung: The North Korean Leader* (New York: Columbia University Press, 1988).

The role of the United States and its allies in the war is the subject of a substantial literature. Concise overall treatment of U.S. policymaking, politics, and tensions with allies can be found in Burton I. Kaufman, *The Korean War: Challenges in Crisis, Credibility, and Command*, 2nd ed. (New York: McGraw-Hill, 1997), an update and substantial condensation of the first edition. On the strategic debate that tied Washington and its commanders in the field in knots, see Rosemary Foot's meticulous reconstructions— *The Wrong War: American Policy and the Dimensions of the Korean Conflict, 1950–1953* (Ithaca, N.Y.: Cornell University Press, 1985) and *A Substitute for Victory: The Politics of Peacemaking at the Korean Armistice Talks* (Ithaca, N.Y.: Cornell University Press, 1990)—as well as Michael D. Pearlman's *Truman & MacArthur: Policy, Politics, and the Hunger for Honor and Renown* (Bloomington: Indiana University Press, 2008); Stanley Weintraub, *MacArthur's War: Korea and the Undoing of an American Hero* (New York: Free Press, 2000), a fast-paced popular treatment; the relevant portions of the MacArthur biographies cited in the literature for chapter 2; and Roger Dingman, "Atomic Diplomacy during the Korean War," *International Security* 13 (Winter 1988–89): 50–91, a crisp review of Washington's hollow nuclear threats. Conrad C. Crane, *American Airpower Strategy in Korea, 1950–1953* (Lawrence: University Press of Kansas, 2000), is essential on an important facet of U.S. war fighting. Martin Russ, *Breakout: The Chosin Reservoir Campaign, Korea 1950* (New York: Penguin, 2000); *Korean War: The Untold Story* (1988; writ., prod., and dir. Carol L. Fleisher; 34 min.), which offers interesting interviews with four American veterans; and Michael Culleen Green, *Black Yanks in the Pacific: Race in the Making of American Military Empire after World War II* (Ithaca, N.Y.: Cornell University Press, 2010), are revealing on the war as the soldiers knew it.

Consequences for the U.S. home front—from intensified political and cultural anxieties to the growing power of the Cold War state—are the subject of Steven Casey, *Selling the Korean War: Propaganda, Politics, and Public Opinion in the United States, 1950–1953* (New York: Oxford University Press, 2008); and Michael J. Hogan, *A Cross of Iron: Harry S. Truman and the Origins of the National Security State, 1945–1954* (Cambridge, U.K.: Cambridge University Press, 1998). For the popular conceptions that attended deepening U.S. involvement in Asia in the 1940s, see Christina Klein, *Cold War Orientalism: Asia in the Middlebrow Imagination, 1945–1961* (Berkeley: University of California Press, 2003); and T. Christopher Jespersen, *American Images of China, 1931–1949* (Stanford, Calif.: Stanford University Press, 1996).

For the effects of war on Koreans, see Kim Dong-choon, *The Unending Korean War: A Social History* (Larkspur, Calif.: Tamal Vista, 2009); and Katherine Moon, *Sex among Allies: Military Prostitution in U.S.-Korean Relations* (New York: Columbia University Press, 1997), chap. 1.

China's response to the Korean War is far better understood now than in 1960, when Allen S. Whiting published his pathbreaking *China Crosses the Yalu: The Decision* to Enter the Korean War (Stanford, Calif.: Stanford University Press, 1968). For insights on decision making and military strategy, see Chen Jian, *China's Road to the Korean War: The Making of the Sino-American Confrontation* (New York: Columbia University Press, 1994); and Shu Guang Zhang, *Mao's Military Romanticism: China and the Korean War, 1950–1953* (Lawrence: University Press of Kansas, 1995). For treatment of Chinese and North Korean forces, see Shu Guang Zhang, "Command, Control, and the PLA's Offensive Campaigns in Korea, 1950–1951, in *Chinese Warfighting: The PLA Experience Since 1949*, ed. Mark A. Ryan, David Michael Finkelstein, and Michael A. McDevitt (Armonk, N.Y.: M. E. Sharpe, 2003), 91–122; Xu Yan, "The Chinese Forces and Their Casualties in the Korean War: Facts and Statistics" (trans. Li Xiaobing), *Chinese Historians* 6 (Fall 1993): 45–58; and Bin Yu, "What China Learned from Its 'Forgotten War' in Korea," also in *Chinese Warfighting*, 123–42. China's relationship with its major ally is treated in Dieter Heinzig, *The Soviet Union and Communist China, 1945–1950: The Arduous Road to the Alliance*, trans. David J. S. King (Armonk, N.Y.: M. E. Sharpe, 2004); Odd Arne Westad, ed., *Brothers in Arms: The Rise and Fall of the Sino-Soviet Alliance, 1945–1963* (Stanford, Calif.: Stanford University Press, 1998); Sergei N. Goncharov, John W. Lewis, and Xue Litai, *Uncertain Partners: Stalin, Mao, and the Korean War* (Stanford, Calif.: Stanford University Press, 1993); and Shen Zhihua, "Sino-Soviet Relations and the Origins of the Korean War: Stalin's Strategic Goals in the Far East," *Journal of Cold War Studies* 2 (Spring 2000): 44–68.

The domestic side of the Chinese war effort is beginning to receive the attention it deserves. For works suggestive of the possibilities, see Hong Zhang, *America Perceived: The Making of Chinese Images of the United States, 1945–1953* (Westport, Conn.: Greenwood, 2002), which is deft on the anti-Americanism among educated youth; Jeremy Brown and Paul Pickowicz, *Dilemmas of Victory: The Early Years of the People's Republic of China* (Cambridge, Mass.: Harvard University Press, 2007), which points to the patterns of social and cultural accommodation and resistance to the new regime; and Ruth Rogaski, "Nature, Annihilation, and Modernity: China's Korean War Germ-Warfare Experience Reconsidered," *Journal of Asian Studies* 61 (May 2002): 381–415, a revealing case study.

The memories and memorials associated with the Korean War are strikingly divergent from country to country. This becomes evident in David R. McCann, "Our Forgotten War: The Korean War in Korean and American Popular Culture," in *America's Wars in Asia: A Cultural Approach to History and Memory*, ed. Philip West, Steven I. Levine, and Jackie Hiltz (Armonk, N.Y.: M. E. Sharpe, 1998), pp. 65–83; Sheila Miyoshi Jager and Rana Mitter, eds., *Ruptured Histories: War, Memory, and the Post–Cold War in Asia* (Cambridge, Mass.: Harvard University Press, 2007); and Philip West and Suh Ji-moon, eds., *Remembering the "Forgotten War": The Korean War through Literature and Art* (Armonk, N.Y.: M. E. Sharpe, 2001).

Vietnam, 1965–1973

The Vietnam War has generated an enormous scholarly literature, far larger than that for any of the other U.S. Pacific conflicts. The attention is easy to explain. The war was long. Its ramifications were felt all across Indochina, and for that matter the world. The controversies surrounding it remain heated. And new sources appear in a steady stream, offering fresh insights, especially on the Vietnamese side of the war and the Nixon years. For a full and up-to-date guide maintained by Edwin E. Moïse, see "Vietnam War Bibliography" at http://www.clemson.edu/caah/history/facultypages/EdMoise/bibliography .html. Gary R. Hess, *Vietnam: Explaining America's Lost War* (Malden, Mass.: Blackwell, 2009), links the enormous literature to the chief points of controversy that have swirled about this war.

A fine set of general accounts provide a helpful point of entry for the uninitiated. Of the many surveys, George C. Herring, *America's Longest War: The United States and Vietnam, 1950–1975*, 4th ed. (Boston: McGraw-Hill, 2002), stands out as a regularly updated classic, while Mark Atwood Lawrence, *The Vietnam War: A Concise International History* (New York: Oxford University Press, 2008), is notable for its lean and wide-ranging coverage. Mark Bradley, *Vietnam at War* (Oxford, U.K.: Oxford University Press, 2009), offers a fresh, crisp introduction to the Vietnamese perspective. An outstanding visual overview is available in *Vietnam: A Television History* (1983; prod. WGBH, Boston; Central Independent Television, Great Britain; and Antenne-2, France; in association with LRE Productions; 13 episodes).

A sense of the origins of the Vietnamese revolution is indispensable to understanding this war. Good places to begin include Neil L. Jamieson, *Understanding Vietnam* (Berkeley: University of California Press, 1993), especially chap. 2, "Confrontation with the West, 1858–1930"; Alexander Woodside, *Community and Revolution in Modern Vietnam* (Boston: Houghton Mifflin, 1976); Hue-Tam Ho Tai, *Radicalism and the Origins of the Vietnamese Revolution* (Cambridge, Mass.: Harvard University Press, 1992); Huynh Kim Khanh, *Vietnamese Communism, 1925–1945* (Ithaca, N.Y.: Cornell University Press, 1982); and Christopher E. Goscha, *Vietnam or Indochina? Contesting Concepts of Space in Vietnamese Nationalism, 1887–1954* (Copenhagen: Nordic Institute of Asian Studies, 1995).

For more specialized treatment, see on the revolution's founding father Pierre Brocheux, *Ho Chi Minh: A Biography* (New York: Cambridge University Press, 2007); and Sophie Quinn-Judge, *Ho Chi Minh: The Missing Years, 1919–1941* (Berkeley: University of California Press, 2002). The watershed marked by the August Revolution is treated by David G. Marr, *Vietnam 1945: The Quest for Power* (Berkeley: University of California Press, 1995); Stein Tønnesson, *The Vietnamese Revolution of 1945: Roosevelt, Ho Chi Minh and de Gaulle in a World at War* (London: Sage, 1991); and Tønnesson, *Vietnam 1946: How the War Began* (Berkeley: University of California Press, 2010). The sweep of change in modern Vietnam is nicely captured in the family history by Duong Van Mai Elliott, *The Sacred Willow: Four Generations in the Life of a Vietnamese Family* (New York: Oxford University Press, 1999). The French film *Indochine* (1992, dir. Régis Wargnier, 162 min.) evokes the social complexities of 1930s Vietnam—and inadvertently exposes Hollywood's scandalous incapacity to take that country seriously.

On the sharpening tensions from the 1940s to 1965 as U.S. Cold War concerns collided with Vietnam's revolution, see Michael H. Hunt, *Lyndon Johnson's War: America's Cold War Crusade in Vietnam, 1945–1968* (New York: Hill and Wang, 1996); Mark Philip Bradley, *Imagining Vietnam and America: The Making of Postcolonial Vietnam, 1919–1950* (Chapel Hill: University of North Carolina Press, 2000); David L. Anderson, *Trapped by Success: The Eisenhower Administration and Vietnam, 1953–1961* (New York: Columbia

University Press, 1991); and Christopher E. Goscha, "Courting Diplomatic Disaster? The Difficult Integration of Vietnam into the Internationalist Communist Movement (1945–1950)," *Journal of Vietnamese Studies* 1 (February–August 2006): 59–103. A controversial U.S. client has recently attracted fresh interest, above all in Seth Jacobs, *America's Miracle Man in Vietnam: Ngo Dinh Diem, Religion, Race, and U.S. Intervention in Southeast Asia, 1950–1957* (Durham, N.C.: Duke University Press, 2004); and Philip E. Catton, *Diem's Final Failure: Prelude to America's War in Vietnam* (Lawrence: University Press of Kansas, 2002).

U.S. war policy has gotten close scrutiny. The place to start on the Johnson administration is the detailed and interpretively engaging treatment by Fredrik Logevall, *Choosing War: The Lost Chance for Peace and the Escalation of War in Vietnam* (Berkeley: University of California Press, 1999). For other perspectives, see Francis M. Bator, "No Good Choices: LBJ and the Vietnam/Great Society Connection," *Diplomatic History* 32 (June 2008): 309–40; George C. Herring, *LBJ and Vietnam: A Different Kind of War* (Austin: University of Texas Press, 1994); and Lloyd C. Gardner, *Pay Any Price: Lyndon Johnson and the Wars for Vietnam* (Chicago: I. R. Dee, 1995). For a journalistic classic, see David Halberstam, *The Best and the Brightest* (New York: Random House, 1972). The documentary *The Fog of War: Eleven Lessons from the Life of Robert S. McNamara* (2003, prod. and dir. Errol Morris, 107 min.) examines a key policymaker turned by the war into a tortured soul.

On the Nixon years, turn to Jeffrey P. Kimball, *Nixon's Vietnam War* (Lawrence: University Press of Kansas, 1998); and Stephen P. Randolph, *Powerful and Brutal Weapons: Nixon, Kissinger, and the Easter Offensive* (Cambridge, Mass.: Harvard University Press, 2007). Kimball has refined his argument in a collection of documents: *The Vietnam War Files: Uncovering the Secret History of Nixon-Era Strategy* (Lawrence: University Press of Kansas, 2004). See also Larry Berman, *No Peace, No Honor: Nixon, Kissinger, and Betrayal in Vietnam* (New York: Free Press, 2001), which sticks close to the documents; and Pierre Asselin, *A Bitter Peace: Washington, Hanoi, and the Making of the Paris Agreement* (Chapel Hill: University of North Carolina Press, 2002), a blow-by-blow chronicle.

The U.S. military effort is the subject of some outstanding treatments, including Gregory A. Daddis, *No Sure Victory: Measuring U.S. Army Effectiveness and Progress in the Vietnam War* (New York: Oxford University Press, 2011); Mark Clodfelter, *The Limits of Airpower: The American Bombing of North Vietnam*, 2nd ed. (Lincoln: University of Nebraska Press, 2006); Eric M. Bergerud, *Red Thunder, Tropical Lightning: The World of a Combat Division in Vietnam* (Boulder, Colo.: Westview, 1993); H. G. Moore and Joseph L. Galloway, *We Were Soldiers Once . . . and Young: Ia Drang, the Battle That Changed the War in Vietnam* (New York: Random House, 1992); Ronald H. Spector, *After Tet: The Bloodiest Year in Vietnam* (New York: Free Press, 1993); David L. Anderson, ed., *Facing My Lai: Moving Beyond the Massacre* (Lawrence: University Press of Kansas, 1998); and Michael R. Belknap, *The Vietnam War on Trial: The My Lai Massacre and the Court-Martial of Lieutenant Calley* (Lawrence: University Press of Kansas, 2002).

For insight on the combatants, see the revealing social and institutional histories by Kyle Longley, *Grunts: The American Combat Soldier in Vietnam* (Armonk, N.Y.: M. E. Sharpe, 2008); Christian G. Appy, *Working-Class War: American Combat Soldiers and Vietnam* (Chapel Hill: University of North Carolina Press, 1993); Ron Milam, *Not a*

Gentleman's War: An Inside View of Junior Officers in the Vietnam War (Chapel Hill: University of North Carolina Press, 2009); Meredith H. Lair, *Armed with Abundance: Consumerism and Soldiering in the Vietnam War* (Chapel Hill: University of North Carolina Press, 2011); Robert K. Brigham, *ARVN: Life and Death in the South Vietnamese Army* (Lawrence: University Press of Kansas, 2006); and Andrew A. Wiest, *Vietnam's Forgotten Army: Heroism and Betrayal in the ARVN* (New York: New York University Press, 2008). Neil Sheehan, *A Bright Shining Lie: John Paul Vann and America in Vietnam* (New York: Random House, 1988), is an engaging study of a dedicated but ultimately frustrated U.S. adviser.

The conduct of Vietnam's anti-American war has been attracting increasing attention. The research of Merle L. Pribbenow II is notable for its fresh insights drawn from new Vietnamese materials. See his "The -Ology War: Technology and Ideology in the Vietnamese Defense of Hanoi, 1967," *Journal of Military History* 67 (January 2003): 175–200; "General Vo Nguyen Giap and the Mysterious Evolution of the Plan for the 1968 Tet Offensive," *Journal of Vietnamese Studies* 3 (Summer 2008): 1–33; and "North Vietnam's Final Offensive: Strategic Endgame Nonpareil," *Parameters* 29 (Winter 1999–2000): 58–71; as well as his translation of Military History Institute of Vietnam, *Victory in Vietnam: The Official History of the People's Army of Vietnam, 1954-1975* (Lawrence: University Press of Kansas, 2002). Other important works on the struggle against the United States include Carlyle A. Thayer, *War by Other Means: National Liberation and Revolution in Viet-Nam, 1954-60* (Sydney, Australia: Allen and Unwin, 1989); Karen G. Turner with Phan Thanh Hao, *Even the Women Must Fight: Memories of War from North Vietnam* (New York: Wiley, 1998); Ang Cheng Guan, *The Vietnam War from the Other Side: The Vietnamese Communists' Perspective* (London: RoutledgeCurzon, 2002); Ang Cheng Guan, *Ending the Vietnam War: The Vietnamese Communists' Perspective* (London: RoutledgeCurzon, 2004); and Luu Van Loi and Nguyen Anh Vu, *Le Duc Tho-Kissinger Negotiations in Paris* (Hanoi: The Gioi, 1996).

The allies that sustained Hanoi through the war are treated in Chen Jian, *Mao's China and the Cold War* (Chapel Hill: University of North Carolina Press, 2001), chaps. 5 and 8; Qiang Zhai, *China and the Vietnam Wars, 1950-1975* (Chapel Hill: University of North Carolina Press, 2000); Xiaoming Zhang, "The Vietnam War, 1964–1969: A Chinese Perspective," *Journal of Military History* 60 (October 1997): 731–62; Yang Kuisong, "Mao Zedong and the Indochina Wars," in *Behind the Bamboo Curtain: China, Vietnam, and the World beyond Asia*, ed. Priscilla Roberts (Washington, D.C.: Woodrow Wilson Center Press, and Stanford, Calif.: Stanford University Press, 2006), pp. 55–96; Mari Olsen, *Soviet-Vietnam Relations and the Role of China, 1949-64: Changing Alliances* (London: Routledge, 2006); and Ilya V. Gaiduk, *The Soviet Union and the Vietnam War* (Chicago: I. R. Dee, 1996), which picks up the Soviet story for 1964–1972.

Grasping the particularities of the southern revolution from one place to another is essential to any appraisal of the war. See David W. P. Elliott, *The Vietnamese War: Revolution and Social Change in the Mekong Delta, 1930-1975*, concise ed. (Armonk, N.Y.: M. E. Sharpe, 2007); David Hunt, *Vietnam's Southern Revolution: From Peasant Insurrection to Total War* (Amherst: University of Massachusetts Press, 2008), which like Elliott deals with My Tho; Jeffrey Race, *War Comes to Long An: Revolutionary Conflict in a Vietnamese Province* (Berkeley: University of California Press, 1972); James W. Trullinger Jr., *Village at War: An Account of Revolution in Vietnam* (New York: Longman, 1980), focusing on the outskirts of Hue; Eric M. Bergerud, *The Dynamics of Defeat: The Vietnam War in Hau Nghia Province* (Boulder, Colo.: Westview, 1991); Pierre Brocheux, *The Mekong Delta: Ecology, Economy, and Revolution, 1860–1960* (Madison: Center for Southeast Asian Studies, University of Wisconsin, 1995); and Mark W. McLeod, "Indigenous Peoples and the Vietnamese Revolution, 1930–1975," *Journal of World History* 10 (Fall 1999): 353–89.

The contention within the United States set off by the war is best surveyed in Rhodri Jeffreys-Jones, *Peace Now! American Society and the Ending of the Vietnam War* (New Haven, Conn.: Yale University Press, 1999); David W. Levy, *The Debate over Vietnam*, 2nd ed. (Baltimore: Johns Hopkins University Press, 1995); and Tom Wells, *The War Within: America's Battle over Vietnam* (Berkeley: University of California Press, 1994). For important aspects of the domestic battle, see David C. Hallin, *The "Uncensored War": The Media and Vietnam* (Berkeley: University of California Press, 1989 [1986]); William L. Lunch and Peter W. Sperlich, "American Public Opinion and the War in Vietnam," *Western Political Quarterly* 32 (March 1979): 21–44; Joseph A. Fry, *Debating Vietnam: Fulbright, Stennis, and Their Senate Hearings* (Lanham, Md.: Rowman & Littlefield, 2006); Randall B. Woods, ed., *Vietnam and the American Political Tradition: The Politics of Dissent* (Cambridge, U.K.: Cambridge University Press, 2003); Charles DeBenedetti assisted by Charles Chatfield, *An American Ordeal: The Antiwar Movement of the Vietnam Era* (Syracuse, N.Y.: Syracuse University Press, 1990); Melvin Small, *Johnson, Nixon, and the Doves* (New Brunswick, N.J.: Rutgers University Press, 1988); Andrew E. Hunt, *The Turning: A History of Vietnam Veterans against the War* (New York: New York University Press, 1999); and Gerald Nicosia, *Home to War: A History of the Vietnam Veterans' Movement* (New York: Crown Publishers, 2001).

General works helpful in tracing the ways the war intersected with societal ferment in the United States include Terry H. Anderson, *The Movement and the Sixties: Protest in America from Greensboro to Wounded Knee* (New York: Oxford University Press, 1995); David Farber, *The Age of Great Dreams: America in the 1960s* (New York: Hill and Wang, 1994); and Mark H. Lytle, *America's Uncivil Wars: The Sixties Era—From Elvis to the Fall of Richard Nixon* (New York: Oxford University Press, 2006). Notable among the documentary films dealing with domestic conflict are *The War at Home* (1979, prod. and dir. Glenn Silber and Barry Alexander Brown, 100 min.); *Chicago 1968* (1995, writ. and prod. Chana Gazit, 56 min.); *Two Days in October* (2005, prod. and dir. Robert Kenner, approx. 80 min.); and *Sir! No Sir!* (2005, dir. David Zeiger, 85 min.) on antiwar activity within the U.S. military.

The war's legacies for American politics and culture have received extensive treatment. Notable works include Arnold Isaacs, *Vietnam Shadows: The War, Its Ghosts, and Its Legacy* (Baltimore: Johns Hopkins University Press, 1997); Robert D. Schulzinger, *A Time for Peace: The Legacy of the Vietnam War* (New York: Oxford University Press, 2006); Michael J. Allen, *Until the Last Man Comes Home: POWs, MIAs, and the Unending Vietnam War* (Chapel Hill: University of North Carolina Press, 2009); Kristin Ann Hass, *Carried to the Wall: American Memory and the Vietnam Veterans Memorial* (Berkeley: University of California Press, 1998); Robert J. McMahon, "Contested Memory: The Vietnam War and American Society, 1975–2001," *Diplomatic History* 26 (Spring 2002):

159–84; and Jeffrey Kimball, "The Enduring Paradigm of the 'Lost Cause': Defeat in Vietnam, the Stab-in-the-Back Legend, and the Construction of a Myth," in *Defeat and Memory: Cultural Histories of Military Defeat in the Modern Era*, ed. Jenny Macleod (Basingstoke, U.K.: Palgrave Macmillan, 2008), 233–50. The reaction of the institution most deeply touched by defeat is adeptly handled by George C. Herring, "Preparing *Not to Refight the Last War*: The Impact of the Vietnam War on the U.S. Military," in *After Vietnam: Legacies of a Lost War*, ed. Charles E. Neu (Baltimore: Johns Hopkins University Press, 2000), 58–84; and Conrad Crane "Avoiding Vietnam: The U.S. Army's Response to Defeat in Southeast Asia" (monograph published by the Strategic Studies Institute of the U.S. Army War College, September 2002).

For the impact on Vietnamese, see Hue-Tam Ho Tai, ed., *The Country of Memory: Remaking the Past in Late Socialist Vietnam* (Berkeley: University of California Press, 2001); Heonik Kwon, *After the Massacre: Commemoration and Consolation in Ha My and My Lai* (Berkeley: University of California Press, 2006); James M. Freeman, *Hearts of Sorrow: Vietnamese-American Lives* (Stanford, Calif.: Stanford University Press, 1989); and Paul James Rutledge, *The Vietnamese Experience in America* (Bloomington: Indiana University Press, 1992). James Tatum offers an arresting comparison in "Memorials of the America War in Vietnam," *Critical Inquiry* 22 (Summer 1996): 634–78.

On the ultimately disastrous impact of the Vietnam War on Cambodia, see David P. Chandler, *The Tragedy of Cambodian History: Politics, War, and Revolution since 1945* (New Haven, Conn.: Yale University Press, 1991); Ben Kiernan, *The Pol Pot Regime: Race, Power, and Genocide in Cambodia under the Khmer Rouge, 1975–79*, 2nd ed. (New Haven, Conn.: Yale University Press, 2002); and Odd Arne Westad and Sophie Quinn-Judge, eds., *The Third Indochina War: Conflict between China, Vietnam and Cambodia, 1972–79* (London: Routledge, 2006).

Conclusion

The aftermath of the U.S. drive into eastern Asia has been a matter of notable concern to both journalists and academics attempting first-cut history. The broad outlines are coming into focus.

For the U.S. retreat from the forward policies of the 1950s and 1960s, see Robert J. McMahon, *The Limits of Empire: The United States and Southeast Asia since World War II* (New York: Columbia University Press, 1999). The ups and downs of relations with China are well covered by Evelyn Goh, *Constructing the U.S. Rapprochement with China, 1961–1974: From "Red Menace" to "Tacit Ally"* (Cambridge, U.K.: Cambridge University Press, 2005); James Mann, *About Face: A History of America's Curious Relationship with China, from Nixon to Clinton* (New York: Alfred A. Knopf, 1999); and Richard Madsen, *China and the American Dream: A Moral Inquiry* (Berkeley: University of California Press, 1995). Michael Schaller, *Altered States: The United States and Japan since the Occupation* (New York: Oxford University Press, 1997), traces the transformation of the other key U.S. regional relationship.

For the former Asian battleground, helpful overviews include Mel Gurtov, *Pacific Asia? Prospects for Security and Cooperation in East Asia* (Lanham, Md.: Rowman & Littlefield, 2002), which offers an acute analysis of the ways U.S. preoccupations have come to diverge from dominant regional trends; Richard Stubbs, *Rethinking Asia's Eco-*

nomic Miracle: The Political Economy of War, Prosperity, and Crisis (New York: Palgrave Macmillan, 2005), a challenging exploration of the impetus international conflict and Cold War rivalry has given to economic development; and Sheila Miyoshi Jager and Rana Mitter, eds., Ruptured Histories: War, Memory, and the Post–Cold War in Asia (Cambridge, Mass.: Harvard University Press, 2007), a collection of rewarding case studies.

Country-specific studies deepen the insight on regional developments as U.S. influence declined. The classic on the postwar Japanese political economy is Chalmers Johnson, MITI and the Japanese Miracle: The Growth of Industrial Policy, 1925–1975 (Stanford, Calif.: Stanford University Press, 1982), but see also the recent assessment by Frances McCall Rosenbluth and Michael F. Thies, Japan Transformed: Political Change and Economic Restructuring (Princeton, N.J.: Princeton University Press, 2010). On contemporary China, Martin Jacques, When China Rules the World: The Rise of the Middle Kingdom and the End of the Western World (London: Allen Lane, 2009), offers behind its sensational title a fresh, thoughtful examination, while Peter H. Gries, China's New Nationalism: Pride, Politics, and Diplomacy (Berkeley: University of California Press, 2004), examines recent popular and official writings. On the Philippines in recent decades, see Benedict Anderson, "Cacique Democracy in the Philippines: Origins and Dreams," in Discrepant Histories: Translocal Essays on Filipino Culture, ed. Vicente L. Rafael (Philadelphia: Temple University Press, 1995), 3–47; Alfred W. McCoy, ed., An Anarchy of Families: State and Family in the Philippines (Madison: University of Wisconsin Center for Southeast Asian Studies, 1993); and Kent Eaton, "Restoration or Transformation? Trapos vs. NGOs in the Democratization of the Philippines," Journal of Asian Studies 62 (May 2003): 469–96. Insights on contemporary Korea can be found in Gregg Brazinsky, Nation Building in South Korea: Koreans, Americans, and the Making of a Democracy (Chapel Hill: University of North Carolina Press, 2007), good on how a "developmental autocracy" led to an authentic democracy; and Charles K. Armstrong, The Koreas (New York: Routledge, 2007), a succinct, well-informed survey of the two Koreas and the Korean diaspora in the context of global politics. William J. Duiker, Vietnam: Revolution in Transition (Boulder, Colo.: Westview, 1995), traces the turn of a war-ravaged country toward a successful growth strategy.

The deepening U.S. involvement in the greater Middle East is the subject of a continuing stream of studies. For overviews, see Douglas Little, American Orientalism: The United States and the Middle East since 1945 (Chapel Hill: University of North Carolina Press, 2002); Rhashid Khalidi, Resurrecting Empire: Western Footprints and America's Perilous Path in the Middle East (Boston: Beacon, 2004); Melani McAlister, Epic Encounters: Culture, Media, and U.S. Interests in the Middle East since 1945, 2nd ed. (Berkeley: University of California Press, 2005); and Geoffrey Wawro, Quicksand: America's Pursuit of Power in the Middle East (New York: Penguin, 2010). More focused studies especially suggestive on the theme of empire include James Mann, Rise of the Vulcans: The History of Bush's War Cabinet (New York: Viking, 2004); Rajiv Chandrasekaran, Imperial Life in the Emerald City: Inside Iraq's Green Zone (New York: Alfred A. Knopf, 2006); and Ahmed Rashid, Descent into Chaos: The United States and the Failure of Nation Building in Pakistan, Afghanistan, and Central Asia (New York: Viking, 2008). For help on historical parallels, see John W. Dower, Cultures of War: Pearl Harbor, Hiroshima, 9-11, Iraq (New York: W. W. Norton and New Press, 2010), on how the thinking and actions of

U.S. policymakers have been grounded in the predicates of empire; Robert K. Brigham, *Is Iraq Another Vietnam?* (New York: PublicAffairs, 2006), a thematic and somewhat fragmented consideration; and Lloyd C. Gardner and Marilyn B. Young, eds., *Iraq and the Lessons of Vietnam, or, How Not to Learn from the Past* (New York: New Press, 2007), a thought-provoking collection in which David Elliott, "Parallel Wars? Can 'Lessons of Vietnam' Be Applied to Iraq?," pp. 17–44, stands out. The documentary *Restrepo* (2010, dir. Tim Hetherington and Sebastian Junger, 93 min.) captures the experience of a platoon in eastern Afghanistan in 2007–8 in a way that calls vividly to mind images from the Vietnam War.

Acknowledgments

In our decade of collaboration on this book, we have accumulated many debts—and not just to each other. Shuhua Fan, Jongnam Na, and Nathaniel Smith first explored these issues with us in a graduate seminar in the fall of 2003. Fan's and Na's dissertations (both completed in 2006) proved especially pertinent. Fan's "Cultural Engineering: The Harvard-Yenching Institute and Chinese Humanities, 1924–1951" contains an instructive chapter on the developments in China during the Korean War, while Na's "Making Cold War Soldiers: The Americanization of the South Korean Army, 1945–1955," provided a reminder of another neglected facet of the Korean War.

Undergraduates enrolled in our jointly taught course on the Pacific Wars (offered spring 2005 and spring 2008) gave us a chance to develop our arguments in detail. We hope they learned as much as we did. Eve Duffy, director of the UNC Program in the Humanities, was good enough to let us test those arguments in a daylong seminar before an attentive audience that raised tough questions.

A number of colleagues did us the great service of a close, discerning reading of the full manuscript: Sherman Cochran, Madeline G. Levine, and Arne Westad, as well as Michael Schaller and Robert McMahon, who evaluated the draft manuscript. We are also grateful to Robert Schulzinger and Frank Ninkovich for comments on our initial book proposal to UNC Press. Andrew Byers, Mark Clodfelter, Miles Fletcher, Richard Kohn, Ronald Spector, and Mark Stoler generously responded to queries about scholarship in their areas of expertise. Will West shared his insights on war memorials in the Mekong Delta. Finally, thanks to Glenn May for searching comments on the introduction and chapter 1 as well as guidance on the literature.

For assistance in securing illustrations, we owe thanks to Linda Corey Claassen, Director, Mandeville Special Collections Library, University of California at San Diego; Sarah Alex, Director of Programs, The Herb Block Foundation; and Beth MacKenzie, Chief, Productions Branch, U.S. Army Center of Military History. Thanks also to William Childress for permission to draw on his poetry and to Sandy Pham for sharing her photograph of the My Lai memorial.

The UNC Press staff did its usual fine job. We are especially grateful to Chuck Grench for steady backing and thoughtful advice, Paul Betz for skillfully orchestrating the editorial work, Vicky Wells for sage guidance on permissions, Heidi Perov for expert help with images, Bill Nelson for cartographic wizardry, Alex Martin for keen copyediting, and Rich Hendel for the terrific design. Well done all!

Finally, we come to the obligatory nod to the spouse or whoever near and dear has suffered on account of the author's neglect, absent-mindedness, or irritability. While all authors go through the motions (as if this one gesture somehow compensates), we want to emphasize that we *really* mean it. Paula and Madeline have in this project, as in all things, borne with us and reminded us of what is important. Our thanks and our love to both!

Sources of Illustrations

Emilio Aguinaldo, probably 1898 or early 1899: From P. Fremont Rockett, *Our Boys in the Philippines: A Pictorial History of the War* (San Francisco: P. Fremont Rockett, 1899), n.p. The quote in the caption is from Stuart C. Miller, *"Benevolent Assimilation": The American Conquest of the Philippines, 1899–1903* (New Haven, Conn.: Yale University Press, 1982), 61.

Miguel Malvar, circa 1902: The original photograph is in the U.S. National Archives (Local Identifier 117-SC-98029).

A burial detail, mid-March 1899: From F. Tennyson Neely, *Fighting in the Philippines: Authentic Original Photographs* (London: F. Tennyson Neely, 1899), n.p.

African American troopers, circa 1898: From U.S. National Archives (Local Identifier 111-RB-2839, ARC Identifier 530699). The quotes in the caption are from *"Smoked Yankees" and the Struggle for Empire: Letters from Negro Soldiers, 1898–1902*, ed. Willard B. Gatewood Jr. (Urbana: University of Illinois Press, 1971), 13 ("our colored brothers") and 14 ("the Devil and the Deep Blue").

All is well on the home front, January 1941: From *Asahigraph*, 1–8 January 1941, reproduced in David C. Earhart, *Certain Victory: Images of World War II in the Japanese Media* (Armonk, N.Y.: M. E. Sharpe, 2008), 147.

Fantasies of revenge, September 1943: From Noyori Shuichi, *Air Raids on the Continental United States*, 2nd ed. (1944), reproduced in David C. Earhart, *Certain Victory: Images of World War II in the Japanese Media* (Armonk, N.Y.: M. E. Sharpe, 2008), 257.

Marine Corps War Memorial, Arlington, Virginia: Prints and Photographs Division, Library of Congress, HALS VA-9-4. Photograph by Jack E. Boucher.

Hiroshima Peace Memorial: Photograph by "Aiden," 24 November 2006, available on WikiCommons.

The sorrow of warriors, 28 August 1950: U.S. National Archives (Local Identifier 111-SC-347803, ARC Identifier 531370). Photograph by Sfc. Al Chang.

Refugees fleeing down the eastern coast of South Korea, early January 1951: Source: U.S. National Archives (Local Identifier 111-SC-356475; ARC Identifier 531397).

Chinese troops below ground during the stalemate war: From *Guangrong de Zhongguo renmin zhiyuanjun* [The glorious Chinese People's Volunteer Army] ([Beijing?]: Jiefangjun huabao, 1959), 129.

A grateful homeland, 1951: Stefan Landsberger's Chinese Propaganda Poster Collection in the Collection of the International Institute of Social History, Amsterdam. "The Institute accepts no liability whatsoever arising from the use of its materials. Users are responsible for conforming to all relevant statutory provisions concerning copyright. The Institute does not intermediate in questions about copyrights held by third parties."

Planning the Dienbienphu campaign, late 1953: From *Ho Chu Tich Song Mai Trong Su Nghiep Chung Ta* (Hanoi: Viet Nam Thong Tan Xa, 1970), 72.

Marine patrol, December 1965: U.S. National Archives (Local Identifier 127-N-A186280, ARC Identifier: 532437). Photograph by LCpl Lookabough.

Leading away a suspected "Viet Cong," August 1965: U.S. National Archives (Local Identifier 127-N-A185020, ARC Identifier: 532431). Photograph by PFC James Durbin.

NLF fighters, date unknown: The photograph by Van Phuong appears in Tim Page, *Another Vietnam: Pictures of the War from the Other Side* (Washington, D.C.: National Geographic, 2002), 101.

Vietnam Veterans Memorial, Washington, D.C.: Prints and Photographs Division, Library of Congress, HABS DC,WASH,643-13. Photograph by Jack E. Boucher. The quote from Lin's proposal in the caption is taken from Kristin Ann Hass, *Carried to the Wall: American Memory and the Vietnam Veterans Memorial* (Berkeley: University of California Press, 1998), 20.

Index

Italic page numbers refer to illustrations and maps.

Castro, Fidel, 200–201

Catholicism: in Philippines, 21, 29; in Vietnam, 196, 198, 200, 204, 217

Cavite, 25

Central Intelligence Agency (CIA), 143, 169, 183; in Vietnam, 199, 201, 298 (n. 31); Vietnam War and, 203, 210, 216, 217, 229

Chaffee, Adna, 45, 53, 255

Chamberlain, Neville, 121

Chang Myon, 267

Chau, Phan Boi. *See* Phan Boi Chau

Cheney, Dick, 274, 277

Chiang Kai-shek: Korean War and, 144, 166, 168; Sino-Japanese War (1937–45) and, 71–72, 125; U.S. support for, 69, 73, 126–27, 179–80, 200, 260; Vietnam and, 187

Childress, William, 149, 150

China, 5, 53; Boxer Rebellion, 15–16, 58, 59; communism and, 1, 62–63, 71, 72, 124–28, 176, 260, 266, 271; development, 1960s and 70s, 266–67, 268; development, into 1990s, 265, 270, 271–72, 302 (n. 16); Great Britain and, 145, 180; Japanese empire and, 60, 66, 68–71; Korea and, 128, 134, 136; missionaries and, 13, 66, 72–73, 75; Nixon and, 229, 233, 259–61, 271; North Korea and, 269; nuclear capability of, 266–67; Philippines War and, 61–62; Sino-Japanese War (1937–45), 71–72, 75, 77, 80, 81, 92, 102, 125; Soviet Union and, 73, 125–26, 153, *163*, 176, 208, 209, 230, 260; U.S. public opinion and, 72, 75, 94–95, 128; U.S. relations with, after Korean War, 179–80; U.S. response to communism in, 126–27, 133, 179, 184; Vietnam and, 125, 192–93, 208, 266; Vietnam War and, 203, 215, 230, 233, 267. *See also* Chiang Kai-shek; Korean War; Mao Zedong; Taiwan

Chinese Americans, 101, 160–61

Chinese Exclusion Act of 1882, 101

Choe, Sang-hun, 178

Churchill, Winston, 187

Civil War, 35, 52, 53, 57

Clark, Mark, 169

Cleveland, Grover, 13

Clifford, Clark, 203, 225

Clinton, Bill, 241, 271–72

Cold War: China and, 127–28, 272; Korean War and, 145, 159, 166, 177; U.S. commitments early in, 177; U.S. policy towards French Indochina and, 188; U.S. strategy during, 122–23, 131, 132, 135, 180–82; U.S. strategy during Nixon years and, 227, 261–62; Vietnam and, 197, 201, 227, 239, 259–60

Combs, Walter R., 36

Communism: in Cambodia, 248; in China, 1, 62–63, 71, 72, 124–28, 176, 188, 260, 266, 271; in Korea, 130–31, 157, 158, 159, 165, 174, 175; in United States, 180–81; U.S. fear of, 121, 122–23, 124, 197, 252, 253; U.S. response to, in China, 126–27, 133, 179, 184; in Vietnam, 188, 190–91, 192, 193, 199, 205, 233, 246–47, 250

Communist International (Comintern), 190

Cortelyou, George B., 19–20

Counterinsurgency, 124, 277–78

Cronkite, Walter, 225–26

Cuba, 13–14, 15, 18, 23, 33, 200–201

Dannenmaier, William D., 120

Day, William R., 20

"Dear John" (song, Shepard and Husky), 159–60

De Gaulle, Charles, 187, 208

Demilitarized Zone, in Korea, 167, 171; in Vietnam, 232, *234*

Deng Xiaoping, 268, 269, 271

Dewey, George, 15, 30, 31

DeWitt, John L., 97

Diem, Ngo Dinh. *See* Ngo Dinh Diem

Dienbienphu, battle of, 193, *194–95*, 224

regime and, 44–45, 56, 58–59, 109, 110, 255; World War II and, 58, 82, 83, 85, 87, 92, 182, 284 (n. 49), 295 (n. 69)

Philippines War (1899–1902), 4, 20; atrocities during, 43, 52; beginning of, 10, 19, 32–35, 281 (n. 1); Filipino losses during, 58, 255, 285–86 (n. 60); Filipino resistance during, 47, 49, 50, 52–54, 55–56, 58–59; forgetting of, 1, 57–58, 276; U.S. Army campaign and, 12, 35–43, 57, 285 (n. 58), 285–86 (n. 60); U.S. public opinion and, 37, 45–49, 55, 57; weapons of, 35. *See also* U.S. Army—in Philippines

Pol Pot, 247, 248–49

Pork Chop Hill (1959 film), 178

Potsdam Proclamation, 106, 108

Potsdam summit, 105, 106

Potter, Paul, 219

Powell, Colin, 241

Pratt, E. Spencer, 30, 31

Puerto Rico, 14, 15

Qing dynasty, 61, 66, 124

Quiet American, The (Greene), 183

Quirino, Elpidio, 182

Qutb, Sayyid, 275

Rambo (aka *First Blood*) (1982 film), 241

Reagan, Ronald, 240, 271

Reischauer, Edwin O., 97

Rhee, Syngman, 267; early life, 129; Kim Il Sung and, 131–32; Korean War and, 133, 135, 166, 170, 171, 263; U.S. support for, 129–30, 131, 139, 173, 175, 198, 200

Ridgway, Matthew B., 145, 146, 158, 167, 168

Rizal, José, 21–22

Roh Mu-hyun, 175, 264

Roosevelt, Franklin Delano, 106, 118, 122, 136; China and, 126; Indochina and, 187; Japanese empire and, 72, 74–76; Korea and, 128; Pearl Harbor attack and, 64–65; World War II in Europe

and, 74, 81, 104; World War II in Pacific and, 76–77, 81, 97, 104, 105

Roosevelt, Theodore, 50, 55; Japanese empire and, 67–69

Root, Elihu, 20, 26, 45, 53, 68

Roxas, Manuel, 182

Rumsfeld, Donald, 274

Rusk, Dean, 129, 225, 259

Russell, Richard, 203

Russo-Japanese War, 66, 68, 128

Ryoso Fujie, 107

Ryukyu (Liuchiu) Islands, 66

Saipan, *84*, 86, 87–88, 101

Samar, *25*, 53, 54, 55, 56

Samoa, 13, 15, 17

Sato Naotake, 104

Schlesinger, Arthur, 256

Schurman, Jacob Gould, 44

Seuss, Dr. *See* Geisel, Theodore Seuss

Shandong, 69

Shangganling (1956 film), 176

Shepard, Jean, 159

Shtykov, Terentii F., 130

Sihanouk, Norodom, 248

Singapore, 30, 73, 82, *84*

Sino-Japanese War (1894–95), 60, 66

Sino-Japanese War (1937–45), 71–72, 75, 77, 80, 81, 92, 102, 125

Sledge, Eugene, 85

Smith, Jacob H., 53, 55

Smith, Oliver P., 144

Smithsonian National Air and Space Museum, 114–15

Solomon Islands, 83–85, *84*. *See also* Guadalcanal

Sorrow of War, The (Bao Ninh), 243

Southeast Asia. *See* Indochina; Japan; Korea; Korean War; Vietnam; Vietnam War; World War II

Southeast Asia Treaty Organization (SEATO), 184, 199

South Korea. *See* Korea; Korean War

South Vietnam. *See* Ngo Dinh Diem; Vietnam; Vietnam War

92, 101, 102, 108; Philippines and, 58, 82, 83, 85, 87, 92, 182, 284 (n. 49), 295 (n. 69); in Southeast Asia, 73, 77, 80, 82, 187; United States entering, 65, 76–78, 79–82; U.S. film and print media sustaining, 94–95; U.S. home front compared with Japanese, 78, 88–101, *93*; U.S. memory of, against Japan, 114–15, *116*; U.S. Pacific victories, 81–88, *84*, 102–3; U.S. public opinion and, 94–95, *99*, *100*; U.S. women and, 95–96. *See also* Pearl Harbor attack; U.S. Army; U.S. Navy

Xuan Thuy, 229
Xu Jiyu, 61

Yamamoto Isoroku, 82
Yamauchi Takeo, 87–88
Yasukuni shrine, 113
Yi dynasty, 128
Yonai Mitsumasa, 103
Yoshida Shigeru, 122, 181–82

Zhang Biwu, 164
Zhou Enlai, 141, 142, 170

H. Eugene and Lillian Youngs Lehman Series

Lamar Cecil, *Wilhelm II: Prince and Emperor, 1859–1900* (1989).

Carolyn Merchant, *Ecological Revolutions: Nature, Gender, and Science in New England* (1989).

Gladys Engel Lang and Kurt Lang, *Etched in Memory: The Building and Survival of Artistic Reputation* (1990).

Howard Jones, *Union in Peril: The Crisis over British Intervention in the Civil War* (1992).

Robert L. Dorman, *Revolt of the Provinces: The Regionalist Movement in America* (1993).

Peter N. Stearns, *Meaning Over Memory: Recasting the Teaching of Culture and History* (1993).

Thomas Wolfe, *The Good Child's River*, edited with an introduction by Suzanne Stutman (1994).

Warren A. Nord, *Religion and American Education: Rethinking a National Dilemma* (1995).

David E. Whisnant, *Rascally Signs in Sacred Places: The Politics of Culture in Nicaragua* (1995).

Lamar Cecil, *Wilhelm II: Emperor and Exile, 1900–1941* (1996).

Jonathan Hartlyn, *The Struggle for Democratic Politics in the Dominican Republic* (1998).

Louis A. Pérez Jr., *On Becoming Cuban: Identity, Nationality, and Culture* (1999).

Yaakov Ariel, *Evangelizing the Chosen People: Missions to the Jews in America, 1880–2000* (2000).

Philip F. Gura, *C. F. Martin and His Guitars, 1796–1873* (2003).

Louis A. Pérez Jr., *To Die in Cuba: Suicide and Society* (2005).

Peter Filene, *The Joy of Teaching: A Practical Guide for New College Instructors* (2005).

John Charles Boger and Gary Orfield, eds., *School Resegregation: Must the South Turn Back?* (2005).

Jock Lauterer, *Community Journalism: Relentlessly Local* (2006).

Michael H. Hunt, *The American Ascendancy: How the United States Gained and Wielded Global Dominance* (2007).

Michael Lienesch, *In the Beginning: Fundamentalism, the Scopes Trial, and the Making of the Antievolution Movement* (2007).

Eric L. Muller, *American Inquisition: The Hunt for Japanese American Disloyalty in World War II* (2007).

John McGowan, *American Liberalism: An Interpretation for Our Time* (2007).

Nortin M. Hadler, M.D., *Worried Sick: A Prescription for Health in an Overtreated America* (2008).

William Ferris, *Give My Poor Heart Ease: Voices of the Mississippi Blues* (2009).

Colin A. Palmer, *Cheddi Jagan and the Politics of Power: British Guiana's Struggle for Independence* (2010).

W. Fitzhugh Brundage, *Beyond Blackface: African Americans and the Creation of American Mass Culture, 1890–1930* (2011).

Michael H. Hunt and Steven I. Levine, *Arc of Empire: America's Wars in Asia from the Philippines to Vietnam* (2012).